Model-Based Product Line Engineering (MBPLE)

Model-Based Product Line Engineering (MBPLE)

The Feature-Based Path to Product Lines Success

Marco Forlingieri
Tim Weilkiens
Hugo Guillermo Chalé-Gongora

WILEY

Published by John Wiley & Sons, Inc., Hoboken, New Jersey.
Published simultaneously in Canada.

Library of Congress Cataloging-in-Publication Data: 2025902944

Print ISBN: 9781394204663
ePDF ISBN: 9781394204670
ePub ISBN: 9781394204687
oBook ISBN: 9781394204694

Cover Design: Wiley
Cover Image: Maria Izabel Thimoteo

Set in 9.5/12.5pt STIXTwoText by Lumina Datamatics

Printed and bound by CPI Group (UK) Ltd, Croydon, CR0 4YY

C9781394204663_250626

MBPLE book Dedications

To Prof. Dr. Danilo Beuche and Marco Ferrogalini, whose mentorship and inspiration shaped my career and introduced me to the world of Product Line Engineering.

To my grandparents, Angelo, Annamaria, and Maria, who remind me daily of the strength and wisdom of my Italian roots.

And to my wife, Maria, and my dog, Kyoto, my companions on every adventure around the world. Your support and love make every journey worthwhile.

Marco Forlingieri

To all the fantastic engineers who are committed to making the world a better place and to my family who make the world a great place for me every day.

Tim Weilkiens

To my parents and siblings, whose example, unconditional love, and support have led me to where I am and made me who I am.

To Geneviève and Anne-Nohemi, for the joy of seeing your smile every morning, and for setting me right whenever I'm wrong. Thanks for making each return home into the best moment of my day. You make life exciting.

Hugo Guillermo Chalé-Gongora

Contents

Foreword

Once upon a time, a unique trio got together: an Italian tool-vendor, a French-Mexican executive, and German subject matter expert (it sounds like the start of a joke, but this is serious stuff, folks!). We come from different backgrounds, possess diverse skills, and pursue distinct goals, but we share one undeniable passion called Model-Based Product Line Engineering (MBPLE).

Several years ago, while working at Renault, Guillermo, the executive, had an intuition: "What if we bring Model Based Systems Engineering (MBSE) and Product Line Engineering (PLE) together?" It was the origin of MBPLE, a concept Guillermo later applied at Alstom and Thales. Marco, now an executive tool vendor, read the work of Guillermo and decided to make PLE and MBSE his main expertise, applying it at Bombardier Transportation and later at Airbus. Tim, the subject matter expert, wrote VAMOS (Weilkiens 2016), a book about modeling the variability with SysML, which captured the attention of the other two, being the first and only source about the topic. The world of systems engineering is small and thanks to International Council on Systems Engineering (INCOSE) we got to know each other at the point that we, the trio, decided to put in writing all the knowledge and expertise gathered about the topic. We wanted to keep the concepts as simple as possible to reach managers, engineers, and students. This is how the idea of this book came to be.

In fact, only a few books exist about product lines, much less about their development, and nothing, so far, about MBPLE. This is because product lines are akin to mythological creatures – mysterious and elusive. Like the legendary Nessie in Loch Ness, the enigmatic UFO sightings or a politician keeping promises once elected, product lines are talked about by some who claim to have experienced them, but fail to prove their existence! And yet, paradoxically, you encounter them in your everyday life. They manifest when you purchase a car, wield a smartphone, drill the wall, dry your hands, board a plane, or even when you turn on the air conditioning.

What is the secret behind product lines? How are they developed? Can someone unveil the product line that, like Aristotle's "first motor," generates countless derived products? Such a revelation proves elusive! Just like a witness to an UFO sighting, the Loch Ness monster or a trustworthy politician, many speak of it, pretending to know the truth, but most, again, are unable to provide concrete evidence.

You might be skeptical, assuming that we, the authors of this book, are merely another group of individuals pretending to have witnessed something incredible without being able to prove it. But what about the five industrial cases on the concrete application of MBPLE from Airbus, Thales, MBDA, Raytheon and Belimo at the end of the book? Or the many references provided throughout this text?

We do not ask you to believe us, we extend an invitation, a summons to join us on this extraordinary expedition, where the mysteries of product lines and their secret recipe await your discovery. Together, let us unravel the enigma, peer behind the veil, and embark on a journey that will forever transform our perception of the way we carry out your business thanks to a deeper understanding of reuse, assets sharing and variability.

Welcome, fellow traveler, to this captivating odyssey and, paraphrasing Ulysses' words in Dante's Divine Comedy (Alighieri 1995), keep in mind that "you were not made to live as brutes, but to follow virtue and knowledge of MBPLE."

Marco Forlingieri
Tim Weilkiens
Hugo Guillermo Chalé-Gongora

References

Alighieri, D. (1995). The Divine Comedy. Originally published in 1320. New York: Knopf, distributed by Random House.

Weilkiens, T. (2016). Variant modeling with SysML. MBSE4U.

Preface

In the field of systems engineering, Product Line Engineering (PLE) has emerged as a transformative approach for managing the complexity of modern product families. First introduced in the 1990s, PLE laid the groundwork for systematically developing families of software and hardware. Over the years, it has evolved to meet the needs of increasingly complex industries, including automotive, aerospace, defense, and beyond.

In today's era of digital transformation, PLE is essential for maintaining competitiveness. The complexity of product development cycles now demands an integrated, model-based approach that enables organizations to achieve digital continuity and efficient lifecycle management. For decades, International Council on Systems Engineering has played a central role in the evolution of systems engineering, embracing emerging disciplines like PLE and adapting to model-based advancements.

Recognizing the importance of PLE in advancing systems engineering, the International Council on Systems Engineering (INCOSE) established the PLE Working Group in 2012. This group plays a critical role in standardizing PLE practices and fostering global collaboration across sectors. Aligned with INCOSE's mission to promote systems engineering, the PLE Working Group has contributed significantly to the evolution of PLE and, more recently, Model-Based Product Line Engineering (MBPLE).

The authors of this book are recognized international experts, bringing extensive experience in both the theory and practical application of MBPLE across industries. Their deep involvement in INCOSE and contributions to major organizations and international standards make them uniquely qualified to present this comprehensive guide.

The publication of ISO/IEC 26550:2015 marked a significant milestone for PLE, providing a foundational standard for product line engineering and management. This was further strengthened by ISO/IEC 26580:2021, which introduced feature-based methods for managing PLE across industries. INCOSE's PLE Working Group has played a vital role in formalizing these standards, ensuring a cohesive framework for PLE across sectors and fostering collaboration within the systems engineering community.

The combination of Model-Based Systems Engineering (MBSE) with PLE – now known as MBPLE – has become a cornerstone of innovation. By leveraging models, MBPLE enables engineers and organizations to manage product family variations and configurations with unprecedented precision and flexibility. This integrated, model-based approach has made it possible to address the complexities of today's product lifecycles, delivering improved digital continuity and competitive advantages.

While the evolution of MBPLE continues to advance, it is accompanied by diverse interpretations and emerging trends, creating a need for clarity and guidance. This book fills a critical gap by offering a comprehensive guide to MBPLE, combining strategic insights with foundational concepts and practical implementation techniques, particularly in Systems Modeling Language (SysML). Through real-world case studies and insights from PLE pioneers, it explores the transformative power of MBPLE, including the potential impact of Artificial Intelligence and its associated opportunities and risks. This book serves as an essential resource for anyone aiming to learn and leverage MBPLE in today's increasingly complex and competitive product development environments.

Ralf Hartmann, INCOSE President

About the Companion Website

This book is accompanied by a companion website.

www.wiley.com/go/forlingieri/mbple1e

This website includes:

- Author Images
- Website content and structure

Part I

Motivation

The first part of the book focuses almost solely on the purpose of Model-Based Product Line Engineering (MBPLE). This emphasis is intentional, based on the authors' experiences that company members often lose sight of the overall purpose of their initiatives. Frequently, they mistake tools and methods (such as digital transformation, modeling, agile practices, or digital twins, to name just a few) for end goals. Avoiding this confusion is crucial for MBPLE due to its transdisciplinary nature, the required investments, and the need to implement it across the whole company.

Chapter 2 begins by drawing a picture of the context in which today's products are developed. The chapter briefly explores complexity and variability as well as their implications on the methods needed to develop and deliver products that are adapted to the needs of different customers. This is the object of Chapter 3, which presents different reuse patterns along with their advantages and disadvantages. Special attention is given to the dangers of implementing unplanned reuse strategies and to the prerequisites that should be in place to ensure a successful implementation of a product line approach.

Chapter 4 explains the difference between document-based engineering and model-based engineering. The growth in the adoption of model-based engineering as well as the perspectives of its evolution are also explored. The chapter presents the benefits and challenges associated with model-based engineering. Chapter 5 is a logical complement to Chapter 4 as it proposes a similar approach to explain the differences between the delivery of single products and the delivery of products in a product-line-based approach. This chapter explains the advantages of transitioning to a programmatic approach to manage the products of a product line as a single entity, as opposed to managing a plethora of separate development projects.

Chapter 6 closes Part I with an analysis of digital threads and digital continuity as enablers to allow managing data during all the stages of the product line life cycle and across the different products of a product line in a consistent way. The chapter also underlines the importance of the openness of IT solutions and the need to connect these in integrated networks to support MBPLE in an effective manner.

1

Introduction

Model-based product line engineering (MBPLE) is a broad topic involving many stakeholders. For most companies, MBPLE's transformational nature concerns almost all engineering activities and operations. Leaders need to understand MBPLE to plan and implement it strategically, as well as to understand and frame its application. But MBPLE principles, concepts, and methods must also be understood by a wider population, including the following:

Process owners who create and adapt MBPLE methods and tools to meet organization-specific requirements.

Engineers who use MBPLE methods directly to create feature models and shared assets supersets.

Engineers and product owners who develop parts of the product line.

Students who learn systems engineering, product line engineering (PLE), and model-based approaches.

This book discusses MBPLE as a central topic, covering all its facets, including the enabling factors for a successful implementation of MBPLE in an organization. For readers who are new to the topic or who would like to acquire a broad understanding of MBPLE, reading the book following the order of the sections might be the best approach. However, readers who are interested in a particular topic or who have previous knowledge of PLE can browse freely through the different sections of the book.

Part I discusses the motivation of MBPLE, which is important for all MBPLE stakeholders. Like all engineering approaches, MBPLE is only a means to an end. Therefore, it is important and helpful to have a good understanding of the purpose of MBPLE.

Part II describes the fundamental concepts of MBPLE, independently of concrete implementations of modeling languages and tools. Like Part I, Part II is also an important reading for all MBPLE stakeholders. The chapters in Part II look at the historical development of model-based approaches and PLE, as well as relevant standards such as ISO/IEC 26550 (ISO/IEC 2015) and ISO/IEC 26580 (ISO/IEC 2021), which provide the framework wherein the MBPLE concepts are presented.

Part III explains the technical implementation of MBPLE and is of particular interest to those who use MBPLE directly. One focus is on the models with SysML, whereby both the widely used SysML v1 and the new SysML v2 are used.

Part IV explains the adoption of MBPLE in organizations, a significant topic for leadership roles. The chapters consider both the investment and return on investment of introducing MBPLE, the processes, the methods, the organization, the information model, and the tool chains. This part is

Model-Based Product Line Engineering (MBPLE): The Feature-Based Path to Product Lines Success, First Edition.
Marco Forlingieri et al.

rounded off by a chapter with an interview of two PLE pioneers, Dr. Danilo Beuche from PTC and Dr. Charles Krueger from Big Lever Software.

Part V intends to show that the book presents MBPLE not only in theory but also in real-life practice. Five chapters focus on industrial cases about adopting MBPLE from five different organizations.

In the appendix, a glossary lists the most important MBPLE terms for reference.

Acknowledgments

It takes a lot of people to write this book, many of whom are directly acknowledged in this book. Thanks to Ralf Hartmann, president of INCOSE, for writing the preface and his continued commitment to the systems engineering community. Many people have agreed to report on their MBPLE approaches within their companies and have written industrial cases in Part V. These contributors include Davi Henrique de Sousa Pinto from Airbus, Dieter Wagner from MBDA, Agnès Guiblin from Thales, James Teaff from Raytheon, and the Belimo's team, consisting of Manuel Pijorr, Alba Pennisi, Markus Hüppi, Daniel Messmer, Mariana Reyes Perez, Mitko Tanevski and Simon Hoffman. Thank you all for your work and the insights you provided in this book. The two PLE pioneers, Dr. Danilo Beuche and Dr. Charles Krueger, took the time to share their views on the world of PLE. Thank you very much for your valuable time and contribution; without your contribution, this book would have not been complete. Many ideas were discussed and matured in the INCOSE PLE Working Group (INCOSE PLE 2024) context. Marco Ferrogalini, who contributed his wealth of experience as Vice President and Head of Modeling and Simulations at Airbus, was involved in the book's initial ideas and structure.

References

INCOSE PLE (2024). INCOSE PLE Working Group. Webpage viewed on 15 July. https://www.incose.org/communities/working-groups-initiatives/product-lines.

ISO/IEC (2015). *ISO/IEC 26550:2015* Software and systems engineering – reference model for product line engineering and management. Geneva ISO/IEC.

ISO/IEC (2021). ISO/IEC 26580:2021 Software and systems engineering – methods and tools for the feature-based approach to software and systems product line engineering. Geneva ISO/IEC. https://www.iso.org/standard/43139.html.

2

Complexity and Variability

2.1 Introduction

As the discipline of systems engineering evolves, it must confront the growing complexity inherent in its expansive scope. This chapter first explores in Section 2.2 the dual drivers of complexity identified by the International Council on Systems Engineering (INCOSE) in its Vision 2035 (INCOSE 2022): technology-driven and scope-driven complexity. Technology-driven complexity is fueled by fast technological advancements, while scope-driven complexity emerges from the increasing size and interdependencies within the development scope. We explore deeper each driver, emphasizing their distinctive impacts on the field.

Section 2.3 addresses the concept of variability driven by customization in product development. Customization, while enhancing individuality and flexibility, often results in a diverse range of product variants.

The combination of complexity and variability are discussed in Section 2.4, two trends that are deeply interrelated and form the challenges in modern product and systems engineering, emerging as a key focus of the chapter. Through a few examples, it illustrates the difficulties of balancing high variability demands with the need to manage complexity effectively.

Ultimately, this chapter contextualizes these concepts within the broader framework of systems engineering, emphasizing the criticality of innovative development paradigms to address the combined challenges of increasing complexity and variability demands in the development of complex systems.

2.2 Complexity

In systems engineering, complexity has always been a key aspect to address. The field itself developed to better handle the increasing scale, interconnections, and complexity in systems development. Professor de Weck (Conservation of Complexity 2023) discussed the rising complexity in today's products and systems, noting that it is much higher than in the past, as highlighted in Figure 2.1. This complexity is intended to lead to enhanced performance and, possibly, increased resilience. It is a common understanding among systems engineers that complexity is escalating each year due to rapidly changing contexts, the growing interdependencies of systems, and more challenging projects taken on by organizations and governments. He also pointed out how monumental achievements like the lunar landing, the International Space Station, 20-hour transoceanic flights, or capturing images of the earliest proto-galaxies post-Big

Model-Based Product Line Engineering (MBPLE): The Feature-Based Path to Product Lines Success, First Edition.
Marco Forlingieri et al.

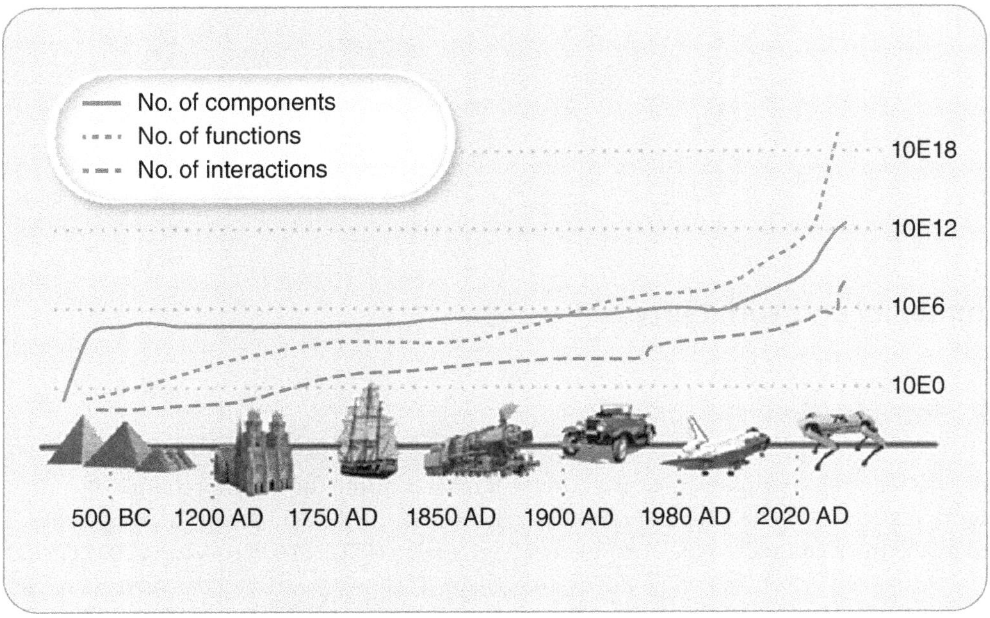

Figure 2.1 Representation of the increasing complexity in history. *Source:* Adapted from INCOSE 2022.

Bang are made possible by the coordinated effort of numerous components, including hardware, software, and human collaboration. However, he also emphasized that many aerospace programs are facing rising costs and challenges in management, partly due to a limited grasp of how system performance, complexity, and the effort needed for design, construction, and validation are interrelated. This can be also explained by what he theorizes as the "First Law of System Science for Conservation of Complexity." In simpler terms, it suggests that the complexity of a system is directly related to expected improvement in its performance, adjusted by the amount of work and resources put into its development and construction (Conservation of Complexity 2023).

In systems engineering, the typical process that aims at managing complexity involves breaking down a "problem" into smaller, more manageable parts, designing solutions for these individual parts, and then reassembling them to form the complete system. This approach is effective for "complicated" systems with fixed interactions among parts, even if they contain many interrelated components and may exhibit unpredictable behavior (INCOSE 2016).

However, this method encounters difficulties when new technologies are integrated into traditional systems and when the scope of these systems expands to ambitious developments. In complex systems, the emergent properties crucial to the system's functionality cannot be fully understood by examining the individual components separately. These properties only become apparent when considering the system as a whole. According to INCOSE's Vision 2035 (INCOSE 2022), the complexity in engineering is continuously escalating, primarily due to two key factors: technology-driven complexity and scope-driven complexity. Other factors contribute to an increase of complexity in systems engineering, such as the complexity of the business context or of the organization in which the systems are developed. However, the focus here is on the complexity intrinsic to the system under development. Let's examine both drivers in detail.

2.2.1 Technology-driven Complexity

Technology-driven complexity arises from the rapid pace of technological advancements and their integration into systems and products. This type of complexity is often characterized by the incorporation of cutting-edge technologies, which, while enhancing capabilities, also add challenges to the system's design, operation, and maintenance, as exemplified in Figure 2.2.

For instance, the implementation of software-defined vehicles in the automotive industry describes the complexity of technology-driven vehicles well. A software-defined vehicle is any vehicle that manages its operations, adds functionality, and enables new features primarily or entirely through software. Tesla cars are the most famous example. Software-defined vehicles are the next evolution of the automotive industry. Their architecture usually divides the vehicle's functions into different server zones, such as infotainment, safety systems, and vehicle control. Each zone integrates advanced technologies like sensor fusion, connectivity modules, and real-time data processing. The challenge lies in harmonizing these technologies to work together, ensuring vehicle performance and safety in diverse driving conditions. This complexity is compounded by the need to constantly update and maintain each server zone over the air to meet evolving technological standards and consumer demands (Burkacky et al. 2023).

2.2.2 Scope-driven Complexity

Scope-driven complexity emerges from the expansion in the scale and interconnectedness of systems. It reflects the transition from developing standalone products to creating systems part of more extensive, often interconnected networks, as illustrated in Figure 2.3.

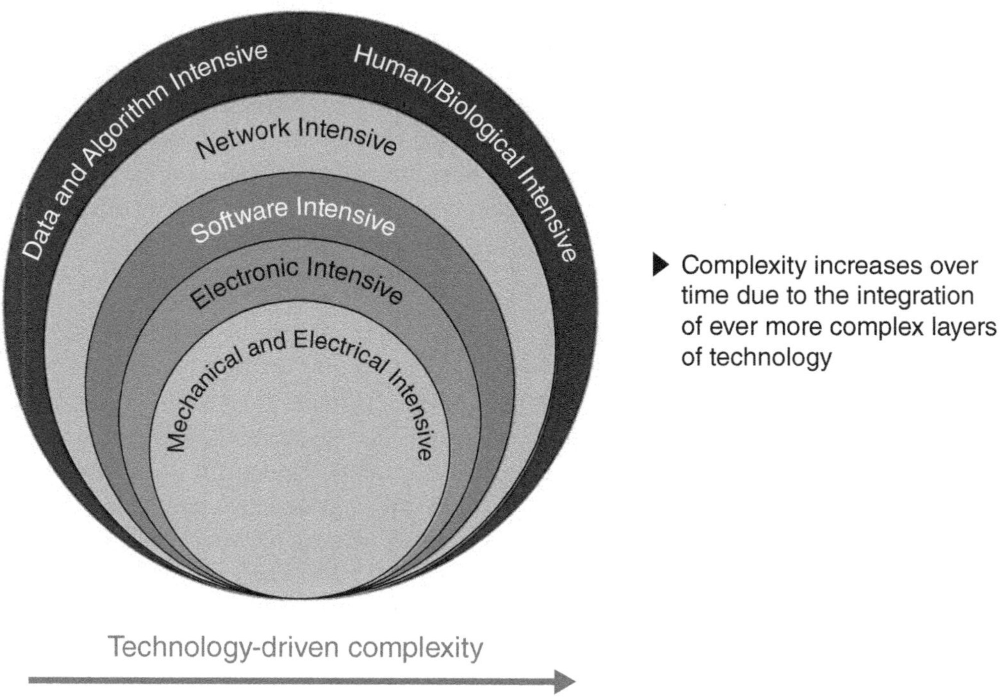

Figure 2.2 Representation of the technology-driven complexity driver. *Source:* Adapted from INCOSE 2022.

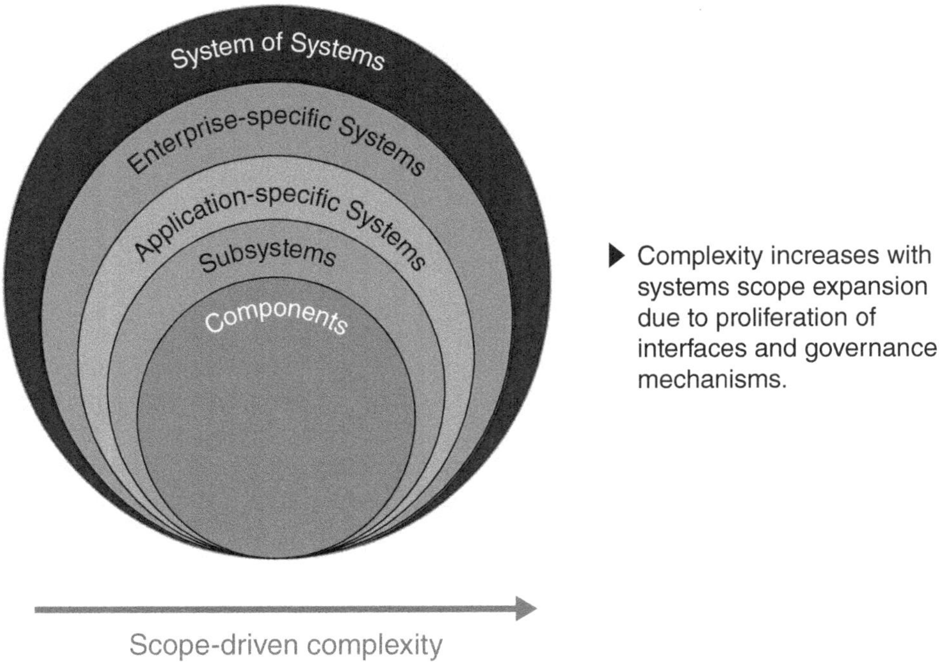

Figure 2.3 Representation of the scope-driven complexity driver. *Source:* Adapted from INCOSE 2022.

Extending the example of software-defined vehicles, scope-driven complexity becomes apparent when these vehicles connect to more extensive networks. Features like over-the-air software updates and vehicle-to-everything communication add layers of complexity. The challenge is ensuring the vehicle's different server zones work well with these external connections, maintaining reliable and secure performance in an interconnected setting. This shows how expanding the scope of vehicle systems naturally makes them more complex.

In summary, understanding complexity in systems engineering involves recognizing the multifaceted challenges posed by technological advancements and expanding project scopes. As we continue to push the boundaries of what is possible, mastery of complexity becomes a critical skill in the engineer's toolkit.

2.3 Variability

In product development, customization refers to the process of tailoring products or systems to meet the specific requirements of a customer or market segment. This often involves modifying or configuring the design, features, functionalities, or even the aesthetics of a product to align with distinct preferences, needs, or operational environments. From a portfolio perspective, customized products or systems exhibit variability, as their characteristics may differ among the members of the product portfolio. Unlike mass production, which focuses on uniformity and scale, customization emphasizes individuality and flexibility, often resulting in diverse product variants. Customization is the primary driver of variability within a product portfolio.

With increasing demand for customization, companies face the double challenge of providing market – or customer-specific variety while mastering the consequences of high variability in engineering and production. Especially in an increasingly saturated market, new products must find ways to differentiate themselves from the competition, like distinctively meeting specific customer needs to enhance customer's satisfaction (Simpson et al. 2005).

However, as observed by Meyer and Lehnerd (1997), focusing on individual customer preferences often leads to overlooking commonality and standardization across product lines. This can result in an overwhelming diversification of products and parts. While offering a comprehensive product variety has merits, it can also incur significant costs and complexity within a company.

Have you ever noticed, while traveling on different flights, even within the exact airline or across various airlines, which the airplane model might be the same, yet many aspects inside differ significantly? For instance, consider the variability in-cabin configuration and layout, the number and style of toilets, infotainment systems, or even the types of movies available during the flight. These differences result from airlines' deliberate customization and high differentiation to enhance their brand identity and customer service offerings. However, this level of variability often becomes a "nightmare" for airplane manufacturers and their suppliers. They frequently face the challenging task of reworking complex systems to accommodate these customizations, sometimes questioning the necessity of altering even minor details, like the exact millimetric position of power and water outlets within the galley of a commercial aircraft!

If not adequately managed, variability can significantly impact the design and development of systems in several ways:

Increased complexity: high variability introduces complexity into the design process, requiring engineers to consider a broader range of variables and potential configurations.

Design flexibility: More flexible design approaches are needed to accommodate changes and variations without extensive redesigns or cost overruns.

Production and supply chain adjustments: Variables impact production processes and supply chains, which need to be adaptable to produce a variety of customized products efficiently.

Increased costs: while customization can lead to higher customer satisfaction and market differentiation, variability often leads to increased production costs and complexity in inventory management.

In summary, customization in product development reflects the dynamic and varied needs of customers and market trends. However, this leads to increased variability, which, if not properly managed, can hinder project success and overall organizational performance.

2.4 The Trade-off Between Complexity and Variability

The increasing complexity in engineering and the escalating demand for customization leading to higher variability are not isolated trends; instead, they are profoundly interconnected and often feed into each other, creating additional challenges in modern systems engineering.

Have you ever considered that a European, South America, or Southeast Asia metro system might be based on the identical product family? This idea was pursued by Bombardier Transportation in 2014 with their "Entry Segment Metro" concept (Forlingieri 2014). They aimed to create a metro design that could be adapted across different regions. However, the project encountered significant challenges and ultimately did not materialize.

One of the primary reasons for this was that metro systems and light rail vehicles often symbolize a city's identity, necessitating unique and strongly differentiated designs. Additionally, the need to comply with diverse local norms and regulations significantly increased the complexity and the potential number of variants required. However, other rolling stock products, such as high-speed trains, may require heavier customization, going beyond style and aesthetics into the specific train architecture (Chalé Góngora et al. 2014).

This example showcases the trade-off between the desire for high customization and the goal of limiting complexity, which arises from the variability of the product variants. The effort to customize a metro system or a light rail vehicle across various geographical and cultural contexts shows how challenging it can be to manage both these aspects effectively.

This applies in particular to a category known as complex products and systems (CoPS). They consist of prime products that demonstrate a high degree of customization and complexity (Hobday 1998). These are high-cost, engineering-intensive items, encompassing a broad range of tailored components, specialized knowledge, and involvement from various organizations. The complexity of CoPS arises not just from their technical difficulties but also from the extensive customization required to meet the unique demands of each project (Forlingieri 2014). Naval, Aerospace, and Civil Engineering are just some of the most representative industries where this category of systems is produced.

The CoPS category is just one of the possible areas where the combination of variability and complexity closely interact.

To conclude, addressing diverse business context factors, specific customer needs, and increasing complexity, particularly within a highly regulated environment, requires new engineering practices and methods. These approaches help to balance variability and complexity in today's systems. You will find some answers later in this book!

References

Burkacky, O., Steiner, F., Deichmann, J. et al. (2023). Getting ready for next-generation E/E architecture with zonal compute. https://www.mckinsey.com/industries/semiconductors/our-insights/getting-ready-for-next-generation-ee-architecture-with-zonal-compute (accessed June 2024).

Chalé Góngora, H.G., Ferrogalini, M. and Moreau, C. (2014). How to boost PLE by using MBSE – a case study of a rolling stock product line. In: *Proceedings of the 5th International Conference on Complex Systems Design and Management (CSDM)* Paris, France: Springer.

Conservation of Complexity: The First Law of System Science (2023). MIT AeroAstro. https://aeroastro.mit.edu/news-impact/conservation-of-complexity-the-first-law-of-system-science/ (accessed January 2024).

Forlingieri, M. (2014). *Platform Planning and Design for Rail Rolling Stock: An Exploratory Study of Platform Development within Bombardier Transportation.* Enschede: University of Twente.

Hobday, M. (1998). Product complexity, innovation and industrial organisation. *Research Policy* 26 (6): 689–710. doi: 10.1016/S0048-7333(97)00044–9.

International Council on Systems Engineering (INCOSE) (2016). A complexity primer for systems engineers.

International Council on Systems Engineering (INCOSE) (2022). Systems engineering vision 2035. https://sevisionweb.incose.org (accessed July 2024).

Meyer, M.H. and Lehnerd, A.P. (1997). *The Power of Product Platforms: Building Value and Cost Leadership.* New York, NY: Free Press.

Simpson, T.W., Siddique, Z. and Jiao, J. (eds.) (2005). *Product Platform and Product Family Design: Methods and Applications.* New York: Springer. 1–15.

3

Reuse Strategies

3.1 Introduction

In today's highly competitive markets, most organizations usually try to leverage previously developed assets for their reuse into a new product. This understanding of reuse, shared by most common folk, is one of the more widespread in the engineering of systems: using again what one has done before to produce a solution that is similar or close to a previous one. The *purpose* of reuse, however, is often much less formalized or even understood: produce the same thing or something similar, only *faster* and *better*. In other words, a reuse strategy should be set to produce clearly stated outcomes, such as improving product characteristics, like quality and performance, or program objectives, like cost-effectiveness, time to delivery, or risk mitigation.

Indeed, in most industrial organizations, practically no system is created from scratch. Engineers are most likely to reuse knowledge from a previous project or product in the form of documents, procedures, diagrams, or models. The problem is that this knowledge, albeit optimal for local usage, is very often partial and sometimes even inadequate when used in a different context. In siloed organizations, this usually results in incompatibilities of engineering artifacts, inconsistent technical data, and duplication of information in different repositories, making the implementation of the principles exposed in Chapters 5 and 6 extremely challenging. In a nutshell, these practices make reuse very problematic at a cross-company level and hamper the creation of well-structured, corporate-wide product lines. Whilst Section 3.2 introduces some of the industrial reuse approaches, Section 3.3 provides a brief analysis of the benefits and risks of those reuse patterns.

3.2 Different Reuse Approaches

As an engineering practice, reuse is well-documented in software and manufacturing, where examples of successful reuse approaches are well known, such as configurable software modules, standard software architectures, flexible manufacturing systems, or automobile platform sharing (Holweg 2008). Reuse is also associated with concepts like modular architectures, system families, and standardization of parts.

The origins of product line engineering (PLE), as the main reuse practice of this book, are often traced back to McIlroy's work on "Mass Produced Software Components" (McIlroy 1968) (see Chapter 10 for a more detailed history of PLE).

Model-Based Product Line Engineering (MBPLE): The Feature-Based Path to Product Lines Success, First Edition.
Marco Forlingieri et al.

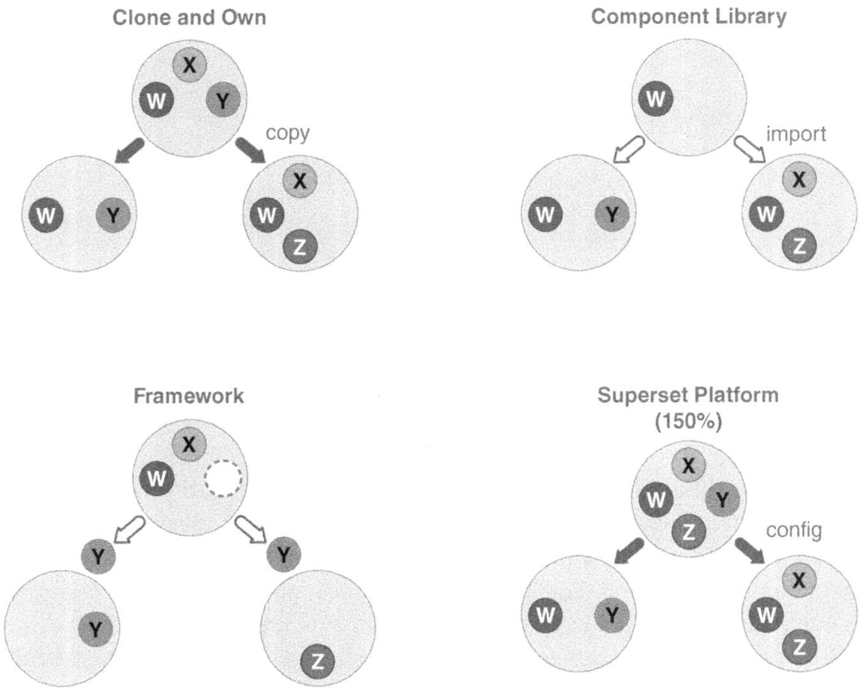

Figure 3.1 Different reuse patterns. *Source:* Adapted from Czarnecki, K.

However, the formalization of PLE and other reuse practices for their application to the engineering of large-scale systems is still scarce and relatively new (International Council on Systems Engineering [INCOSE] 2019) despite historical, *de facto*, or casual reuse in industry, like the reutilization of existing specification documents, technical drawings, or test procedures, and the existence of some reports on successful industrial applications (Chalé Góngora et al. 2014; Flores et al. 2013; Gregg et al. 2016). Figure 3.1 represents a spectrum of different reuse patterns explained in the sections below.

3.2.1 Clone and Own

Usually associated with the search for short-term benefits, clone-and-own (or branch-and-merge) approaches are the easiest to implement since engineering teams are usually independent and able to manage engineering assets as they like. There is practically no sharing among the different branches, and separate efforts to maintain each individual branch are required. This approach might be a suitable scheme for businesses in which single product instances are delivered over very large periods of time. It might also be appropriate for companies that want to reuse existing products to enter a new market or propose a groundbreaking application in an opportunistic way. The success of this approach relies on mastering the technical debt and on top-class configuration management processes.

3.2.2 Component Library and Framework

Component library and framework approaches produce more substantial benefits than the clone-and-own approach. The component library approach is based on the definition of *standard components*. Besides the need to master the interactions and interdependencies amongst the components, the biggest challenge of the component library approach is to ensure that the emerging properties of the composed product are those expected by the customers. In the framework approach, efforts would instead be dedicated to the definition of *standard interfaces* in such a way that any component that complies with the standard can potentially be used to "compose" a particular product. The Autosar (Automotive Open System Architecture) framework (Autosar 2024) is a well-known example of a standardized software framework supporting a composable approach for electric and electronic system architectures in the automotive industry.

In practice, these two approaches are carried out simultaneously to foster compsability and ease of integration. They are adapted to products evolving in markets that require the delivery of a rather stable set of functionalities over time. These functionalities can be allocated to dedicated components that would evolve at a slow pace, while isolating those components that support fast-evolving functions or technologies. The main difficulties of the component library and framework approaches are that the evolution of standard components must be thoroughly planned and controlled and that managing the definition of standard interfaces can be a complicated task in large-scale systems.

3.2.3 Superset Platform

The superset platform approach is closely related to advanced PLE approaches proposed in this book, as explained below. In this approach, a "platform" of asset supersets is designed and made available for its use in customer projects. This is done through the configuration of the supersets to match the needs of a given customer. The term 150% is used to illustrate the fact that the supersets contain more than what it would take to define a single customer solution, which would sum up to 100%. The benefits of this approach include substantial reuse and automation of the production of engineering assets, which requires capabilities to control variability efficiently, master the dependencies amongst the supersets, and control the configuration mechanism of specific products to keep this from becoming a complex task.

3.3 Quick Benefits Versus Risk Analysis of Reuse Patterns

To decide which reuse pattern should be implemented in a given organization, a business case must be established, taking into consideration the business context and strategy of the organization. The business case should consider the cost-effective investment of engineering resources and time evidenced by the elimination of low-value, trivial, repetitive, demotivating, and energy-consuming tasks. This liberatory effect should translate into a more profitable investment of energy and time in high-value activities and innovation. Examples of possible activities and outcomes include, but are not limited to, improving products, reducing organizational complexity, reducing time to market and lead time, reducing engineering costs and efforts, exploring possibilities, and advancing business objectives. Chapter 21 presents the elements that can be used to build a compelling business case for MBPLE.

When the products within a portfolio are engineered as individual, unique solutions, clown-and-own techniques usually result in duplication and divergent engineering efforts for every "branch" that is created. Since controlling the consistency of the different branches usually relies on tacit knowledge and interpersonal communication, it is inevitably an error-prone activity. This difficulty (usually known as "branching hell") increases in organizations in which each discipline adopts ad-hoc techniques for managing the variation among the different products of the portfolio, introducing further inconsistencies and misunderstandings. This way of working systematically translates into process-induced complexity, which adds on top of the intrinsic complexity of the products and of the business contexts in which organizations evolve.

What sets mature PLE practices apart from the approach mentioned above is their holistic nature and the systems engineering groundings that support them. PLE can be defined as the engineering of a product line (i.e. a family of similar products with variations in features and functions) as a single entity, using a shared set of engineering assets and an efficient means of production, taking advantage of the commonality shared across the family, while efficiently and systematically managing the variation among the products (more details are given in Chapter 5). This implies that a programmatic approach must be put in place to manage the portfolio of customer projects (i.e. those that benefit from the shared assets supersets of the product line) as a single entity too, instead of managing a multitude of individual projects separately. Such an approach enables an organization to perform informed trade-offs and make balanced cost-benefit decisions regarding investments, with a view on short-term expectations and long-term goals, particularly business profitability.

The consolidation of shared asset supersets within disciplines eliminates duplication, inconsistencies, and divergence across the products of the family, on the one hand. On the other hand, consistent transdisciplinary management of variation across the different supersets and across the product line life cycle, made possible by its formalization in a variability model, helps avoid miscommunication and misalignment amongst disciplines (Chalé Góngora and Greugny 2017). Although this delivery approach might be appealing and appear as sheer common sense, it represents a true breakthrough and, for many organizations, a major shift that requires changes in governance and organizational structures, as well as strong commitment from all functions, disciplines, and leadership. These aspects will be further developed in Part IV of this book: Adoption of MBPLE.

To conclude, PLE relies on processes that help manage the life cycle of the portfolio of products of an organization (as well as the underlying reusable assets used to perform the architecting, design, and evolution of the portfolio) in order to maximize the benefits of reuse. Reusing assets, however, should be the result of a well-documented decision process, meaning that implementing PLE should require upfront investment and forethought. And yet it is safe to postulate that, in most organizations, one could find examples where reusing an asset actually proved to be less profitable over the system life cycle than developing a new one: while the initial engineering cost of the asset might have been low, the overall costs induced by debugging, repair, validation, warranty expenses, or penalties slowly but surely end up consuming the originally planned profits (Wymore and Bahill 2000; Chalé Góngora et al. 2014). To put it simply, copy-pasting assets from one project to another without an overarching strategy cannot be considered PLE (or engineering, for that matter), and it cannot yield by itself all the potential benefits of PLE.

References

Autosar (2024). Automotive open system architecture. www.autosar.org (accessed 4 July 2024).

Chalé Góngora, H.G., Ferrogalini, M. and Moreau, C. (2014). How to boost PLE by using MBSE – a case study of a rolling stock product line. In: *Proceedings of the 5th International Conference on Complex Systems Design and Management (CSDM)*, Paris, France: Springer.

Chalé Góngora, H.G. and Greugny, F. (2017). Where the big bucks (will) come from – implementing product line engineering for railway rolling stock. In: *27th Annual INCOSE International Symposium, Adelaide, Australia*. San Diego: INCOSE.

Flores, R., Krueger, C., and Clements, P. (2013). Second generation product line engineering – a case study at general motors. In: *Systems and Software Variability Management: Concepts, Tools, and Experiences* (ed. R. Capilla, J. Bosch, and K. Kang), 317–341. Springer.

Gregg, P., Susan, and Clements, P. (2016). The best of both worlds: agile development meets product line engineering at Lockheed Martin. In: INCOSE 2016 International Symposium, Scotland, UK. INCOSE, San Diego.

Holweg, M. (2008). The evolution of competition in the automotive industry. In: Build To Order (ed. G. Parry and A. Graves) London: Springer.

International Council on Systems Engineering (INCOSE) (2016). Panel: An industry-wide concern: how to improve your business with product line engineering–challenges and opportunities. Moderator: Chalé Góngora, H.G. Presenters: Unger, C., Wozniak, L., Jarry, H., Schoonover, P., Tirumalai, S. and Czarnecki, K. Edinburgh, Scotland: INCOSE, San Diego.

International Council on Systems Engineering (INCOSE) (2019). Feature-based systems and software engineering: a primer.

McIlroy, M.D. (1968). Mass produced software components. In: *Software Engineering: Report of a Conference Sponsored by the NATO Science Committee, Garmisch, Germany*, 7–11, Scientific Affairs Division.

Wymore, A.W. and Bahill, A.T. (2000). When can we safely reuse systems, upgrade systems or use COTS components. *Journal of Systems Engineering* 3 (2): 82–95.

4

From Document-based to Model-based Engineering

4.1 Introduction

The increasing use of models in engineering is not a new topic. However, the adoption rate remains modest, with document-based engineering still prevailing in many sectors. As discussed in Chapter 2, with the escalating complexity of systems and the organizations developing them and the ever-accelerating pace of developments, adopting models is the most effective alternative to document-centric engineering.

Section 4.2 discusses the challenges of document-based engineering, and Section 4.3 presents model-based engineering (MBE) as an approach to overcoming these challenges.

4.2 Document-based Engineering

The number of documents increases, as does the number of dependencies between their contents. A text document might reference a figure from a spreadsheet, or a presentation may use a figure from a text document, and so on (Figure 4.1).

With increasing complexity and demands for system capabilities, along with growing constraints on quality improvement and cost-effectiveness, attempting to apply "old" practices and tools to overcome these challenges would be ill-advised. Here, "practices and tools" encompass mechanical and software tools, methods, and modeling languages. Our progress in systems engineering must not lag behind the need for system capabilities.

Figure 4.2 illustrates the "gap of missed improvements." Commonly, the systems we develop surpass the capabilities of the tools used to create them. Project heroes often bridge the gap – people who, through their dedication and expertise, enable organizations to develop great systems. As systems evolve, this gap widens.

This strain becomes apparent in organizations where the gap grows too large. Symptoms include employees reaching their limits, experts leaving the company, and a shift from proactive to reactive management. Such organizations accumulate technical debt, which, if unrecognized, diverts resources to "firefighting" rather than improving engineering tools. This "vicious circle" exacerbates problems over time as the capabilities of engineering tools remain stagnant.

Any improvement, including that of engineering tools, often follows a "hockey stick" curve, where performance initially declines before rising and achieving the desired enhancements.

Model-Based Product Line Engineering (MBPLE): The Feature-Based Path to Product Lines Success, First Edition.
Marco Forlingieri et al.

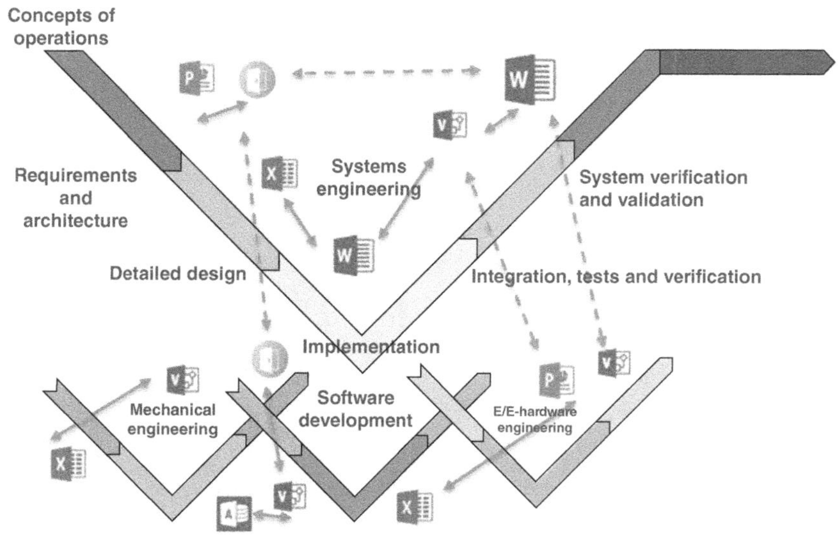

Figure 4.1 Documents along the engineering V models.

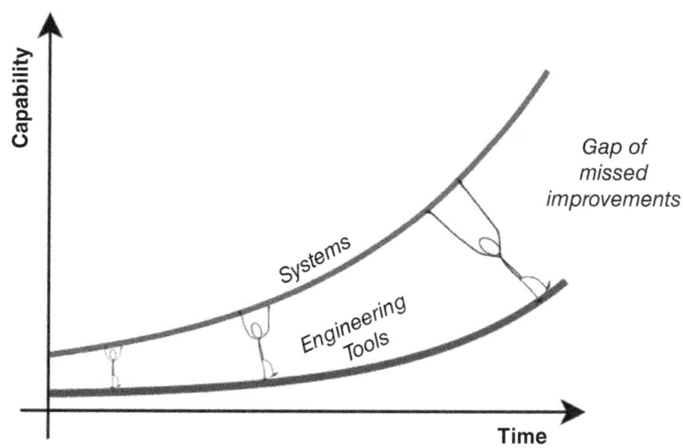

Figure 4.2 Gap of missed improvements.

4.3 Model-based Engineering

The introduction of MBE is generally regarded as an improvement in engineering tools and practices. There are many advantages of MBE. In a nutshell, it allows us to capture knowledge formally or semi-formally, making valuable engineering information accessible to machines. With this, machines can then support engineering processes. If information is stored in digital documents, machines can "understand" and support the document structure, such as layouts, page counts, graphics, and references. However, they do not understand the meaning – or the semantics – of the contents.

If machines understand the semantics of engineering information, they can help ensure better quality control throughout the development process, as models can be automatically checked for consistency, completeness, and correctness. This reduces the risk of errors and helps to ensure that the final product will meet all requirements.

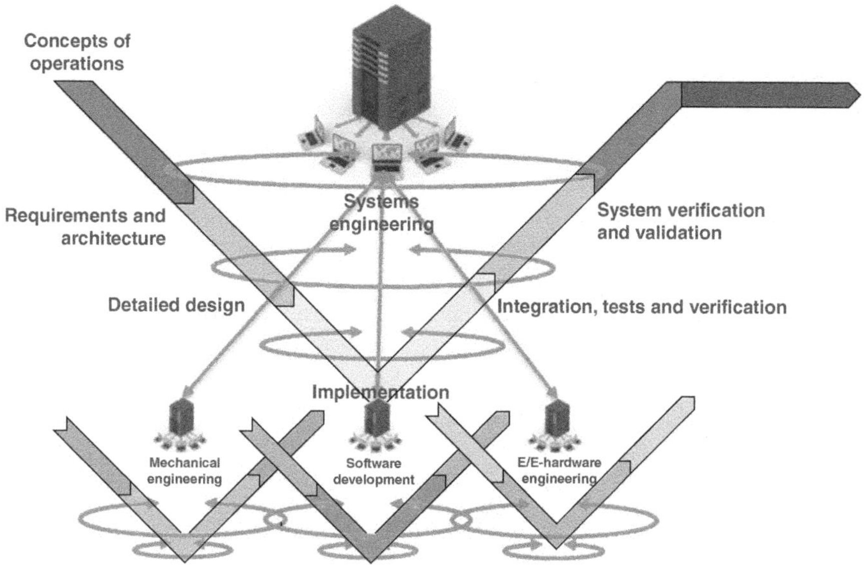

Figure 4.3 Models along the engineering V's.

MBE also allows greater collaboration between different stakeholders, as everyone can understand, work, and see changes in real time using the same model. This can help reduce interpretation errors and misunderstandings that may occur when working with traditional document-based approaches. The model serves as a single source of truth for the entire project and ensures all stakeholders have access to the latest information. Figure 4.3 shows, in contrast to Figure 4.1, the usage of models in engineering.

Manifold advantages exist; nevertheless, it is fair to state that the investment is also high. Introducing a model-based approach requires investments in people's training, process adaptation, and licenses of the necessary software tools. It is widely accepted that MBSE brings benefits or a return on investment, but it should also be noted that there is little proven evidence to date (Henderson and Salado 2021). No evidence does not mean absence.

The increased usage of model-based approaches occurs in many engineering disciplines. For example, in mechanical and electrical engineering, the shift from drawing boards to computer-aided design (CAD) (including electronic computer-aided design [ECAD] and mechanical computer-aided design [MCAD], or in software engineering, from source code in simple text editors to development environments that understand the semantics of the code and provide support functions, or the modeling of software with the Unified Modeling Language (Object Management Group [OMG 2007).

The shift from document-based to model-based systems engineering (MBSE) can be well observed in the vision documents published by the International Council on Systems Engineering (INCOSE)[1]. It clearly states that MBSE is "systems engineering enhanced by the usage of models over documents." For those who do not know, INCOSE is the leading worldwide organization for systems engineering. The vision documents state the consolidated opinion of the systems engineering community about how the future of systems engineering will look. The development of the three visions 2020, 2025, and 2035 clearly shows how the systems engineering community anticipates the importance of MBSE, embraces it, and then takes up the capabilities that build on it.

1 www.incose.org.

In 2007, INCOSE published its 2020 vision (INCOSE 2007). Also, in the same year, MBSE was already a hot topic because it was the year when SysML v1.0 was officially released by OMG (2017). However, although the community intensively discussed it, MBSE approaches were not widely adopted in the industry. The vision forecasted the state of systems engineering for 13 years in the future in 2020. It addresses model-based as follows:

"In many respects, the future of systems engineering can be said to be "model-based". A key driver will be the continued evolution of complex, intelligent, global systems that exceed the ability of the humans who design them to comprehend and control all aspects of the systems they are creating."

The year 2020 has already passed, and in retrospect, the forecast was appropriate. Seven years later (in 2014), INCOSE published its next vision for 2025 (INCOSE 2014). The vision 2025 strengthens the statement about MBSE by saying: "MBSE will become the "norm" for systems engineering."

The latest INCOSE Vision 2035, published in 2022, adds to this list of forecasts "a family of unified, integrated MBSE-systems modeling and simulation frameworks" by 2035 (INCOSE 2022).

That statement adds simulation, which is an important purpose of model-based approaches. If machines understand the content, they can simulate aspects to support or even drive analysis, verification, and other engineering tasks.

Only the transition from document-based to descriptive MBSE, which already offers many advantages, lays the foundation for comprehensive simulations, analyses, and the use of artificial intelligence technologies. These technologies can all help close the gap in Figure 4.2.

So, what exactly is "model-based," you might be asking yourself by now? It may be obvious in the first view, but it can raise several questions in the second view. For example, using SysML seems to be "model-based," but what if you just draw the diagrams in a drawing tool? Is a spreadsheet "model-based"? You will find answers and a discussion of the definitions of MBSE and models in Chapter 8.

References

Henderson, K. and Salado, A. (2021). Value and benefits of model-based systems engineering (MBSE): Evidence from the literature. *Systems Engineering* 24 (1): 51–66. https://doi.org/10.1002/sys.21566.

International Council on Systems Engineering (INCOSE) (2007). *Systems Engineering Vision 2020*. San Diego: International Council on Systems Engineering.

International Council on Systems Engineering (INCOSE) (2014). *Systems Engineering Vision 2025*. San Diego: International Council on Systems Engineering.

International Council on Systems Engineering (INCOSE) (2022). *Systems Engineering Vision 2035*. San Diego: International Council on Systems Engineering. https://www.incose.org/about-systems-engineering/se-vision-2035 (accessed 20 April 2023).

Object Management Group (OMG) (2007). 'OMG System Modeling Language Version 1.0, formal/07-09-01'. Object Management Group.

Object Management Group (OMG) (2017). 'Unified Modeling Language Version 2.5.1, formal/17-12-05'. Object Management Group.

5

From Single Product to Product-line-based Delivery Approach

5.1 Introduction

Companies across all industrial sectors are constantly striving to deliver better (safer, more reliable, more attractive) products at a faster pace and with higher profits in extremely competitive markets. Delivering the appropriate product with ever shorter time-to-market and at competitive costs becomes not only a critical factor for survival in historically saturated markets but also to get a foothold in new emerging markets. There are many different ways to face this challenge. However, in both product-push markets, where companies can manufacture off-the-shelf products ready for the delivery to customers, and in more traditional tender-driven markets, organizations are increasingly recognizing the necessity to transition from traditional project-oriented methodologies to a more holistic and efficient product-line-based approach.

This chapter explains the critical importance of this shift, beginning with displaying the challenges derived from project-oriented delivery approaches in Section 5.2. These challenges often manifest as limitations in scalability, adaptability, and resource optimization, hindering an organization's ability to remain competitive.

Section 5.3 shows how the concept of product-line development emerges as a central solution to these challenges. A product-line-based delivery approach is finally introduced in Section 5.4. This approach contrasts strongly with the isolated and often siloed nature of project-oriented approaches, offering a more integrated and efficient path to product creation.

In Section 5.4, we introduce the concept of product line and other ancillary concepts such as product platform and product family. Section 5.5 concludes by underlining how organizations can exploit the synergies of commonality and variability within their product lines, leading to enhanced innovation, reduced time-to-market, and greater cost-effectiveness.

This chapter aims to provide the motivation for a change in the delivery approach, highlighting how a product-line-based methodology is not merely a response to the challenges of project-oriented approaches but a strategic move towards sustained success and market leadership.

5.2 Project-oriented Approaches

In many organizations, projects serve as the foundation of their operations. Even when organizations have a centralized engineering function and release their products incrementally, they often deliver each product as a standalone project, resulting in a lack of synergies across products (Young and Clements 2017). While standalone projects offer advantages such as temporary organization

Model-Based Product Line Engineering (MBPLE): The Feature-Based Path to Product Lines Success, First Edition.
Marco Forlingieri et al.

with framed resource allocation and clear time-based deliverables, they can also lead to a siloed culture with limited collaboration and minimal reuse of solutions across projects. Consequently, the overall utilization of time and resources within the company may become inefficient when considering the collective scope of all projects. Organizations that adopt a project-oriented approach to manage each project as a single entity, and face challenges when trying to manage a portfolio of products due to the limited synergies within the portfolio.

In this setup, each product is often developed and evolved in isolation from others, or the best-case scenario, begins as a copied version of a similar product. This "clone" is then modified to meet the unique requirements of the new product or customer. Unfortunately, this project-centric approach does little to capitalize on the shared aspects or commonality among products in a portfolio after the cloning process. This approach, known as "clone-and-own" (see Chapter 3), also offers minimal benefits during the maintenance and repair of a product, where data indicate that most products utilize up to 90% of the project resources (Young and Clements 2017). In the end, all this translates into a loss of knowledge and investments across projects.

Within project-oriented environments, especially in large projects within the naval, rolling stock, aerospace, and defense sectors, specific customer requirements are often the primary driving force behind product development. As introduced in Chapter 2 for the complex products and systems (CoPS) category, these requirements emerge from a detailed and competitive bid process, often beginning with calls for tenders and culminating in the award and negotiation of customer specifications. For each tender, companies design or adapt an existing product to meet these specific and detailed customer requirements. This leads to design and sourcing activities being heavily customized for each individual project, which, along with complex systems and project organizations, make reuse challenging.

This situation often results in an excessive number of hours dedicated to parallel product developments. Sometimes, engineers discover the potential for reuse almost inadvertently. For example, opportunities for reuse are identified only after specific customer requests are raised or when an engineer who worked on a previous project identifies similar requirements, leading "by accident" to carryover of functions or components from past projects (Forlingieri 2014).

5.3 Shifting Toward a More Efficient Paradigm

Although organizations recognize the need for reuse within their product portfolios, the implementation of these strategies faces numerous barriers related to project constraints, the mindset of people, and the nature of the product itself, similar to the CoPS category discussed in Chapter 2.

In many industries, there is a constantly growing need for systems that are qualitatively better, safer, and more cost-effective, with shorter times to market. Engineers work hard to make their systems simpler and easier to use while incorporating the latest innovations. Moreover, as previously mentioned, in most industries, systems are rarely built entirely from scratch. Engineers often reuse elements from previous projects or products, including documents, processes, or models (Chalé Góngora et al. 2014), in an effort to improve quality, reduce costs, and speed up delivery.

While software development often relies on well-established reuse practices, the formalization of reuse techniques in systems engineering is relatively recent development. There is still a lot to learn about reuse practices in real-world industrial settings (see Chapter 3), even though engineers have been informally reusing requirements and design artifacts for a long time.

Platform strategies are common practices in the industry aimed at reducing resources such as cost and time during all stages of product development through systematic reuse. In particular, in the automotive industry, they refer to standardization and differentiation strategies for product development, production process, and procurement based on the reuse of underbody structures, which usually include the front floor, underfloor, engine compartment, and frame (Muffatto 1999).

Product platforms enable the transfer of technology and the reuse of assets across different projects, significantly cutting down lead time and engineering hours for each new product compared to creating a new design from scratch (Forlingieri 2024).

Standardized and pre-tested components lead to better product performance and lower risk, thanks to the benefits of accumulated learning and experience. This approach, also known as composability, helps companies manage the increasing demand for diverse and customized products while keeping complexity in check. Especially in stable markets that do not often experience product disruption, establishing a strong product platform can give companies a dominant position in the market and open doors to new opportunities. Platform solutions are strategic means that can provide a technological edge and facilitate the use of common assets in various products or projects. However, the move toward strategic reuse, proactively planned and supported by product platform solutions, often encounters resistance from key players in project-oriented organizations, namely project managers and engineering managers.

If you are reading this chapter, it is likely that you are involved in a project or have experience working on one. You are aware that the project manager holds the reins of authority in this temporary organizational setup. The scenario we are about to explore is a familiar one in the context of projects, especially when a company aims to implement reuse strategies within a project-oriented culture.

Let us assume that the centralized engineering function of a rolling stock manufacturer came up with the idea of developing a product platform to offer enhanced adaptability for future customizations and upgrades. The platform promises long-term industry leadership. However, the project manager faced a tough decision: Adopting this platform would mean facing the "lead penalty"–a delay in investment returns until the break-even point was reached, resulting in increased initial costs and project timelines. The project manager's primary obligation is to ensure that the project remains within its allocated budget and schedule!

The project manager's performance is evaluated solely on the success of the current project. Investing resources in a platform that would yield benefits for future projects appears to be a risky and unappealing move. This scenario, while specific to rolling stock development, mirrors similar dilemmas across various industries, illustrating the often-difficult balance between short-term project objectives and long-term business benefits.

Project managers are not the only actors who can pose obstacles in promoting reuse practices within project-oriented organizations; middle management and, to a certain extent, engineers can also play a significant role in it. The "Not-Invented-Here" syndrome is a notable example where engineers might be skeptical about reusing solutions developed by others in a different project. This skepticism often comes from the belief that externally developed solutions may not meet the specific needs of their project. This might result in unnecessary duplication of engineering efforts, inconsistencies in technical data, and missed opportunities for learning and innovating.

To address these challenges, forward-thinking organizations have turned to a product-line-based delivery approach. This approach aims to maximize commonality within and across product lines, fostering collaboration, innovation, and efficiency. Rather than treating each product as an isolated project, these organizations focus on developing common and variable assets that can be reused across multiple products and on managing these as a single entity. The organization's structure, policies, and development processes are also adapted to a product line-based delivery approach.

By allocating most resources to the product line itself, rather than to specific projects, organizations can establish a centralized hub of expertise. This concentration of resources promotes collaboration and knowledge sharing among functions and teams, breaking down the barriers between projects and fostering a culture of continuous improvement. Since team members have a clear view on long-term objectives and roadmaps and on short-term deliveries expected by customer projects, they are better equipped to find the right balance when making technical decisions.

So far, we have introduced some new concepts, such as “Product Platform” and “Product Line.” It is now time to define these concepts and shed light on them.

5.4 Product Platform, Product Family, and Their Derived Products

The concept of “product platform,” or simply “platform,” is now a familiar term among R&D engineers and product managers across various industries. Its widespread usage and implementation have led to diverse interpretations. Broadly speaking, platform thinking involves recognizing and leveraging similarities across products and target markets to create and deliver new offerings. It enables companies to structure and develop a product platform, which is essential “a collection of subsystems and interfaces forming a common foundation from which a variety of derivative products (also known as “member products”) can efficiently evolve” (Meyer and Lehnerd 1997).

Terms such as “product platform,” “product family” (or “product line”), and “member products” are often used in this context. It is crucial to understand that these terms have hierarchical differences and are not interchangeable, with the exception of “product family” and “product line,” which can be used synonymously (Forlingieri 2014). A product line is defined as a set of products that share common features, functions, or characteristics and are developed from a common set of core assets in a prescribed way (ISO/IEC 2015). A member product is a product that is part of a product line” (ISO/IEC 2015). A product platform, which is technically a composable product-line architecture is therefore neither the same as a member product (quite intuitive at this point!) nor the same as a product line; it is one possible way to implement product lines, and it refers to the common basis of all individual products within a product line.

For instance, in automotive, sharing underbodies “platforms” between car models can lead to a decrease in capital investment by up to 50%, particularly in welding equipment, and a 30% reduction in product lead time (Simpson et al. 2005). A prime example of a product platform from the late 1990s is Volkswagen. Many are familiar with Volkswagen’s Platforms A and C, which included essential components such as the floor group, drive system, running gear, and parts of the cockpit. This platform is effectively shared across four brands: Volkswagen, Audi, Seat, and Skoda. In simple terms, models developed using Platform A or C is what we call product lines, from which various member products can be created (Simpson et al. 2005).

For simplification, in this case, we can refer to the member products as the finished and configured cars, which customers ultimately purchase from the dealership.

5.5 Product-line-based Delivery

To understand the concept of product-line-based delivery, it is a prerequisite to introduce two key dimensions of the approach, first defined in the ISO 26550 (ISO/IEC 2015): domain engineering and application engineering. While the terms have been quite used in the software domain, they may result in misleading system development, probably due to their software domain-related origin.

Domain engineering consists of the phase where the product line is consistently defined in terms of features and related domain assets (aka shared assets). On the other hand, application engineering represents the phase where a product is configured out of the product line by selecting the in-scope features and deriving the related domain assets into application assets for their usage in the resulting products. As illustrated in Chapter 2, the high level of customization required by a certain type of system does not permit pure product standardization. The only way to boost reuse is the implementation of a product-line-based development where the reuse is not only focused on the product itself but also on the related engineering assets (Chami et al. 2017).

Product-line delivery approaches always require the strategic development of engineering assets that can serve multiple products. Figure 5.1 simplifies the differences between a single-product development and a product-line development.

In the first approach, products A's and B's requirements, design, and realization assets are developed in parallel in an isolated manner. In contrast, in a product-line development, both common and variable assets are developed with the intent to serve both products A and B, avoiding duplication and rework.

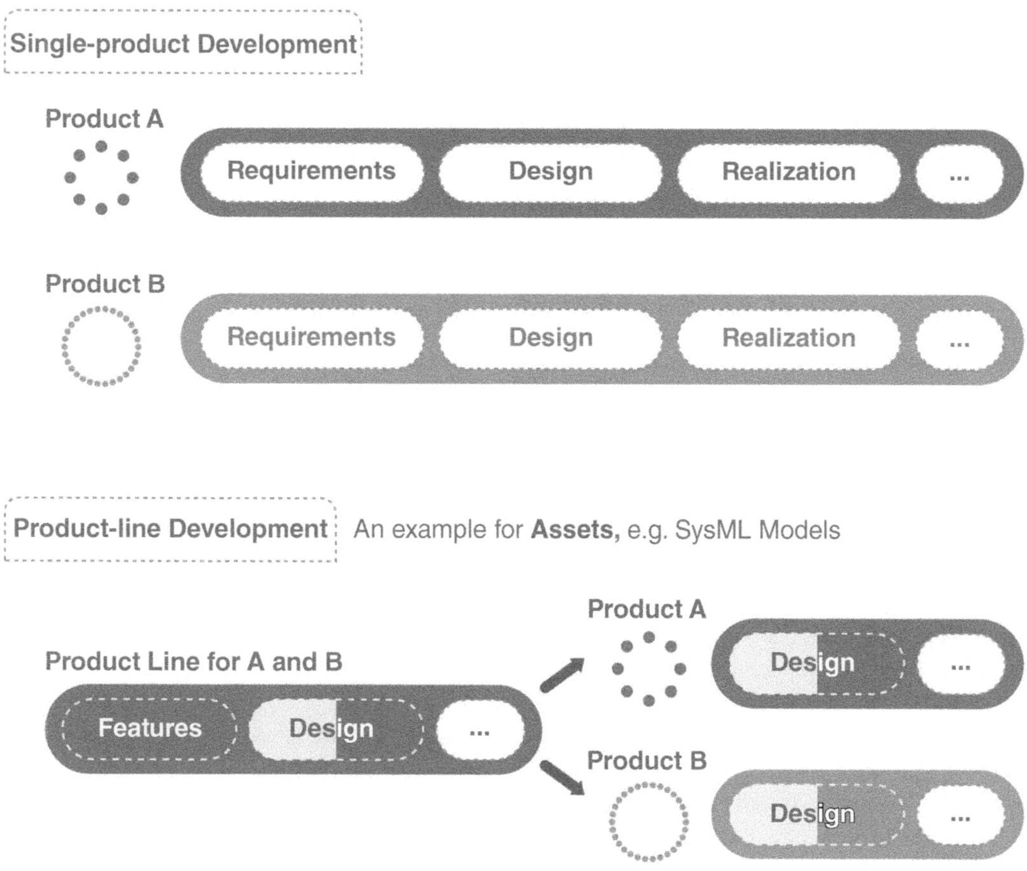

Figure 5.1 Differences between single-product development and product-line development.

By embracing a product-line-based approach, organizations can unlock several advantages:

- Collaboration and synergies: as teams align around the product line and share knowledge, resources, and best practices. This collaborative environment fosters innovation, accelerates development cycles, and ultimately leads to improved product quality.
- Reuse of verified and validated engineering assets: rather than reinventing the wheel for each product, organizations can leverage existing assets that have undergone rigorous testing and validation. This not only saves time and resources but also reduces the risk of errors and improves overall product reliability.
- Strategic collaboration within the supply chain: by aligning processes, standards, and requirements across the product line, organizations can establish stronger relationships with suppliers, partners, and other stakeholders that are committed not just to a single product but to a product line. This collaboration streamlines the development and delivery of multiple member products, enhances supply chain efficiency, and drives overall competitiveness.
- Smoother identification of defects and solutions: in traditional project-oriented development, if a defect is identified, all impacted projects must individually address and rectify the issue. In contrast, within a product-line-based development, the defect can be fixed within the product line itself, benefiting all member products. This defect resolution approach not only saves time and resources but also ensures consistent product quality across the entire product line.
- Efficient allocations of experienced engineers: rather than spreading these valuable resources thinly across multiple projects, they can be dedicated to the product line (out-of-cycle development), where their expertise can be fully utilized. This concentration of knowledge leads to higher-quality outputs and faster development cycles.

These are just some of the advantages that can arise from the shift of organizations from project-oriented to product-line-based delivery. More insights are shared in Chapter 21.

References

Chalé Góngora, H.G., Ferrogalini, M., and Moreau, C. (2014). How to boost PLE by using MBSE – a case study of a rolling stock product line. In: *Proceedings of the 5th International Conference on Complex Systems Design and Management (CSDM)*, Paris, France: Springer.

Chami, M., Forlingieri, M., and Oggier, P. (2017). Model-based variability management solution with SysM. *Prostep Journal*, 2017_01.

Forlingieri, M. (2014). Platform planning and design for rail rolling stock: an exploratory study of platform development within Bombardier transportation. University of Twente, Student Theses. https://essay.utwente.nl/66384/.

Meyer, M.H. and Lehnerd, A.P. (1997). The power of product platforms. In: *Building Value and Cost Leadership*. New York, NY: Free Press.

Muffatto, M. (1999). Introducing a platform strategy in product development. *International Journal of Production Economics*, 60–61: 145–153.

Simpson, T.W., Siddique, Z., and Jiao, J. (eds.) (2005). *Product Platform and Product Family Design: Methods and Applications*, 1–15. New York: Springer.

Young, B. and Clements, P. (2017). Model-based engineering and product line engineering: combining two powerful approaches at Raytheon. In: *27th Annual INCOSE International Symposium (IS 2017)*, Adelaide, Australia.

6

Digital Continuity and System Life Cycle Management

6.1 Introduction

Digital continuity, as a key enabler of system life cycle management, ensures that as the system evolves, all stakeholders – from designers to operators – can depend on a single source of truth. It serves as the thread that weaves through the life cycle, connecting disparate pieces of data into a coherent whole. This chapter explores how digital continuity becomes a necessity when dealing with variability spread across the multiple assets of a product line. It shows that without the continuity of engineering data, developing and managing product lines and their member products would be impossible.

Section 6.2 reintroduces the concept of complexity and its demand for a digital continuity of the engineering data. Section 6.3 provides the basic concepts of the system life cycle and its importance across engineering domains. The integration of various engineering disciplines and domains – mechanical, electronic, and software – is no longer optional but required to build complex systems. Section 6.4 shows how, in this context, the integration of diverse engineering tools and data presents a significant challenge, despite the advantages that it brings. The chapter then discusses the role of frameworks such as the Open Services for Life Cycle Collaboration (OSLC 2021) and other frameworks like modeling and simulation information in a collaborative systems engineering context (ISO 2021). Finally, it concludes with Section 6.5, where the need of a digital continuity becomes even more critical due to the third-dimensional aspect added by the product line variability in the development artifacts.

6.2 The "Eternal Return" of Complexity

The "Eternal Return" is a Nietzschean philosophical concept that states that time repeats itself in an infinite loop, with exactly the same events continuing to occur in exactly the same way, over and over again, for eternity (Nietzsche 1883). Similarly, the concept of "complexity" is treated in this book!

Building on the concepts of complexity introduced earlier, it is clear that the role of engineering has been transformed. While the technical and creative facets remain valued, they are now part of a larger, more integrated approach. The integration of advanced information technology

Model-Based Product Line Engineering (MBPLE): The Feature-Based Path to Product Lines Success, First Edition.
Marco Forlingieri et al.

solutions – simplifying tools and tool chains – into every stage of development is not just a response to complexity but a proactive strategy to cope with it.

In the past, engineers could focus separately on discrete components of a product. Today, they must consider how these components interact with and affect each other and the entire system – and even beyond, the system's operational environment. In fact, we can say that systems engineering for today's systems require a continuous digital fabric as a foundation to connect every aspect of the system.

6.3 System Life Cycle and Multiple Domains

ISO/IEC/IEEE 15288 (2023) is a standard that defines a set of processes for systems engineering. This standard is crucial in providing a structured framework for the life cycle of systems, from their initial concepts through retirement. The standard defines in detail the technical process that must be put in place for the successful delivery of systems as well as the life cycle stages of a system (ISO/IEC/IEEE 2023).

During these stages, a myriad of data is generated, ranging from requirements and design documents to test reports and maintenance logs. The integrity and availability of this information are critical for the continuous progression from one stage to the next.

As we explore the varied domains, disciplines, and techniques involved in system development – mechanical, electronic, software, modeling, and simulations, to name a few – it becomes evident that the data produced must be consistent and managed throughout the entire life cycle of the system. This requirement extends beyond the confines of individual disciplines, necessitating an environment where data generated during each stage is not only reliable but also accessible across all domains (Eigner and Stelzer 2009). In single-system developments, this leads to the need for system life cycle management.

At each life cycle stage of the system, several domains are, in fact, involved in the production of engineering assets. Their consistency and management become crucial along the system engineering life cycles.

The production of data in each stage from multiple domains is a complex task. Each domain may use specialized tools and methods to produce and manage its data, but it is imperative that this data must remain synchronized along the system development. Inconsistencies or inaccuracies in the data can lead to errors, delays, and increased costs, which highlights the importance of digital continuity.

Without it, consistency and efficiency can hardly be ensured, as each stage builds upon the accuracy and completeness of the information generated in the previous stages.

As we progress through the ISO/IEC/IEEE 15288 life cycle stages, the collaborative effort of multiple disciplines contributes to the success of system development. This collaboration is fueled by the data each domain generates, relies on, and contributes to. The harmonization of this data across the life cycle is not just beneficial but essential, forming the backbone of an integrated, multidisciplinary approach to systems engineering in the digital era. In addition, data production and exchange extend beyond the confines of individual enterprises, incorporating suppliers and other stakeholders into the fold. This extended enterprise further justifies a digital continuity of data that allows for seamless data exchange and collaboration, ensuring that all entities contribute effectively to the product's key success factors: time-to-market, cost, and quality (Eigner and Stelzer 2009).

6.4 Digital Continuity and Its Challenges

One of the most pressing challenges in systems engineering today remains the fragmentation across the engineering tools and data landscape (International Council on Systems Engineering 2022). As mentioned earlier, the goal is to integrate tools and data from various domains and vendors, creating a federation across domain-specific tools to enable collaboration and analysis.

For instance, the Department of Defense (DoD) has set forth engineering foundational principles to guide future developments and facilitate data creation and management (DoD 2023). These principles are the following:

- Formalizing the development, integration, and use of models: This involves using digital models to inform decision-making at both enterprise and program levels, which is expected to facilitate more informed decisions, greater insight, and increased transparency.
- Providing an enduring, authoritative source of truth: This principle emphasizes the need for digital threads, which are data-driven architectures linking information from across the product life cycle. These threads are envisioned to be the primary data and communication platforms for a company's products.
- Incorporating technological innovation: The adoption of technological advancements is crucial to improve engineering practices.
- Establishing a supporting infrastructure: This involves creating infrastructure to support various activities, enable collaboration, and facilitate communication across stakeholders.
- Transforming the workforce: It's essential to equip and encourage the workforce to adopt and support digital engineering across the product life cycle.

However, implementing these principles comes with several challenges:

- Integrating life cycle models and heterogeneous environments: Ensuring consistency and traceability across various models that describe different aspects of the system at different life cycle stages is a significant challenge.
- Maintaining "authoritative sources" for the entire system: This involves managing consistency across domain models and tools, and ensuring that changes in one domain are accurately reflected in related domains.
- Managing consistency across domain models and tools: It is necessary to facilitate data consistency across life cycle models, which can be challenging as models and their constituents evolve over time.
- Enabling cross-life cycle digital viewpoints for stakeholders: Digital threads should provide digital continuity, establish digital relationships across different life cycle models, and create a federated life cycle information model overlaid on various domain-specific models.
- Digital connectivity: Creating effective digital connectivity across authoritative sources of truth is crucial. This involves creating a web of links across all data sources, where each link carries certain semantics.

Central to these principles is the concept of the digital thread – a data architecture that provides a reliable communication platform across the product life cycle.

The Open Services for Life Cycle Collaboration (OSLC) framework (OSLC 2024) plays a crucial role in facilitating the implementation of data continuity in engineering. It promotes an open and federated environment for engineering collaboration, allowing different tools and systems to interact seamlessly. This interoperability is vital for the engineering data continuity, as it necessitates the integration of diverse tools and data sources across various engineering domains.

OSLC's contribution lies in its standardization of interfaces, which simplifies the integration of disparate tools by allowing them to share and exchange data in a predictable manner. This standardization enhances interoperability and reduces the complexity of integrating various systems. A significant benefit of OSLC is the support it offers for cross-domain data integration, which is a key challenge in implementing digital threads.

Furthermore, OSLC lays the groundwork for data continuity by providing a foundational framework that supports the creation of a data-driven architecture. This architecture links various datasets, models, and systems across the product life cycle, offering a comprehensive view of the product development process.

The integration and interoperability facilitated by OSLC lead to more informed decision-making and increased efficiency in engineering processes. Stakeholders gain access to a broader range of data and insights, reducing redundancy and rework due to improved data consistency and accessibility.

In essence, OSLC is instrumental in addressing the challenges of implementing digital threads by promoting open standards, enhancing cross-domain collaboration, and establishing a unified and interconnected engineering environment (Gery 2023).

There are several frameworks that can complement or serve as alternatives to OSLC. For example, MoSSEC (2021) facilitates the sharing of model context across various domains, overcoming traceability challenges during the transfer of information from one domain to another within the realm of modeling and simulation. Similar to OSLC, it provides a framework for collaboration across distributed datasets. MoSSEC's primary goal is to document and convey the who, what, when, where, and why of modeling and simulation data whenever it is exchanged. This approach offers a more detailed and encompassing strategy compared to the Functional Mock-up Interface.

6.5 Digital Continuity for System Variability

Digital continuity, summarized as the integration of life cycle models and the management of authoritative data sources, presents significant challenges. These complexities are amplified when dealing with not just a single complex system but multiple system variants issued from a product line. Eigner and Stelzer (2009) identify the system life cycle and the multiple domains as two critical dimensions of system development.

As Figure 6.1 shows, the development of product lines introduces a third dimension, the system variants – or simply variability. If not managed correctly, engineering assets can quickly duplicate and grow in an exponential and inconsistent manner.

The central challenge lies in handling the commonality and variability in the engineering data of system variants. Each variant, while being a member of a broader product line, possesses its unique configuration and set of interdependencies. Managing these effectively calls for a strategic approach to maintaining a single source of variability and enhanced configuration management capabilities (as further explained in Chapter 19). This ensures that all reusable assets within the product line are consistently managed and their interrelations

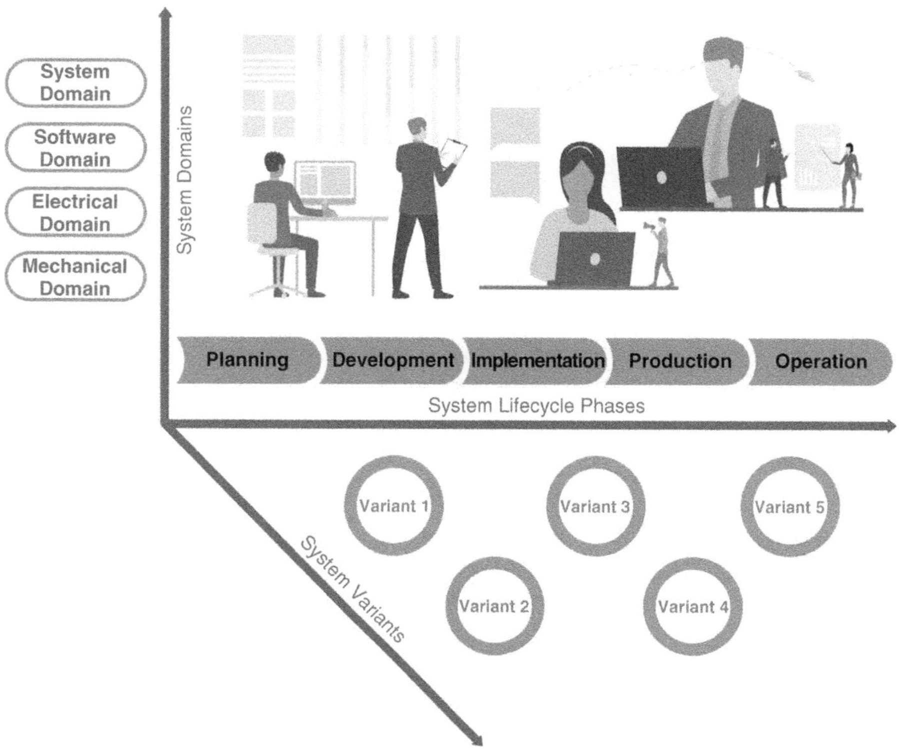

Figure 6.1 System domains, life cycle phases, and variants.

meticulously overseen, as highlighted by Forlingieri (2022). Configuration management is the discipline that covers those important aspects. Chapter 18 offers a complete example of digital continuity in the MBPLE context, while Chapter 19 explores further into configuration management for product lines.

Let's explain this concept with a simple example. Figure 6.2 illustrates an aircraft product line that utilizes a set of shared assets. These assets are used in different aircraft variants (aka member products) related to seating capacities ranging from 150 to 180 or 124 to 156 seats, as an example. We assume that most of the requirements will be the same, but many will vary across the member products, impacting also design, testing, and discipline-specific assets.

The example illustrates that with digital continuity in place, it becomes possible to monitor and propagate changes across product line assets (aka shared assets), aircraft variant requirements, and other related assets, rather than navigating through a collection of disconnected clone-and-own data sets.

In such a complex environment, the importance of digital continuity goes beyond being just an optional element; it becomes an essential prerequisite. Digital continuity plays a critical role in enabling efficient reuse practices, above all in product line engineering, allowing for accurate product configurations, and facilitating comprehensive analyses of the impacts of changes.

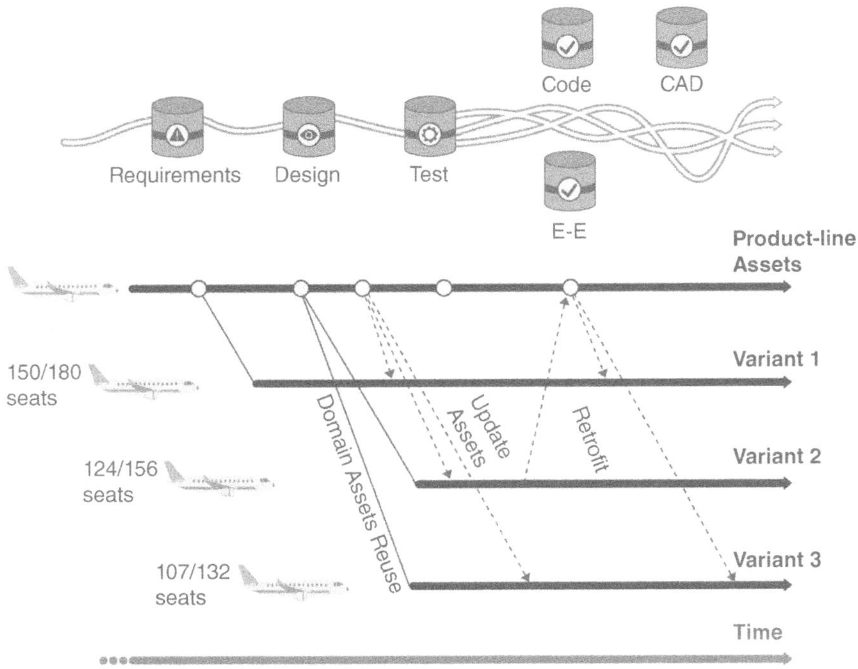

Figure 6.2 Example of digital continuity across multiple variants.

References

Eigner, M. and Stelzer, R. (2009). Product lifecycle management: *Ein Leitfaden für Product Development und Lifecycle Management*, 2e. Berlin: Springer.

Forlingieri, M. (2022). The four dimensions of variability and their impact on MBPLE: how to approach variability in the development of aircraft product lines at airbus. In: *Proceedings of the 16th International Working Conference on Variability Modeling of Software-Intensive Systems (VAMOS 22)*: 23–25 February 2022, Italy. ACM, Vamos.

Gery, E. (2023). Digital threads – benefits, challenges, and best practices. *Presented at the AOSEC Conference*, October 2023.

International Council on Systems Engineering (INCOSE) (2022). Systems engineering vision 2035. https://sevisionweb.incose.org (accessed July 2023).

ISO (2021). Industrial automation systems and integration – product data representation and Exchange – application protocol: for modelling and simulation information in a collaborative systems engineering context (MoSSEC) (ISO 10303–243:2021).

ISO/IEC/IEEE 15288 (2023). Systems and software engineering – system life cycle processes.

Nietzsche, F.W. (2006). *Thus Spoke Zarathustra: A Book for all and None*. Originally 1883–1885. Cambridge: Cambridge University Press.

Office of the Under Secretary of Defense for Research and Engineering (DoD) (2023). *DOD Instruction 5000.97 Digital Engineering, December 2018*. Washington, DC: Office of the Under Secretary of Defense for Research and Engineering.

OSLC Core Version 3.0 (2021). Part 1: Overview. In: *OASIS Project Specification 02* (ed. J. Amsden and A. Berezovskyi), 23 April 2021, OASIS Open Project.

Part II

Foundations of MBPLE

The second part of this book provides an overview of the foundations of Model-Based Product Line Engineering (MBPLE). It begins by presenting a brief history of MBPLE in Chapter 7, including its origins in the object-oriented methodologies of the end of the twentieth century.

The main foundations of MBPLE are then presented in Chapter 8. Systems Engineering (SE), Model-Based Systems Engineering (MBSE), and Product Line Engineering (PLE) define the basic elements that, combined in a holistic approach, provide the means to improve the efficiency of product development. Chapter 8 introduces the key MBPLE concepts, which are further developed in the rest of Part 1.

The main concepts of MBPLE are described in Chapter 9. Concepts such as *features, feature models, shared asset supersets*, and *member products* are explained in terms that facilitate understanding before moving to the more formal definitions later in the book. These concepts are based on published standards, noticeably *ISO/IEC, 2021. ISO/IEC 26580:2021 Software and systems engi neering – Methods and tools for the feature-based approach to software and systems product line eng ineering*.

Chapter 10 focuses on the importance of modeling languages for MBPLE. These languages support the definition of shared reusable assets of different nature, as well as the formalization of the variability of product lines through feature models. Instead of presenting specific modeling solutions, the chapter outlines the requirements for such modeling languages (including interoperability requirements) and elaborates on the role of SysML v2 in the landscape of modeling languages for MBPLE.

The last chapter of Part II (Chapter 11) presents a short analysis of international standards related to MBPLE. These standards cover the domains of PLE, SE, MBSE, methods and tools, and data formalization and exchange. The goal of Chapter 11 is not to dress an exhaustive panorama of available standards but rather to point to those standards that are central to MBPLE and to which the reader can refer for further details.

7

Past, Present, and Future of MBPLE

7.1 Introduction

The landscape of software engineering has experienced a remarkable evolution since the 1960s, a journey marked by significant milestones, groundbreaking methodologies, and the emergence of key paradigms that have shaped the modern digital world. As we dive deep into the heart of this transformative journey in Section 7.2, we will explore the profound changes initiated by the advent of object-oriented languages and methodologies in the 1990s. This period not only introduced new programming languages into real-world projects but also marked the debut of object-oriented design and analysis, planting the first seed of what would lead to model-based product line engineering (MBPLE) today.

The narrative then transitions to Section 7.3, drawing a parallel between the cloning of "Dolly" the sheep and the clone-and-own practices prevalent in software development at the time. This era underscored the challenges and limitations of early software product line development, highlighting the need for more sophisticated and sustainable methodologies.

In Section 7.4, we witness the evolution of product line engineering (PLE), characterized by the systematic use of feature models and engineering assets. This section examines the shift toward a more efficient, PLE-oriented approach to software development, signifying a major advancement in the discipline.

In Section 7.5, the chapter expands its focus beyond software to encompass systems engineering. The introduction of model-based systems engineering (MBSE) and the SysML represents a pivotal shift, indicating the beginning of a new era where software engineering principles begin to intersect with systems engineering, leading to the emergence of MBPLE.

Finally, Section 7.6 explores the synergistic relationship between PLE and MBSE, detailing the efforts to model variability within SysML and the challenges of integrating PLE and MBSE practices.

7.2 Everything Started with Software Engineering

Since the software crisis of the 1960s and the NATO Software Engineering Conferences (Naur and Randell 1969), the field of software engineering has undergone significant evolution. The late 1980s and early 1990s, in particular, prefigured a new era of coding and software development methodologies. During this period, object-oriented design and analysis made their debut in the software engineering landscape. Early on, there was considerable debate among experts regarding how design methods, which had gained popularity in the 1980s, could be adapted to the flourishing

Model-Based Product Line Engineering (MBPLE): The Feature-Based Path to Product Lines Success, First Edition.
Marco Forlingieri et al.

Figure 7.1 A type of methodologist you would have encountered during the "Methods War."

object-oriented paradigm. This period saw a proliferation of methodologies and notations designed to support object-oriented methods, leading to intense debates and disagreements among methodologists, a time humorously named the "Methods War" (Scott and Fowler 1997). A joke from this era summarizes the atmosphere: "What's the difference between a methodologist and a terrorist? You can negotiate with a terrorist!" (Scott and Fowler 1997). Figure 7.1 epitomizes the mood of the time!

Among these debates, three pioneers of object-oriented modeling – Grady Booch, Jim Rumbaugh, and Ivan Jacobson, collectively known as the "Three Amigos" – emerged. Their contributions led the object management group (OMG) to initiate a task force aimed at creating a unified modeling notation. This effort culminated in the successful development of the unified modeling language (UML) (OMG 1997), highlighting that despite variations in methods, the notations employed showed remarkable consistency.

Concurrently, the 1990s witnessed the emergence of other significant movements within the software engineering field. Among these, feature-oriented domain analysis (FODA), conceptualized by Kang et al. (1990), represented the earliest methodology within the feature model family. FODA's primary aim is the identification of prominent or distinguishing features of software systems. These features, visible to users, delineate the domain's scope and give the methodology its name. They encapsulate both the commonalities within the domain and the distinctions between related systems, serving to define the domain through a spectrum of mandatory, optional, or alternative characteristics (Kang et al. 1990).

The introduction of object-oriented languages marked a pivotal moment in software engineering. It opened avenues for component reuse in software development. This shift facilitated the creation of configurable software, with feature models gaining popularity in the software product line community. This community focused on strategies that enable developers to create software that could serve multiple products rather than just one. Central to these methodologies is the use of models to delineate the variations and similarities among the resulting products or implementation fragments (Beuche et al. 2004).

The foundation of modern model-based software product line engineering can be traced back to the innovations of UML and FODA, marking the genesis of modern software development methodologies and beyond.

7.3 The First Generation of Software Product Line Development: The "Dolly" Era

The origins of PLE, are often traced back to McIlroy's (1968) work on "Mass Produced Software Components." However, it was again in the 1990s that the discipline started to form consensus and its application became more visible. During this time, a worldwide event unfolded that seemed to leap from the pages of science fiction into reality. "Dolly" the sheep emerged as the first mammal

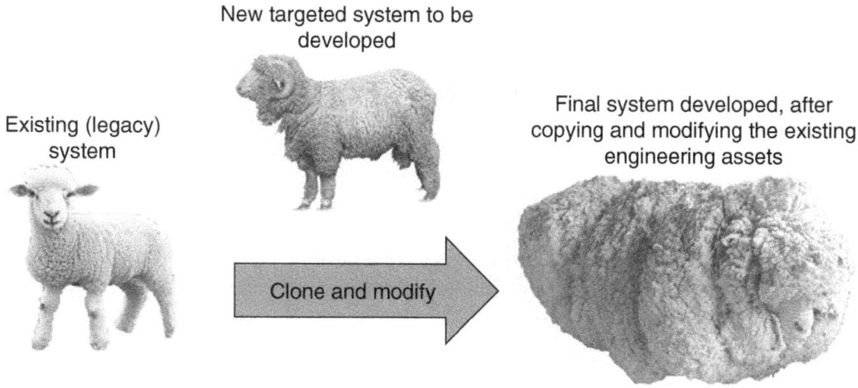

Figure 7.2 Example of a bad result of clone-and-own practices.

successfully cloned from an adult cell, a feat that paralleled the cloning practices within the software industry, albeit with starkly different complexities and implications. In fact, in the software development landscape, the practice of cloning, characterized by copying software codes and components for the creation of new applications within product lines, was still prevalent. This approach was not only limited to the software code itself but also included other engineering assets such as requirements and test artifacts.

Beyond investing in technical design and developing domain artifacts, adopting PLE often requires changing processes, organizational structures, and tools, leading to significant investments. As discussed in Chapter 3, instead of using a PLE approach, software systems are frequently created by "cloning" existing ones. This involves copying and modifying the requirements, architecture, and code of previous systems. This "clone-and-own" method became popular because it allows for quick adaptation to new technologies and meets the demands of fast development cycles.

Despite the reuse and some successes in the industry, this approach presents several limitations, which are introduced in Chapter 3 and detailed in Chapter 21. Talking about our "Dolly," Figure 7.2 exemplifies the result of uncontrolled clone-and-own practices.

These operational challenges inherent in first generation, product-centric software product line development significantly limit an organization's ability to achieve its strategic objectives. The obstacles include difficulties in meeting deadlines, offering competitive value within controlled costs, ensuring product quality, and expanding the product portfolio's breadth and depth (Lanman et al. 2011).

7.4 The Second Generation of Software Product Line Development

It was in the 2000s that the systematic use of feature models in combination with engineering assets led to the first successful realization of PLE, primarily in automotive (Flores et al. 2012) and defense (Lanman et al. 2011), also called the second generation of software product line development.

According to Lanman et al. (2011), the significant transformation, known as the second generation of product line development, lies in the recognition that it is far more efficient to approach software product line engineering as the development of a production mechanism – a unified system designed to automate the production of all products within a product line – instead of as the creation of numerous interconnected products (similarly to the product-centric approach). This profound, albeit nuanced, realization of the PLE breakthrough emphasizes the importance of concentrating on this singular production method rather than on the extensive array of products.

The second generation of product line development owes much to experts who established foundational principles for the field. In the US, Northrop and Clements' book, Software Product Lines: Practices and Patterns (Northrop and Clements 2001), laid significant groundwork. In Germany, Beuche and Papajewski pioneered a PLE software, pure::variants derived as an outcome of the Consul method (Beuche et al. 2004). Krueger in the US developed Gears by Big Lever (Krueger 2001), marking, similar to Beuche and Papajewski, one of the initial PLE solutions.

Meanwhile, Pohl et al. (2005) introduced an alternative approach to capturing variability through orthogonal variability modeling (OVM), a concept detailed in their work on software product line engineering. On the academic front, institutions such as Carnegie Mellon University in the US, the Waterloo University in Canada, and the Universities of Magdeburg, Duisburg-Essen, and Braunschweig in Germany emerged as key players in advancing the field.

This research contributed to establishing the first norm, ISO/IEC 26550 (ISO/IEC 2015). While this standard was a step towards formalizing PLE, it still lacked a well-defined and formalized PLE approach, which can be adopted by industry practitioners (more details in Chapter 11). Despite its limitations, the standard represents a significant milestone in the evolution of PLE's. However, the Common Variability Language initiative (Øystein et al. 2013) did not achieve the same success. This initiative aimed to create a unified approach to variability modeling but failed due to disagreements among tool vendors and other key stakeholders. This scenario was similar to the "methods war" period, where methodologists were at odds. As a result, a universally accepted variability or feature modeling notation has not emerged, and after over a decade, the "PLE arena" is still dominated by tool-specific solutions.

7.5 From Software Product Lines to System Product Lines

In the early 2000s, the International Council on Systems Engineering (INCOSE) played a pivotal role in evangelizing and promoting systems engineering across various industries. This included the development of ISO 15288, which saw further revisions in 2023 (ISO/IEC/IEEE 15288 2023), and the publication of the *Systems Engineering Handbook*, now in its fifth edition (Walden et al. 2023). During this period, system engineers began recognizing the need for a more formalized approach to architecting systems consistently. They considered UML (OMG 1997) for its potential applicability in system analysis and definition. This consideration led OMG to establish a new task force aimed at creating a modeling language that could extend UML to support system development. Kobryn et al., along with a team of experts from various industries, tool vendors, and academic institutions, introduced the SysML language under OMG in 2007, which has now reached its 1.7 version (OMG 2022). This marked the beginning of the MBSE era, a fundamental shift with no point of return.

As we discussed in the previous section, the advancements of PLE in the software field and the increasing importance of the systems engineering discipline produced interest in a few experts and companies on the possibility to apply PLE in systems development. The idea was not completely new; in fact, the automotive industry had already introduced the use of "car configurators," in the early 1990s, though mainly for manufacturing and not for the engineering of the vehicle. At this stage, MBSE and SysML were at their beginning, so the primary focus on PLE was to look at all those engineering assets produced in several domain-specific repositories and try to identify what varies and map it to those optional or alternative features. Textual requirements were the first natural candidates, but the possibility to reuse CAD models and other PLM artifacts also started to be considered. Bombardier and Alstom in railway (Chami et al. 2017; Chalé Góngora et al. 2014), Thales (Dubois et al. 2012), and US DoD (Clements et al. 2014) in aerospace and defense, General Motors (Flores et al. 2012) in automotive are among the pioneers of the application of PLE n system development.

At this stage, PLE predominantly relied on a document-based approach, yet initial proofs of concept (PoC) and feasibility studies for integrating SysML models were underway. During this period, Hause and Hummell (2015) and Chalé Góngora et al. (2014) introduced the concept of MBPLE, combining PLE and MBSE for the first time.

They were among the first to formalize the concept of a 150% model for SysML assets, presenting initial examples of how to define variation points within SysML use cases, blocks, and parts, and including textual requirements as additional assets within the MBPLE scope. Chalé Góngora et al. (2014), presenting a real-life product family case from the rolling stock industry, outlined a new way of working for MBSE and PLE. They showed how variability can be defined in requirements, system use cases, and system/subsystem architectures (both functional and structural), with the variability model serving as a central reference for defining variation points in the assets (Chalé Góngora et al. 2014).

Several similarities are identified in these initial conceptualizations of the MBPLE approach between those two key references (Hause and Hummell 2015; Chalé Góngora et al. 2014):

- Both sets of authors recognized the potential of integrating MBSE and PLE in response to the increasing complexity of systems.
- Both referenced ISO/IEC 26550 as the standard for PLE and SysML as the language for MBSE.
- Both adopted the OVM notation for creating variability models, a different approach from feature modeling.
- Both highlighted the strong dependency of the approach on tools and tool chains.

At that time, we, the authors of this book, had the chance to actively contribute to the introduction of MBPLE within our respective organizations: Forlingieri at Bombardier Transportation, Weilkiens at Oose, and Chalé at Alstom, recognizing the need to promote this emerging discipline also within the INCOSE PLE Working Group (INCOSE PLE 2024).

7.6 The Liaison Between PLE and MBSE

The absence of methods and a formalized approach to modeling variability within SysML prompted Weilkiens (2016) to develop VAMOS, a technical guide dedicated to modeling and managing variability within SysML models. Although this approach did not explicitly address PLE, it established foundational principles for defining variation beyond the reliance on specific tools.

Forlingieri and his colleagues at Bombardier Transportation addressed a gap left by VAMOS, specifically the creation of variability models and feature models to support the reuse of SysML models (Chami et al. 2017). This development signifies the gradual convergence of essential elements in this field. At the same time, Chalé and Greugny further elaborated on the application of MBPLE to support a "composable" approach for architecture definition in railway rolling stock, providing additional elements for the business case of MBPLE (Chalé Góngora and Greugny 2017).

Additionally, the work of Young and Clements (2017) deserves recognition for showcasing the application of MBSE and PLE within Raytheon in the defense industry. Echoing the endeavors of Hummell and Hause (2015) and Chalé Góngora et al. (2014), their publication provides an example of tool application, this time using a feature modeling approach. It illustrates the model transformation from the comprehensive 150% SysML model to the specific 100% model, guided by various feature configurations.

The period spanning 2020 to 2022 will go down in history as challenging years due to the COVID-19 crisis, yet these years were pivotal for MB-PLE. In 2021, the ISO/IEC 26580 standard (ISO/IEC 26580 2021) was released, providing better guidance on applying PLE in system development using a feature-based approach. Concurrently, Airbus launched its largest digital transformation program in engineering, known as Digital Design Manufacturing & Services (DDMS) (Forlingieri and Ferrogalini 2020), which acknowledged MBSE and PLE as key pillars of this transformation. This initiative spurred progress in the field, leading to significant publications such as "The Four Dimensions of Variability with MBPLE at Airbus" (Forlingieri 2022), detailed in Chapter 17. This work formalizes essential considerations for adopting MBPLE in complex systems.

This momentum for MBPLE facilitated productive collaboration between two of us, Weilkiens and Forlingieri, culminating in the establishment of the first tool-agnostic methodological foundations for MBPLE. They leverage the recently published ISO/IEC 26580 standard and the insights from VAMOS, as well as the experiences gained at Airbus, as shown in "Two Variant Modeling Methods for MBPLE at Airbus" (Forlingieri and Weilkiens 2022), As elaborated in Chapter 15, the approach introduced two complementary methods for modeling variation in SysML models, supported by a feature-based (MB)PLE. Furthermore, the publication outlines essential guidelines for MBPLE adoption, emphasizing the significance of implementing a feature-based PLE, enabling variant modeling in SysML, and separating the methodological discussions from tool dependencies (Forlingieri and Weilkiens 2022).

The following year, Forlingieri and his previous MBPLE team at Airbus advanced their efforts by introducing a methodological approach to model variability, supported by the Airbus MBSE architecture framework, MOFLT (Madeira, de Sousa Pinto, and Forlingieri 2023). This approach illustrates the modeling of variability and variation points across different abstraction layers such as operational, functional, logical, and technical. It emphasizes the importance of a model-based architecture framework as "the backbone" of the feature-based PLE approach.

Another significant boost to the discipline was provided by advancements in the release of SysML v2 (OMG 2023) notation. SysML v1 does not offer a specific notation to facilitate variability modeling, posing a "challenging liaison" (Forlingieri and Weilkiens 2023).

In contrast, SysML v2 introduces the capability to define variation and variants within the model, thereby unlocking multiple opportunities for reuse. These advancements are discussed in more detail in Chapter 15.

In 2023, the world quickly embraced artificial intelligence (AI) with the emergence of open foundation models like OpenAI. While AI was not new to technical audiences, it became popular among non-experts as well.

This technological disruption offers new opportunities in both MBPLE and systems engineering. Chapter 20 explores potential use cases, highlighting the synergy between AI and MBPLE (AI4MBPLE).

This book aims to consolidate theory, practical contributions, and real-world experiences, providing comprehensive guidance on its application. Three decades after the introduction of object-modeling notations and feature models, these concepts have merged and evolved beyond their initial software applications. It is important to recognize the significant contributions of the pioneers in feature modeling, UML and related fields.

References

Beuche, D., Papajewski, H., and Schröder-Preikschat, W. (2004). Variability management with feature models. *Science of Computer Programming* 53 (3): 333–352.

Chalé Góngora, H.G. and Greugny, F. (2017). Where the big bucks (will) come from–Implementing Product Line Engineering for Railway Rolling Stock. In: *INCOSE 2017 International Symposium, Adelaide*, Australia. San Diego, CA: INCOSE.

Chalé Góngora, H.G., Ferrogalini, M., and Moreau, C. (2014). How to boost PLE by using MBSE – A case study of a rolling stock product line. In: *Proceedings of the 5th International Conference on Complex Systems Design and Management (CSDM)*, Paris, France: Springer.

Chami, M., Forlingieri, M., and Oggier, P. (2017). Model-based product line engineering solution with SysML-variability management approach. *Prostep Journal*, 01–2017.

Clements, P., Gregg, S., Krueger, C. et al. (2014). 'Second generation product line engineering takes hold in the DoD. 27. 12-18. https://www.researchgate.net/publication/291850759_Second_Generation_Product_Line_Engineering_Takes_Hold_in_the_DoD.

Dubois, H., Ibanez, V., Saratxaga, C. et al. (2012). The product line engineering approach in a model-driven process. (ERTS2012), Feb 2012, Toulouse, France. HAL Open Science. chrome-extension://efaidnbmnnnibpcajpcglclefindmkaj/https://hal.science/hal-02263430/document.

Flores, R., Krueger, C., and Clements, P. (2012). Mega-scale product line engineering at general motors. In: *Software Product Line Conference 2012*.

Forlingieri, M. (2022). The four dimensions of variability and their impact on MBPLE: how to approach variability in the development of aircraft product lines at Airbus. In: *Proceedings of the 16th International Working Conference on Variability Modelling of Software-Intensive Systems (VaMoS'22)*. Florence, Italy: ACM.

Forlingieri, M. and Ferrogalini, M. (2020). Transforming airbus through product line engineering foundation and real-life implementation. In: *The 14th ESA Workshop on Avionics, Data, Control and Software Systems (ADCSS)*, October 2020.

Forlingieri, M. and Weilkiens, T. (2022). Two Variant Modeling Methods for MBPLE at Airbus. In: *INCOSE Symposium* 2022, Detroit.

Hause, M. and Hummell, J. (2015). Model-based product line engineering—enabling product families with variants. In: *2015 IEEE Aerospace Conference*, Big Sky, MT, USA.

INCOSE PLE (2024) *INCOSE PLE Working Group*. https://www.incose.org/communities/working-groups-initiatives/product-lines (viewed 15 July 2024).

ISO/IEC 26550 (2015). Software and systems engineering—Reference model for product line engineering and management.

ISO/IEC 26580 (2021). Software and systems engineering—Methods and tools for the feature-based approach to software and systems product line engineering.

ISO/IEC/IEEE 15288 (2023). Systems and software engineering—System life cycle processes.

Kang, K., Cohen, S., and Hess, J. et al. (1990). Feature oriented domain analysis (FODA) feasibility study. *Technical Report CMU/SEI-90-TR-21, Software Engineering Institute, Carnegie Mellon* University, Pittsburgh, USA.

Krueger, C. (2001). Easing the transition to software mass customization. In: *Proceedings of the 4th International Workshop on Product Family Engineering, Bilbao*, Spain: Springer-Verlag.

Lanman, J.T., Kemper, B., and Rivera, J., et al. (2011). Employing the second generation software product-line for live training transformation. *Interservice/Industry Training, Simulation, and Education Conference (I/ITSEC)*.

Madeira, R.H., de Sousa Pinto, D.H., and Forlingieri, M. (2023). Variability on system architecture using airbus MBPLE for moflt framework. In: *INCOSE International Symposium*, 33 pp. 601–615.

McIlroy, M.D. (1968). Mass produced software components. In: *Software Engineering: Report of a Conference Sponsored by the NATO Science Committee, Garmisch*, Germany, 7–11 Oct. 1968.

Naur, P. and Randell, B. (1969). Report on a conference sponsored by the NATO science committee: software engineering, *Garmisch, Germany*, 7–11 Oct. 1968, Jan. 1969.

Northrop, L.M. and Clements, P. (2001). Software product lines: Practices and Patterns. Carnegie Mellon University.

Object Management Group (OMG) (1997). Unified Modeling Language (UML) 1.1.

Object Management Group (OMG) (2022). OMG System Modeling Language Version 1.7, formal/22-08-02. OMG.

Object Management Group (OMG) (2023). OMG System Modeling Language Version 2.0, ad/2023-02-11. OMG.

Øystein, H., Wąsowski, A., and Czarnecki, K. (2013). CVL: Common Variability Language. In: Proceedings of the 17th International Software Product Line Conference (SPLC'13), New York, NY, USA, pp. 277.

Pohl, K., Böckle, G., and Linden, F. (2005). *Software Product Line Engineering: Foundations, Principles and Techniques*. Springer.

Scott, K. and Fowler, M. (1997). *UML Distilled: Applying the Standard Object Modeling Language*. Addison Wesley Object Technology Series. London: Addison Wesley.

Walden, D., Garry J. Roedler, Kevin J. Forsberg et al. (2023). *Systems Engineering Handbook: A Guide for System Life Cycle Processes and Activities*, 5e. Sane capability to define vaDiego, CA, USA: INCOSE.

Weilkiens, T. (2016). Variant Modeling with SysML. MBSE4U.

Young, B. and Clements, P. (2017). Model based engineering and product line engineering: combining two powerful approaches at Raytheon. In: 27th Annual INCOSE International Symposium (IS 2017), Adelaide, Australia.

8

Shifting to a Model-based Approach

8.1 Introduction

Model-based product line engineering (MBPLE) touches a range of disciplines, including systems engineering, product line engineering (PLE), and model-based systems engineering (MBSE). It also interfaces with various other engineering and non-engineering disciplines involved in developing a product line. The shift from document-based to model-based engineering, as described in Chapter 4, illustrates the demand for modeling and the shift from PLE to MBPLE.

Section 8.2 briefly introduces systems engineering, and Section 8.3 adds the model-based aspect and discusses the shift from systems engineering to MBSE. Section 8.4 consequently discusses the shift from PLE to MBPLE.

8.2 Systems Engineering

The International Council on Systems Engineering (INCOSE) defines systems engineering as follows:

"Systems Engineering is a transdisciplinary and integrative approach to enable the successful realization, use, and retirement of engineered systems, using systems principles and concepts, and scientific, technological, and management methods" (INCOSE 2023).

The definition sounds clear! However, if you are not already familiar with the discipline, you may not know what systems engineering really is or what a systems engineer does.

The accomplishment of a systems engineer lies in ensuring that everything results in a successful system. Other engineering disciplines have concrete outputs like software, mechanical, or electrical components, while systems engineering has documents and models. The achievement is hard to grasp and is only truly recognized when it is absent.

Although two decades ago, systems engineering was mainly associated with the aerospace and defense industries, today it is applied in almost any company that develops complex systems.

INCOSE drives the systems engineering discipline. Its publication, "*Systems Engineering Handbook*," covers the core topics and tasks of systems engineering (INCOSE 2023). It is based on the ISO/IEC 15288 standard (ISO/IEC/IEEE 2023), which defines systems engineering processes in four process groups:

1. Agreement processes: for example, acquisition and supply;
2. Organizational project-enabling processes: for example, infrastructure management;

Model-Based Product Line Engineering (MBPLE): The Feature-Based Path to Product Lines Success, First Edition.
Marco Forlingieri et al.

3. Technical management processes: for example, risk management;
4. Technical processes: for example, requirements and architecture definition.

The standard does not have an explicit process for product lines, but several processes cover the topic. For more details, see Chapter 24.

8.3 Model-based Systems Engineering

In simple terms, MBSE is "systems engineering using models to perform tasks." While documents still hold value, they are primarily derived from or exported from models to present different views of the model information. Still, documents shall not be the single source of engineering information. Chapter 4 discusses the need for MBSE in more detail.

INCOSE defines MBSE as "the formalized application of modeling to support system requirements, design, analysis, verification, and validation activities beginning in the conceptual design phase and continuing throughout development and later life cycle phases" (INCOSE 2007).

Although somewhat dated, the definition of MBSE by INCOSE originated during the early stages of MBSE as a viable alternative to document-intensive systems engineering. An alternative definition that complements rather than contradicts it highlights that MBSE is still systems engineering and emphasizes the purpose of the application of models:

"Model-based systems engineering is systems engineering with the formal application of models to make engineering information accessible to machines to support the stakeholders" (Weilkiens 2022).

While document-based approaches can also facilitate structured work and clear representations, they are not as efficient or effective as model-based approaches. One of the primary goals of modeling is to allow machines to access engineering information and provide support throughout the engineering process. While machines can read text documents, drawings, and slides, they can only interpret the semantics of the documents. They can help with formatting, organizing the texts, managing references, and so forth. The semantics remain unknown to machines. Even with advances in natural language processing and artificial intelligence, it is difficult for machines to process the information. In contrast, an MBSE model is based on a modeling language with systems engineering semantics, enabling rigorous and unambiguous content to be accessible by machines.

The systems modeling language (SysML) is certainly the most widely used language in MBSE, but it is not the only one: MBSE is not SysML, and SysML is not MBSE. SysML is developed by the Object Management Group. As this book is being written, the language is in the process of changing from SysML v1 to SysML v2. The book primarily uses SysML v2 but also shows the use of SysML v1 (OMG 2022, 2024).

MBSE is a large topic and not the focus of this book. There are many publications on the subject. The following books provide a few good examples to dive deeper into the topic.

- *Handbook of Model-Based Systems Engineering* (Madni et al. 2023): This is a comprehensive volume on various aspects of MBSE.
- *SYSMOD: The Systems Modeling Toolbox* (Weilkiens 2020): Description of common MBSE methodology.
- *A Practical Guide to SysML* (Friedenthal et al. 2014): Textbook about SysML v1.
- The *Absolute Beginners Guide to SysML v2* (Weilkiens and Muggeo 2024) provides an introduction to the next-generation systems modeling language SysML v2.

8.4 From PLE to MBPLE

PLE is an approach to software or product development that focuses on efficiently creating a family of related products with shared characteristics or features. Instead of developing each product from scratch, PLE emphasizes the reuse of common assets and processes across the product line.

PLE refers to products, while systems engineering refers to systems. The *INCOSE* handbook states that "product" is equivalent to "system," "product line" is equivalent to "system family," and "product line engineering" is equivalent to "system family engineering" (INCOSE 2023).

A product is an entity that an organization sells and becomes a system when integrated and operated in its intended environment. The ISO/IEC 26550 standard explicitly mentions that "product" is equivalent to "system-level products" (ISO/IEC 2015).

PLE is, therefore, not an alternative to systems engineering but rather an admixture. Just like systems engineering, PLE is also transdisciplinary. It must be well integrated into the organization and its engineering activities.

In traditional software or product development, each new product is typically developed independently, resulting in redundant efforts and increased time and costs. PLE aims to address these challenges by establishing a systematic approach to product development, enabling organizations to manage variability and leverage commonalities within a product line effectively. Chapter 5 discusses the shift from project-oriented to product-line-oriented delivery approaches in more detail.

As anticipated in Chapters 3 and 5, some of the key concepts of product line development include:

1. Variability: Product lines consist of products with common features and features that exhibit variability. PLE provides mechanisms to manage this variability, allowing companies to configure and customize products based on customer requirements or portfolio planning.
2. Commonality: PLE identifies and promotes reusable assets within the product line. By maximizing commonality, companies can streamline development efforts, reduce duplication of effort, and improve overall efficiency.
3. Domain engineering: Domain engineering involves analyzing the problem or opportunity space, identifying the commonalities and differences within the product line, and designing core components that can be reused across products. It focuses on creating a reusable foundation for the product line.
4. Application engineering: Application engineering involves developing specific products within a product line using the reusable assets created during domain engineering. It focuses on customizing and configuring the product to meet specific customer requirements.

Although the topic of PLE affects all product areas, most publications, methods, and tools only deal with software PLE.

A common PLE approach described in the ISO/IEC 26580 standard is feature-based PLE (ISO/IEC 2021). The terminology in this standard differs in part from the ISO/IEC 26550 standard (ISO/IEC 2015). The terminology in this book follows the standards but sometimes uses other terms if we, as authors, believe this alteration could facilitate their understanding.

Since a product line is more extensive in scope than a single system, to effectively implement PLE and, in particular, the feature-based PLE approach, models are essential. The motivation used to "elevate" MBSE as the way to move forward in systems engineering (abandoning document-based systems engineering) applies even more strongly to PLE. In other words, we can define the axiom: If "MBSE will become the norm for systems engineering" (INCOSE 2014), then "MBPLE will become the norm for PLE".

The symbiosis of MBSE and PLE is proving to be a particularly advantageous strategy (Chalé Góngora et al. 2014). This combination is a "win–win" for both disciplines. On the one hand, MBSE significantly contributes to ensuring the consistency of PLE assets. On the other hand, PLE significantly increases the potential for reusing MBSE models. This reciprocal relationship increases the efficiency of each approach and promotes a more robust and scalable development process.

You cannot expect the variability defined in a feature model to be implemented correctly in all engineering artifacts if these are scattered across umpteen documents and you hardly get any machine support. Models can be used to design extremely complex interrelationships more effectively and reliably.

We can consequently define MBPLE as "the application of feature-based PLE in combination with MBSE," where architecture models are central, but not exclusive for realizing the product line and its member products.

While the feature-based PLE approach ensures a single and independent source of variability across the engineering assets, the MBSE approach secures digital continuity and consistency across all the engineering models in scope.

Chapter 9 presents the concepts of MBPLE in more detail. The glossary in Annex A defines all PLE and MBPLE terms used in this book.

References

Chalé Góngora, H.G., Ferrogalini, M., and Moreau, C. (2014). How to boost PLE by using MBSE – a case study of a rolling stock product line. In: *Proceedings 5th International Conference on Complex Systems Design and Management CSDM*. Paris: Springer.

Friedenthal, S., Steiner, R., and Moore, A. (2014). *A Practical Guide to SysML*, 3e. Burlington: Morgan Kaufmann.

International Council on Systems Engineering (INCOSE) (2007). *Systems Engineering Vision 2020*. INCOSE.

International Council on Systems Engineering (INCOSE) (2014). *Systems Engineering Vision 2025*. INCOSE.https://www.incose.org/docs/default-source/se-vision-2025/se-vision-2025/incose-se-vision-2025.pdf (accessed 20 April 2023).

International Council on Systems Engineering (INCOSE) (2023). *INCOSE Systems Engineering Handbook*. 5e. Hoboken, NJ: John Wiley and Sons.

ISO/IEC (2015). *ISO/IEC 26550:2015 Software and Systems Engineering – Reference Model for Product Line Engineering and Management*. London: ISO/IEC.

ISO/IEC (2021). *ISO/IEC 26580:2021 Software and Systems Engineering – Methods and Tools for the Feature-Based Approach to Software and Systems Product Line Engineering*. London: ISO/IEC. https://www.iso.org/standard/43139.html.

ISO/IEC/IEEE (2023). *ISO/IEC/IEEE 15288:2023 Systems and Software Engineering – System Life Cycle Processes*. doi: 10.1109/IEEESTD.2023.10123367.

Madni, A.M., Augustine, N., and Sievers, M. (eds.) (2023). *Handbook of Model-Based Systems Engineering*. Switzerland: Springer.

Object Management Group (OMG) (2024). 'OMG System Modeling Language Version 1.7, formal/24-01-07'. Object Management Group.

Object Management Group (OMG) (2024). 'OMG System Modeling Language Version 2.0 beta 2, ptc/24-02-03'. Object Management Group. Available at: https://www.omg.org/spec/SysML.

Weilkiens, T. (2020). *SYSMOD – The Systems Modeling Toolbox*. 3e. MBSE4U.
Weilkiens, T. (2022). *Definition of MBSE-Revised*. https://mbse4u.com/2022/01/11/definition-of-mbse-revised (accessed 20 April 2023).
Weilkiens, T. and Muggeo, C. (2024). *Don't Panic! – The Absolute Beginner's Guide to SysML v2*. INCOSE UK (Don't Panic!).

9

MBPLE Concepts and Definitions

9.1 Introduction

This chapter provides an overview of the key concepts of model-based product line engineering (MBPLE). Feature models are the main source for formalizing product variability, which is determined by features and feature configurations. The shared assets supersets contain all elements used to specify, develop, and validate a concrete physical product. These include systems modeling language (SysML) models and other engineering artifacts, such as simulation models, CAD models, and so on. The shared assets supersets support the variability formalized in the feature model through "internal" variations.

The definitions are based on standards (ISO/IEC 2021, 2015) but also contain additions and, in some cases, modified names that we believe are easier to understand. Figure 9.1 shows the cornerstones of MBPLE. The product line is the overarching concept that includes variability models, shared assets supersets, product models, and product portfolios.

Chapter 26 formally defines the terms in an information model, and Chapters 13–15 present their applications.

9.2 Variability Model

A variability model contains both a feature model and feature configurations to fully represent the scope of a product line.

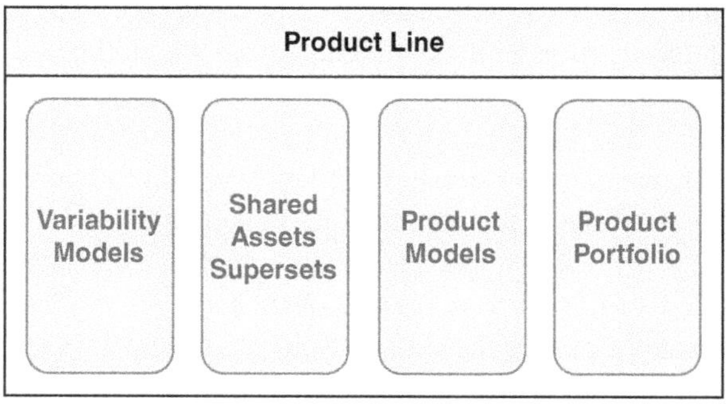

Figure 9.1 MBPLE cornerstones: variability, shared assets, products models, and product portfolio.

Model-Based Product Line Engineering (MBPLE): The Feature-Based Path to Product Lines Success, First Edition.
Marco Forlingieri et al.

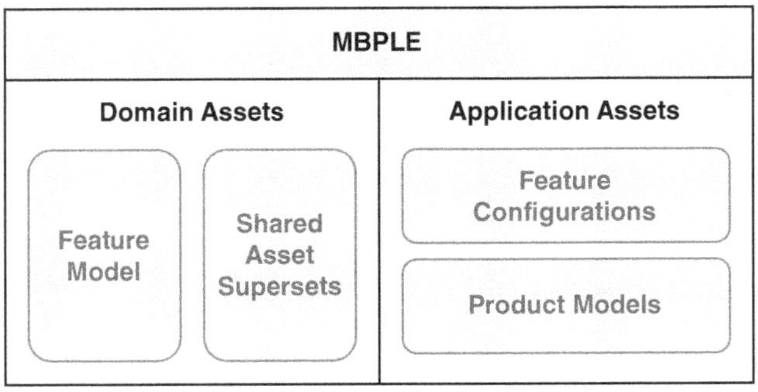

Figure 9.2 Domain and application assets.

The feature model defines the available features and their interdependencies, establishing the possible variations within the product line. Meanwhile, feature configurations are specific combinations of these features that define individual products within the product line. In essence, feature configurations express the product line's realized variability. They detail how the abstract possibilities of the feature model are translated into concrete products.

In practice, the variability model is often implemented by the project or workspace of the product line engineering (PLE) tool in which the features and feature configurations are defined.

In summary, a variability model includes both a feature model and feature configurations to capture a product line's intended variability.

ISO/IEC 26580 has a compliant but different view of the concepts (Figure 9.2). The standard distinguishes between domain assets and application assets, or domain engineering and application engineering. Domain engineering is about the specification and management of the product line's commonalities and variabilities, while application engineering is about the specification and management of individual products.

It is particularly noteworthy, in this view, that the feature model is a domain asset and the feature configurations are an application asset, while the concept of the variability model combines both. Both views are valid and not contradictory.

9.3 Feature Model

A feature model specifies a product line's variability. It is the "single source of variability." A feature model consists of features with feature constraints. The feature configurations include the selection of features to express the member product's needs (Figure 9.3). The ISO/IEC 26580 standard calls the feature tree the feature catalog, and a feature configuration a bill of features (ISO/IEC 2021).

The features are organized in a hierarchical tree, starting with a root feature from which the tree spans the subfeatures (Figure 9.4). The view is called a feature tree. The term feature tree is often used synonymously with feature model.

A feature is a product's characteristic that differentiates it from other products within the same product line (ISO/IEC 2021). The characteristic is visible to the product line's stakeholders.

The definition of a feature also implies that a feature does not specify a product characteristic without any variability. Therefore, the feature model does not cover all product characteristics, only the variability. If a characteristic itself does not indicate variability, the variability is specified by the subfeatures. However, there are different practices in the industry and different definitions of the feature concept. For example, the definition of a feature in feature-oriented domain analysis includes the common characteristics of the product (Kang et al. 1990). This book follows the definition given in ISO/IEC (2021), which only considers the variability.

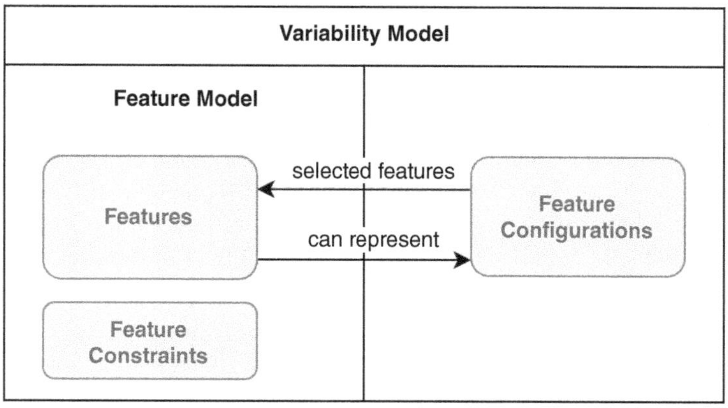

Figure 9.3 Definition of feature model.

A feature has an identifier, a name, a description, and a binding time. Of course, further properties can be defined if appropriate. The list mentioned here includes only the essential properties.

The binding time of a feature indicates in which life cycle phase the feature is set or decided for a given product. The life cycle stages according to ISO/IEC/IEEE 15288 are shown in Figure 9.5 (ISO/IEC/IEEE 2023). The stages "Concept" and "Retirement" are typically irrelevant for the binding time. The binding time can have one of the values "Development," "Production," or "Operation." For example, suppose that, in a drone product line, the binding time of a feature related to the number of engines is "Development" and that two subfeatures specify an option for four or six engines. In this case, the feature is integrated into a product during the design phase, and the production gets a variability-free input specification for this feature. The decision is made during the design phase, and the production gets a clear specification for four or six engines. Maybe you have two different production sites, Factory A builds a quadcopter and Factory B builds a hexacopter. The variation, including the decision for an option, is not set during the production stage but indeed affects the manufacturing system.

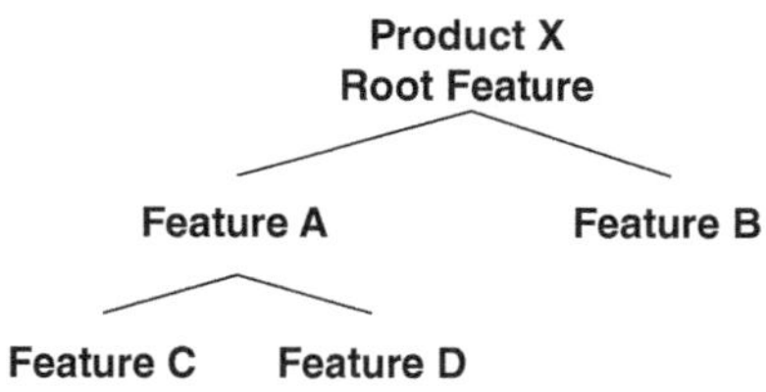

Figure 9.4 Example feature tree.

If the binding time is "Production," the decision to set a given feature for a product, such as a drone's body color, is made during the production phase. The input for the production phase from the design phase includes unbound features about the color options such as red, white, blue, and black. The decision about the concrete color of the drone is made during production, for example, based on customer orders.

The same principle can be applied to the binding time "Operation." For example, if the drone provides a standard and a long-distance battery, the binding time of the type of battery feature can be "Operation." The drone's user can change the battery type during the operation phase. Consequently, the procedure for changing the batteries must be provided to the users and documented in the user manual, and so forth.

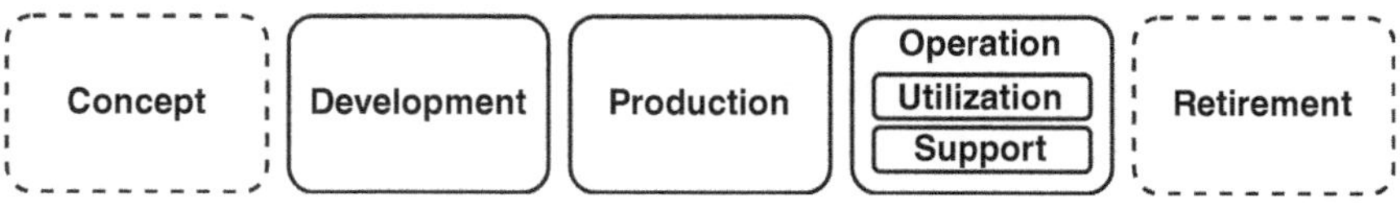

Figure 9.5 Life cycle stages. *Source:* Adapted from ISO/IEC, 2023.

Features are organized like a tree, which means a feature can have subfeatures that are owned or referenced by the parent feature. Additionally, the subfeature relationship specifies how many of the subfeatures can be selected in a feature configuration. This is called cardinality, specified by a lower bound and an upper bound. For example, the cardinality range [1.1] specifies exactly one possible selection [0.1] specifies none or one, and [1.4] specifies that one to four features can be part of the product. An upper bound of "*" means that there is no upper limit. A cardinality range with a lower bound of 1 specifies a mandatory feature, which means it must be selected for all products. Mandatory features with cardinality [1.1] have no variability themselves but can have subfeatures with variability. The cardinality range with a lower bound of 0 specifies an optional feature.

For example, the feature "batteryKind" is a mandatory subfeature of the root feature that represents the whole product line and has the cardinality [1.1]. Subfeatures can be grouped into a set of alternative subfeatures. The set also has a cardinality that specifies how many subfeatures can be selected. For example, the feature "batteryKind" has two alternative subfeatures, "standardBattery" and "longDistanceBattery." Each subfeature is optional and has a cardinality of [0.1], but the alternative set has the cardinality [1.1], meaning exactly one subfeature of the set must be selected. It is an exclusive-or (XOR) feature group.

A feature can also reference another feature. In that case, the feature is a proxy for the referenced feature. It can be used to reuse a feature in another branch of the feature tree. However, it can also be used across feature trees by referencing a feature from another feature tree or the entire feature tree itself. In Figure 9.6, "Feature D" is used in two different branches of the tree, and the feature tree of "Product Y" is put below "Feature E."

A feature constraint is a Boolean expression about features that must be true for all member products. It can be any kind of expression. The following two are commonly used constraints.

Conflicts: If one of the features in a *conflicts* feature constraint is selected, none of the other features linked by the constraint may be selected.

Requires: If the source feature of a *requires* feature constraint is selected, the target feature shall also be selected.

Any other kind of feature constraint combination can be defined. For example, if Feature A is selected but not Feature B, then a valid feature configuration must select Features C and D.

A feature configuration is a valid set of selected features of a feature tree. Valid means that all feature constraints are met, all cardinality bounds are met, and all variability decisions are made except for features with binding times in future life cycle stages. A feature configuration also refers to a life cycle stage. The ISO/IEC 26580 standard calls the feature configuration the bill of features (ISO/IEC 2021).

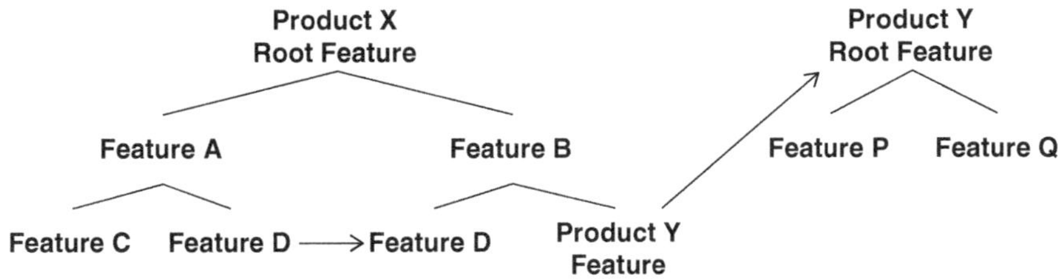

Figure 9.6 Proxy features.

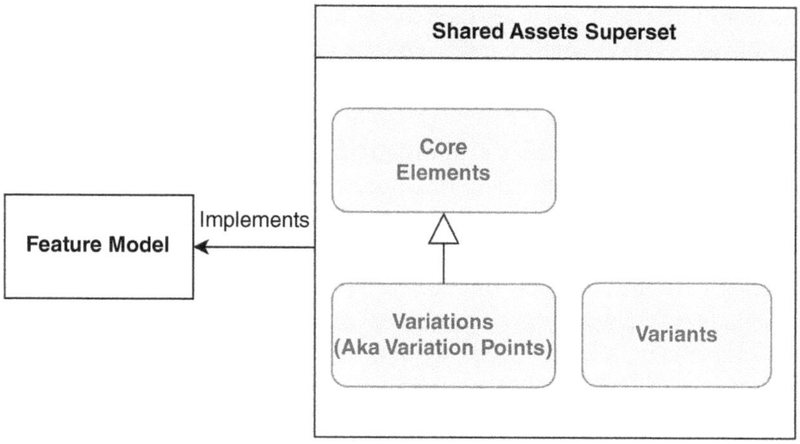

Figure 9.7 Definition of shared assets supersets.

9.4 Shared Assets Supersets

The shared assets supersets are collections of engineering artifacts implementing a feature model for a given product line. They consist of core common elements, variation (also known as variation point), and variant elements that implement variability (Figure 9.7).

The shared assets supersets point to the feature model specifying the variability. Since the feature model is independent of the supersets, different supersets could implement it.

The supersets contain all assets required to engineer a product. It includes the common assets used for all member products and the variants that relate to features and are only used for some member products. A shared asset is a digital engineering artifact, such as requirements, architecture descriptions, CAD models, simulation models, and so forth. A shared assets superset is only a logical construct. It is not, in reality, a repository in its own right since it consists of several different artifacts stored in different engineering repositories.

All engineering artifacts on different levels can be shared assets, which include, for example, a single architecture description element like an interface definition and the whole product architecture description. A shared asset has its own life cycle and can be considered by configuration management as a configuration item or as part of a configuration item (see Chapter 19).

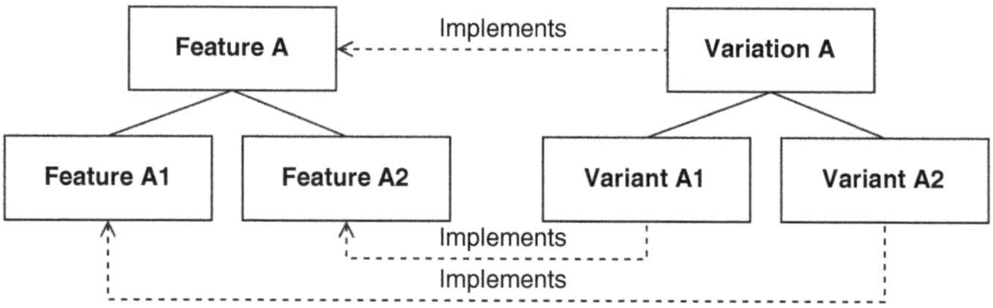

Figure 9.8 Relationship of feature model and shared assets superset elements.

Some elements of the shared assets are used for all member products. They are called core elements. Unlike the feature model, which only considers variability, the shared assets supersets contain all the elements necessary for all member products.

A node feature in the feature tree specifies variability. The corresponding parts that implement variability within the shared assets are called variations. They represent the point where variation happens, which is why they are also called variation points. The variations are the glue elements between features and variant elements in the shared assets supersets. Many variations can be linked with the same feature because the variability expressed by a feature can impact many assets. Setting or selecting a feature "triggers" the variation to which it is linked; this, in turn, results in the transformation of the appropriate design choice linked to the selected feature.

A variant also implements a feature. The variation with the linked variants mirrors the appropriate part of the feature tree (Figure 9.8). The variations and variants that implement a single feature together define a part of a corresponding member product. This can be a mixture of SysML elements, CAD models, simulation models, or any other engineering artifacts. Variations and variants are not the physical member product parts themselves.

9.5 Product Models

A product model is the complete set of variations and variants that implement the feature configuration for a given member product of the product line. It can be initially automatically derived from a feature configuration of the appropriate shared assets, which contain the core elements and the variations and variants according to the selected features of the feature configuration. Theoretically, a complete generation of the product model would be possible. In practice, however, the model is usually refined even further in an iterative way. For example, if additional variants that are not managed in the product line for various reasons are specified at later stages.

Again, the product model consists of various engineering models, such as SysML system models, CAD models, simulation models, and so on.

9.6 Member Products

Member products are not digital engineering assets. They are actual physical instances of the product line built from the product model.

Member products are distinct yet interconnected entities within a product line. They represent the various manifestations of a core product concept, tailored to cater to different market segments or customer needs.

Each member product, while unique in its specifications and features, shares a common foundation with the rest of the product line.

This shared foundation typically includes core technologies, design principles, and operational frameworks. Developing member products is a strategic process, allowing businesses to diversify their offerings while maintaining production efficiency and quality consistency. It enables organizations to explore new market opportunities without deviating significantly from their established domain of expertise. In essence, member products embody a product line's flexibility and adaptability.

They illustrate how a single, cohesive product strategy can create a diverse yet harmonious portfolio of products catering to a wide range of consumer needs and preferences.

References

ISO/IEC (2021). ISO/IEC 26580:2021 Software and systems engineering – methods and tools for the feature-based approach to software and systems product line engineering.

ISO/IEC (2015). ISO/IEC 26550:2015 Software and systems engineering – reference model for product line engineering and management.

ISO/IEC/IEEE (2023). ISO/IEC/IEEE 15288:2023 Systems and software engineering – system life cycle processes.

Kang, K., Cohen, S., Hess, J. et al. (1990). *Feature-Oriented Domain Analysis (FODA) Feasibility Study (No. CMU/SEI-90-TR-021)*. Software Engineering Institute, Carnegie Mellon University.

10

MBPLE Modeling Languages

10.1 Introduction

The term "model-based" highlights the need for modeling languages, at least in the definition of the term "model" defined in this book. This chapter discusses modeling languages within the context of model-based product line engineering (MBPLE). Chapter 4 explains the need for modeling and describes the characteristics of a modeling language. Chapters 13–15 provide examples of how different modeling languages are applied to specify variability.

Modeling languages formalize features and shared assets. A product portfolio's member products are typically outside the scope of models because they are real-world products. In this book, modeling languages for feature and variable shared assets are generally called variability modeling languages.

Section 10.2 defines the terms "model" and "modeling language." Section 10.3 provides an overview of variability modeling languages, Section 10.4 provides an overview of feature modeling languages, and Section 10.5 provides an overview of shared assets modeling languages. The sections propose requirements for those languages and discuss the unique role of systems modeling language (SysML) v2. Finally, Section 10.6 covers the topic of model interoperability.

10.2 Models and Modeling Languages

Herbert Stachowiak describes in his book *Allgemeine Modelltheorie* three fundamental characteristics of a model (Stachowiak 1973):

1. Mapping: Models are representations of things.
2. Reduction/Abstraction: Models are not 1:1 mappings. An illustrative example is a map. Lewis Caroll, in his book *Sylvie and Bruno Concluded* (Carroll 2015), writes about two individuals talking about the making of a map and its scale. By increasing the scale step-by-step, they finally agreed to create a map with a scale of 1:1 miles. This provokes the disappointment of the farmers living in that area, who object that now the map covers the entire land and blocks the sunlight.
3. Pragmatism: Models are created for a purpose.

Typically, the common definitions of the term "model" are true but, in most cases, not sufficient to define a model in the engineering context. First, we require the model to be digital, excluding analog models. Of course, analog models are also valuable, but they are neither the focus of MBPLE

Model-Based Product Line Engineering (MBPLE): The Feature-Based Path to Product Lines Success, First Edition.
Marco Forlingieri et al.

nor MBSE. This first requirement for model-based engineering (MBE) models (MBEML-1) refers to Stachowiak's definition, while the second requirement (MBEML-2) calls for digital assets:

MBEML-1: Basic Characteristics: An engineering model shall conform to the three model characteristics defined by Stachowiak: representation, simplification, and pragmatism, ensuring the model accurately reflects, simplifies for understanding, and serves the intended practical purpose within the modeling domain.

MBEML-2: Digital Assets: An engineering model shall exclusively comprise digital assets.

The third requirement of an engineering model calls for machine accessibility, whereby "access" means that a machine can read and write the model and also understand the concepts according to the domain of the model. For example, a machine accessing an MBSE model can identify requirements, architectural elements, and the satisfying relationship between them and can point out gaps in satisfying traceability. Likewise, a machine accessing MBPLE models can identify features or variants.

MBEML-3: Machine Accessible: The engineering model shall be machine accessible, meaning that machines must be capable of reading and writing it and understanding its concepts in accordance with its domain.

The requirements summarized led to our definition of an MBE model, which equally applies to MBSE, MBPLE, and other engineering disciplines. The definition is based on (Weilkiens 2022).

An MBSE model is a digital model that represents systems and their environments and is based on a modeling language that covers concepts of engineering.

A modeling language is a rule-based system of signs. A sign has a meaning (semantics), a representation (concrete syntax), and a structure (abstract syntax). The rules constrain the use and combination of the signs. For example, SysML v2 defines the sign "part definition." The simple, informal semantics is that a part definition represents a modular unit of structure. The formal semantics are quite complex and skipped here. The concrete syntax specifies a graphical notation (rectangle with different compartments) and a textual notation (part def). The abstract syntax defines the properties and relationships of the part definition data element in the model repository.

10.3 Variability Modeling Languages

A language for modeling variability goes beyond simply capturing the variability of the system; it is a comprehensive modeling language that includes support for variability among other features, as is the case with SysML v2.

Around 2012, the OMG tried to develop and standardize the common variability language (CVL) (OMG 2012). However, as mentioned in Chapter 7, since the initiative did not materialize, CVL was never finalized. To date, no common standardized and tool-independent variability language exists.

The architecture of modeling languages includes three pillars: abstract syntax, concrete syntax, and semantics. In addition to the engineering model requirements MBEML-1, MBEML-2, and MBEML-3, the following lists high-level requirements for each of these pillars for variability modeling languages.

VML-1: Semantics: The variability modeling language shall cover the semantics of variability concepts grounded in the standard ISO/IEC 26580:2021 (ISO/IEC 2021).

VML-2: Concrete Syntax: The variability modeling language shall cover graphical or textual notation elements common in the PLE domain.

VML-3: Abstract Syntax: The variability modeling language shall define an abstract syntax that makes variability concepts available to machines.

The variability concepts related to MBPLE are defined in Chapters 9 and 26. They are based on common concepts and ISO/IEC standards. However, they can, of course, differ in different areas of application and do not claim to be complete or unique.

A model created by a modeling language that satisfies the above requirements can be understood by human readers familiar with PLE. Machines can, in turn, read the model data and interpret the semantics.

10.4 Feature Modeling Languages

A feature modeling language is a special variability modeling language and, therefore, satisfies the requirements in Section 10.2, whereby the variability concepts are limited to features. The concepts are defined in Chapters 9 and 26.

A feature tree is a common concrete syntax for features (see Figure 14.4), and a matrix is a common concrete syntax for feature configurations (see Figure 14.6).

In the MBPLE landscape, there is no standard language for modeling features. There is an almost common agreement on the concrete syntax of feature trees, but they differ in the details, for example, how to depict mandatory features or alternative feature sets.

The feature semantics are also slightly different in the various approaches. However, the standards ISO/IEC 26550 and ISO/IEC 26580 define a solid foundation (ISO/IEC 2015, 2021). For example, ISO/IEC 26580 defines a feature as a characteristic that distinguishes a product from other products. At the same time, the definition of a feature in feature-oriented domain analysis (FODA) also includes characteristics common to all products (Kang et al. 1990).

Feature tree approaches are typically purely graphical and do not specify an abstract syntax. Without an abstract syntax, they are not considered as modeling languages according to the definition given above. A proprietary abstract syntax is probably defined for the implementation of a feature tree tool, but it is not easily accessible for other tools because there is neither a documented open abstract syntax nor a standard (see Section 10.5 about model interoperability).

Examples of feature tree approaches are FODA (Section 14.1.2; Czarnecki et al. 2005) and implementations in tools like PTC pure::variants (PTC 2024), Gears (BigLever 2024), or FeatureIDE (METOP 2020).

OVM is a variability modeling language (Pohl et al. 2005) often mentioned as an implementation of ISO/IEC 26550. Their history is related, but OVM itself is not part of the standard. The feature modeling language OVM is briefly described in Section 13.4.

10.5 Shared Asset Modeling Languages

Shared assets are digital artifacts required for the development of products. Modeling languages for shared assets are defined by "native" modeling languages implemented in the various engineering tools, like SysML or Modelica, or by tool-specific modeling languages used in simulation, requirements management, or CAD tools, to mention a few.

Often, these languages do not provide explicit support for modeling variability and do not satisfy the requirements given in Section 10.2. However, an exception is SysML v2, which accommodated the great need for PLE concepts due to its timeliness. The role of SysML v2 in the context of PLE is presented in Section 10.5.

Many modeling languages and tools for shared assets come from a time when the specification of product lines did not play a dominant role in engineering. Therefore, product lines were not explicitly supported by these languages and tools. Over time, the need for variant modeling has increased. The direct method is a common approach to implementing variability afterward in languages and tools that do not explicitly support variability (Section 15.1.1). This consists of plugins that access a feature model, manage the variability of shared assets, provide filters, and perform transformations of the modeled assets. However, variability is so essential to MBPLE not to be explicitly considered by engineering model languages. Otherwise, specific engineering tools alone would not have sufficient knowledge of the overall variability of the product line to provide effective support and perform validations (e.g. consistency checks).

10.6 SysML v2

The requirements for SysML v2 were developed when there was already a high demand for modeling variability. Therefore, SysML v2 explicitly supports variability concepts based on the standard ISO/IEC 26580 (ISO/IEC 2021). However, it does not provide the modeling of features; it only provides the variability of shared assets. The modeling of shared assets is covered in detail in Chapter 15.

SysML plays a special role in model-based engineering. In general, a SysML model describes the overall system and has relationships to many specific engineering modeling tools. It is usually considered the backbone of an engineering environment. Therefore, including variability modeling in SysML is an important step forward. Thanks to this, the variability modeling in SysML models will no longer rely on non-standard approaches.

10.7 Model Interoperability

Model interoperability is not a specific MBPLE topic. However, by the very nature of MBPLE, there is a strong need for a broad exchange between feature and shared asset models. The following example illustrates the core and challenge of model interoperability ('Model Interoperability' 2023).

A variation in a shared asset model has a relationship named R to a feature in a feature model. The relationship crosses the models' borders and requires a model interoperability approach (Figure 10.1).

If the shared asset model owns the relationship, the target element must also be part of the model as a proxy for the fundamental feature in the feature model. Technically, the target of the relationship cannot be in another model repository. Figure 10.2 shows the feature proxy element. The relationship R is a relationship from the variation. There is another technical relationship between the feature proxy and the feature element. The proxy must be consistent with the feature, requiring a technical solution to keep them in sync.

The concrete implementation of Figure 10.2 in a model could be, for example, a link attached to the variation element that points to the feature. Link management and synchronization with the

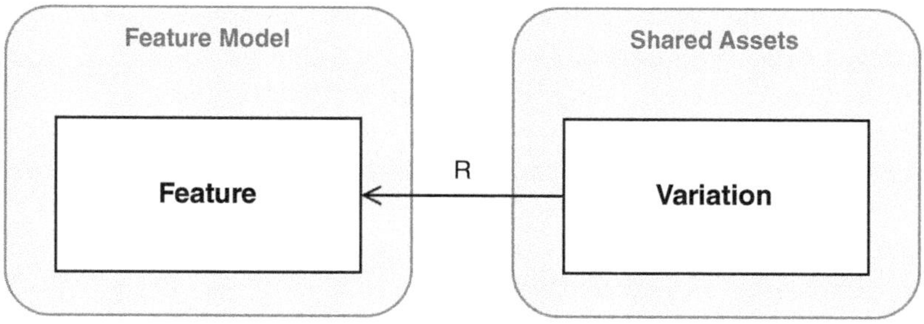

Figure 10.1 Cross-model relationship between variation and feature.

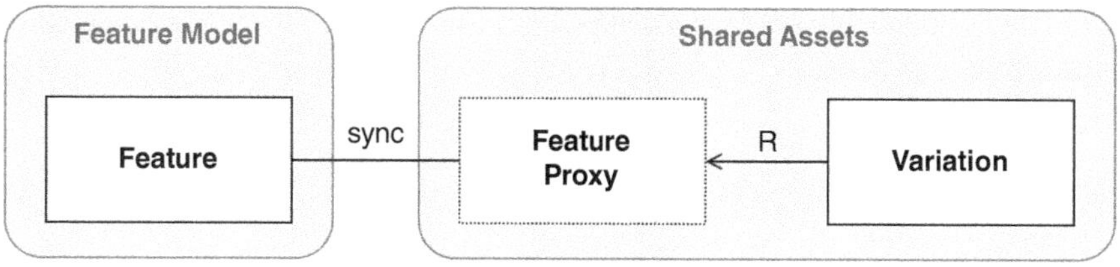

Figure 10.2 Proxy element for cross-relationships.

feature model are proprietary implementations of the tool in which the shared asset resides. Examples of possible implementation mechanisms to support interoperability include:

- Open Services for Lifecycle Collaboration is a standardized interoperability technology that could be used to link shared assets with features (OASIS 2021).
- The variability exchange language was an attempt to standardize a data format for exchanging variability information (OASIS 2018). Unfortunately, the project is currently on hold.
- If the feature model is created with SysML v2 (see Chapter 13), the standardized SysML v2 API could be used to provide the feature information to other engineering tools.

References

BigLever (2024). Biglever Software Gears. https://biglever.com/solution/gears/ (accessed 25 July 2024).

Carroll, L. (2015). *Sylvie and Bruno: Fully Illustrated Edition*. Originally published In 1889.

Czarnecki, K., Helsen, S., and Eisenecker, U. (2005). Formalizing cardinality-based feature models and their specialization', *Software Process Improvement and Practice*, 10 (1): 7–29.

ISO/IEC (2015). ISO/IEC 26550:2015 software and systems engineering – reference model for product line engineering and management. ISO/IEC.

ISO/IEC (2021). ISO/IEC 26580:2021 software and systems engineering – methods and tools for the feature-based approach to software and systems product line engineering. ISO/IEC: https://www.iso.org/standard/43139.html.

Kang, K., Cohen, S., Hess, J. et al. (1990). Feature-oriented domain analysis (FODA) feasibility study. CMU/SEI-90-TR-021. Software Engineering Institute, Carnegie Mellon University: http://resources.sei.cmu.edu/library/asset-view.cfm?AssetID=11231 (accessed 7 January 2023).

METOP (2020). *FeatureIDE*. https://www.featureide.de/ (accessed 10 January 2023).

Model Interoperability (2023). In: *Handbook of Model-Based Systems Engineering*. ed Madni, A. M. Switzerland AG: Springer.

OASIS (2018). *OASIS* Variability exchange language *(VEL)*. https://www.oasis-open.org/committees/tc_home.php?wg_abbrev=vel (accessed 23 July 2023).

OASIS (2021). OSLC Core Version 3.0. https://docs.oasis-open-projects.org/oslc-op/core/v3.0/os/oslc-core.html (accessed 17 February 2024).

Object Management Group (OMG) (2012). *Common Variability Language* (CVL)-OMG Revised Submission. New York: Object Management Group.

Pohl, K., Böckle, G., and van der Linden, F.J. (2005). *Software Product Line Engineering: Foundations, Principles and Techniques*. New York: Springer.

PTC (2024). *PTC pure::variants*. Available at: https://www.ptc.com/en/products/pure-variants (accessed 25 July 2024).

Stachowiak, H. (1973). *Allgemeine Modelltheorie*.

Weilkiens, T. (2022). Definition of MBSE model. https://mbse4u.com/2022/01/18/definition-mbse-model/ (accessed 18 February 2024).

11

The MBPLE Foundation in the Standards

11.1 Introduction

Establishing standards for systems engineering concepts, terminology, processes, and methods is crucial as we explore the complex landscape of systems engineering (Friedenthal et al. 2015). These standards act as beacons in the vast sea of systems engineering, guiding professionals through complexity but requiring them to know how to deal with it and adapt to specific circumstances. This analogy emphasizes that while standards provide direction and a foundation, the real skill lies in interpreting and applying them dynamically to meet the unique needs of each organization, project, or context.

Section 11.2 begins with the main PLE-specific standards such as ISO/IEC 26550 (ISO/IEC 2015) and the ISO/IEC 26580 (ISO/IEC 2021) standards, also including the only standard covering the method and tool part for the discipline ISO/IEC 26560 (ISO/IEC 2019).

They emphasize a paradigm shift in systems engineering to adopt product line engineering (PLE) for the efficient and effective development of "system product lines" or "system families." The focus is no longer on (single) system engineering but on system family engineering.

Section 11.3 continues by covering the key standard in systems engineering, ISO/IEC/IEEE 15288 (ISO/IEC/IEEE 2023), and focusing predominantly on standards for model-based assets and their interoperability.

Figure 11.1 simplifies and highlights the key-related standards.

11.2 PLE Standards

ISO/IEC 26550 (ISO/IEC 2015) was established to formalize the application of PLE, primarily having a return on experience in the software domain. Despite being a significant milestone, it remains overly software-centric and generic to a degree that may lead to interpretational challenges during its practical application.

Subsequently, ISO/IEC 26580 (ISO/IEC 2021) was introduced as an extension to its predecessor and addressed the gaps, which frequently complicate the application of ISO/IEC 26550 (ISO/IEC 2021).

Noteworthy enhancements include the incorporation of feature-based PLE as a standard methodology for defining and managing variability alongside a more coherent and practicable PLE mechanism. Figure 11.2 illustrates a simplification of the standard with its main concepts.

Model-Based Product Line Engineering (MBPLE): The Feature-Based Path to Product Lines Success, First Edition.
Marco Forlingieri et al.

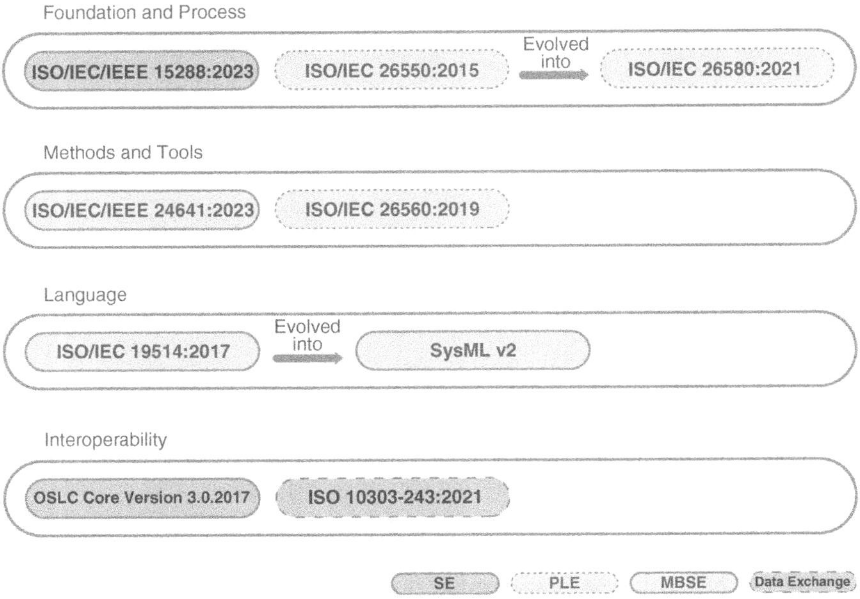

Figure 11.1 Standards associated with MBPLE.

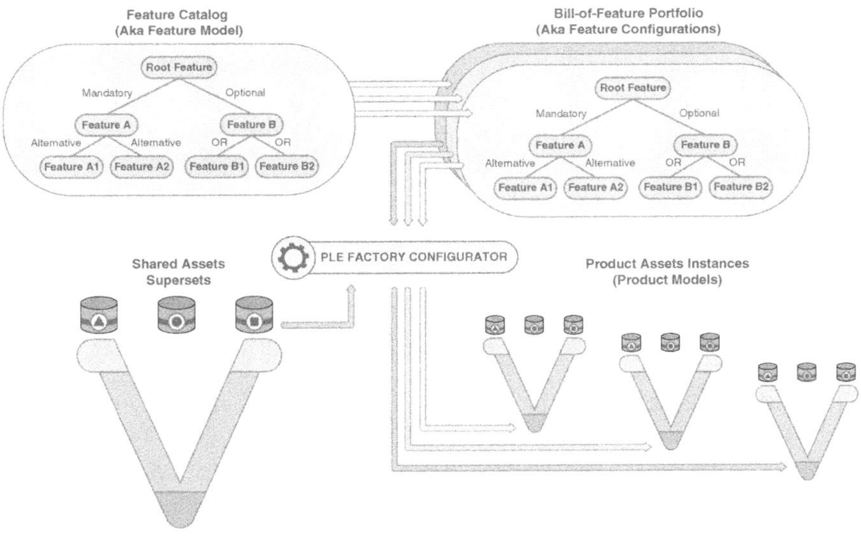

Figure 11.2 Featured-based PLE. *Source:* Adapted from ISO/IEC 26580.

Currently, model-based product line engineering (MBPLE) has not been delineated in any standard, given that the subject is still addressed separately within PLE and model-based standards. However, we see this book as a key contribution toward the establishment of a new standard that could formalize the discipline in the foreseeable future.

11.3 Systems Engineering Foundation, Model-based and Interoperability Standards

The ISO/IEC/IEEE 15288 (ISO/IEC/IEEE 2023) standard is often regarded as the cornerstone of systems engineering standards, addressing the comprehensive needs of the industry and embedding the core principles of systems engineering. In its latest version and its elaboration within the *INCOSE Systems Engineering Handbook* (Walden et al. 2023), it is highlighted that in many cases, systems engineering is performed in the context of a product line and that the discipline of PLE fills with processes, methods, and tools the gaps of systems engineering when it is elevated to systems family engineering.

In model-based systems engineering (MBSE), the ISO/IEC/IEEE 24641 (ISO/IEC/IEEE 2023) standard focuses on the capabilities and methodologies of tools for MBSE and software engineering. Although it does not introduce additional life cycle processes for systems and software, it specifies an MBSE reference model, including considerations for cognitive aspects of modeling and model management, thereby supporting and enhancing system and software life cycle processes.

Concerning standardized language, although there is no specific standard for feature modeling within PLE, Object Management Group (OMG)'s ISO/IEC 19514 (ISO/IEC 2017) standard defines the systems modeling language (SysML), which is on the edge of evolving into SysML v2 (OMG, 2023), currently nearing its final publication phase. This development will be explored further in subsequent chapters.

As already discussed in Chapter 6, for data representation and exchange, examples include the OSLC core version 3 by OASIS (OASIS, 2017), which sets the framework for Open Services for Lifecycle Collaboration and its domain-specific implementations. Meanwhile, ISO 10303–243 (ISO, 2021) specifies the protocol for modeling and simulation information within a collaborative systems engineering context.

It is important to note that numerous other standards could influence the adoption and implementation of MBPLE and that this chapter does not aim to provide an exhaustive list of all possible standards but to stress the significance of adopting a multidisciplinary and multistandard approach when embracing the MBPLE paradigm. The next part of the book (III) opens with Chapter 12, which is dedicated to the MBPLE paradigm.

References

Friedenthal, S., Moore, A. and Steiner, R. (2015). *A Practical Guide to SysML: The Systems Modeling Language*, 3e. The MK/OMG Press.

ISO (2021). Industrial automation systems and integration – product data representation and exchange – application protocol: for modelling and simulation information in a collaborative systems engineering context (MoSSEC) (ISO 10303-243:2021).

ISO/IEC (2000). International standards for quality management. Geneva, Switzerland: International Organization for Standardization (ISO)/International Electrotechnical Commission (IEC). (ISO/IEC 9000:2000)

ISO/IEC (2017). Information technology – Object Management Group systems modeling language (OMG SysML) (ISO/IEC 19514:2017).

ISO/IEC (2019). Software and systems engineering – tools and methods for product line product management (ISO/IEC 26560:2019).

ISO/IEC (2021). Software and systems engineering – methods and tools for the feature-based approach to software and systems product line engineering (ISO/IEC/IEEE 26580:2021).

ISO/IEC/IEEE (2015). Software and systems engineering – reference model for product line engineering and management (ISO/IEC/IEEE 26550:2015).

ISO/IEC/IEEE (2023). Systems and software engineering – System life cycle processes (ISO/IEC/IEEE 15288:2023).

ISO/IEC/IEEE (2023). Systems and software engineering – methods and tools for model-based systems and software engineering (ISO/IEC/IEEE 24641:2023).

Object Management Group (OMG) (2023). OMG system modeling language Version 2.0, ad/2023-02-11. OMG.

OSLC Core Version 3.0 (2021) Part 1: Overview (ed. Amsden, J. and Berezovskyi, A). OASIS Project Specification 02.

Walden, D.D. (2023). *Systems Engineering Handbook: A Guide for System Life Cycle Processes and Activities*, 5e. INCOSE, San Diego, CA, USA.

Part III

Implementation of MBPLE

Part III is entirely dedicated to the technical aspects of Model-Based Product Line Engineering (MBPLE). Readers who have started their MBPLE journey and feel ready to begin the architecture definition and the formalization of asset supersets of their product lines will find invaluable information and the core technical elements of MBPLE in this part of the book.

Chapter 12 offers a general overview of the MBPLE approach, outlining four key steps to move from single-system, document-based, and siloed developments to a collaborative, model-based engineering of a family of systems. Chapter 13 follows up with a presentation of the methods and basic concepts for creating feature models. The chapter bridges the gap between the theoretical concepts presented in previous chapters and their implementation in engineering tools, stressing the central role of feature models in variability management and in the improvement of model interoperability. Feature-oriented domain analysis (FODA) and the orthogonal variability model (OVM) are also briefly discussed.

Chapter 14 continues with an exploration of feature configurations. The concept of feature constraints is presented as a means to limit the number of possible feature configurations. The chapter concludes with a discussion about the integration of feature configurations into large product lines. Chapter 15 then dwells on the techniques for modeling shared assets. Two different techniques are proposed: the *direct* method (in which variants are explicitly defined in the models) and the *clean* method (in which variation points are included within model elements), both illustrated through practical examples. To link the concepts presented in the two previous chapters, Chapter 16 provides a comprehensive approach to deriving product models from feature configurations and shared assets.

Part III continues with the topic of variability management by discussing the different dimensions of variability in Chapter 17: co-variability (of products, manufacturing and services), variability in the development process, variability in different layers of abstraction, and variability in the levels of the system hierarchy.

Chapter 18 explores digital end-to-end continuity. The chapter stresses the importance of digital continuity to derive assets in a consistent way and perform effective impact analysis during the product line life cycle. To illustrate this, an example showing the introduction of a new feature is provided. Chapter 19 introduces the critical role of configuration management (CM) in MBPLE to ensure effective and consistent product development throughout the product line life cycle. The chapter describes the specifics of CM for MBPLE and the importance of keeping under control the evolution of the variability and the assets of the product line, and mastering the dependencies between the product line assets and those of the multiple member products.

Chapter 20 closes Part III with an exploration of the application of artificial intelligence in MBPLE, including opportunities and threats.

12

The MBPLE Paradigm

12.1 Introduction

The *Capability Maturity Model Integrated (CMMI) for development* (Software Engineering Institute 2007) extends on the classical definition of a process provided by the quality management standard (ISO/IEC 2000) and defines a development process as "a set of activities, methods, practices, and transformations that people use to develop and maintain systems and associated products." If we adopt the wording from describing the development and maintenance of "systems and associated products" to "product lines and member products," we align closely with the product line engineering (PLE) definition provided in this book's glossary. However, when consulting ISO/IEC/IEEE 15288 (ISO/IEC/IEEE 2023), a cornerstone document for systems engineering processes, there is little focus on product lines or system product lines, and no direct process guidance is offered for their development. This gap suggests a necessary shift in paradigm – a term which, in the context of science as defined by Kuhn, refers to a "universally recognizable scientific achievement that temporarily provides model problems and solutions to a community of practitioners" (Kuhn 1962). While the shift in paradigm is progressing for model-based systems engineering (MBSE), progressively establishing itself as the new way of doing systems engineering, the same cannot be said for PLE yet. MBPLE benefits from the synergies of MBSE and PLE and aims to become a new paradigm for developing system product lines. After systems engineering became model-based and digital collaboration predominant, the last shift remains: the move from MBSE (single) to model-based system family engineering, that is, MBPLE. As we discussed in Chapter 11, this paradigm lies at its firm foundation, the PLE, model-based, and interoperability standards.

This book aims to argue convincingly that MBPLE, with its four main steps introduced in Sections 12.2–12.5, is the most logical method for developing product lines and its derived products. It is important to mention that the steps do not differ between a PLE or MBPLE approach. As introduced in Chapter 8, the main difference lies in the centrality of the models as main shared assets to be developed, managed, and reused within a PLE approach. This chapter is the beginning of the journey into this new paradigm and presents the four key steps of the MBPLE approach, as shown in Figure 12.1.

12.2 Step 1: Define Feature Models

The journey of MBPLE begins with the definition of feature models. These models formally represent a product line's variability, capturing the different features that can be included in a product and how they relate to each other. Features are organized hierarchically, illustrating parent–child

Model-Based Product Line Engineering (MBPLE): The Feature-Based Path to Product Lines Success, First Edition.
Marco Forlingieri et al.

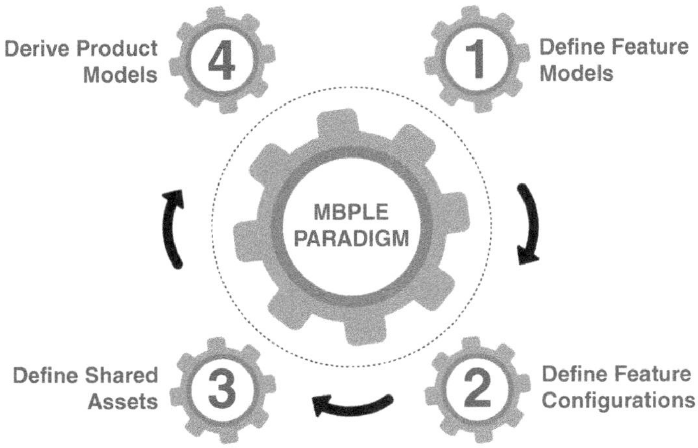

Figure 12.1 MBPLE four-step approach.

relationships, and are further defined by constraints that formalize compatibility or conflict between them. This step is critical as it lays the groundwork for understanding the scope of variability within the product line. It facilitates stakeholders' involvement by aligning the product line's capabilities with their needs and constraints. Features play a crucial role in aligning market needs with how an organization plans to transform these needs into business opportunities, on the one hand, and with what the organization is capable of delivering through its product line, on the other hand (Chalé Gongora et al. 2014; Chalé and Greugny 2017). Features serve a dual purpose: first, to enhance communication among all involved parties by making the variations within the product line clear and easy to grasp; and second, to steer the creation of engineering assets by offering a definitive reference for understanding these variations and their constraints (Forlingieri and Weilkiens 2022). Chapter 13 provides a full explanation of the feature model.

12.3 Step 2: Define Feature Configurations

After establishing a comprehensive representation of the product line through feature models, the next phase involves defining feature configurations for individual member products. This process is guided by the feature models developed in Step 1, allowing for the tailoring of products to meet specific customer requirements.

Feature models specify the available features and identify incompatible combinations due to constraints imposed for technical or economic reasons. Allowing every conceivable configuration could be prohibitively expensive, making these constraints essential (Forlingieri and Weilkiens 2022). The activity entails choosing which features will be included in the member product and setting appropriate parameter values, thereby defining the product's unique configuration. This step is instrumental in refining the product line's scope for each member product, ensuring that each meets its intended purpose and market needs. The topic of feature configurations is further developed in Chapter 14.

12.4 Step 3: Define Shared Assets

The next step focuses on defining the product line shared assets. These assets encompass a wide range of elements, from requirements and design models to source codes, each linked to specific product line features (Forlingieri and Weilkiens 2022). This linkage is crucial to systematically manage variation points within the assets systematically. The scope of the shared assets within the MBPLE paradigm extends beyond merely MBSE models, since it encompasses all engineering assets required to develop the product line and its member products. The model-based approach ensures consistency among all those assets, while the feature model guides the engineers in defining the variation in their specific engineering domain assets. This process culminates in creating what is often referred to as 150% assets, from which the specific (100%) assets for each member product are derived. Chapter 15 illustrates Step 3 with details and examples.

12.5 Step 4: Derive Product Models

The final step in the MBPLE approach is about turning the abstract feature configuration into a tangible product. This involves deriving the necessary shared assets, as defined and linked in Step 3, according to the specific feature configuration selected for the member product. The outcome is the product models fulfilling the needs of the member product (Forlingieri and Weilkiens 2022). This ensures that the final product is not only aligned with the stakeholder's requirements but also leverages the product line's full potential by maximizing the reuse of predefined assets and feature configurations. In principle, any engineering asset or system can be reused at least partially to satisfy the future needs of other customers. However, the efforts required to do this depend on how much "built for reuse" these assets or systems are. So, anchoring such a paradigm in engineering processes is central for an organization. Manufacturers in industries such as automotive, aerospace, defense, rail, and electronics rarely produce just a single variant of their products. If they do, they could soon go out of business. The product models are further developed in Chapter 16.

12.6 Extending the Four Steps for a Real-world Execution of MBPLE

The "MBPLE Factory" is based on the feature-based PLE factory described in the standard ISO/IEC 26580 (ISO/IEC 2021). The real-world execution order of the four steps might be different, iterative, and incremental.

To recap, we have the four key steps defined above that can be summarized as:

1. Define feature models: Create a feature tree to specify the variable characteristics of the product line.
2. Define feature configurations: The feature configurations define the set of valid feature combinations for the intended member products of the product line.
3. Define shared assets: The shared assets supersets are all digital engineering artifacts required to define the member products.
4. Derive product models: Based on a feature configuration, a product model could be automatically derived from the shared assets. It can also be done manually or a mix of both.

However, in practice, a tailoring job that needs to be done to implement MBPLE within an enterprise setting. For instance, we provide a sequence of process steps that extend the initial simplified four-step approach:

1. Define the product line scoping
2. Define feature models

3. Define feature configurations
4. Define shared assets
5. Derive product models
6. Verify the product line
7. Customize the product models (if needed)
8. Verify the member products
9. Produce the member products
10. Validate the member products
11. Evolve and decommission the product line

It is important to note that those combined 11 steps are not exhaustive in representing a complete MBPLE real-world approach. For instance, further adaptation and tailoring shall be performed to integrate the approach into the systems engineering processes of an organization willing to embark on this journey. Chapter 24 provides a description of the MBPLE process and the steps highlighted here.

References

Chalé Gongora, H.G., Ferrogalini, M. and Moreau, C. (2014). How to boost PLE by using MBSE – a case study of a rolling stock product line. *Proceedings of the 5th International Conference on Complex Systems Design and Management CSDM*, Paris, France: Springer.

Chalé Gongora, H.G. and Greugny, F. (2017). Where the Big Bucks (will) come from – implementing product line engineering for railway rolling stock. *INCOSE 2017 International Symposium, Adelaide, Australia*. San Diego, CA: INCOSE.

Forlingieri, M. (2022). The four dimensions of variability and their impact on MBPLE: how to approach variability in the development of aircraft product lines at Airbus. *Proceedings of the 16th International Working Conference on Variability Modelling of Software-Intensive Systems (VaMoS'22)*, 23–25 February 2022, Florence, Italy: ACM.

Forlingieri, M. and Weilkiens, T. (2022). Two variant modelling methods for MBPLE at Airbus, *INCOSE International Symposium*, 32 (1): 1097–1113.

ISO/IEC (2000). International standards for quality management. Geneva, Switzerland: International Organization for Standardization (ISO)/International Electrotechnical Commission (IEC) (ISO/IEC 9000:2000).

ISO/IEC/IEEE. (2023). Systems and software engineering – system life cycle processes. (ISO/IEC/IEEE 15288:2023).

Kuhn, T.S. (1962). *The Structure of Scientific Revolutions*. Chicago: University of Chicago Press.

Software Engineering Institute (SEI) (2007). Capability maturity model integrated (CMMI) for development, version 1.2. Pittsburgh, PA, USA: Software Engineering Institute (SEI)/Carnegie Mellon University (CMU).

13

Define Feature Models

13.1 Introduction

This chapter provides insight into implementing a feature model. Chapter 10 introduces the concepts and Chapter 27 presents the feature information model. The definition of feature models is the first step of the model-based product line engineering (MBPLE) four-step approach (Figure 13.1).

First, the basic techniques for modeling feature models are described. The core element is a feature tree. Different types of feature trees and their relationships are introduced. Subsections provide an overview of feature-oriented domain analysis (FODA), orthogonal variability model (OVM), and feature modeling tools.

Section 13.2 covers the basic concepts. Section 13.3 describes how to specify a feature model with FODA, and Section 13.4 covers use of OVM. The chapter concludes with overview of feature modeling tools in Section 13.5 and provides another example of a feature model for a drone product line in Section 13.6.

13.2 Basic Concepts

The basic principle of applying a feature model is first demonstrated with a simple example to reduce distraction and put the focus on the concepts. Section 13.6 provides a more real-world example of a drone feature model.

A simple example is a "tiny Product Line Engineering (PLE) wall" comprising three different bricks: a standard brick (P), a large brick (L), and a standard dark brick (E). Figure 13.2 is a sketch of the tiny wall product.

Since customers opt for more variety, two slightly different tiny walls are developed and offered: a wall with two small bricks instead of the dark one and a wall with a sandy brick instead of the dark one (Figure 13.3).

In addition to the customer requests, the product management plans another L-brick variation that can be implemented by three very small bricks instead of the large lower left brick (Figure 13.4).

Product line scoping defines the product line and its member products. It also includes the definition of features and feature configurations, which are largely derived from the planned member products. More insights about the product line scoping are provided in Chapter 24.

Model-Based Product Line Engineering (MBPLE): The Feature-Based Path to Product Lines Success, First Edition.
Marco Forlingieri et al.

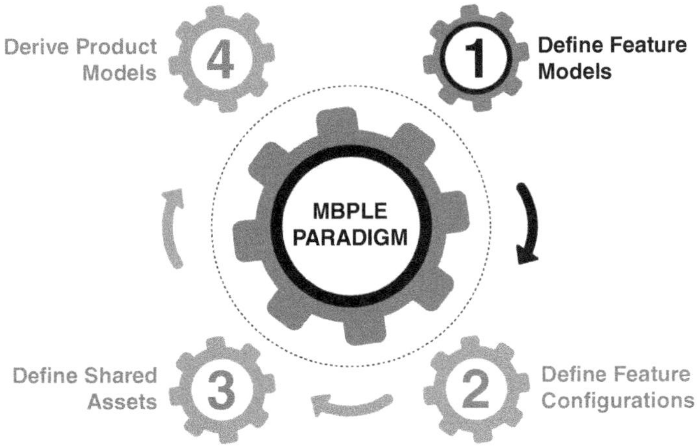

Figure 13.1 MBPLE four-step approach "define feature models."

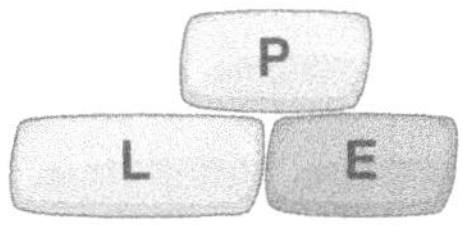

Figure 13.2 Product "tiny PLE wall."

Figure 13.3 Products "tiny PLE wall" and "tiny PLESandy wall."

Figure 13.4 L-brick variations

The first step of the MBPLE process presented in Chapter 9 is defining the feature model, typically depicted by a feature tree (Figure 13.5). The representation is based on the notation for feature trees proposed by Czarnecki et al. (2005).

The root feature represents the whole feature tree of the product line. Its identifier is "PLEW-F1," the name is "tiny PLE wall," and the binding time is "production." The textual description of the feature states, "the tiny PLE wall specifies a product line of walls for an illustrative example in the MBPLE book."

The lower right brick feature PLEW-F1.2 is an owned mandatory subfeature of the root feature PLEW-F1 with three owned subfeatures that are part of an exclusive-or (XOR) feature group – alternative features – which means exactly one of the features must be selected by a feature configuration. Another feature is the lower left brick PLEW-F1.1, which is also an owned mandatory subfeature with two subfeatures in an XOR feature group.

The feature PLEW-F1.1.2 (three very small bricks) cannot be combined with the feature PLEW-F1.2.2 (two small bricks). This is specified by the conflicts feature constraint between the two nodes in the feature tree.

The feature PLEW-F1.1.3 has a parameter property. Instead of having many features for each valid parameter value, it is only one and the feature parameter is set when selected for a feature configuration. Different feature configurations can select different parameter values. The feature sets the mass of a standard brick. The mass of other brick sizes can be derived appropriately.

A single feature model specifies the variability for all model layers on the same level (Figure 13.6). Here, layers are, for example, based on the common requirements, functional, logical, and physical approach (RFLP). However, it can also be used in any other layer approach.

The system levels also play an important role in defining the feature models. For example, the system, subsystem, and component levels follow the system's decomposition. Each element of a

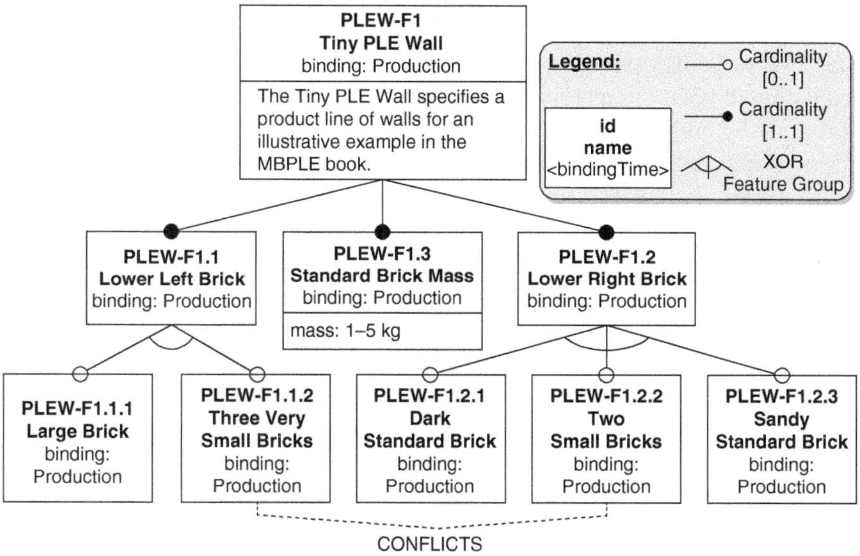

Figure 13.5 Feature tree "tiny PLE wall."

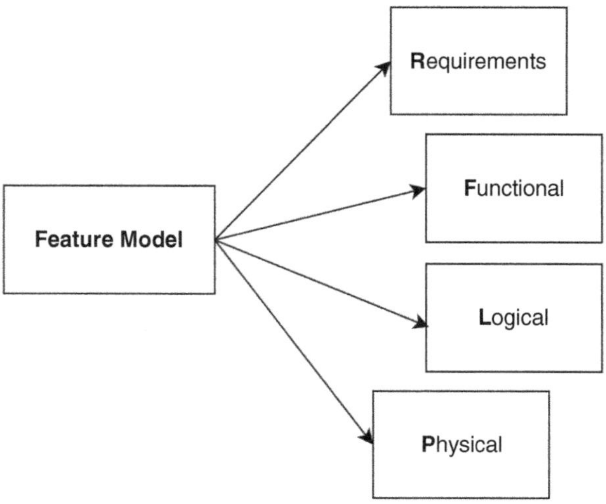

Figure 13.6 One feature model for all RFLP layers.

decomposition could have its own feature model: a feature model for subsystem A, one for subsystem B, and so on (Figure 13.7).

A feature in a feature tree can also be the root element of another feature tree. For example, the root feature of a subsystem feature model in a system feature model. In this way, feature trees can be composed of many feature trees, or a large one can be broken down into several smaller ones.

The feature model on the system level can have feature constraints on features from different subsystem feature models. To do this, however, the feature model must have access to all features of the lower feature model. If another organization owns a feature model on a detailed level, it might not be fully accessible by the feature model on the higher level. Chapter 14 shows an example of this scenario.

The feature model in Figure 13.5 defines the set of valid member products of the product line. Typically, not all valid member products are also planned member products of the product portfolio. The oversimplified example of the tiny PLE wall has only two features, PLEW-F1.1 and PLEW-F1.2, with variability represented by their subfeatures. However, they have already resulted in six unconstrained potential member products. You get the number of unconstrained potential member products by multiplying the number of variable options of each feature.

The number of unconstrained potential member products is often cited as an example of the explosion of possible combinations. It sounds impressive, but it is irrelevant because nobody would ever build all these combinations. The set of unconstrained potential member products is only theoretical and contains undesirable combinations that are invalid due to unfulfilled feature constraints.

You must consider the feature constraints to get the set of valid member products. Figure 13.5 depicts one conflicting feature constraint between two features in the feature tree, which results in a set of valid member products with five elements. There are two features with two, respectively, three options ($2 \times 3 = 6$), and the conflicts feature constraint in the feature model excludes one combination ($6 - 1 = 5$). If the upper bound of the cardinality of a feature relationship or feature group is greater than 1, it changes the number of options. The product of the set of valid member products could be built.

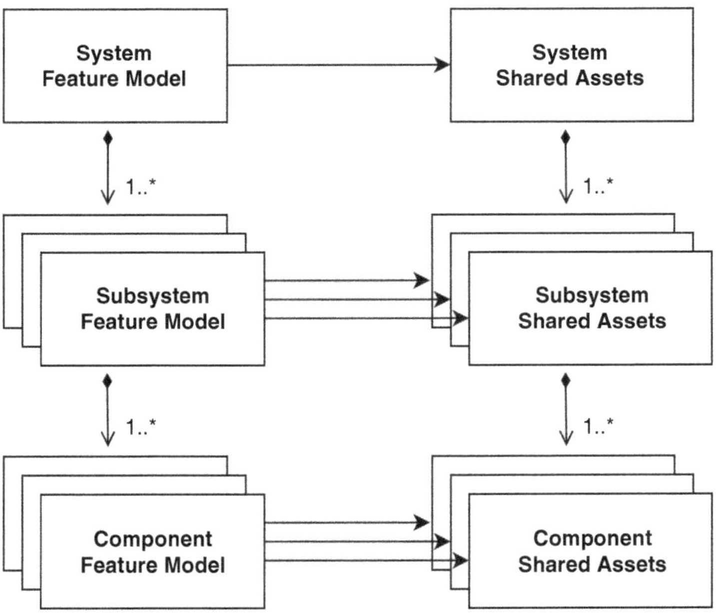

Figure 13.7 Multilevel feature models.

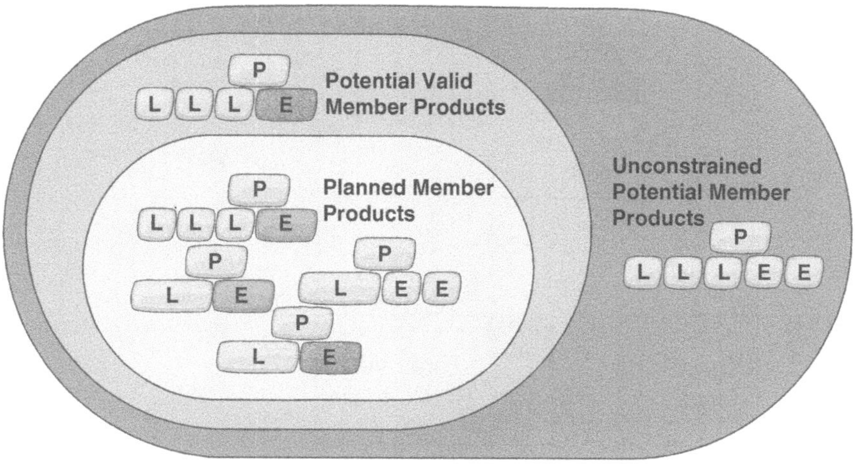

Figure 13.8 Member product sets.

The set of planned member products includes only those valid member products that should be engineered and built. The "tiny PLE wall" product portfolio excludes the combination of three tiny bricks with the sandy brick from the set of valid member products. The combinations of the planned member products are specified as feature configurations presented in Chapter 14. Figure 13.8 shows the different member product sets.

13.3 Feature-Oriented Domain Analysis

A common and old concept of feature modeling is the FODA by Kang et al. (1990). FODA also defines a notation for feature trees, similar to the notation used above in Figure 13.5. Since it is not a full modeling language, it only specifies how to draw feature trees. Tools can add the missing data structures layer to provide feature tree modeling, but it still remains a tool-specific proprietary solution.

The FODA feature tree is the mother of the feature trees. The concept is used in many variant descriptions and modeling approaches. Later, Kang extended FODA to the feature-oriented reuse method, which incorporates the marketing perspective in addition to the requirements and architecture perspective (Kang et al. 1998).

FODA originates from the software engineering discipline but is independent of software and can also be applied to other disciplines, including systems engineering.

13.4 Orthogonal Variability Model

The OVM is described by Pohl et al. (2005). An OVM captures the variability of software artifacts in a separate model. OVM has its roots in software engineering but could also be applied to systems engineering models. It also provides a variability notation, as shown in Figure 13.9. The node with the VP symbol represents a variation point. The nodes with the V symbol represent variants. The dashed lines depict optional variants. Solid lines depict mandatory variants.

OVM uses terms from the shared assets domain (Chapter 14) to model features such as variants.

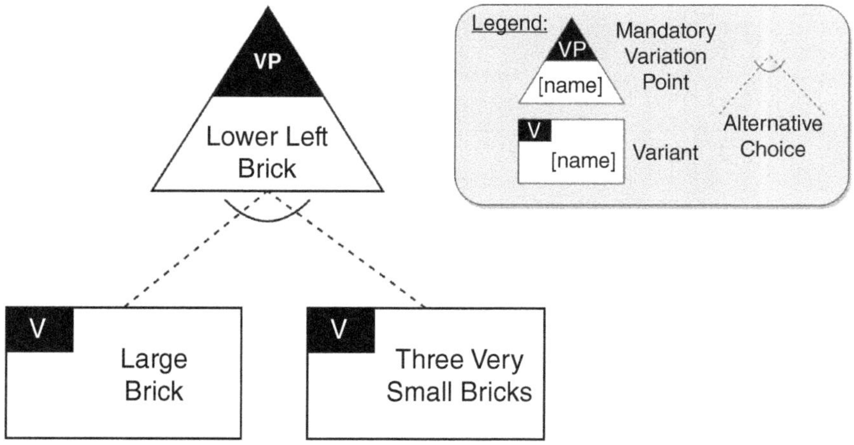

Figure 13.9 Example of OVM.

13.5 Feature Modeling Tools

Of course, there are commercial tools with which feature models can be created. For example, pure::variants from PTC (PTC 2024) and Gears from BigLever (BigLever 2024). Chapter 27 provides more information about the PLE tools, while Chapter 29 features an interview with PLE pioneers from the two companies.

The tools follow the basic concept of feature modeling but implement them proprietarily with their own extensions and in their own format. As mentioned in Chapter 10, FODA and OVM, for example, have specifications on what the notation should look like. Still, the so-called abstract syntax, which means the data format of the feature model, is not specified or even standardized.

As a proxy for feature modeling tools, we show the open-source tool FeatureIDE as an example here in order to appear neutral toward the tool market (METOP 2020). FeatureIDE is not as powerful as the commercial tools, but it is sufficient to show the use of a PLE tool here.

Typically, PLE tools provide a feature tree view and several dialogs for specifying the details of a feature or feature relationship. The terms used and feature tree notation can differ from those provided in Chapter 10, but the basic concept is the same. Figure 13.10 shows the feature tree from Figure 13.5 in the tool FeatureIDE.

Applying the feature information to all kinds of shared assets is an important and challenging task. The cylinders depicted in Figure 13.11 are different tools, possibly from different vendors, with different repositories. Exchanging the feature model information to the shared assets superset models requires interoperability between the tools.

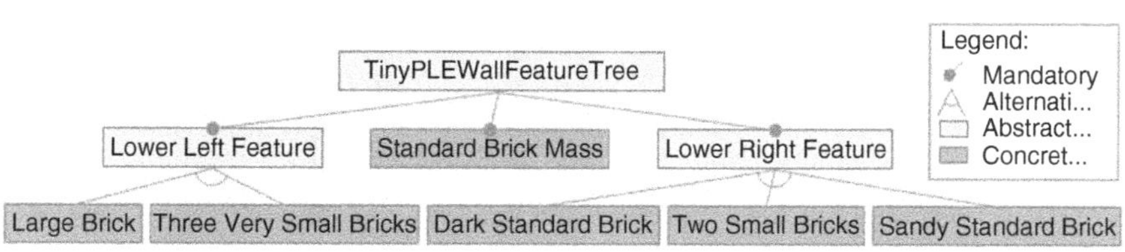

Figure 13.10 FeatureIDE feature tree.

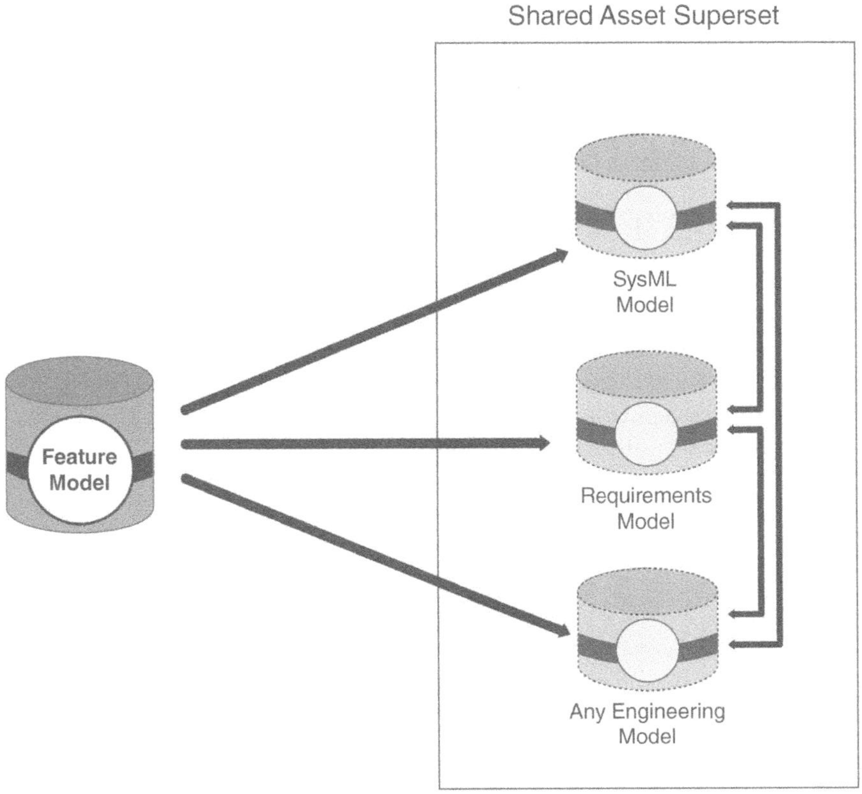

Figure 13.11 Feature model connections.

Technically, the engineering tools must be able to get the feature information from the feature modeling tool. Additionally, they must be able to understand the information and appropriately apply it to their engineering data. Alternatively, a specific PLE tool can do the job independently from the other tools by retrieving the feature information from the feature model tool and managing the shared asset variability in the other engineering tools. Of course, the PLE tool needs access to the tools by an API or plugin to realize such synergy.

The variability exchange language is an initiative to specify a standardized format for exchanging feature models (OASIS 2018). However, the project has not yet been completed. The exchange still takes place proprietarily and depends on the interfaces offered by the tools used. Often, the feature model tools offer various plug-ins for the engineering tools to establish the connection and make the appropriate changes in the engineering model.

Although systems modeling language v2 (SysML v2) does not explicitly provide feature modeling, it could be used for it, and the SysML v2 Application Programming Interface (API) provides standardized access to the feature model data.

13.6 Drone Product Line Example

The "tiny PLE wall" is an oversimplified example that demonstrates the concepts of MBPLE. The "drone product line" example is closer to real-world projects, although, of course, it omits many details that are outside the book's scope.

Imagine an organization that develops various types of drones. They offer both standard products for sale and customized solutions. Their product portfolio includes:

- Standard consumer drones.
- Delivery drones for transporting small goods to hard-to-reach places, such as islands or ships.
- Surveillance drones for tasks like locating and monitoring forest fires.

The feature tree contains one feature constraint: the feature "six engines" requires the feature "long distance battery."

The product line for a forest fire detection system (FFDS) also references the feature model of the drone product line in Figure 13.12. The feature constraint explicitly defines here that the feature in the FFDS for "long-time monitoring" missions requires the feature "long-distance battery" in the included drone feature model (Figure 13.13).

After explaining the concept of features and feature models, the next chapter will shift focus to the other "side of the coin": feature configurations.

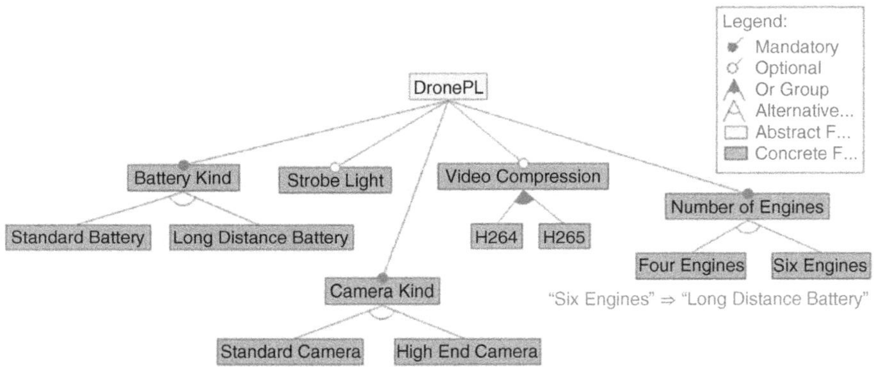

Figure 13.12 Drone product line feature tree.

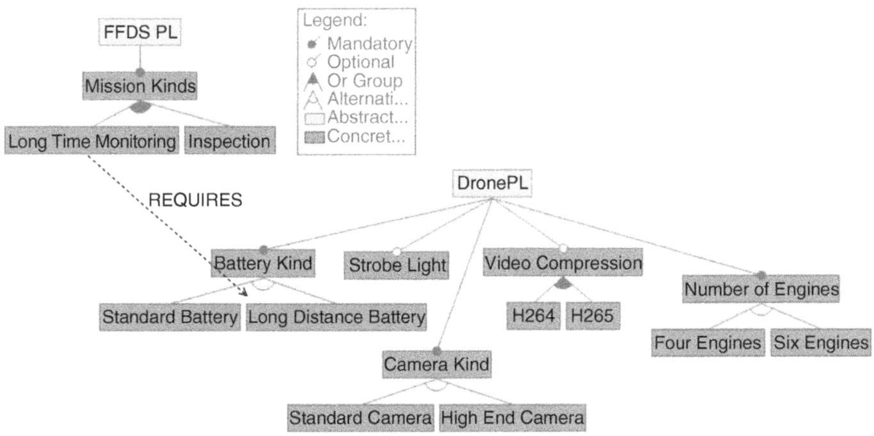

Figure 13.13 Cross-feature model feature constraint.

References

BigLever (2024). *BigLever Software Gears*. Available at: https://biglever.com/solution/gears/ (accessed 25 July 2024).

Czarnecki, K., Helsen, S. and Eisenecker, U. (2005). Formalizing cardinality-based feature models and their specialization. *Software Process Improvement and Practice* 10 (1): 7–29.

Kang, K., Cohen, S., and Hess, J. et al. (1990). Feature-Oriented Domain Analysis (FODA) Feasibility Study. *Technical Report CMU/SEI-90-TR-21*, Software Engineering Institute, Carnegie Mellon University, Pittsburgh, USA. http://resources.sei.cmu.edu/library/asset-view.cfm?AssetID=11231 (accessed 7 January 2023)

Kang, K.C., Kim, S., Lee, J., *et al.* (1998). FORM: A feature-; oriented reuse method with domain-; specific reference architectures. *Annals of Software Engineering* 5 (1): 143–168.

METOP (2020). FeatureIDE. https://www.featureide.de/ (accessed 10 January 2023).

OASIS (2018). *OASIS Variability Exchange Language (VEL)*. https://www.oasis-open.org/committees/tc_home.php?wg_abbrev=vel (accessed 23 July 2023).

Pohl, K., Böckle, G. and van der Linden, F.J. (2005). *Software Product Line Engineering: Foundation, Principles and Techniques*. 413–434. Springer.

PTC (2024). PTC pure::variants. Available at: https://www.ptc.com/en/products/pure-variants (accessed 25 July 2024).

14

Define Feature Configurations

14.1 Introduction

This chapter presents the modeling of feature configurations, building upon the foundational concepts introduced in Chapter 9, and the detailed feature information model presented in Chapter 26. The definition of feature configurations is the second step of the model-based product line engineering (MBPLE) four-step approach (Figure 14.1).

The chapter outlines the basic techniques in Section 14.2 and covers feature configurations in product line engineering (PLE) tools in Section 14.3.

14.2 Basic Concepts

Chapter 13 has already shown that the unconstrained potential feature combinations typically do not correspond to the number of planned products in the product line. These combinations increase exponentially with the number of variability. As a simple example, just take 10 features, each with three selection options. This already leads to 50 049 possible combinations. Significantly fewer of these are only valid if feature constraints declare some invalid. However, the number of valid combinations will certainly still be much higher than the number of different products that the product line is supposed to create. The planned set of member products is an outcome of the product line scoping.

Feature configurations specify the planned combinations, which means the planned products of the product line. A feature configuration is a valid selection of features.

Feature configurations are often represented within a matrix view, where the rows depict the features and the columns depict the feature configurations. The cells show the selection of a feature in a feature configuration. The root feature is omitted in the matrix, as it is always selected by all feature configurations of the feature model. Figure 14.2 shows a feature configuration matrix for our simple "tiny PLE wall" example from Chapter 13.

A feature configuration can also be represented by a feature used in another feature model. Figure 14.3 shows the feature configurations from Figure 14.2, represented by features as part of the feature model. They are an exclusive-or (XOR) feature group of subfeatures of the root feature and play a special role in the tree. Selecting a feature configuration implies selecting the corresponding features.

Let us assume our "tiny PLE wall" is part of another product line, "PLE house." The "PLE house" feature tree is depicted in Figure 14.4. The root feature of the "tiny PLE wall" feature model is

Model-Based Product Line Engineering (MBPLE): The Feature-Based Path to Product Lines Success, First Edition.
Marco Forlingieri et al.

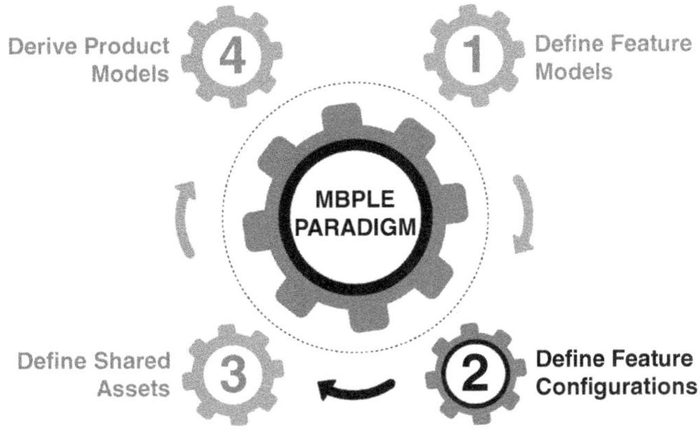

Figure 14.1 MBPLE four-step approach "define feature configurations."

	2SmallBricksTinyPLEWall	3VerySmallBricksTinyPLEWall	DarkBrickTinyPLEWall	SandyBrickTinyPLEWall
PLEW-F1.1 Lower Left Brick	●	●	●	●
PLEW-F1.1.1 Large Brick	●		●	●
PLEW-F1.1.2 Three Very Small Bricks		●		
PLEW-F1.2 Lower Right Brick	●	●	●	●
PLEW-F1.2.1 Dark Standard Brick		●	●	
PLEW-F1.2.2 Two Small Bricks	●			
PLEW-F1.2.3 Sandy Standard Brick				●
PLEW-F1.3 Standard Brick Mass	2 kg	2 kg	4 kg	3 kg

Figure 14.2 Feature configurations map.

referenced and used as a subfeature of the "PLE house" root feature. The reference is depicted by a rectangle with a dashed borderline.

All features of the "tiny PLE wall" feature tree could be used here. However, typically, only the defined feature configurations of the used feature model are of interest. They represent the planned configurations created by the experts of the corresponding product line. Therefore, only the corresponding products are available and can be used within the parent product line.

A "PLE house" feature configuration can select sub-features of the Door and Roof (not shown in Figure 14.4) and select one of the "tiny PLE wall" feature configurations.

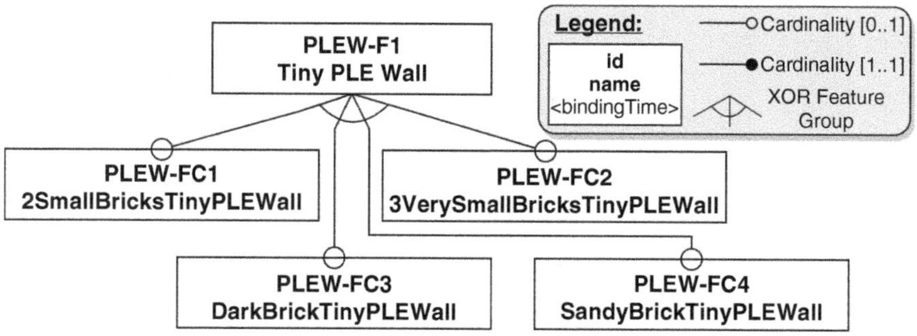

Figure 14.3 Feature tree with feature configurations.

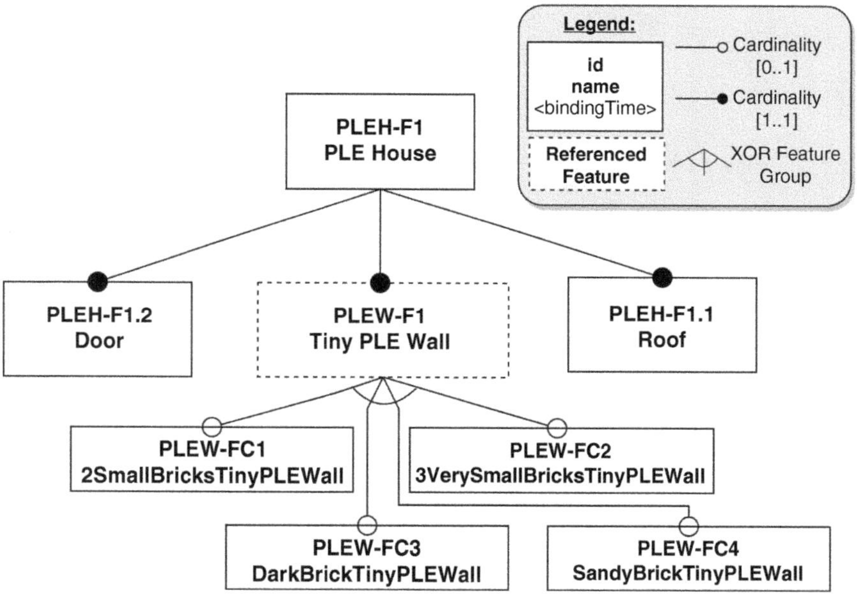

Figure 14.4 PLE house feature tree.

Similar to features, feature configurations can also affect all layers of a level, such as the requirements, functional, logical, and physical layers, and might include the scope of different system levels.

14.3 Feature Modeling Tools

A feature modeling tool also provides the capability to specify feature configurations in addition to the feature tree. The usual view and editor for feature configurations is a matrix. You will find such opinions in commercial feature modeling tools like pure::variants from PTC (PTC 2024) or Gears from BigLever (BigLever 2024).

Figure 14.5 shows the matrix reproduced from Figure 14.2 in the tool FeatureIDE (METOP 2020). The parameter settings of the feature "standard brick mass" are configured in the tool, but not visible in the configuration matrix.

Features	2SmallBricksTin...	3VerySmallBrick...	DarkBrickTinyPL...	SandyBrickTinyP...
⌄ TinyPLEWallFeatureTree				
⌄ Lower Left Feature				
Large Brick	+	−	+	+
Three Very Small Brick	−	+	−	−
Standard Brick Mass	+	+	+	+
⌄ Lower Right Feature				
Dark Standard Brick	−	+	+	−
Two Small Bricks	+	−	−	−
Sandy Standard Brick	−	−	−	+

Figure 14.5 FeatureIDE configuration matrix.

During the features selection, the PLE tools check whether the feature constraints are fulfilled since only valid combinations can be chosen.

Feature configurations do not have to be always complete. Depending on the binding time, feature decisions can also be made later. For example, a feature with a binding time of "production" must not be decided within the "design" phase. The concept of partial feature configurations is explained in Chapter 9.

Similar to what was discussed in Chapter 13, the challenge consists of transferring the information about the feature configuration and individual features in all affected models and making use of it.

References

BigLever (2024). BigLever Software Gears. https://biglevehom/solution/gears/ (accessed 25 July 2024).

METOP (2020). FeatureIDE. https://www.featureide.de/ (accessed 1 October 2023).

PTC (2024). PTC pure::variants. https://www.ptc.com/en/products/pure-variants (accessed 25 July 2024).

15

Define Shared Assets

15.1 Introduction

The chapter describes how to model shared assets with Systems Modeling Language (SysML). The main part uses the latest version of SysML v2, but SysML v1 and other modeling languages are also presented. Chapters 9 and 27 define the concept of shared assets and the superset. The definition of shared assets is the third step of the model-based product line engineering (MBPLE) four-step approach (Figure 15.1).

Section 15.2 presents the basic principle with two different approaches to model variable shared assets. The direct approach is covered in Section 15.2.1 and the clean approach in Section 15.2.2. Section 15.2 closes by showing the impact of variability across multiple layers and levels in Section 15.2.3.

Section 15.3 shows the modeling of shared assets with SysML v2, and Section 15.4 shows the modeling with SysML v1. Section 15.5 briefly demonstrates the modeling of shared assets without SysML.

15.2 Basic Principle

There are three basic approaches for modeling shared assets that implement the variability of the feature model.

The first approach is mentioned here only for the sake of completeness. It is not a real MBPLE approach, but the one used when there is no established MBPLE with no explicit management of commonalities between similar products. Assets are copied and pasted and then further developed (a clone-and-own approach). Sometimes, this may seem to be the best way for the project because it is quick and easy, but it can lead to more effort and missed synergies. The disadvantages of the approach versus the advantages of using product line engineering (PLE) are described in detail in Part I of this book (in particular in Chapter 3).

The other two approaches are real MBPLE approaches, presented in Sections 15.2.1 and 15.2.2. They were first published under these names in the paper (Forlingieri and Weilkiens 2022).

Methodologies in general and also the MBPLE methodology in this book follow a logical top-down sequence. In practice, work is usually carried out simultaneously from top to bottom and from bottom to top.

For example, shared assets are usually already in place when a product line is set up. Therefore, they exist before the features.

Model-Based Product Line Engineering (MBPLE): The Feature-Based Path to Product Lines Success, First Edition.
Marco Forlingieri et al.

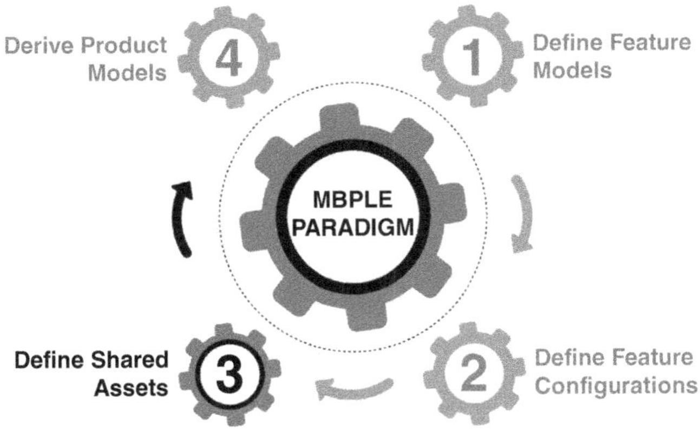

Figure 15.1 MBPLE four-step approach "define shared assets."

Just as features and feature configurations are identified during product scoping, the existing shared assets must also be analyzed during asset scoping to examine their use in the product line.

15.2.1 "Direct Method" to Create Shared Assets

The first real PLE approach is called the "direct method." All variants are specified directly at the appropriate point in the model and are labeled as variants.

If the modeling language does not explicitly cover the concept of variability, this can lead to inconsistencies. For example, a model of a vehicle specifies three different engines in the same position within the vehicle. Without explicit variability modeling, this is a technically invalid model. Depending on the tool and language, this can lead to problems.

Figure 15.2 shows all variants of "the tiny PLE wall" in a blueprint view of a fictional wall modeling tool.

The direct approach is easily applicable. The variant is added like any other artifact. The bottom positions of the wall now have more than one brick option. The variation points (also known as variations) are depicted as tags in Figure 15.2.

In addition to the ease, another advantage of the direct approach is that you can see everything at a glance. Figure 15.2 shows the common core and all variant elements. It's like putting each product's blueprints on top of each other. Showing everything at once is practical, but it can also easily have the disadvantage of making it confusing or hiding aspects.

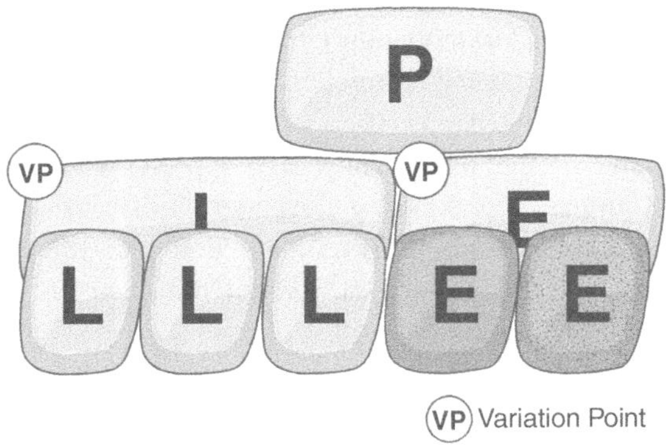

Figure 15.2 Direct method shared assets "tiny PLE walls."

The blueprint model in Figure 15.2 specifies which different kinds of bricks are located on the wall's lower left and right sides. Without processing the variability information, the model is wrong. If the blueprint model does not have a built-in capability for variability modeling, it could lead to issues. For example, a wall modeling tool could complain that placing more than one brick at the same location is not allowed.

If the tool for the wall specification supports different views of the data, the specification data could be depicted in different views, each showing only one or a few variants to make it more overseeable. But the data behind the views is still squeezed. The shared assets superset created by the direct approach does not represent real products. You need an additional technology that manages the variability. Together with the feature model and selected feature configurations, such technology can transform the shared assets into a product model, which means a model that specifies only a single product.

The direct approach is component-oriented rather than systems-engineering-oriented. However, it is easily applicable and can be a good choice in the project's early exploration phases or when variation is added to existing legacy assets.

15.2.2 "Clean Method" to Create Shared Assets

The second approach is called the "clean method." The variants are not directly added to the model like in the direct method. Instead, first, the point of variation is identified. In the wall example, it is the lower left and right brick of the wall. Second, the commonality of all variants is explicitly specified. The common element is a variation element. Here, the commonality is the concept of a brick with a tag in the middle of the front and a specific size. The immutable asset and the variations together form the core of the shared assets superset. The core is part of all member products. The variants are specified separately and linked with the appropriate variation in the core (Figure 15.3). The variation links to the variants and the appropriate feature in the feature model. A variation is also called "variation point."

The modeling language and tool must be able to separate common specifications (the variations) from ad hoc specifications (the variants), including the relationship between them. Otherwise, the direct method can be used.

15.2.3 Multilayer and Multidiscipline Shared Assets

We have already discussed the topic of multilevel and multilayer in Chapter 13 when defining the feature models. It also applies to shared assets. The terms layer and level are used differently. In Figure 15.4, we use the term layer for the horizontal structure (RFLP) and the term level for the

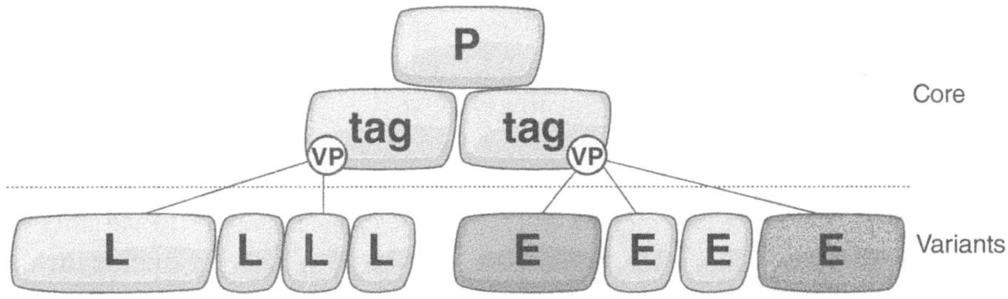

Figure 15.3 Clean method shared assets superset "tiny PLE walls."

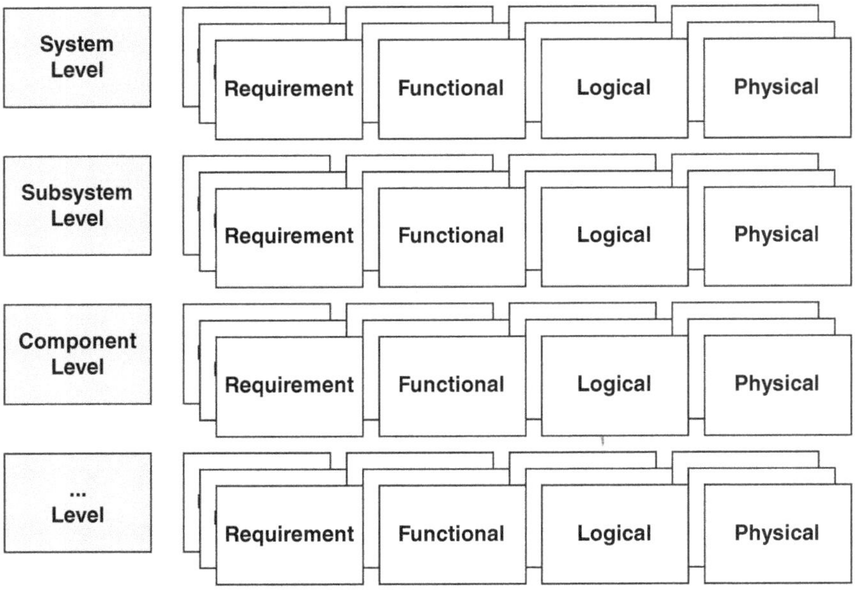

Figure 15.4 Multilevel and multilayer shared assets.

vertical decomposition level. RFLP and the names of the decomposition levels are only examples and can be replaced by any other terminology. The concept remains the same.

In addition to multiple layers and levels, each cell can contain several models and tools. Overall, it is a multidimensional space with many different relationships between the individual layers, levels, and models within a cell. It illustrates the challenge of engineering projects in the real world.

This could be a challenging engineering space, even for a single system. But here we are talking about a product line, i.e. a large number of systems.

The variability is defined in the feature model or, as in Chapter 13, in several feature models and affects all shared assets, which are distributed in this multidimensional engineering space.

15.3 Modeling of Shared Assets with SysML v2

An essential capability of SysML v2 (OMG 2024b) is the built-in concept of variation and variants. Any definition or usage element can be a variation. The definition and usage elements in SysML v2 cover the most required kinds of elements used in technical systems engineering processes, like requirements, parts, ports, interfaces, actions, states, and so forth. A variation defines a list of design choices, which are the variants. The SysML v2 concept of a variation misses the link to features since features are not part of SysML v2 (see Chapter 13). A variant in SysML v2 is always a usage element because it is a design choice with a context.

Behind the scenes of the SysML v2, the variations and variants are not model elements on their own but are ends of a variant membership relationship (Figure 15.5). The relationship connects a definition or usage element (the variation) with exactly one usage element (the variant). It denotes the usage element as a design choice for the variation element. Typically, a variation includes more than one variant. There is one variant membership relationship for each variant. Finally, it depends on the user interface of the modeling tool and how we can create variations and variants. Still, very

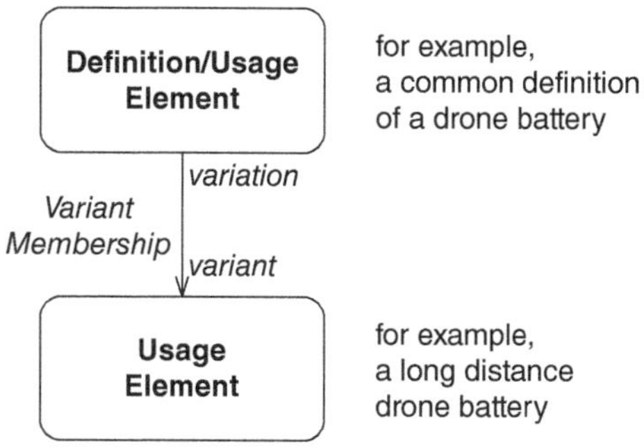

Figure 15.5 Variant membership relationship.

likely, as modelers, we will not explicitly work with the variant membership relationship, except if we access the model data using scripts or other model-data-based approaches.

The variation element is always abstract because, without the choice of one of its variants, there is no instance specified by the variation. The variants must conform to the variation. That means if the variation is a definition element, the variants are implicitly defined by the variation. If the variation is a usage element, the variants subset the variation. The subsections below provide concrete examples to illustrate the concept.

Variations and variants need a link to the appropriate features in the feature model. The feature model is outside of a SysML v2 model, and the link between variations or variants and the features requires additional technology to manage the relationship across the models. For example, a plugin from a feature model tool vendor in a SysML v2 modeling tool could connect the SysML elements and the features. The plugin can access the feature model and control the SysML v2 model, for example, display filtered views based on feature configurations that only show elements that are valid for the selected features.

Since modeling variations and variants with SysML uses the specialization mechanism, the clean approach fits very well, and the following sections use only the clean method. The application of the direct method with SysML v2 is briefly discussed. Section 15.4 describes applying the clean and direct method with SysML v1.

The shared assets superset is modeled as a library package in SysML v2. It contains the shared assets organized in subpackages. It does not cover the whole shared assets superset, but only the SysML assets. There might be other shared assets in other models like computer-aided design (CAD), product life cycle management (PLM), or simulation models.

```
library package Drone_SharedAssetsSuperset {
     package DroneBattery { …
     package DroneEngine { …
```

Section 15.3.1 presents the variability modeling of SysML v2 part structures. Section 15.3.2 focuses the variability modeling of behavior, while Section 15.3.3 addresses the variability modeling of requirements.

15.3.1 Modeling of Shared Assets: Parts

Chapter 13 specifies the feature model for the drone product line, which includes the mandatory feature "batteryKind" with two alternative subfeatures, "standardBattery" and "longDistanceBattery," and a mandatory feature about the number of engines, which can be four or six.

Figure 15.6 depicts an abstract definition of a drone battery that specifies some properties and two concrete specializations of the abstract definition for a standard and a long-distance battery. The package "DroneBattery_Parts" is contained in the package "DroneBattery" in the shared assets superset library package, which is not shown in Figure 15.5. The example focuses on a limited set to highlight only the variability aspect.

The battery definitions are specified by model elements without any explicit variability. A shared asset is not required to vary. It is just a digital artifact of the engineering process used for the member products. Implicitly, the model in Figure 15.6 already contains a touch of variability because it specifies two different kinds of drone batteries with different capacities. But it does not specify how they are used. It is only a library of part definitions like a parts catalog.

Next, variability is added to the shared assets by constraining their usage according to the feature model. The variations are organized in a separate package named "DroneBattery_Variations." The element "droneBatteryVariation" is a part and a variation. It specifies two design choices as variants, each of them is linked to the appropriate features in the feature model (Figure 15.7). The links between the variants and the features implicitly include the relationship between the variation and the feature. Therefore, it is not explicitly modeled. Since these relationships are created between elements in different models and tools, the link cannot be done directly, but requires a technology that establishes and maintains the connection.

The variants in Figure 15.7 depend on the feature model, but the part definitions of the drone battery in Figure 15.6 have no dependency on features. Following the principle of separation of concerns, they can be stored in separate packages in the shared assets superset and can also be used in other contexts.

The shared assets superset also contains a package "Drone_ProductLine" with elements specifying the complete SysML part of the drone product line. The following Figure 15.8 shows only some elements of it. The battery of the drone product line specializes in the drone battery variation. The

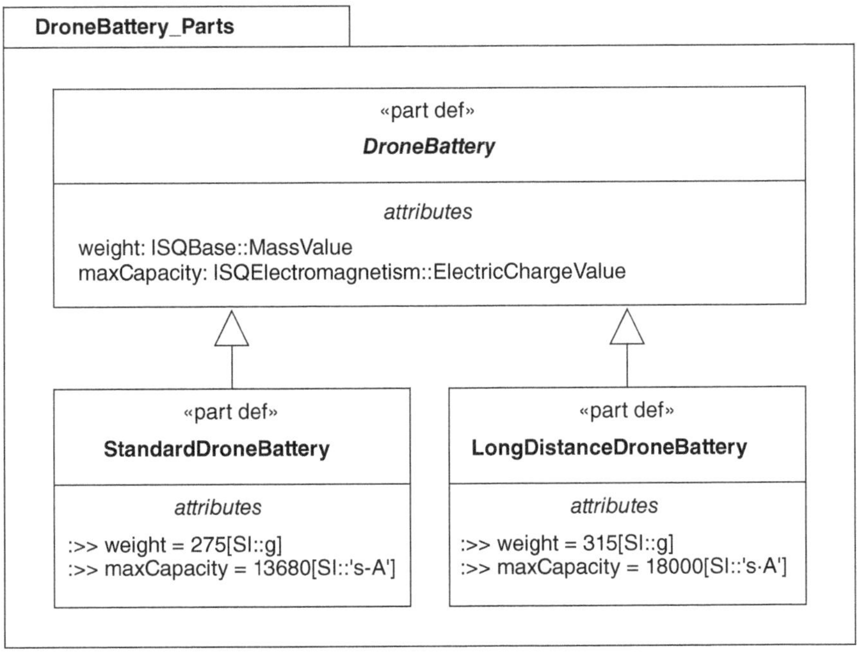

Figure 15.6 Shared assets for drone batteries.

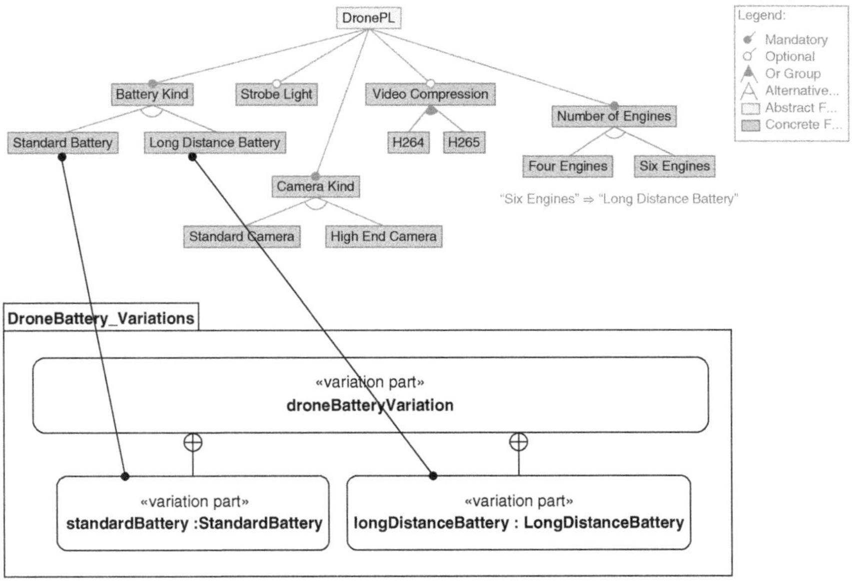

Figure 15.7 Variation of the drone battery.

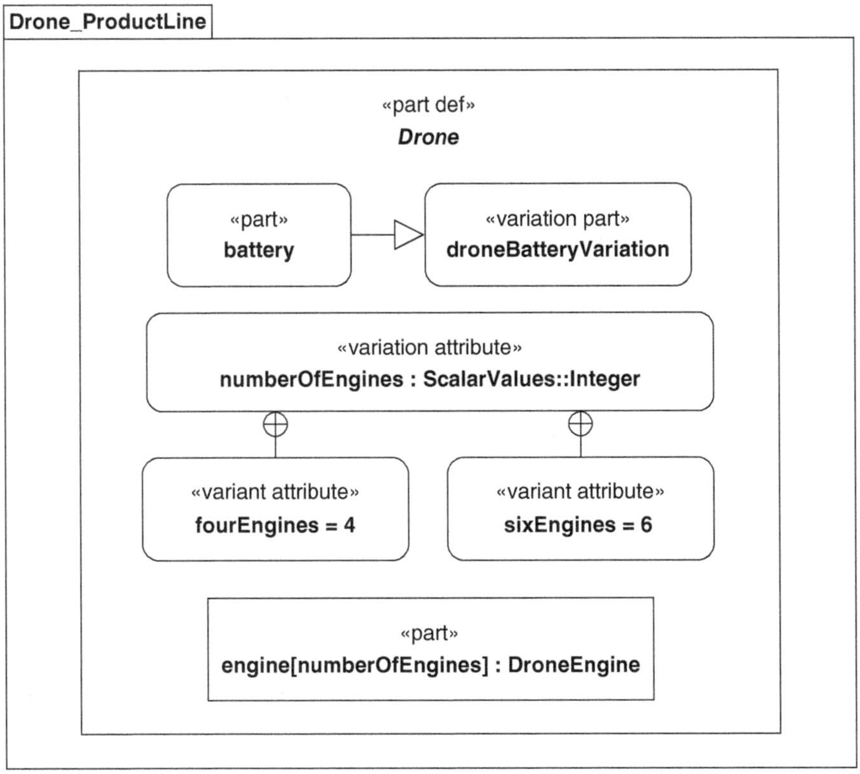

Figure 15.8 Definition of the drone product line.

top-level element is the product itself, which includes all variations. Here, it is the part definition of "Drone."

Another feature of the drone product line is the number of engines. The variation is directly specified inside the drone specification (`variation attribute numberOfEngines`). For the sake of simplicity, the variability is only specified by the number used for the multiplicity of the engine part (`part engine[numberOfEngines] : DroneEngine`).

The feature model specifies a feature constraint between the feature "numberOfEngines" and "batteryKind": six engines require a long-distance battery. The constraint can also be considered in the SysML model between the variants, but it is redundant to the feature model. If possible, the modeling principle of avoiding redundancy should be followed. Redundant elements must be kept synchronized to ensure the consistency of the model. Someone has to do this reliably.

Anyhow, the following textual syntax shows an example of the variability constraint that mirrors the feature constraint between variants.

```
abstract part def Drone {
  // Battery specializes the variation
  part battery :> droneBatteryVariation;
  // Engines
  variation attribute numberOfEngines : ScalarValues::Integer {
    variant attribute fourEngines = 4;
    variant attribute sixEngines = 6;
  }
  assert constraint {
    (numberOfEngines == numberOfEngines::sixEngines) and
    (battery == DroneBattery_Variation::droneBatteryVariation::longDistanceBattery)
  }
  part engine[4..numberOfEngines]: DroneEngine;
}
```

Technically, the number of engines has more impact on the specification of the drone than a simple change in its multiplicity. For example, the drone might need different bodies according to the number of engines and different flight control software. The shared assets superset also contains the assets for the special bodies and the software (Figure 15.9).

The different bodies and software applications do not appear in the feature model. They are not selectable product line features but variants implementing the product feature "numberOfEngines."

This relationship should be modeled in the constraint so that the constraint looks as follows. As mentioned above, the relationship to the battery type is redundant and is already covered by the feature constraint in the feature model.

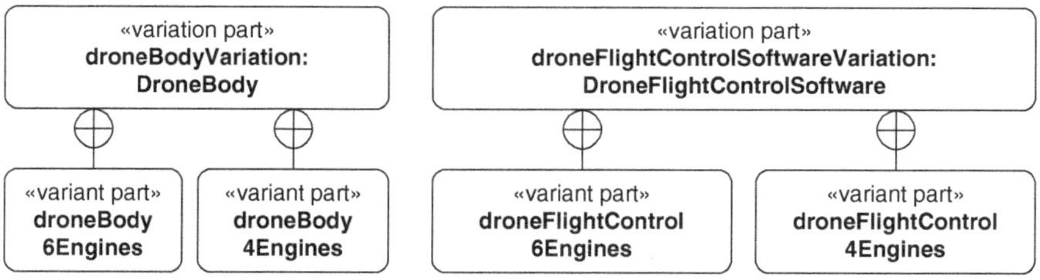

Figure 15.9 Drone body and flight control software variations.

```
assert constraint {
((numberOfEnginesVariation == numberOfEnginesVariation::sixEngines) and
(battery == DroneBattery::DroneBattery_Parts::DroneBatteryVariation::longDistanceBattery) and
 (body == DroneBody::DroneBody_Parts::DroneBodyVariation::droneBody6Engines) and
 (flightControl == DroneFlightControl::FlightControlVariation::flightControl4Engines)) or
 ((numberOfEnginesVariation == numberOfEnginesVariation::fourEngines) and
(body == DroneBody::DroneBody_Parts::DroneBodyVariation::droneBody4Engines) and
 (flightControl == DroneFlightControl::FlightControlVariation::flightControl6Engines))
}
```

So far, the example has been modeled using the clean approach. The variation element represents the commonality and the variants, the specializations. The direct approach with SysML means "not using the variation and variant concepts of SysML v2." Therefore, it does not make sense to apply the direct approach if the modeling language explicitly supports the modeling of variability. Section 15.4 illustrates the direct approach with SysML v1, which does not support variability modeling in its notation.

If you were to model the drone with the variability in battery type and number of engines using the direct method, it would look like in the example below. The (non-SysML) variation points are not displayed, but they can still filter out the corresponding parts via an external technology based on the feature configuration.

```
part def Drone {
  part standardBattery : StandardBattery;
  part longDistanceBattery : LongDistanceBattery;

  part fourEngine[4] : DroneEngine;
  part sixEngine[6] : DroneEngine;
}
```

15.3.2 Modeling of Shared Assets: Behavior

The behavior elements of SysML have the same foundation as the structural model elements. Therefore, the basic approach for modeling behavior variability is the same as for structures.

The drone product line has a feature, "Flight Patterns," with three subfeatures: "Fly Observation Patterns," "Fly Camera Patterns," and "Fly Fun Patterns" (Figure 15.10).

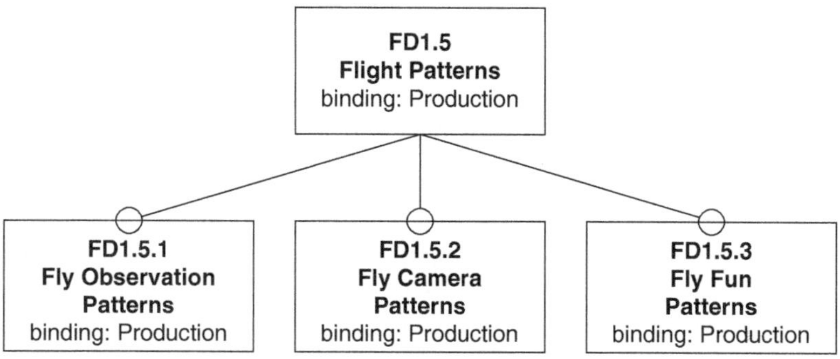

Figure 15.10 Feature flight patterns.

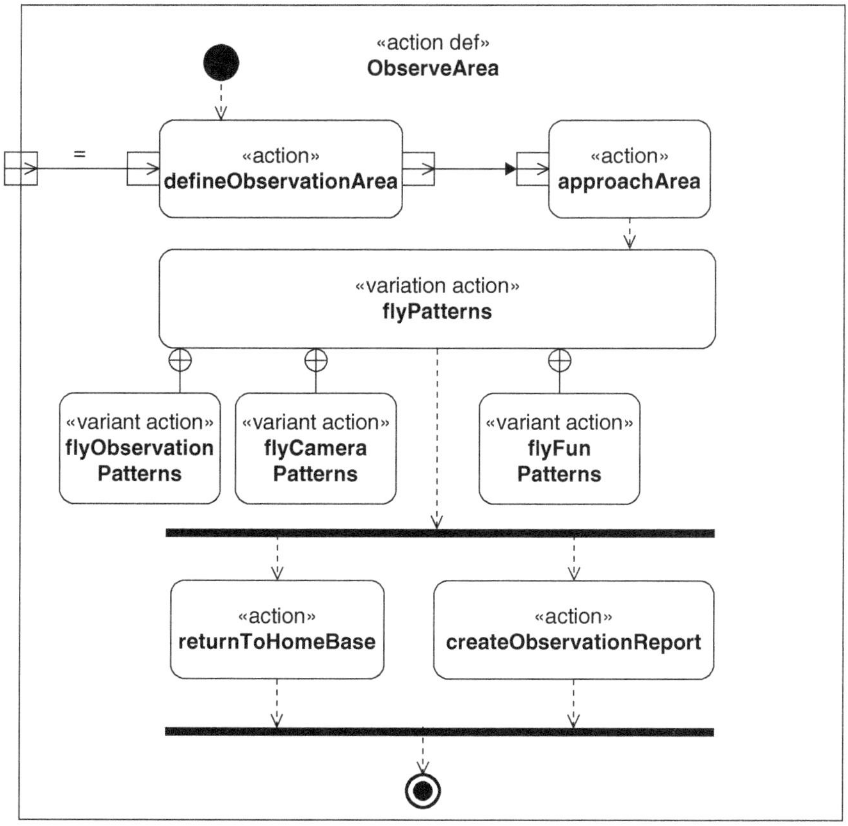

Figure 15.11 Flight pattern actions.

Figure 15.11 shows different flight pattern actions corresponding to the features. The details are omitted here because the flight pattern algorithms are unimportant for the variability aspect.

The use of variation and variants corresponds to the clean approach again. This is a good example that shows why the direct approach is not always possible. The same action modeled according to the direct approach could lead to a nonvalid SysML v2 model, as the fork node must not have multiple incoming successions.

The same scenario leads to the analogous formal problem in SysML v1. Figure 15.12 shows the invalid SysML model.

15.3.3 Modeling of Shared Assets: Requirements

Also, variations and variants of requirements can be modeled similarly to the modeling of structure and behavior variability. In the example below, the requirement definition maximum takeoff weight (MTOW) generally defines a takeoff weight requirement for drones. The two requirement usages specify concrete weights. The following SysML textual notation shows parts of the definition of the drone requirement specification, including the variation of the takeoff weight requirement according to the product feature "numberOfEngines."

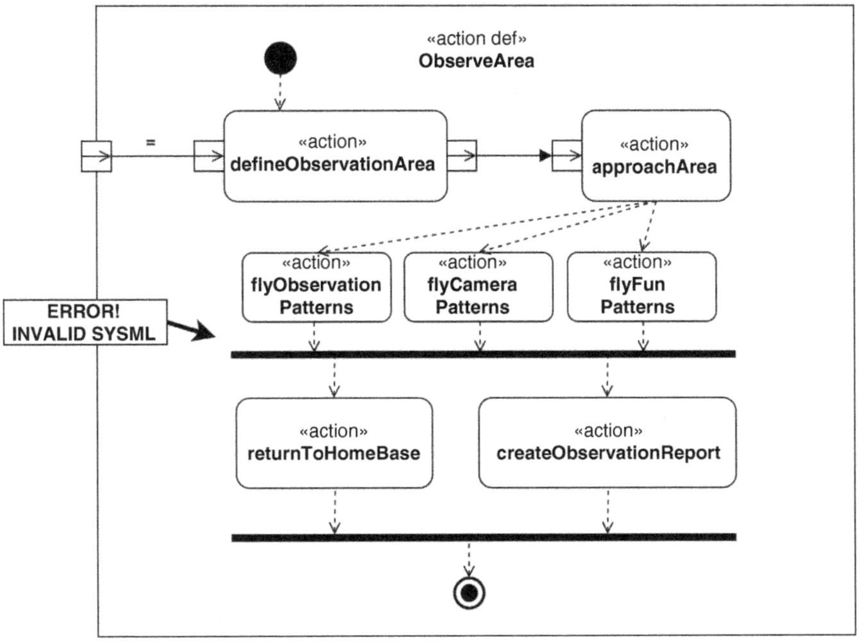

Figure 15.12 Invalid SysML model scenario usage of the direct approach.

```
requirement def <'D-REQ-22'> MTOW {
        subject drone : Drone;
        doc /*
             * The maximum takeoff weight (MTOW) for a drone shall not exceed [X] kilograms.
             * This includes the weight of the drone itself, its battery, payload, and any
             * additional attached equipment. [X] depends on the number of engines.
            */
        attribute mtow : ISQ::MassValue;
        require constraint {drone.massActual <= mtow}
}
requirement def <'D-REQ-23'> MTOW_Quadcopter :> MTOW {
        doc /*
             * The maximum takeoff weight (MTOW) for a quadcopter equipped with 4 engines shall
             * not exceed 15 kilograms.
            */
        :>> mtow = 15[SI::kg];
}
requirement def <'D-REQ-24'> MTOW_Hexacopter :> MTOW {
        doc /*
             * The maximum takeoff weight (MTOW) for a hexacopter equipped with 6 engines shall
             * not exceed 25 kilograms.
            */
        :>> mtow = 25[SI::kg];
}
requirement droneStakeholderRequirements {
        subject drone : Drone;
        require droneEngineStakeholderRequirements;
        require droneBatteryStakeholderRequirements;
        variation requirement maximumTakeoffWeight {
                variant requirement mtqw_Quadcopter: MTOW_Quadcopter;
                variant requirement mtqw_Hexacopter: MTOW_Hexacopter;
        }
}
```

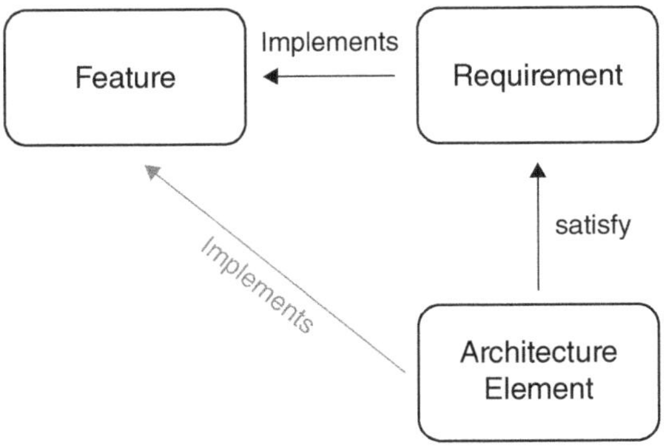

Figure 15.13 Feature, requirement, and architecture element.

The requirements are linked with features in the feature model. The requirements are, in turn, satisfied by architectural elements. These also have corresponding variability and are modeled as variants with relationships to the corresponding features.

Figure 15.13 shows these relationships between the elements. Conceptually, the "implements" relationship between the architecture element and the feature can be omitted. It is sufficient that only those shared assets are linked with features that are directly derived from them, such as the requirement. But not the parts that are conceptually derived from the requirements. If the shared asset model has implemented clean traceability, it is sufficient to link the source elements with the features to calculate all derived elements.

In this way, if the feature is updated, complete traceability to all impacted shared assets is secured.

15.4 Clean and Direct Approach with SysML v1

SysML v1 (OMG 2022a) does not have explicit model elements for the modeling of variants. However, it is possible to use SysML v1 to model variability. For example, the variability modeling of software-intensive systems (VAMOS) approach (Variant Modeling with SysML) provides a set of stereotypes (profile) for a variability language extension for SysML v1 (Weilkiens 2016).

Figure 15.14 shows variations and variants of the drone example. The stereotypes "variation" and "variant" are from the VAMOS profile. They are applied to packages that contain all elements that belong to a variation or variant. The meaning of variations and variants is slightly different from their semantics in SysML v2. Since they are attached to a grouping element, they also play the role of features that are implemented by the elements inside the packages.

The core elements are defined in a separate package named "Drone_Core." Figure 15.15 depicts some core system architecture breakdown structure elements with variation points. The VAMOS variation point corresponds to the variation concept of SysML v2. It marks a single shared asset as an element with design choices.

The variants are specializations of variations which correspond to the variant concept of SysML v2. Figure 15.16 shows the definition of the battery variants.

The modeling above follows the clean approach. The core and variant elements are clearly separated. The common parts of the variable elements are extracted and modeled as abstract core elements, such as the block DroneBattery.

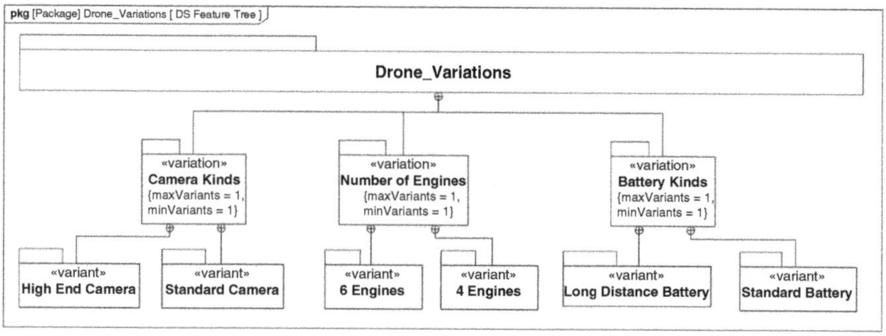

Figure 15.14 Variations and variants with SysML v1.

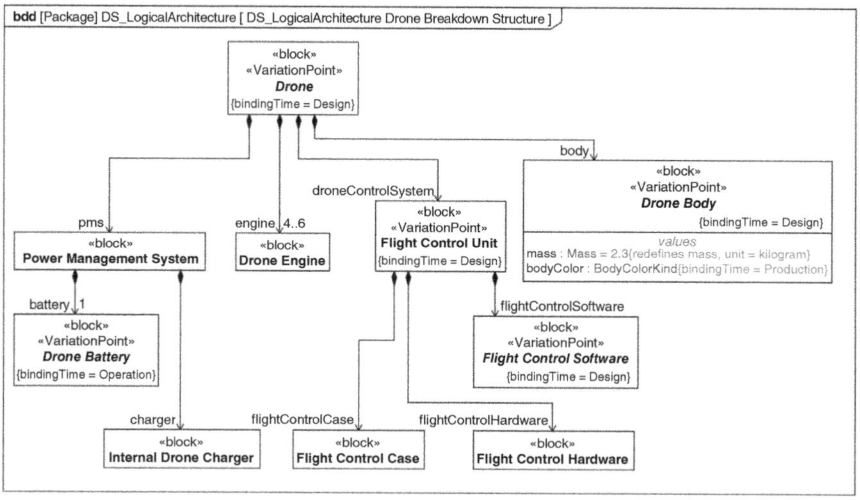

Figure 15.15 Drone core system architecture breakdown with variations.

The direct approach does not require a strict separation of core and variant elements. Figure 15.17 defines the drone system architecture using the direct approach. The architecture does not define a valid system without considering the variability represented by the variation points. It is a drone with two different batteries and 4 and 6 engines, which means 10 engines, two bodies, and so forth. The variation points tag the variable elements and link them with the features. A variability tool could transform the model into a valid product model based on a feature configuration. However, a SysML v1 tool cannot interpret the variability out-of-the-box. For example, if it provides analysis functions such as a mass roll-up pattern, it will calculate incorrect values because all variant components are considered.

Even in this simple example, the internal block diagram might look confusing when all parts and connectors are displayed (Figure 15.18). Of course, this can be displayed more clearly in several internal block diagrams, for example, only by showing the parts and connectors of one feature configuration.

15.5 Non-SysML Shared Assets

A shared assets superset does not contain only systems engineering assets but also elements from other engineering disciplines.

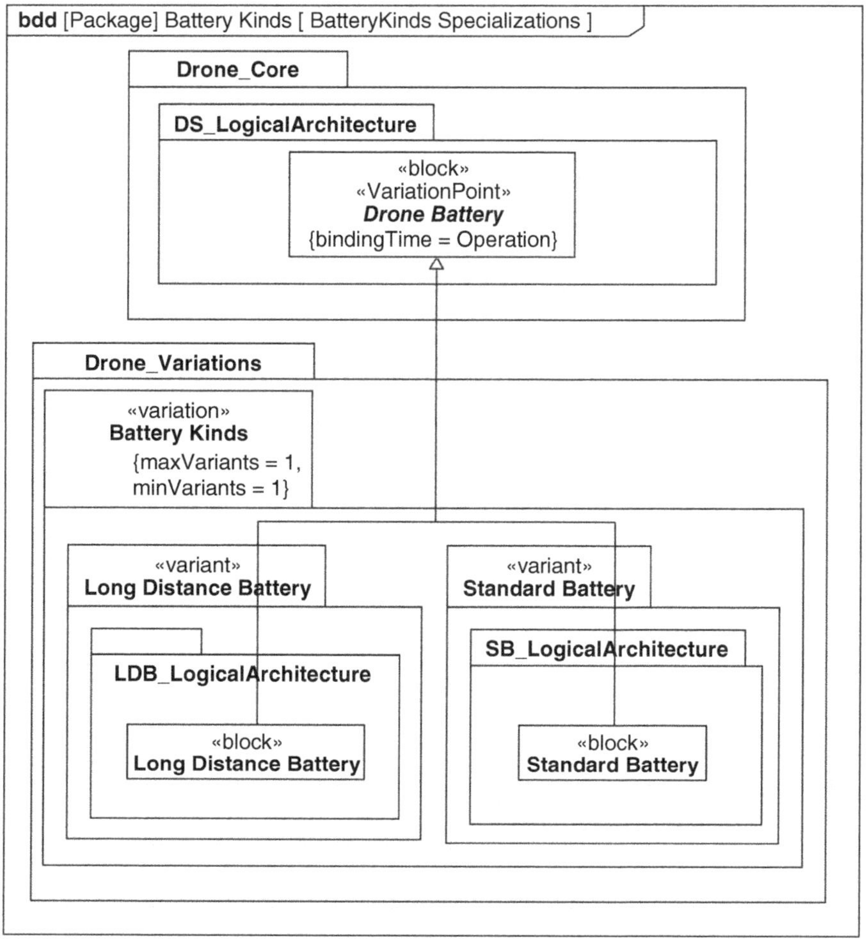

Figure 15.16 Drone battery variants.

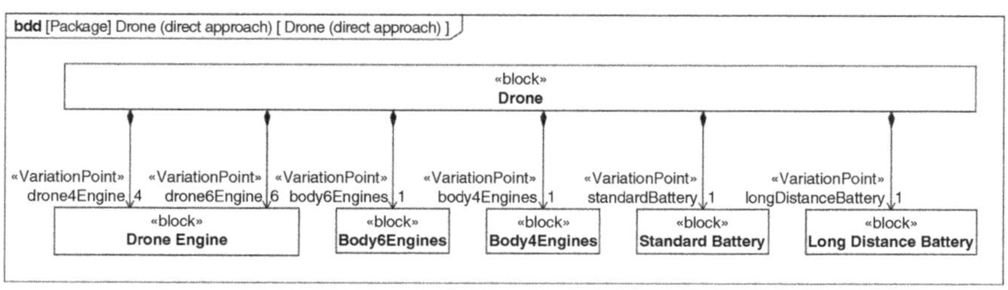

Figure 15.17 Drone system architecture with direct approach.

The following is an extract from the drone product line system requirements specification. Requirements could also be modeled with SysML, but they are specified in a text document here, to emphasize their textual form (similar to a requirements set in a dedicated requirements management system). The textual syntax of the requirements, and in particular, the variants and variation points, are not based on a standard but on a project-specific guideline. The variation points

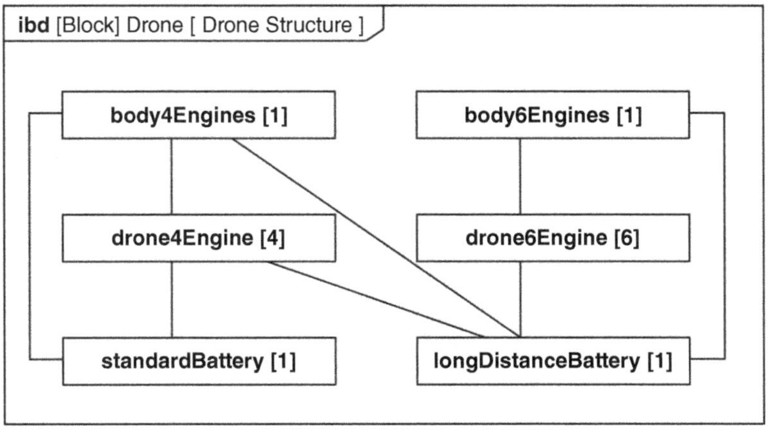

Figure 15.18 Drone internal block diagram with direct approach.

are inside curly brackets and point to the appropriate feature. The variability is modeled by applying the direct approach because specifying variability is not explicitly supported by the tool and language.

Therefore, the specification contains requirements with the same identifier (REQ-TPW2, REQ-TPW3). In sum, the requirement list shown below is not valid. It only becomes valid when a feature selection is made, and the unwanted requirements are removed from the list with the help of the variation points and feature configurations. Alternatively, the variant requirements could get special identifiers like REQ-TPW2a and REQ-TPW2b. However, the complete list of requirements is only valid once the variants have been transformed.

Requirement ID	Requirement text
REQ-TPW1	The top brick shall be a standard brick with a black tag "P" in the middle of the front.
REQ-TPW2	The lower left brick shall be an extra-wide brick with a black tag "L" in the middle of the front {v: F1.1.1}.
REQ-TPW2	The lower left brick shall be three very small bricks with a black tag "L" in the middle of the front of each brick {v: F1.1.2}.
REQ-TPW3	The lower right brick shall be a dark standard brick with a black tag "E" in the middle of the front {v: F1.2.1}.
REQ-TPW3	The lower right brick shall be two small bricks with a black tag "E" in the middle of the front of each brick {v: F1.2.2}.
REQ-TPW3	The lower right brick shall be a sandy standard brick with a white tag "E" in the middle of the front {v: F1.2.3}.

It is also possible to use the clean approach by applying special rules to the standardized requirement text. In the example below, the rule is as follows: The text of a variation requirement is enclosed by square brackets (REQ-TPW2). The deviating requirements are given the same requirement identifier with a subnumber (REQ-TPW2.1, REQ-TPW2.2). The variation and the variants reference the feature ({v: F1.1}, ...). Without the variant subrequirements, it is a valid, complete requirement specification. However, it is abstract because the variation requirements are not specific enough.

Requirement ID	Requirement text
REQ-TPW1	The top brick shall be a standard brick with a black tag "P" in the middle of the front.
REQ-TPW2	[The lower left brick shall be a composite of one or more bricks with a total size of an extra-wide brick and a black tag "L" in the middle of the front of each brick {v: F1.1}].
REQ-TPW2.1	The lower left brick shall be an extra-wide brick with a black tag "L" in the middle of the front {v: F1.1.1}.
REQ-TPW2.2	The lower left brick shall be three very small bricks with a black tag "L" in the middle of the front of each brick {v: F1.1.2}.
REQ-TPW3	[The lower right brick shall be a composite of one or more bricks with the total size of a standard brick and a tag in the middle of the front of each brick {v: F1.2}].
REQ-TPW3.1	The lower right brick shall be a dark standard brick with a black tag "E" in the middle of the front {v: F1.2.1}.
REQ-TPW3.2	The lower right brick shall be two small bricks with a black tag "E" in the middle of the front of each brick {v: F1.2.2}.
REQ-TPW3.3	The lower right brick shall be a sandy standard brick with a white tag "E" in the middle of the front {v: F1.2.3}.

References

Forlingieri, M. and Weilkiens, T. (2022). Two Variant Modeling Methods for MBPLE at Airbus, *INCOSE Symposium 2022*, Detroit.

Object Management Group (OMG) (2024a). 'OMG System Modeling Language Version 1.7, formal/24-01-07'. OMG.

Object Management Group (OMG) (2024b). OMG System Modeling Language Version 2.0 beta 2, ptc/24-02-03. OMG. https://www.omg.org/spec/SysML.

Weilkiens, T. (2016). *Variant Modeling with SysML*. MBSE4U.

16

Define Product Models

16.1 Introduction

This chapter completes the description of modeling variability. Chapters 13 and 14 describe the definition of feature models and feature configurations, Chapter 15 discusses the modeling of shared assets, and also focuses on how product models for the specification of member products are derived from them.

The derivation of product models is the fourth step of the model-based product line engineering (MBPLE) four-step approach (Figure 16.1).

Section 16.2 presents the basic principles, Section 16.3 describes how to model a product model with Systems Modeling Language (SysML) v2, and Section 16.4 presents the modeling with SysML v1.

16.2 Basic Principles

A product model is a product specification based on a feature configuration. It sets together the shared assets appropriate to the selected features within the feature configuration. According to ISO/IEC 26580 (ISO/IEC 2021), the product model is referred to as a "product asset instance."

A tool could automatically derive a product model: With the selected features, the feature configuration contains the design decisions for the variations in the shared assets superset. Depending on the specific shared asset model, the selected variant can be used and the others discarded. Even if it is done automatically, in the real world, the product model is often further developed and completed with elements that are not fully integrated into the overall product line model.

A product model is an input specification for production and resolves only those variant choices that belong to the binding time "design" (Figure 16.2). The choices with binding time "production" are made during production. A handover artifact for the operation stage, in addition to the product itself, could consist of a handbook that describes the design choices with binding time "operation," for example, the option of how to replace a battery with a different kind.

The shared assets superset of "the tiny PLE wall" example includes two variations. With the information from the feature configuration "3VerySmallBricksTinyPLEWall," a tool could automatically transform the shared assets into a product model specifying only a single member product (Figure 16.3).

This requires that the selected variants of a variation are automatically integrated into the product model, and those not selected are removed to create a consistent model. It is quite simple

Model-Based Product Line Engineering (MBPLE): The Feature-Based Path to Product Lines Success, First Edition.
Marco Forlingieri et al.

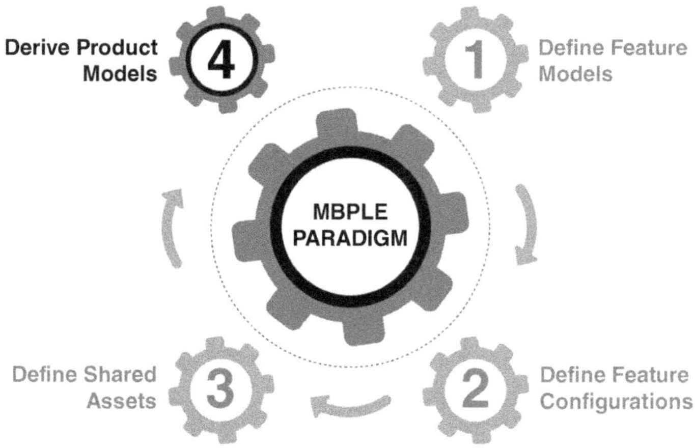

Figure 16.1 MBPLE four-step approach "define product models."

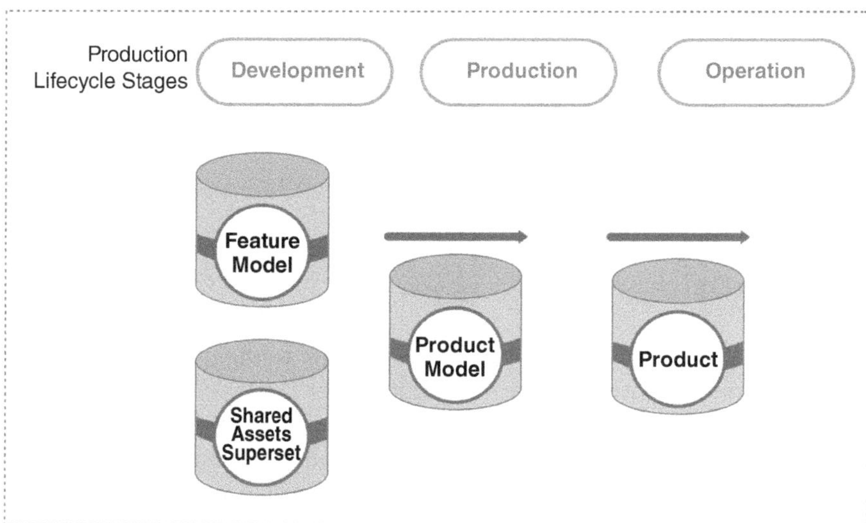

Figure 16.2 Handover artifacts.

in our fictitious wall model (Figure 16.3). Since our focus here is to facilitate the understanding of the approach and not of the technical system. Conceptually, the transformation could be done automatically, but this depends primarily on the capabilities of the modeling languages and tools used.

Typically, a product model is created in each modeling tool used for shared assets. For example, a SysML modeling tool, a CAD tool, and a requirements management tool together form the complete product model (Figure 16.4).

SysML models often play the role of the backbone in an engineering environment. The product model in a SysML model could be the glue that binds all the others together to a fully traceable specification. The arrows from the SysML product model to the others indicate that relationship in Figure 16.4. However, in the implementation of the MBPLE approach, it is not mandatory to use SysML.

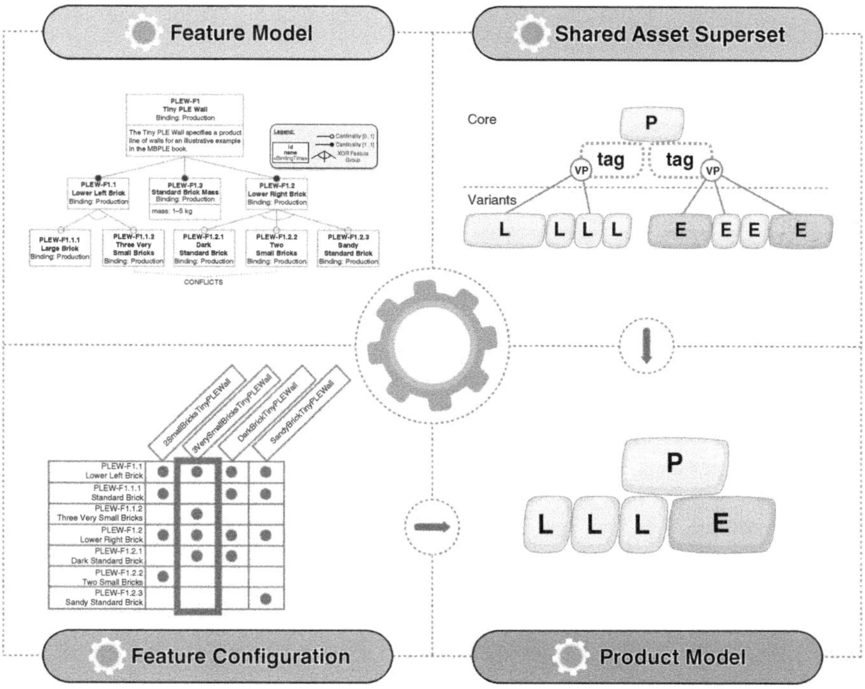

Figure 16.3 Tiny PLE wall product model.

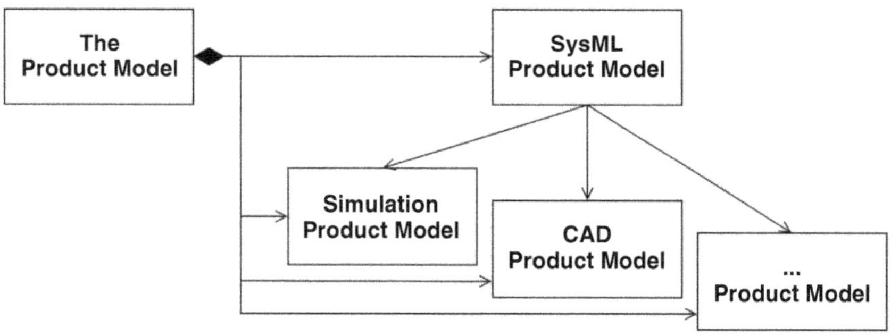

Figure 16.4 Product model.

The path from the shared assets to the product assets in the product model is usually a one-way street. If changes are made in the product model, these cannot be automatically incorporated into the corresponding shared assets model. Chapter 18 further details this aspect.

Suppose that whoever is working on the product model decides to change the bottom left bricks and make the center brick a dark brick as well (Figure 16.5). It is only a minor change, but the transformation that created the product model from the shared assets is unidirectional and will not automatically update the shared assets model.

If the update does not impact the existing "3VerySmallBricks" variant but adds another one, "3VerySmallBricksWithADarkOne," this would also result in a change in the feature model. Even with a bidirectional transformation, the decision should be made in advance. An automatic transformation that adapts the feature model is imaginable but very challenging.

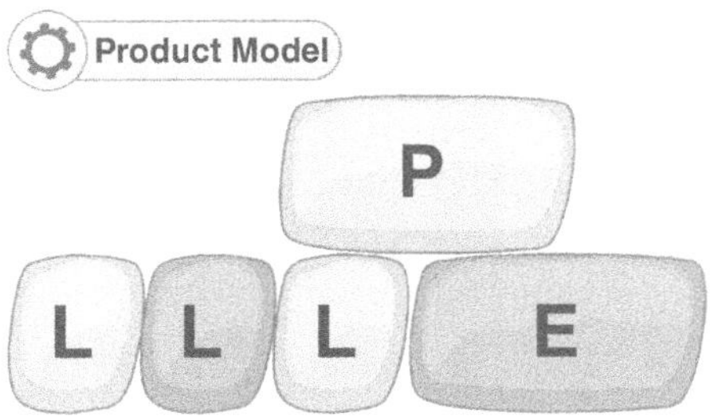

Figure 16.5 Product model change.

There are several options:

1. The change can be manually transferred to the shared asset and feature models. This may require communication and agreement across departmental boundaries, as other people may be responsible for the shared assets superset and the feature model than those responsible for the product model.
   In any case, it is important not to skip this step. It is very likely not necessary for current product development but for future developments. So, it is a task that could be easily pushed out of the project plan.
2. The engineering process can prohibit changes to the product model and require that changes be made only to the source, the shared assets superset, and the feature model, and that the product model be regenerated.
   This would be a clean approach. It is particularly beneficial for this approach that the transformation to the product model is as completely automatic as possible, as otherwise, the effort involved in this iterative approach can quickly become unreasonably high if several changes must be made.
3. The shared assets superset is not updated. This could be useful if the change only affects the specific product and should not become part of the product line.
4. It could also be a valid approach not to map the complete product specifications in the product line but only selected areas. The missing parts are added to the product models outside the product line development.

16.3 Modeling of Product Models with SysML v2

In this section, we look at SysML v2 shared assets supersets and the derivation of a corresponding SysML v2 product model. The product model can be derived from the shared asset models in many different ways. Two approaches are shown below:

- Generation of a product model that is independent of the shared assets superset.
- Generation of a product model that uses elements of the shared assets superset and is therefore directly dependent on it.

A product line engineering (PLE) tool could create a product model based on a feature configuration and shared assets. It looks like a "normal" system model, for example, the structural model of an XDrone product, which has a long-distance battery and six engines.

```
part def 'Forest Fire Observation Drone' {
  part longDistanceBattery : LongDistanceBattery;
  part sixEngine[6] : DroneEngine;
}
```

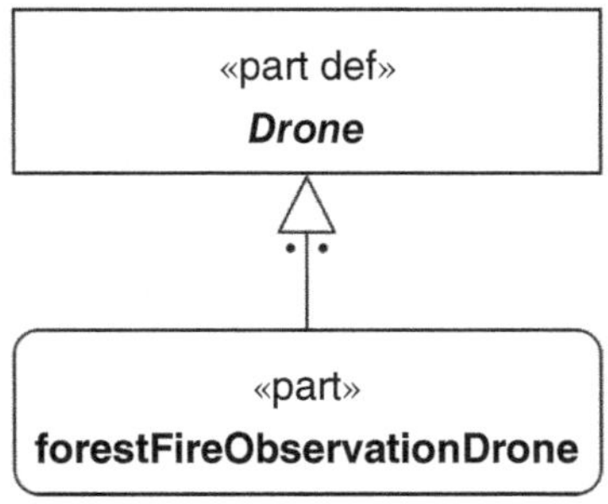

Figure 16.6 Member product "forestFireObservationDrone" defined by the product line "drone."

If the shared assets superset is created with the direct approach, it is simply a filtering transformation and probably the setting of some parameters (see features with parameters in Chapters 13 and 14).

If the shared assets superset is modeled with the clean approach as described in Chapter 15, the product model can keep links to the shared assets. Since modeling variability according to ISO/IEC 26580 (ISO/IEC 2021) is part of the language SysML v2 (OMG 2024b), modeling the product model with variability is relatively simple.

First, the product must be defined. It is a specialization of the product line element from the shared assets model. In the example of the drone, the product line element is the "drone" (see in the previous chapter Figure 15.8). In the following, we define the product of a forest fire observation drone. In SysML v2, the defined by relationship is a kind of specialization. Figure 16.6 shows the member product "forestFireObservationDrone" defined by the product line "drone."

The product model element is linked with the appropriate feature configuration. As mentioned in previous chapters, the relationship must be established using a corresponding technology that connects SysML models with feature models.

For each variation in the shared assets supersets of the product line element, the corresponding variant must now be selected according to the feature configuration. The selection is made in the model by redefining the variation and binding the corresponding variant. The redefinition is indicated by ":>>" in the textual notation of SysML v2. The following Figure 16.7 shows some of these redefinitions in the product model for the forest fire observation drone.

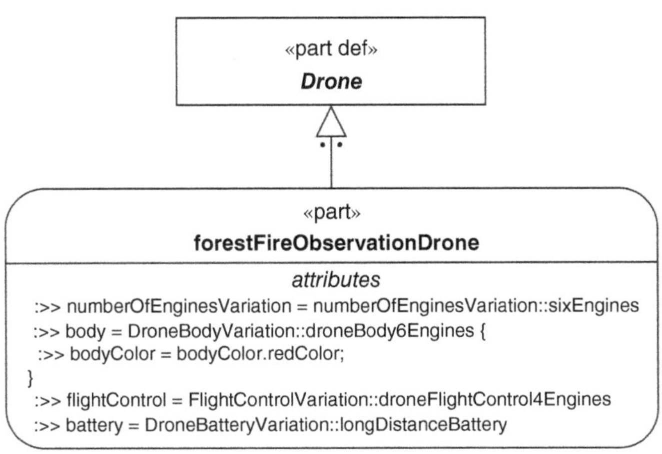

Figure 16.7 Resolving the variability.

It is easy to imagine that such a product model could also be created automatically by a PLE tool, at least in this simple example. At the same time, additional changes that are not created by the transformation could also be implemented.

16.4 Modeling of Product Models with SysML v1

Chapter 15.4 describes the modeling of shared assets with SysML v1 (OMG 2024a). Using the clean approach, they are located in core and variation packages to separate the common core elements from the variable elements.

As described in the previous section for SysML v2, a PLE tool can also generate a SysML v1 product model from a shared assets superset that is independent of the shared assets.

It is also possible to create a SysML v1 model that is linked with the shared assets superset. The VAMOS approach (Weilkiens 2016) describes a "way" to model it. The product models are inside another package. VAMOS calls the product model a variant configuration (see terminology comparison table in Appendix A). Figure 16.8 shows parts of the definition of the forest fire observation

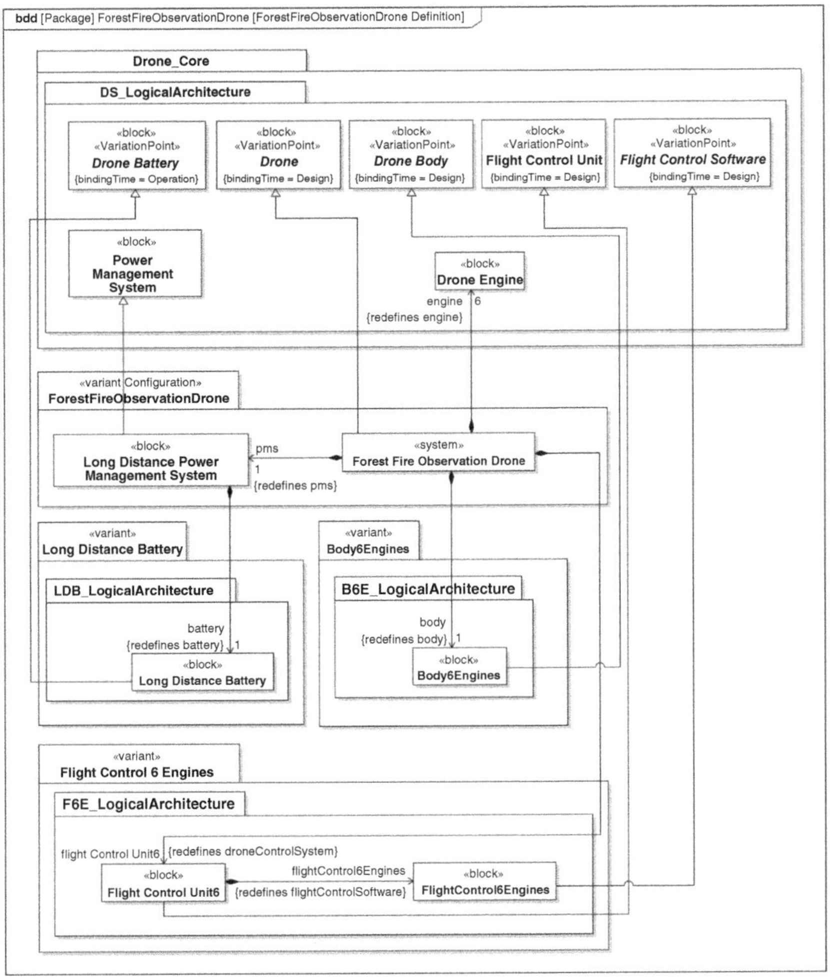

Figure 16.8 Forest fire observation drone variant configuration (product model).

drone variant configuration (product model). At first glance, the model is more complex than the same situation in the SysML v2 model. This is primarily because the modeling of variability is not explicitly supported by SysML v1. Variability is primarily modeled using generalization relationships and redefinition.

The basic principle is that the root element of the product model (forest fire observation drone) specializes the root element of the shared assets superset (done). Selected variants redefine the common features; for example, `battery : LongDistanceBattery redefines battery : DroneBattery`.

References

ISO/IEC (2021). ISO/IEC 2658 0: 2021 Software and systems engineering – methods and tools for the feature-based approach to software and systems product line engineering. London: ISO/IEC. https://www.iso.org/standard/43139.html.

Object Management Group (OMG) (2024a). 'OMG System Modeling Language Version 1.7, formal/24-01-07'. Object Management Group.

Object Management Group (OMG) (2024b). 'OMG System Modeling Language Version 2.0 beta 2, ptc/24-02-03'. Object Management Group. https://www.omg.org/spec/SysML.

Weilkiens, T. (2016). *Variant Modeling with SysML*. MBSE4U.

17

The Four Dimensions of Variability

17.1 Introduction

In this chapter, we show how it is key for companies that aim at implementing model-based product line engineering (MBPLE) to digitalize, harmonize, and enhance the end-to-end development of complex systems. Forlingieri (2022) taking the example of Airbus, shows how such digitalization initiatives often include manufacturing and after-sales services, going beyond the development of the system of interest (e.g. the engineered product) itself. In particular, he identifies four crucial dimensions to be considered during the modeling and management of variability within an MBPLE approach (Forlingieri 2022). These include the following:

Co-variability in product, manufacturing, and services: This dimension addresses how the variability, in one area, such as product design, can impact manufacturing processes and services. It requires a holistic approach to manage the interdependencies effectively (Section 17.2).

Variability in the development life cycle: It refers to the differences that can arise at various stages of the development process, from initial design to final production. It emphasizes the need for flexible strategies for modeling the variability that can adapt to changes and challenges throughout the system life cycle (Section 17.3).

Variability in layers of abstraction: This dimension focuses on the different levels of abstraction, from operational concept (OpsCon) to detailed implementation. Managing variability at each layer ensures that the overall vision aligns with practical execution (Section 17.4).

Variability in system hierarchy levels: It pertains to the complexity inherent in systems that are composed of numerous interconnected parts. Understanding and managing the variability at different levels of the system hierarchy is essential for ensuring its consistency and cascading along the entire system (Section 17.5).

Finally, Section 17.6 discusses how, for companies in sectors that develop complex systems, addressing these dimensions of variability within an MBPLE approach becomes crucial. The impact is not only on the product line itself but also the process, method, and tools used to develop it. In Chapters 13–16, we read how the system life cycle, layers of abstraction, and system breakdown are interrelated with the four-step approach. This chapter mainly focuses on their relevance to the aerospace and automotive industries, but these dimensions can be extended to other industrial contexts as well. Figure 17.1 illustrates a simplification of those dimensions for an aircraft development example.

Model-Based Product Line Engineering (MBPLE): The Feature-Based Path to Product Lines Success, First Edition.
Marco Forlingieri et al.

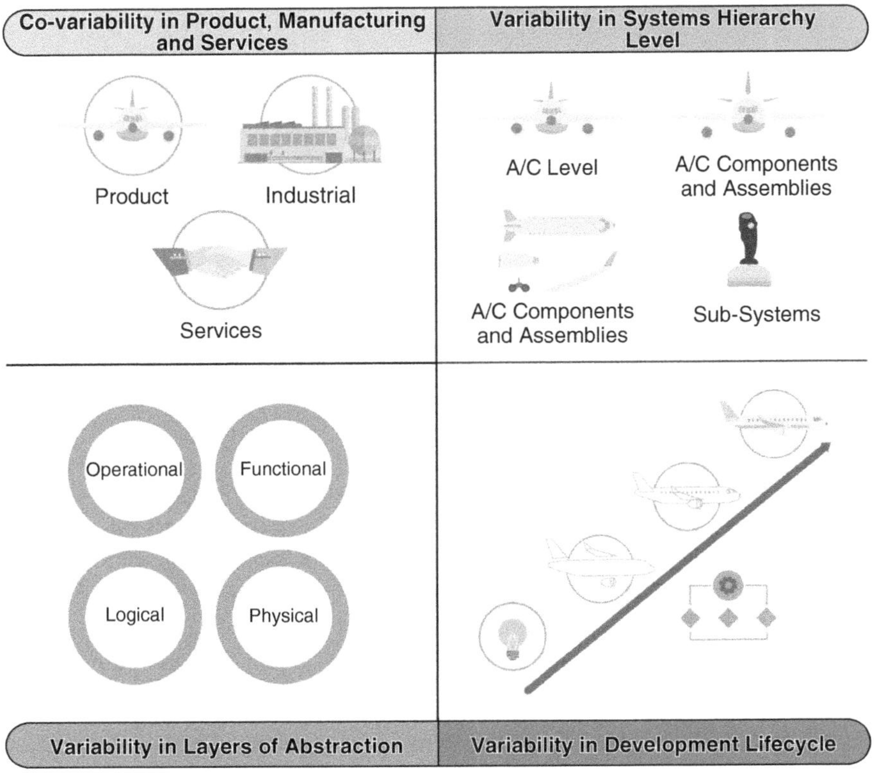

Figure 17.1 Simplified example of the four-variability dimensions.

17.2 From Co-Development to Co-Variability

Forlingieri (2022), using the Airbus example, stresses the importance in the aerospace industry of integrating the development of aircraft, industrial systems, and related after-sales services. This approach, called "co-development" (Michaelis 2013), is essential when adopting platform or product line strategies. For example, the installation process and industrial tooling machinery, including working stations and the devices for lifting and mounting the engine and pylon within an aircraft, can vary significantly among different models. This variation is a result of the traditional development approach, where the final assembly line (FAL) adapts its processes and tooling based on the specific aircraft type being assembled. Similarly, the development of engine maintenance services often requires customization to the specific aircraft, with maintenance instructions and procedures tailored accordingly.

In co-development, the product line's scope includes the aircraft, its manufacturing, and the extended services, making it crucial to identify and assess the "co-variability" from the aircraft, FAL, and related services in the early phases of development. This early assessment of co-variability is pivotal for engineering the aircraft efficiently, ensuring standardization across the FAL, and enabling the reuse of services, thus fostering a more integrated and efficient development process.

In the automotive industry, the concept of co-variability in products, manufacturing, and services is equally important. The development of vehicles, their manufacturing systems, and associated services are brought together under a unified development strategy. This approach ensures that vehicles are designed with manufacturing and serviceability in mind from the outset. For instance, the assembly line processes, tooling, and service protocols for different models or variants within a vehicle line-up might require customization to accommodate specific features or technologies. By applying a co-development strategy, automakers can streamline the engineering process, standardize production lines, and enhance service efficiency. This includes developing modular platforms and the related manufacturing tooling and services. Co-development emphasizes the need for early identification and management of co-variability across products, manufacturing processes, and services for those companies that develop complex systems.

17.3 Variability Along the Development Life Cycle

In the aerospace industry, the development life cycle of aircraft encompasses several phases, ranging from the feasibility of launching a new program to the qualification and delivery of the aircraft to airlines (Forlingieri 2022). This progression mirrors the general system life cycle phases defined by ISO/IEC/IEEE 15288 (ISO/IEC 2023). During the feasibility phase of a new aircraft development program, the evaluation of new technologies and their interdependencies with the aircraft architecture is a critical activity. Key variability inputs, such as fuselage type, mileage range, passenger capacity, and overall weight targets, are collected and assessed for their impact on the design and performance of the aircraft.

However, other types of variabilities, such as cabin layouts and configurations, may not be prioritized in the early stages but become crucial during the concept and design phases. These elements are significant because of the value they bring to customers, influencing their experience and satisfaction with the aircraft. Additionally, customer-specific features, including those related to country-specific qualifications, might be addressed in later phases.

Similarly, in the automotive industry, the development life cycle of vehicles follows a phased approach, from initial feasibility studies to the final delivery to customers. During the early phases, crucial decisions regarding the vehicle's design, technology integration, and performance targets are made. Variability in aspects like engine options, drivetrain configurations, and vehicle dimensions are key considerations. As the development progresses, the focus shifts to more customer-centric variabilities, such as interior design, infotainment systems, and customization options, which significantly influence buyer preferences.

Understanding the importance of each type of variability at different stages of the life cycle is vital for the successful development of a complex system. This approach ensures that all critical factors are considered at the appropriate times, facilitating a smooth development process and aligning product offerings with market demands and customer expectations.

17.4 Cascading Variability Along Layers of Abstraction

In the development of complex systems using a systems engineering approach, it is unavoidable to consider multiple layers of abstraction or viewpoints (Wirtz and Bouffaron 2020). For example, defining the OpsCon is a vital step to comprehend the operational context of the system of interest (SOI) and its interdependence with other entities. Variability at the operational layer can have cascading effects on other abstraction layers, including functional, logical, and technical layers (Forlingieri 2022).

For instance, the adoption of innovative optional features in aerospace, such as "electrical taxi-in, taxi-out, and pushback operations," which allow aircraft to taxi and push back from the gate without using the main engines, relying instead on auxiliary power (Forlingieri 2022). This feature introduces variability not only in how aircraft operations are conducted but also impacts lower abstraction layers. It necessitates additional functions like "avoid on-ground collision" or "provide auxiliary power for autonomous pushback," which must be integrated into the system. These functions, in turn, can be realized through various system solutions, introducing further variability at the logical and technical layers.

Similarly, in the automotive industry, the cascading of variability along different levels of abstraction is key in development. A practical example is the implementation of an "autonomous emergency braking" (AEB) system. Depending on the operational scenario (e.g. driving in a high-density area), the scope of AEB systems may necessitate additional functional requirements for identifying and responding to pedestrians in various scenarios, including low-light conditions and unpredictable movements. This requires the integration of more complex logical and technical solutions, such as high-definition cameras, infrared sensors, and sophisticated image processing algorithms, to accurately detect pedestrians and calculate the necessary response. Effectively managing the variability introduced by this new system and the different scenarios – from the operational level, where drivers and vehicles interact with more dynamic environments, to the technical level, involving advanced sensor technology and data processing – is critical for developing vehicles that provide enhanced safety for both occupants and pedestrians, meeting the comprehensive safety norms.

In both examples, the aircraft manufacturer and the automaker will continue to develop systems with and without the new innovative features. Thus, understanding and managing the variability introduced at each layer – from operational to technical – becomes of primary importance.

17.5 Breaking Down the Systems and Their Variability

Systems engineering requires an in-depth understanding of system decomposition or hierarchy levels. The approach involves the breakdown of the SOI into several systems, which are further decomposed into subsystems and components (Eisner 2005). Such a hierarchical structure is crucial for managing variability in the development of systems product lines. Variability cascades top–down from the upper level to the lower level, but it can also be generated bottom–up as solutions from subsystem product lines provided by suppliers.

For example, the integration of advanced propulsion systems in new generations of aircraft introduces significant variability. This could include the adoption of more efficient, environmentally friendly propulsion technologies, such as hybrid-electric engines or fully electric propulsion systems. At the aircraft level, this introduces operational variability in terms of range, fuel efficiency, and environmental impact. At the subsystem level, additional variability must be considered for the propulsion system itself, which may involve different types of engines (e.g. turbofan, turboprop, electric motor) and energy sources (e.g. conventional jet fuel, electricity, hydrogen fuel cells). In turn, in the propulsion system, the variability in engine technology and energy source options influences product line decisions at higher levels, including aircraft design, performance specifications, and market positioning.

Similarly, in the automotive industry, the transition to autonomous driving technology illustrates a systems engineering challenge that encompasses multiple levels of system hierarchy. Starting at the vehicle level, the adoption of autonomous driving introduces operational variability in terms of vehicle control, safety features, and user interaction. At the subsystem level, significant variability arises in the sensor suite (e.g. cameras, LiDAR, radar) and the onboard computing platform, each of which may offer different levels of performance, resolution, and data processing capabilities. Those subsystems might allow variability in technology choices and configurations, which then influences the broader vehicle product line.

In conclusion, the analysis of the impact of variability, during systems decomposition, facilitates the modeling of it and the development of multi-level product lines.

17.6 The Four Dimensions and the MBPLE Implementation

The four dimensions of variability play a crucial role in the development of product lines, guiding both the elicitation and modeling of variability through an MBPLE approach. Forlingieri (2022) highlights that these dimensions also influence the selection of methods and processes in MBPLE implementation. Some important decisions that are influenced by the four dimensions of variability include the following:

- the use of a single feature model versus multiple feature models for the development scope;
- the use of proxy features to prevent duplication across system levels and layers of abstraction;
- the adoption of partial configurations during the initial stages of development when making all variability choices is not feasible;
- the maintenance of consistent asset modeling across various abstraction layers and system hierarchy levels.

For additional insights and detailed examples, "The four dimensions of variability and their impact on MBPLE" (Forlingieri 2022) serves as a valuable resource.

References

Eisner, H. (2005). *Managing Complex Systems.* Hoboken: Wiley.

Forlingieri, M. (2022). The four dimensions of variability and their impact on MBPLE: how to approach variability in the development of aircraft product lines at Airbus. In: *Proceedings of the 16th International Working Conference on Variability Modelling of Software-Intensive Systems (VaMoS'22),* 23–25 February 2022, Florence, Italy. ACM.

ISO/IEC/IEEE (2023). Systems and software engineering – system life cycle processes. (ISO/IEC/IEEE 1528 8: 2023).

Michaelis, M. (2013). Co-development of products and manufacturing systems using integrated platform models. ICED23, 24–28 July 2023, Bordeaux, France.

Wirtz, J. and Bouffaron, F. (2020). Applying MBSE at airbus helicopters: the airbus MBSE architecture framework in CATIA no magic based on SysML. *Tag des Systems Engineering 2020* – digital, 18–20 November 2020.

18

Digital End-to-end Continuity with MBPLE

18.1 Introduction

As outlined in Chapter 6, digital continuity is a fundamental requirement for implementing model-based product line engineering (MBPLE). Specifically, it serves in defining and reusing shared assets throughout the development of product lines and facilitates the analyses of change impacts during the evolution of the product line.

Digital continuity within MBPLE is equivalent to maintaining the continuity of data or assets, extending from feature models to all relevant domain assets (e.g., requirements, source codes, CAD models). Additionally, Chapter 6 introduces standards such as Open Services for Lifecycle Collaboration (OSLC) and Modelling and Simulation information in a Collaborative Systems Engineering Context (MoSSEC) that support the digital linkage and information exchange across different domains.

Section 18.2 explores the significance of digital repositories for a product line, which houses and manages these shared assets along with their interdependencies. These repositories are crucial for linking features to assets and for the consistent transformation of assets from the product line to the member product scope. Section 18.3 focuses on the centrality of the Systems Modeling Language (SysML) (Object Management Group [OMG] 2024a,b) models during the entire product line development and transformation of the shared assets including their digital continuity. Central is also how such continuity supports the evaluation of changes within the product line and its subsequent evolution (Section 18.4). Section 18.5 enriches the chapter with an illustrative example that demonstrates the management of new feature introductions, providing a simple yet effective visualization of the workflow.

Finally, as reiterated in this book, adopting MBPLE is not an "overnight activity." Hence, Section 18.6 shows how in the real world, digital continuity may not be fully and immediately established, allowing for temporary manual data exchange methods until full digital continuity is implemented.

18.2 The Digital Repositories of a Product Line

As the shared assets are stored across various repositories connected to the tools (or included with the tools) used for defining or modeling these assets, interfaces between these digital repositories, based on interoperability standards, must be developed to ensure complete traceability between

Model-Based Product Line Engineering (MBPLE): The Feature-Based Path to Product Lines Success, First Edition.
Marco Forlingieri et al.

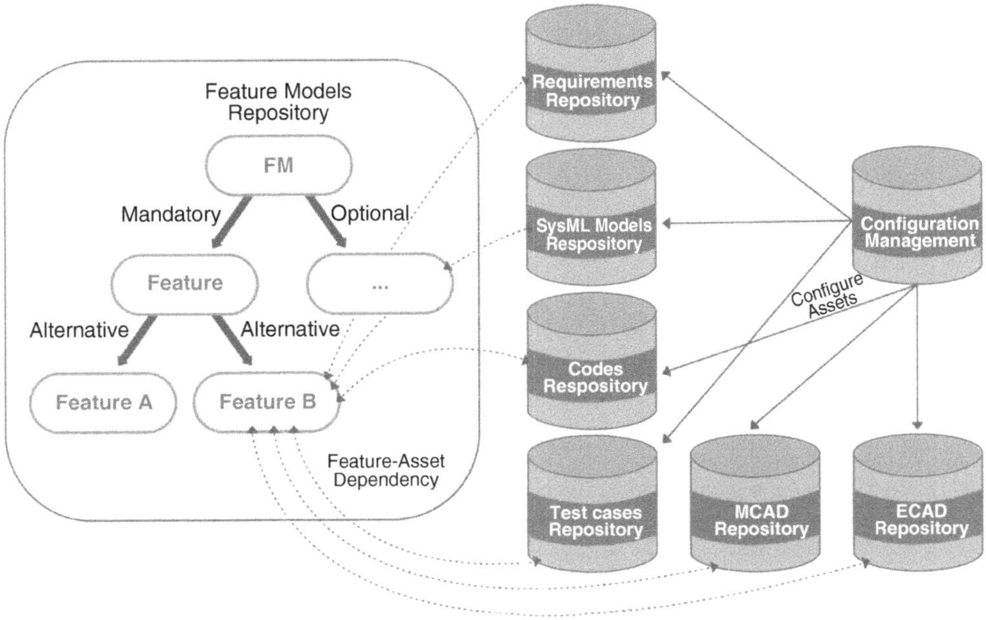

Figure 18.1 Overview of the feature model and shared assets links across digital repositories.

assets, as illustrated in Figure 18.1. This figure provides a simplified illustration of the connections between different asset repositories, including the feature model repository.

MBPLE initially necessitates the definition of the feature model that captures and formalizes the single source of variability, serving as a reference for its application across multiple assets in scope. As explained in the previous chapters, the feature model consists of the formalization of the product line's variability. A feature, as part of the feature model, may be associated with in-scope assets within various repositories, exemplified by "Feature B" in the figure.

The feature model includes all possible variation points and variants within the product line, across every level of system decomposition (system, subsystem, components, etc.), and within all assets in scope (Chalé Góngora et al. 2014). A fundamental component of this approach is the establishment of thorough and consistent feature-asset dependencies across multiple assets, while adhering to the constraints among variants and preserving the relationships between objects as specified by the information model utilized. The variability depicted in the feature model might affect a specific domain or not, which determines whether a feature-asset dependency exists. For example, a feature might be associated with a variable requirement or set of requirements, a part, or action of the SysML v2 model, lines of source code, and test cases up to the three-dimensional (3D) objects, as demonstrated in Figure 18.1. However, this figure is merely illustrative; a feature usually does not encompass all these asset dependencies, but rather, it is more accurate to state that a feature model might include features with various asset dependencies. Without digital repositories and their interlinking, consistently defining and managing variability across the shared assets becomes time-consuming and unsustainable for the product line development team. This underscores the crucial role of a configuration management solution that operates in sync with the product line engineering (PLE) tool. Indeed, while the PLE tool handles the feature models and their configurations, a configuration management solution is tasked with controlling, versioning, and configuring the shared assets for the product line.

18.3 Transforming Shared Assets Consistently Through the MBSE Model

Due to the extensive range of assets covered by the MBPLE scope, the maintenance of the assets consistency becomes a central task. This includes not only managing variability but also ensuring there are no conflicting or duplicated engineering data. Within MBPLE, the model-based systems engineering (MBSE) model is central, providing a consistent approach for transforming assets from the so-called 150% models (product lines) to the 100% models (product variants). Utilizing an MBSE approach to capture the comprehensive architecture of a product line offers the advantage of documenting architecture information and design decisions within a unified model repository. Within this model, different views are established to deliver relevant information to each stakeholder. Consequently, the model holds the superset architectural elements, while the varied views represent the distinct architectural alternatives for each product variant.

Employing SysML to record the comprehensive architecture of a product line facilitates the capture of architecture information and design decisions within a central model repository. As previously discussed, all requirements are stored in a designated repository, which remains synchronized with the SysML architectural models' repository. The logical and technical system architectural models can also serve as a basis for defining a physical architecture in CAD or for generating a consistent bill of materials. This also involves linking their dedicated repository to the SysML repository.

It is important to identify which assets should include a variation and which should not, considering asset-feature dependencies. Sometimes, it's preferable not to directly implement variations in the assets to avoid redundant transformation and effort, which often leads to inconsistencies. For instance, if the MBSE approach delineates multiple architecture layers such as operational, functional, logical, etc., it is advisable to avoid applying variations at the operational layer. Consequently, post-model transformation, the operational analysis continues to reflect the 150% view, including all common and variable assets. Despite this drawback, the superior quality achieved by avoiding inconsistencies in variation definitions across layers compensates for it (Madeira et al. 2023). Likewise, as illustrated in Figure 18.2, if requirements are connected to model assets and both have feature-asset dependencies, a decision must be made on whether to maintain both links or if an automated mechanism could indirectly cascade the variability and trigger the transformation. If not, it must be verified that the linking scheme remains consistent prior to the transformation.

18.4 Evolving the Product Line

As previously discussed, within the lexicon of PLE, the notion of a 150% product family frequently arises, denoting a product line scope that is typically broader than the scope required for a singular product, which is designated as 100%. Product lines, like individual products, evolve over time. Establishing digital continuity across all scoped assets significantly simplifies the product line development team's tasks. Consider the simplified drone example presented in Figure 18.3. Initially, a product line named "Drone Product Line v1" was developed, from which three basic drone member products were derived, accommodating the variability demanded by diverse customers. Each member product, while sharing substantial commonalities, is distinct from the others. Following market demands for new surveillance capabilities in the drone, the development

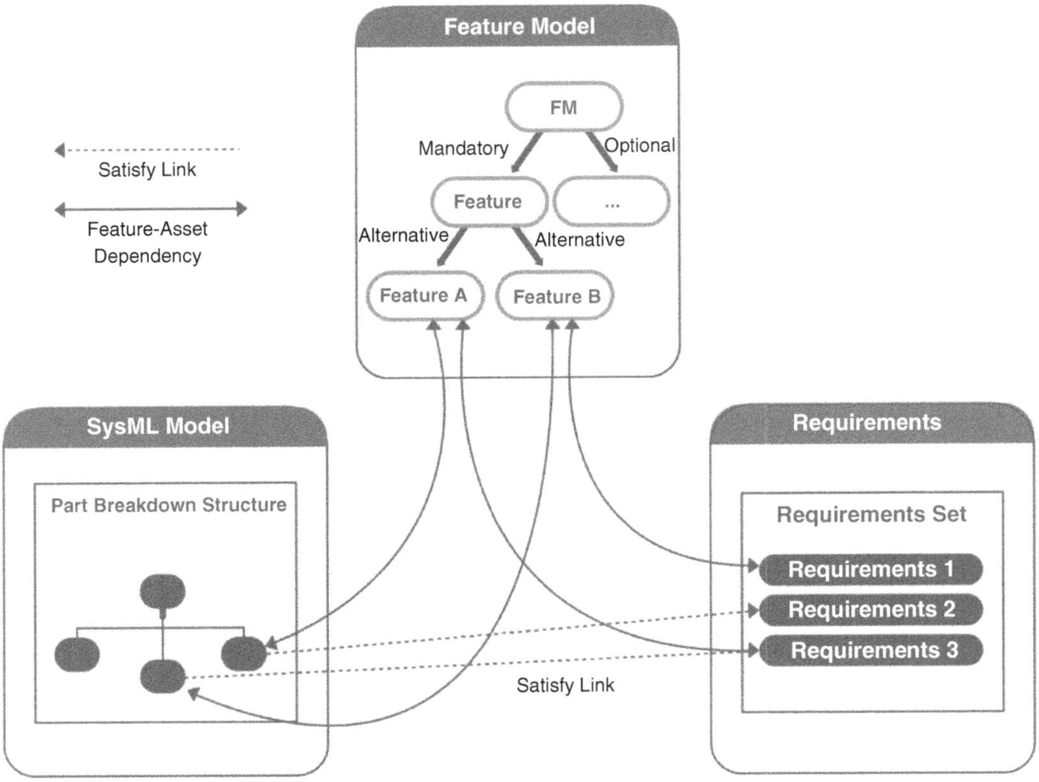

Figure 18.2 Example of the two types of links, the satisfy link and the feature-asset across assets.

team expanded the original product line into "Drone Product Line v2" by adding new features related to surveillance, thereby broadening the product line's scope. Consequently, both Basic and Surveillance drones could be derived from v2. Alternatively, the team might have opted to maintain separate product lines, though not in this case. This approach could be pertinent when a product line becomes too extensive and costly to sustain or when commonalities are minimal. Typically, during the analysis of gaps between the new features or requirements to be developed and the existing product line (also known as the gap analysis phase), the product line development team determines the path to follow. As illustrated in Figure 18.3, this pattern is reiterated with the inclusion of drone payload capabilities, aligning all member products under a unified product line and shared assets. In real-world product line development, member products might include customizations absent in the product line. While not always advisable, this practice is sometimes unavoidable. This highlights that a product line possesses a lifecycle independent of its member products, although, throughout their existence, multiple synchronization points may arise where adjustments made at the product line level (as shown in Figure 18.3) or at the member product level are shared and potentially implemented. Thus, the product line may be enriched by experiences coming from various member products (Chalé Góngora et al. 2014). Digital repositories facilitating end-to-end continuity of shared assets and product models are crucial for conducting gap analyses when new features are requested, thereby supporting the evolution of the product line while continually tracking the derivation of member products across different versions. Chapter 19 covers the topic within "configuration management."

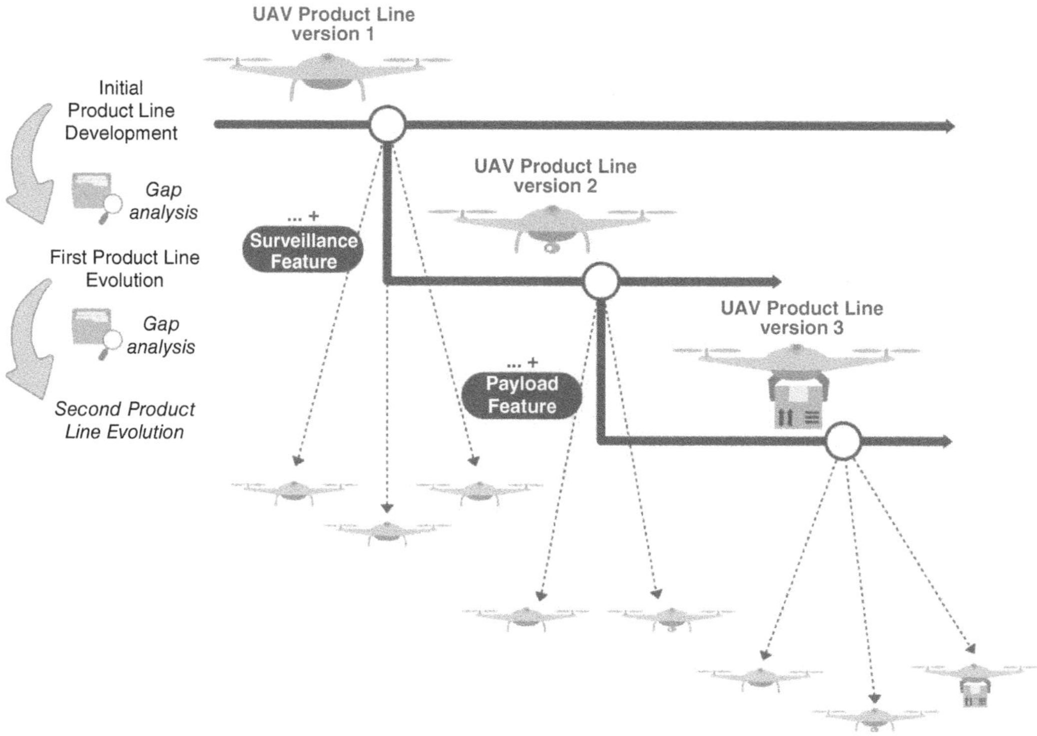

Figure 18.3 Simplified evolution of a drone product line along the development time and its related member products.

18.5 The Journey of a New Product Line Feature

At this point, the benefit of establishing digital continuity for assets within the MBPLE approach should be clear. The following example focuses on the impact analysis when new features are integrated into the existing digital continuity of assets.

Drawing from the earlier drone example, Figure 18.4 illustrates the typical traceability between a feature and its associated assets that include variations. As previously discussed, assets such as requirements, SysML models, and CAD models are often interconnected – a practice highly recommended for traceability not only in product lines but also in the development of standalone products.

For instance, integrating a "payload feature" in a new generation of drones, as shown in Figure 18.5, can introduce substantial variability, affecting everything from the drone's structure to new software functionalities and interactions with external systems essential to the overall "delivery" mission. Introducing a new feature typically necessitates the creation of new requirements, alterations to SysML models, and the development of new MCAD and ECAD models. The capacity for such comprehensive impact analysis and the precise identification of assets affected by the introduction of new features with variations are made possible by implementing a system across tools and repositories that ensures such continuity. Interoperability, based on standards such as OSLC (OSLC 2021) and MoSSEC (ISO 2021) is an important piece of the "puzzle."

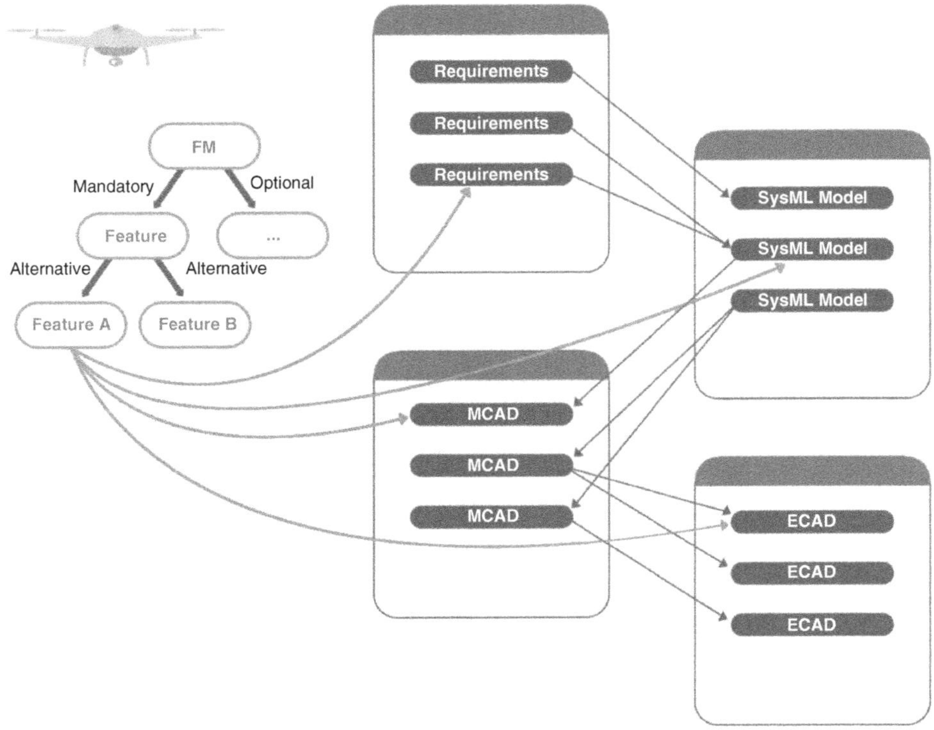

Figure 18.4 Example of digital continuity between a feature and other shared assets.

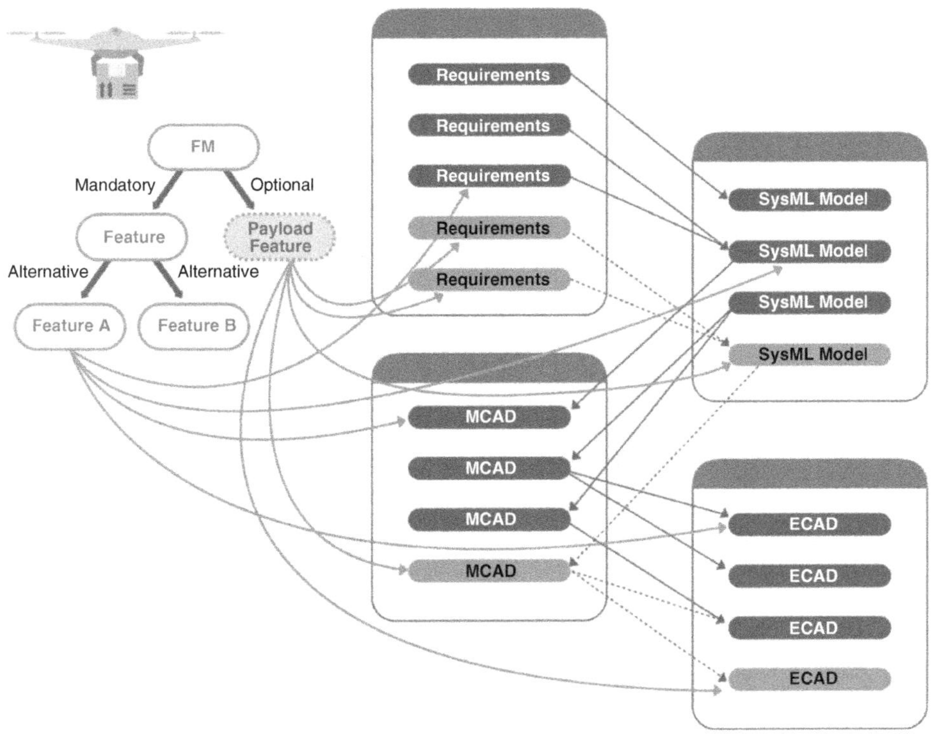

Figure 18.5 Example of impact of new feature to the existing digital continuity already in place.

18.6 Manual Workarounds? Only If Temporary

In Chapter 23, we cover in detail the adoption of MBPLE. Here, we provide a hint: MBPLE adoption should be incremental within an organization. In other words, it is not necessary to wait for all asset repositories to be perfectly linked and synchronized, or for the comprehensive tool chain to be fully implemented. Although crafting a clear roadmap for MBPLE adoption is crucial, it is equally important to apply the MBPLE approach to those assets that are more mature and already have established connections between repositories. Nevertheless, manual workarounds to bridge the gaps in repository connections are acceptable as temporary solutions.

For instance, suppose a feature model has dependency links with a SysML model and a 3D modeling tool, but the connection between the SysML model repository and the MCAD repository has not yet been established. How can we ensure that the MCAD model remains consistent with the SysML architecture model? The dependencies between feature assets alone do not guarantee such consistency. In this scenario, Figure 18.6 illustrates how a manual workaround using XML or similar exchange formats can ensure the consistency of variations implemented for the SysML model and the MCAD. In the example, the SysML structure, including the variation, is exported and then imported into a 3D modeling tool. This method also enhances the quality of the assets transformation from 150 to 100% instances.

To conclude, digital continuity is a critical enabler of a successful implementation of MBPLE. While it is already a key enabler of success in single-product development, it becomes essential when the variability dimension is added, leading to links across variable assets that are used in different member products. Establishing and controlling those links across different asset versions, by

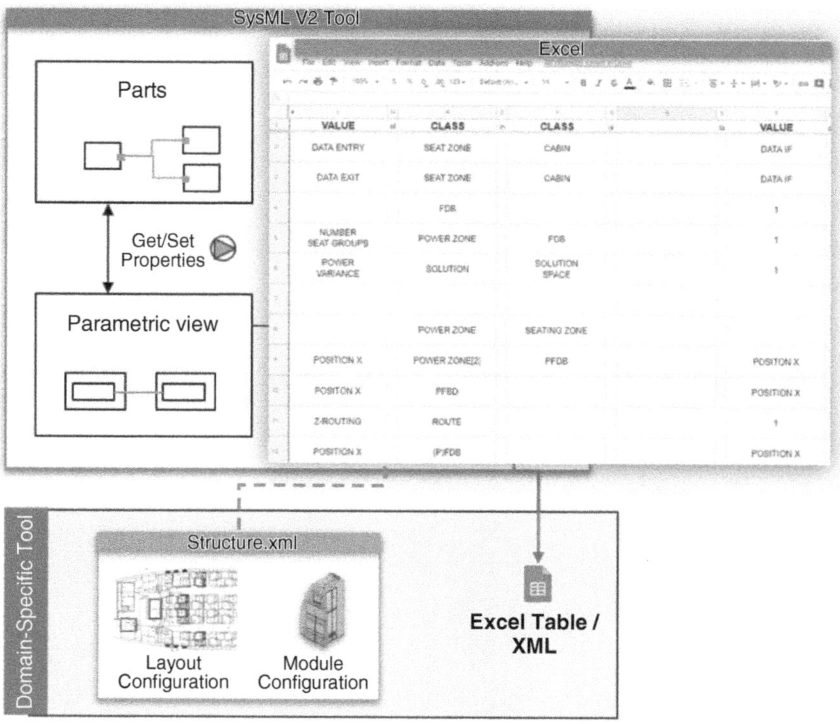

Figure 18.6 Example of data exchange between the SysML v2 model repository and another domain-specific repository.

keeping consistency and implementing the single source of variability represented by the feature model, without digital continuity can lead to the worst "nightmares" for the systems engineers responsible for the product line and its derived member products!

References

Chalé Góngora, H.G., Ferrogalini, M. and Moreau, C. (2014). How to boost PLE by using MBSE – a case study of a rolling stock product line. *In: Proceedings of the 5th International Conference on Complex Systems Design and Management CSDM*, Paris, France. Paris: Springer.

ISO (2021). Industrial automation systems and integration – product data representation and exchange – application protocol: For modelling and simulation information in a collaborative systems engineering context (MoSSEC). (ISO 10303-243:2021).

Madeira, R.H., De Sousa Pinto, D.H., and Forlingieri, M. (2023). Variability on system architecture using airbus MBPLE for MOFLT framework. *INCOSE International Symposium*, 33, pp: 601–615.

Object Management Group (OMG) (2024a) 'OMG System Modeling Language Version 1.7, formal/24-01-07'. OMG.

Object Management Group (OMG) (2024b) OMG System Modeling Language Version 2.0 beta 2, ptc/24-02-03. OMG. https://www.omg.org/spec/SysML.

Weilkiens, T. (2016). *Variant Modeling with SysML*. MBSE4U.

OSLC Core Version 3.0 (2021). *Part 1: Overview*. (eds. Jim Amsden and Andrii Berezovskyi). OASIS Project Specification 02, 23 April 2021.

19

Configuration and Model Management for MBPLE

19.1 Introduction

The feature models and shared asset supersets contain many elements, often numbering in the thousands. Like any single product, a product line and its member products are governed by configuration management (CM) rules.

This chapter first introduces general CM terms and principles in Section 19.2, laying the groundwork for building CM for product lines described in Section 19.3. Sometimes, people confuse CM with product line engineering (PLE). While they share similarities in selecting items to create a valid set, a valid set of configuration items (CI) and a valid set of features are distinct.

Section 19.4 covers CM in model-based product line engineering (MBPLE), highlighting key CM aspects for feature models, feature configurations, shared assets, and product models for the product line and the resulting member products. While Section 19.5 briefly recalls the importance of digital continuity and traceability in CM, Section 19.6 provides additional information on the CM consideration of models. This leads to Section 19.7, which emphasizes the importance of model organization and management, aiming to organize models and their elements for effective use by both humans and machines.

The chapter concludes with Section 19.8, which offers an outlook on the future CM standard, ISO/IEC 26581, and its significance for MBPLE.

19.2 General CM

A project produces many engineering artifacts, each with its own life cycle from creation to incremental development, freezes, and deletion. CM aims to ensure the integrity of all artifacts (ISO/IEC/IEEE 2023) by controlling their changes.

An important CM task is identifying the artifacts and their versions that compose the whole. The "immutable" temporal set is called a baseline, which is agreed upon as an officially reviewed version approved by the team. From a baseline, one or multiple branches can be created. A branch is an intermediate "piece of work" between two baselines. The versioned artifacts are CI, the objects under version and control.

Figure 19.1 depicts a simple example. The three technical assets, shown as a set of requirements, Systems Modeling Language (SysML) models, and CADs (A1, A2, and A3), have different versions developed over time. The assets (dotted lines) here are the CI. Baseline B1 is a set of selected versioned items, including A1 in version v1, A2 in v2, and A3 in v1. Baseline B2 is another set of

Model-Based Product Line Engineering (MBPLE): The Feature-Based Path to Product Lines Success, First Edition.
Marco Forlingieri et al.

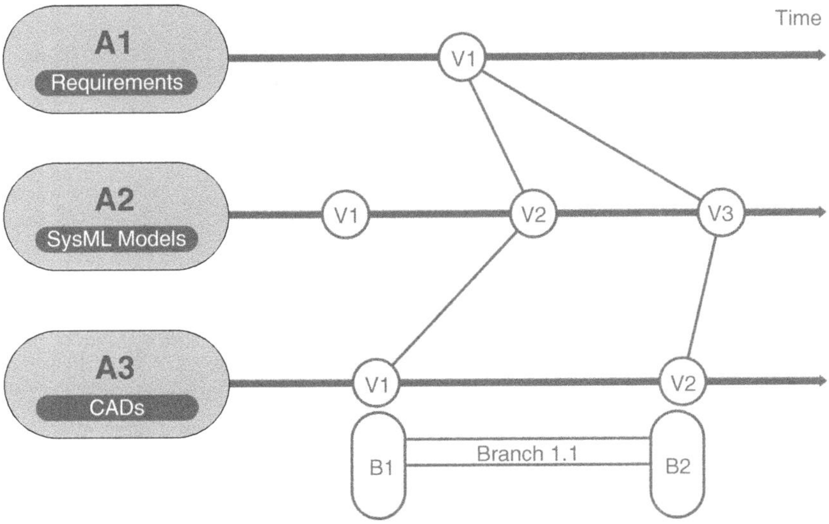

Figure 19.1 CM basic concepts.

versioned items. Branch 1.1 is the temporary version of the assets created from B1, which, after version control, review, and approval, becomes B2.

The fundamental concepts of CM are simple. However, establishing effective CM in an enterprise is both an organizational and technical challenge.

CM affects all engineering artifacts, requiring all stakeholders to agree on a CM process, including the technical implementation and organizational procedures such as who can decide about baselines, freezes, changes, etc.

Integrating all areas and artifacts means that different tools must work together to control the versions. In addition to integrating diverse areas, the number of artifacts to be versioned can also pose a scaling problem.

19.3 CM of Product Lines

CM comes into play when considering the MBPLE discipline in a life cycle, as all the assets of a product line need to be managed in terms of product line evolution, change control, and maintenance.

CM is not a substitute or an alternative to PLE; it is a key enabler for managing the evolution of the product line and its assets over time. A product line evolves like a single product does, meaning different baselines and branches are supported by CM, as with a single product. However, there are some important differences to highlight.

19.3.1 Variation in Time versus Variation in Space

A product line adds to the typical variation in time, which is controlled by versioning the CI produced over time and their differences, the variability of the CI, or variation in space. While variation in time is temporary and does not translate into the needs of a member product, variation in space expresses the needs of the different member products derived from the product line. To summarize, CM focuses on variation in time, while PLE focuses on variation in space, which we call variability.

19.3.2 Product Line versus Member Product Life Cycle

While CM applied to a single product only covers its life cycle, dealing with PLE involves managing the CM of the product lines and their member products. In theory, and ideally (or more easily in software development), all modifications are performed on shared asset supersets, the feature model, and/or the feature configurations. This means that product models should be "read-only" after being derived with a PLE approach.

If avoiding changes and customizations in the product models is possible, it is desirable but often unrealistic due to specific customer requirements, as explained in Chapter 24. Hence, CM is usually applied to both the product line and member product life cycles.

In the next paragraph, we will look at some simple scenarios where CM works in synergy with MBPLE.

19.3.3 CM in the Development of a Product Line

The CM of a product line during its development stage does not differ from the CM of a single product's assets. As long as product models are not derived from the shared assets supersets, Figure 19.1 is still valid. The difference lies in the introduction of additional assets like feature models and feature configurations as CI. The shared assets also represent the variability of the product line, which is why more elements are managed under CM than in single product development.

However, it is a common practice for the engineers working on the product line to start deriving product models from the shared assets based on feature configurations superset for several reasons. For instance, they might need to perform simulations or share the product model with other stakeholders. This can be done through the preview of the product model, supported by the main PLE tools, without generating a new product model artifact (e.g. to compare the results of different configurations). In some cases, however, generating a new product model artifact is necessary (e.g. for the simulation of the product model).

Figure 19.2 represents the second case, where the product models A3 (CADs) are derived from B1 to perform simulations on the product models. In this case, we introduce the second dimension, variation in space. At this temporary stage, it is highly recommended not to change the product models but to make changes on the shared assets supersets and re-derive the product models.

It is a good practice to label product models with the ID of the shared assets baseline they belong to. Since these product models can be kept in the CM system as "read-only" while other baselines of the same artifact are produced, it is important to track them back to the "source baseline" (B1). In Figure 19.2, the product model A3 stands for the type of CI (CAD), PM1 for the product model variant, and B1 for the shared assets superset baseline.

19.3.4 CM in the Derivation of a Member Product

In this second case, we analyze when CM is applied to the life cycle of a member product derived from a product line. Once the product line and its shared assets superset have reached a good maturity for product models to be generated (e.g. not just for simulation purposes but to start the development of the member products), CM is applied to the product models, as illustrated in Figure 19.3 with B2. Similarly to Figure 19.2, the generated product model for the member product is traceable to its shared assets supersets baseline (B2 labels). This is like the nationality in our passport, which shows where we come from.

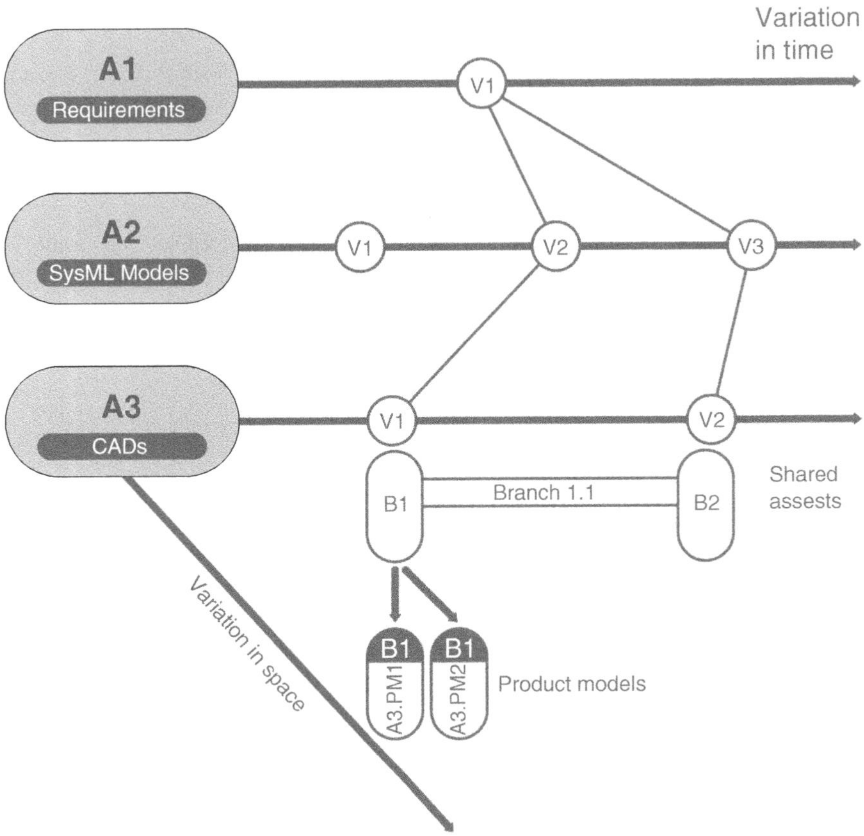

Figure 19.2 CM extended concepts for the product line.

The key difference is that, in a nonideal world, changes are performed on the product models, and different baselines are created. Limiting the changes to only those parts mandated by specific customer needs and tracking these changes along the life cycle of the product model are key activities. We strongly recommend evaluating whether features that result from specific customer requirements can be elevated to the product line level and added to it (see Section 19.4) instead of treating them by default as customizations, hence only applicable to the member product.

Once the member product is developed, maintenance is done for the member product, and any resulting defects must be fixed in both the member product and the product line, or only in the member product if they are just related to the customized part of the product model. This is the price to pay when changes are also performed on the product model.

19.3.5 CM in the Maintenance and Evolution of a Product Line

New features can be added to a product line to serve new markets or customer needs. Defects can also be fixed on product lines when identified in the derived member products. Both scenarios require changes to be performed on the shared assets supersets, feature models, and feature configurations.

In the first case, the product line changes will only serve new member products and will not impact the existing derived member products from the current product line baseline. The work

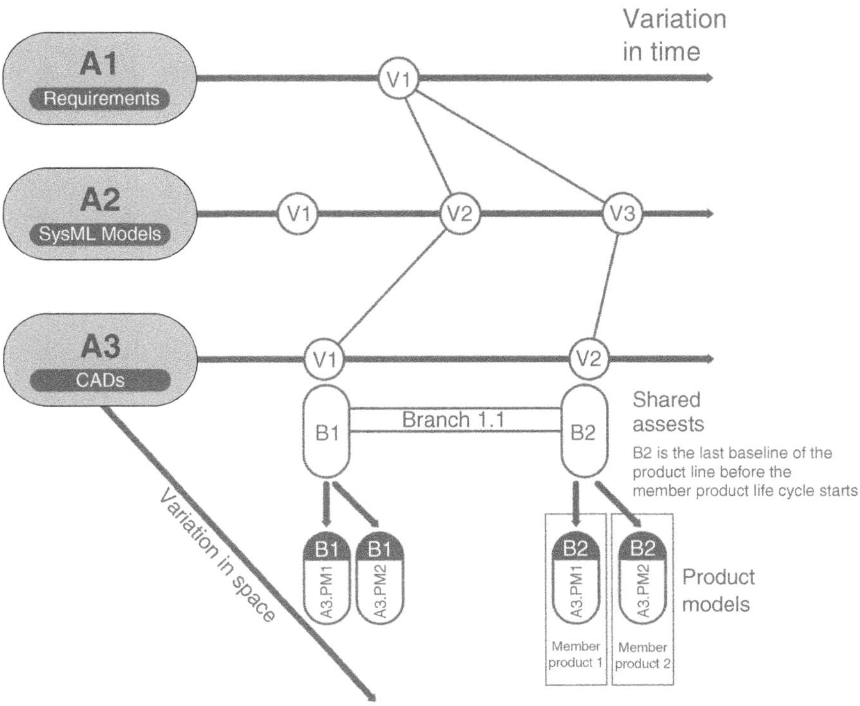

Figure 19.3 CM extended concepts for the member product.

starts from the latest product line baseline and follows the same approach described in Sections 19.3.1 and 19.3.2. In the second case, the fixes are the following:

- Option 1: Performed only on the shared assets supersets if no customization was required for the derived product models (read-only) and updated on all derived member products for the CI in scope.
- Option 2: Performed on both shared assets supersets and product models if customization was originally required for the product models. As mentioned before, this option leads to double the effort needed to fix the defects.

19.4 CM for MBPLE

This section covers CM in MBPLE, highlighting key CM's aspects for feature models, feature configurations, shared assets, and product models for the product line and the resulting member products.

19.4.1 Feature Models as CI

Differently than for a single product, product lines developed with MBPLE include feature models as CI. This is done according to the CM approaches described in Section 19.3. Each time a feature is added, modified, or deleted, a new version of the whole model could then be generated. An update might consist of adding a feature, deleting a feature because it became obsolete, or changing an existing feature (Lameh et al. 2023). For instance, instead of changing the whole "feature model 1," it can be versioned, according to the CM rules, to a new version, "1.1," which can eventually become a new baseline.

19.4.2 Feature Configurations as CI

Feature configurations are also considered CI. New versions of the same feature configuration can be generated similarly to the feature models. This can happen when the feature models are updated or when the previous baseline of the feature configuration is a "partial configuration." Partial configurations help derive the product models from the shared assets supersets in multiple steps. Instead of generating product models based on a feature selection in one go, you can also add in-between steps. This usually happens when not all the information on the feature selection is available at a specific time and life cycle phase.

19.4.3 Shared Assets as CI

Shared assets as CI are the main example used in Section 19.3 and have already been described in detail. However, it is important to highlight the challenge posed by the dependency of artifacts on many projects (member products) compared to a single product development project.

If a core shared asset of the product line changes, this impacts all member product assets (product models). This is technically challenging, as many artifacts stored in different repositories must be made dependent on each other. It is particularly an organizational challenge, as many teams and managers with sometimes conflicting goals are involved. While the product line manager primarily focuses on the product line as a whole, a manager of an individual project prioritizes his/her own product together with its associated deadlines and requirements. For example, a positive change in the product line can benefit five member products but negatively affect two member products of the same portfolio.

19.4.4 Product Models as CI

Product models as CI are also covered in Section 19.3. However, it is key to complement the topic with some considerations.

First, it is a good practice to keep the product model as "read-only." When this is not possible, it is recommended to develop the product model in a modular way and isolate those parts of the model that will undergo customization after the product model is derived.

Traceability must be maintained between the product model and the shared assets to track changes in the product models. In some cases, it is possible to bring back and implement the changes that were made only in the member product at a later time in the most suitable baseline of the product line.

19.5 Maintaining the Digital Continuity

As shown in Figure 19.1, engineers deal with more than one model. In the context of MBPLE, there is at least a feature model and some engineering models as shared asset supersets. These models are linked with each other. For example, a shared assets superset model needs information about variability from a feature model. This traceability is added to the typical links that exist between assets in a single product development (e.g. requirement <<verified by>> test case) as described in Chapter 6.

Another traceability link is between the shared assets superset and the derived product models. This can be done simply by labeling the product model with the corresponding baseline ID, as shown in Section 19.3. However, a better practice involves establishing dependencies between the shared assets supersets and the product models once these are derived (e.g. through automatic generation of the dependency).

One challenge is the specific technical connection of the models. Various approaches exist, including standards such as REST or Open Services for Lifecycle Collaboration and tool-proprietary solutions ('Model Interoperability' 2023).

The overall architecture of the "Model of Models" should be explicitly designed and controlled. This is the only way to master the dependencies and enable a digital thread. Chapter 18 covers the topic of "digital end-to-end continuity with MBPLE" in detail.

19.6 CM for Models

The paper "Model lifecycle management for MBSE" defines model lifecycle management (MLM) as "a governance process synchronizing the create, read, update, and delete (CRUD) operations on heterogeneous models within the supporting modeling tools and model repositories throughout the system development life cycle" (Fisher et al. 2014). In addition to the CRUD operation within a model, MLM should also cover the management of the model's life cycle, which includes considering the versions of the MBSE tools.

Three types of CI can be distinguished. Whether and how the conceptual distinction is considered depends on the project requirements.

Generally, a model stores information. If the information piece is under configuration control, it is called an information CI (ICI). A requirement or a part specification could be an ICI. Independent of the concrete kind of modeling, it is information that exists in different versions. Depending on the modeling language, information is represented in a model by one or more model elements. If you use SysML for the modeling of the specification of parts, it could be represented by a part definition. The conceptual ICI is implemented by one or more model CI (MCI) in the model.

Both the conceptual and model levels have no physical manifestation, which is located on the repository level. For example, a SysML model can be stored in a tool-specific database. It could also be exported to an XMI file, which is a pure text file containing the model in an XML representation. In addition to the ICI and MCI, we also have a repository CI. Figure 19.4 shows the three different kinds of CIs in the context of models.

Assume you create a system architecture model with SysML for a product line. The products must be in operation for at least 20 years, including maintenance and further development. This also requires that the system architecture model still be accessible in 20 years' time.

The main focus of CM is on the conceptual level. You want to manage the versions of a feature. The versions of the corresponding model elements go hand in hand with this. This means all model elements representing the information get the corresponding version. In practice, the model elements are versioned, not the information elements, which only exist conceptually.

Typically, a repository contains several model elements and, therefore, has its own versioning, which is less related to the model element's versions.

It is important to note the connection, for example, to obtain the information in the future that a model element in version 37 is stored in the repository in version 12, and therefore, it is known which tools can be used to load and read this repository.

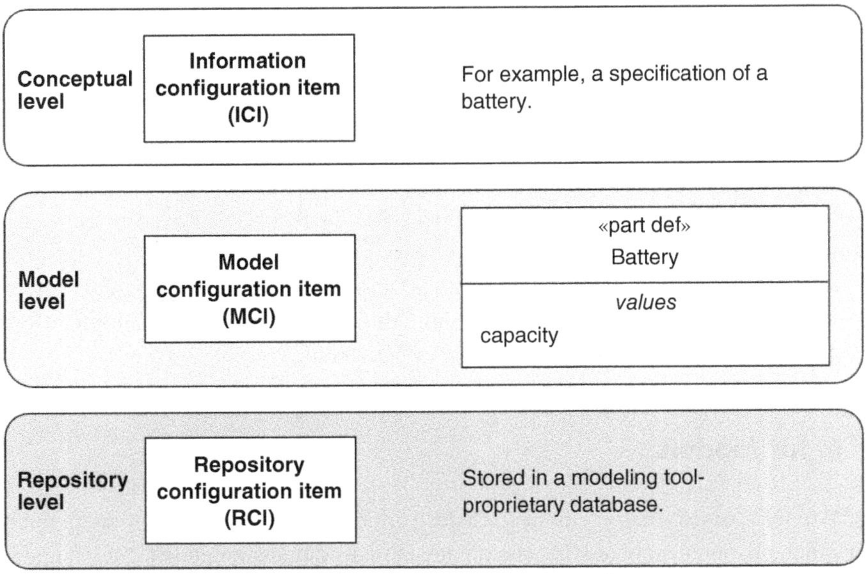

Figure 19.4 Configuration items of a model.

Ensure that the information lifecycle requirements are met. For example, the information in the model can be accessed until the end of its life. It cannot be taken for granted that models from today can still be opened in, say, ten years. The associated tool may no longer be available in the version or be unable to be opened because it has to access a license server of the tool vendor for this purpose, which is no longer operated, and so forth.

19.7 Model Organization and Management

The elements of a model can be organized by many criteria. For instance, the model elements of the drone shared assets can be organized by engine elements, flight-control elements, power management elements, and so forth.

The organization units of models are, typically, folders. The semantics of a folder is a container and a namespace for elements. It has a name and constraints that member elements have distinguishable unique names. Folders can have subfolders and create a hierarchical structure. Usually, each level is one-dimensional, and only one criterion can be applied.

An illustrative example of a folder-based organization in the real world is a cutlery drawer. The drawer is the root folder with many subcompartments, typically organized by knife, fork, spoon, etc. However, this striking example already shows a challenge in the organization: all spoons in one compartment or soup and teaspoons separately? Is expensive silver cutlery separated from everyday cutlery? Is it sorted first by material and then by type, or vice versa?

We are sure many people are familiar with this problem and the similar challenge of organizing files in folders on a hard drive. While there are often several grouping criteria, folder-based organizations only allow one per level. This topic is also critical for deriving product models from the shared assets supersets. For instance, if the model is organized as a large interdependent chunk each and every time, the product model derivation is performed for the entire model. If the model is modularized, the product model can be generated just for the module under scope.

In a SysML model, packages are the folders. The core concept can be found in almost all modeling languages and tools. In addition to the one-dimensional organization, there are also other possibilities. For example, tags can assign several criteria per element on one level and enable a multi-dimensional organization of the elements.

Organization of shared assets – a SysML example: This example describes organizing shared assets in a systems engineering model with SysML. Covering other shared asset models, such as simulation and CAD models, would exceed the book's scope.

In SysML, the model organization units are packages. The following package structure proposal is based on system modeling method ([SYSMOD] Weilkiens 2020). The top-level structure criteria are engineering-oriented: core elements, variant elements, and product models. The next level is organized by domain criteria. This pattern can be repeated on a detailed level. Figure 19.5 shows the package structure pattern with a simple example. Note the recursive style of the package

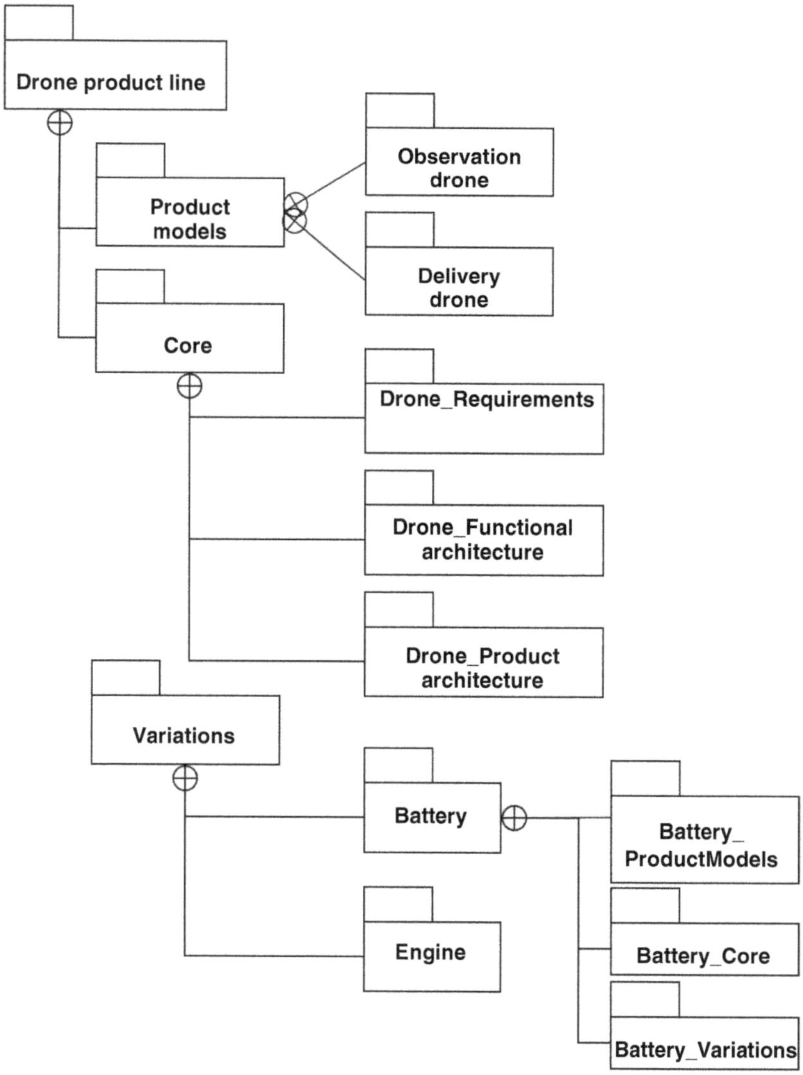

Figure 19.5 Organization SysML shared assets.

pattern: the whole structure repeats for the package battery since the same recursive pattern of the overarching system is applied.

19.8 ISO 26581: A New CM Standard for PLE

ISO/IEC 26580 (ISO/IEC 2021) focused primarily on the PLE factory elements operating at a fixed point in time, emphasizing variation in space but not in time. In the previous sections, we discussed how assets, evolving over time, become CI. Hence, in a PLE approach to derive complete product models, the versions of all assets must be perfectly aligned at a specific point in time.

This CM gap in the discipline of PLE necessitates a new standard to complement the existing ISO/IEC 26580 (ISO/IEC 2021). Therefore, the INCOSE PLE Working Group (INCOSE PLE WG 2024), under the responsibility of Dr. Charles Krueger, is leading the development of such a standard. This new standard aims to facilitate the controlled evolution of PLE assets over time and guarantee the reproducibility of any previously configured and released member product.

The future standard will describe the tools and methods that create an overarching CM solution for the product line and its members, aggregating and aligning the constituent traditional CM systems.

References

Fisher, A., Nolan, M., Friedenthal, S. et al. (2014). 3.1.1 Model lifecycle management for MBSE. In: *INCOSE International Symposium* 24 (1), pp. 207–229. 10.1002/j.2334-5837.2014.tb03145.x.

INCOSE PLE WG (2024). Product Line Engineering Working Group Webpage. https://www.incose.org/communities/working-groups-initiatives/product-lines (accessed 24 July 2024).

ISO/IEC (2021). Software and systems engineering – methods and tools for the feature-based approach to software and systems product line engineering (ISO/IEC/IEEE 2658 0: 2021).

ISO/IEC/IEEE (2023). Systems and software engineering – system life cycle processes (ISO/IEC/IEEE 1528 8: 2023).

Lameh, J., Dubray, A., and Jankovic, M. (2023). Towards a configuration management integration to feature models in model-based product line engineering. In: *Proceedings of the International Conference on Engineering Design, ICED23* (24–28 July 2023), Bordeaux, France.

Model Interoperability (2023). *Handbook of Model-Based Systems Engineering (ed.* A.M Madni, N. Augustine, M. Sievers). Springer.

Weilkiens, T. (2020). SYSMOD – *The Systems Modeling Toolbox: Pragmatic MBSE with SysML,* MBSE4U Book Series.

20

MBPLE and Artificial Intelligence

20.1 Introduction

Artificial intelligence (AI) has significantly influenced various fields, especially since the release of ChatGPT. This impact extends to systems engineering and model-based product line engineering (MBPLE).

Artificial intelligence is a broad subject area, and when non-experts discuss it nowadays, they usually refer to ChatGPT. Section 20.2 first provides an orientation in the field and explains some key terms related to AI in general.

Section 20.3 shows the application of large language models (LLM), such as ChatGPT. Section 20.4 presents two types of "AI assistants" for using LLMs to support MBPLE activities. Section 20.5 combines these two into one "super" MBPLE assistant and shows its capabilities in a concrete application use case. Finally, Section 20.6 discusses opportunities and threats that may arise from using AI in MBPLE.

20.2 AI Foundation

This section explains the numerous abbreviations related to artificial intelligence: AI, machine learning (ML), deep learning (DL), GenAI, LLM, and ChatGPT. The focus is on AI for systems engineering (AI4SE) and LLMs. AI4SE means using AI to support systems engineering activities. There is also systems engineering for artificial intelligence, which is about using systems engineering approaches for developing AI systems.

The following subsections explain them briefly.

20.2.1 Artificial Intelligence

The broadest term in Figure 20.1 is AI. Understanding AI begins with defining what "intelligence" means. Marvin Minsky describes intelligence as a complex combination of simpler processes (Minsky 1988). Russell and Norvig propose a two-dimensional definition of AI, considering first whether AI aims to imitate human behavior or rationality and second whether it focuses on external actions or internal thought processes (Russell and Norvig 2020). The Turing Test, formulated by Alan Turing, evaluates an AI's ability to exhibit human-like behavior (Turing 1950).

Model-Based Product Line Engineering (MBPLE): The Feature-Based Path to Product Lines Success, First Edition.
Marco Forlingieri et al.

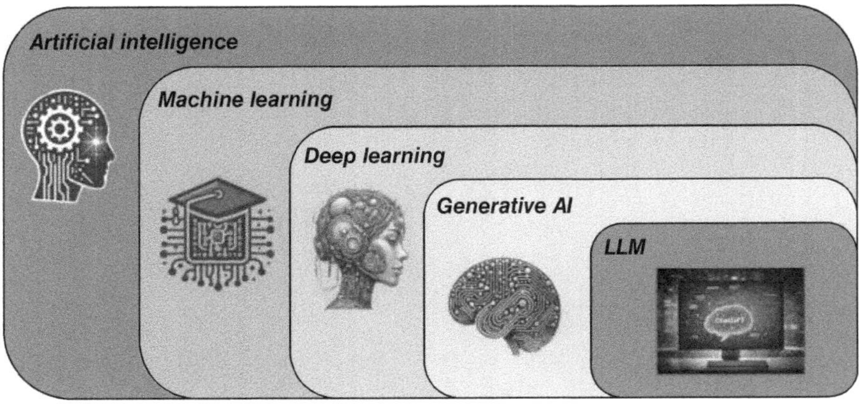

Figure 20.1 AI terminology. *Source:* Adapted from Rosenberg et al., 2024 / with permission of Model Based Systems Engineering 4 You.

Russell and Norvig identify four essential capabilities for an AI: natural language processing, knowledge representation, automated reasoning, and machine learning.

20.2.2 Machine Learning and Deep Learning

Machine learning (ML) is a branch of AI that focuses on learning and making decisions based on data. There are different methods to achieve this; one of the most popular is the neural network approach.

Neural networks are a type of ML model designed to mimic the way the human brain works. They consist of interconnected nodes, or "neurons," which process and transmit information. When these networks have many layers of neurons, they are considered as DL models. Deep learning allows for more complex data analysis and has been particularly successful in tasks such as image and speech recognition.

20.2.3 Generative AI and LLMs

Generative AI (GenAI) is a subfield of DL. It creates new content, such as text, images, and audio, by learning from datasets and generating data that resembles the training data.

Large language models, such as ChatGPT, are a subset of GenAI focused on text. GPT, or generative pre-trained transformer, is the basis of ChatGPT. This advanced language model, developed by OpenAI[1], is characterized by natural language processing and text generation.

ChatGPT's capabilities span multiple domains, including conversational dynamics, creative and technical writing, educational applications, and code generation. ChatGPT falls into the "acting humanly" AI category defined by Russell and Norvig and focuses on human-like interactions and natural language processing.

ChatGPT is certainly the most famous LLM, but there are also others, such as Google Gemini[2], xAI Grok[3], Meta Llama 3[4], or Mistral[5].

1 openai.com.
2 gemini.google.com.
3 x.ai.
4 ai.meta.com/blog/meta-llama-3/.
5 mistral.ai.

20.3 Communication with an LLM

Large language models turn natural languages into an interface between man and machine. Chatting with an LLM such as ChatGPT is based on prompts, i.e. a statement that prompts the LLM for a response. Processing a prompt in an LLM involves tokenizing the text, converting tokens into numerical values, and generating responses based on these values.

OpenAI has published a guide with six strategies for writing effective prompts (OpenAI 2024):

1. Write clear instructions: Specify detailed information and provide examples.
2. Provide reference text: Include references or ask the AI to base its response on specific texts.
3. Split complex tasks: Break down complex tasks into simpler steps.
4. Give the model time to "think": Encourage the AI to consider tasks deeply.
5. Use external tools: Create outputs for external tools that can be fed back into the AI.
6. Use a test suite: Monitor AI responses over time to ensure consistency and accuracy.

In most cases, an LLM can also be addressed via an API. In this case, more parameters, such as the so-called temperature, can typically be set, which controls how "creative" the responses are.

One aspect of LLM behavior is the phenomenon of "hallucinations," where an LLM generates incorrect or fabricated information. This differs from human lying, which involves conscious intent, whereas AI hallucinations arise from improperly learned data. However, both phenomena can overlap; for instance, false knowledge can underpin human lies, and an LLM might deliberately produce false information under certain conditions. That is why it is recommended that organizations adopt governance mechanisms to control and mitigate such risks.

20.4 AI4MBPLE

The application of AI, or more precisely, LLMs, supporting MBPLE activities can be further categorized as using AI as a domain expert assistant or as an MBPLE methodology assistant. A similar approach is described for MBSE in the book "AI Assisted MBSE with SysML" (Rosenberg et al. 2024).

The LLM does not care much about the distinction. Separating concerns helps focus and write concise prompts.

20.4.1 AI as a Domain Expert Assistant

Using AI as a domain expert assistant means using the broad and deep knowledge of ChatGPT and similar LLMs to identify additional engineering artifacts, such as more potential features for a feature model.

This book uses a simple example of a drone product line. The following prompt provides the existing feature model and asks for additional features using the LLM's knowledge. The prompt contains the following important properties, among others: providing a context, showing an example, and giving clear instructions.

Prompt:

We are working on a feature model for a drone product line according to ISO/IEC 26580.

The features' hierarchical structure is depicted as a list in textual notation, as in the following example. Constraints about valid feature selections are given in square brackets.

Feature1 [Constraints: Select exactly one subfeature]
Subfeature1.1
Subfeature1.2
Subfeature 1.2.1

Below is the existing feature model. Propose additional features, including subfeatures, constraints, and changes to the existing feature model. Use the same textual notation for the enhanced feature model.

DroneFeature
Number of Engines
Four Engines
Six Engines
Battery Kinds
Standard Battery
Long Distance Battery

Response from ChatGPT:
Here is the enhanced feature model for the drone product line, including additional features, subfeatures, constraints, and changes to the existing feature model. I have added some common features and constraints that might be relevant for a drone product line:

DroneFeature [Constraints: Select at least one subfeature from Number of Engines, Battery Kinds, Camera Types, and GPS Capabilities]
Number of Engines [Constraints: Select exactly one subfeature]
Four Engines
Six Engines
Battery Kinds [Constraints: Select exactly one subfeature]
Standard Battery
Long Distance Battery
Camera Types [Constraints: Select exactly one subfeature]
Standard Camera
High-Resolution Camera
Thermal Camera
GPS Capabilities [Constraints: Select at least one subfeature]
Basic GPS
Advanced GPS with Real-Time Tracking
Flight Modes [Constraints: Select at least one subfeature]
Manual Mode
Autonomous Mode
Follow Me Mode
Sensors [Constraints: Select at least one subfeature]
Collision Avoidance Sensors
Altitude Hold Sensors
Obstacle Detection Sensors
Connectivity [Constraints: Select at least one subfeature]
Wi-Fi Connectivity
Cellular Connectivity
Satellite Connectivity

Payload Capacity [Constraints: Select exactly one subfeature]
Light Payload
Medium Payload
Heavy Payload
Control Options [Constraints: Select at least one subfeature]
Remote Control
Mobile App Control
Voice Control
Durability Features [Constraints: Select at least one subfeature]
Water Resistant
Dust Proof
Shock Resistant

We sent the prompt to ChatGPT 4o without any additional training (also called zero-shot). Currently, a challenge in a real-world project is the limit of the prompt's size, which could be a problem for a large feature model. This is just a simplified example, but it shows how you can use domain knowledge to identify gaps, generate more ideas, or generate content quickly. It emphasizes the potential of training the LLM as a domain expert within an organization (e.g. learning legacy specifications, competitive solutions, best practices, etc.). We all have experienced the challenge of chasing the right domain expert, who is always overloaded by support requests, projects, or on leave.

20.4.2 AI as a MBPLE Methodology Assistant

ChatGPT has also learned methodological knowledge. As there are different approaches, it is important to clearly describe the context in the prompt and provide an example.

The following demonstrates the links of a simple system model with the previous feature model, turning the system model into a shared assets superset. The prompt has been sent in the same thread as the previous one for the feature model, which means that the feature model is already known and does not need to be specified.

The prompt contains an example of modeling variations in Systems Modeling Language (SysML) v2 and linking them to features. Finally, the prompt provides a very simple system model and asks for changes and additions based on the link to the feature model.

Prompt:
Consider the feature model and define the corresponding variations with a link to the respective feature, similar to the following example for a vehicle:

```
part def Vehicle{
  variation wheel : Wheel {
    doc /* Link to Feature */
    variant wheelStandard : StandardWheel;
    variant wheelX : XWheel;
  }
}
part def Wheel;
part def StandardWheel;
part def XWheel;
```

Change the parts of the given SysML v2 model to variations if the suitable features exist.

```
part def Drone {
  part battery : Battery;
  part engine : Engine;
  part frame : Frame;
}
part def Battery;
part def Engine;
part def Frame;
```

The answer is only given here in a shortened form, as the whole answer is not important to demonstrate the principle.

Response from ChatGPT:

Here is the revised SysML v2 model incorporating variations linked to the respective features in the enhanced feature model:

```
part def Drone {
  variation battery: Battery {
    doc /* Link to Battery Kinds Feature */
    variant standardBattery: StandardBattery;
    variant longDistanceBattery: LongDistanceBattery;
  }
  variation engine: Engine {
    doc /* Link to Number of Engines Feature */
    variant fourEngines: FourEngines;
    variant sixEngines: SixEngines;
  }
  variation camera: Camera {
    doc /* Link to Camera Types Feature */
    variant standardCamera: StandardCamera;
    variant highResolutionCamera: HighResolutionCamera;
    variant thermalCamera: ThermalCamera;
  }
variation flightMode: FlightMode {
    doc /* Link to Flight Modes Feature */
    variant manualMode: ManualMode;
    variant autonomousMode: AutonomousMode;
    variant followMeMode: FollowMeMode;
  }
}
[...]
```

20.5 The "Super" Assistant: Combining Domain Expert and MBPLE Methodology

Have you ever experienced the excitement of discovering that your team includes a systems engineer or MBSE expert who is also a domain expert in your industry? It is a rare and valuable discovery. Now, imagine if your best domain expert and the most experienced MBPLE expert could train an LLM to become the ultimate team member you've always dreamed of. In the next sections, we explore the feasibility of such a scenario.

20.5.1 The Creation of a Feature Model for a New Product Line based on Existing Product Specifications

The use case we present here consists of two activities that can be supported by a third MBPLE expert, which we call the "super" assistant because it combines both the system domain expertise and the knowledge of the methodology. We divide the use case into three parts, answering the following questions:

1. How to create an initial feature model from an existing specification of a legacy product that contains some variability but was not originally intended to serve a product line?
2. How to add new features, necessary to develop the product line?
3. How are the existing requirements impacted by the new features, and how are the new (added or updated) requirements in the original specification identified?

Large organizations often start a product line using a brownfield approach, leveraging existing assets from large legacy systems. This strategy can benefit from the MBPLE approach (Essoussi et al. 2024).

The example used is a simplified requirements specification of the drone in PDF format that includes the following requirements:

Req. 1 - The system shall autonomously navigate the drone from the shore to the designated ship location.

Req. 2 - The system shall ensure safe takeoff and landing of the drone on the ship's deck.
Req. 3 - The system shall allow for manual override and control of the drone by an operator.
Req. 4 - The system shall provide real-time tracking of the drone's location during delivery.
Req. 5 - The system shall provide additional continuous monitoring of the item to be delivered via camera if required by the customer.

Req. 6 - The system shall be capable of carrying payloads up to 10 kg.
Req. 7 - The system shall complete a delivery within a maximum time of 30 minutes.
Req. 8 - The system shall operate within a range of up to 10 km from the shore if equipped with 4 engines and within a range of up to 20 km if equipped with 6 engines.
Req. 9 - The system shall maintain stable flight in winds up to 25 km hour.
Req. 10 - The system shall be able to operate in temperatures ranging from −10 to 40 °C.
Req. 11 - The system shall ensure a battery life sufficient for at least one round trip.
Req. 12 - The system shall include collision avoidance technology to prevent accidents.
Req. 13 - The system shall be equipped with either Radio communication systems or with 5G to ensure constant contact with the operator.
Req. 14 - The system shall secure the payload to prevent loss during flight.
Req. 15 - The system shall comply with all relevant aviation and maritime safety regulations.

In the next section, we present a step-by-step approach that includes a short LLM training with prompt engineering (behind the scenes) necessary for the LLM to execute our use case.

20.5.2 A Step-by-Step Approach

The approach can be summarized in the following steps:

(1) **Training the LLM with free-text prompts:** It consists of teaching the LLM what a feature model is and how features can be identified and extracted from a set of requirements. It is usually done through trial and error.

(2) **Importing the legacy specification:** The requirements contained in a PDF document specification are uploaded using a model based on LLM user interface that has been built for the exclusive purpose of this book.
(3) **Identifying and exporting the feature model:** Features are extracted from the legacy requirements and organized into a consistent feature model, which represents the system's variability. This model is then exported as a CSV file. The features are labeled with a tool-specific notation to facilitate import, as a standard variability modeling language does not yet exist.
(4) **Importing and visualizing the feature model in a product line engineering (PLE) tool:** The feature model is imported as a CSV file in the PLE tool. This is because the PLE tool is not connected via API with the LLM solution.
(5) **Adding new features and exporting the resulting feature model:** New features are added to the first feature model and exported as a CSV file.
(6) **Importing and visualizing the new feature model in the PLE tool:** Same step as before (4), but this time the feature model includes the new added features.
(7) **Understanding impact on existing requirements:** It focuses on capturing which requirements are impacted by the introduction of the new features.

IBM watsonx (IBM watsonx 2024) is the commercial platform used in this example. It includes several LLMs and prompt labs to facilitate the creation of AI-driven tasks and services. The Llama 3 70-b instruct LLM is used here[6]. Once the feature model is generated as a CSV file, PTC pure::variants (PTC pure::variants 2024) is used as a PLE tool to import and visualize the feature model. The solution presented in this book is created solely to simulate the activities performed by the "super" domain and MBPLE methodology expert assistant. Integrating the AI solution with the PLE tool would streamline the entire process.

20.5.3 The Super Domain and MBPLE Expert in Action

Step 1 consists of training the model with free-text prompts, and it is good practice to refine the prompts until the desired outcome is reached. The following example shows the first prompt used.

Prompt (zero-shot):
<|begin_of_text|><|start_header_id|>system<|end_header_id|>
You are an MBPLE super assistant working on requirements specifications. Do not respond in markdown.
Information is provided below, delimited by triple backticks.
...
Shore-to-ship Drone

The system shall provide additional continuous monitoring of the item to be delivered via camera if required by the customer.
The system shall be capable of carrying payloads up to 5 kg.
The system shall operate within a range of up to 10 km from the shore if equipped with 2 engines and within a range of up to 20 km if equipped with 4 engines.
The system shall secure the payload to prevent loss during flight.
...

6 ai.meta.com/blog/meta-llama-3/.

<|eot_id|>Create a hierarchy of features with a minimum of 3 levels and a maximum of 5 levels.
The first level is always one feature and is the parent of the features of the second level. The name of this feature is always the title of the requirements list (example: Shore_to_shipDrone). The first feature at level one can only have ps:mandatory (stands for mandatory relation) or ps:optional (stands for optional) with its children features.
The second level should have around a minimum of 3 and a maximum of 5 features, either ps:mandatory or ps:optional. The second level features can have with their children features of level 3 the following relations ps:mandatory (stands for mandatory relation) or ps:optional (stands for optional) or ps:or (stands for at least 1 feature within the group under the same parent must be selected, not mutually exclusive) or ps:alternative (features under the same parent features are mutually exclusive).
The third level and eventual fourth and fifth levels follow the same rules of the second level.
Respond only in a valid CSV format, with 4 columns,
- name of the feature, column title “Unique Name” (all feature names under this column cannot have spaces between words but only underscore “_”)
- the parent name of the feature, column title “Parent Unique Name”
- the relation between parent and child feature, column title “variation Type” (use the variation types starting with “ps:”
- Exact copy of column 1 “Unique Name” but with new title “Visible Name”.
<|start_header_id|>assistant<|end_header_id|>

First result (invalid):
“Unique Name”,”Parent Unique Name”,”Variation Type”,”Visible Name”
“Shore_to_shipDrone”,””“,””“,”Shore to ship Drone”
“Delivery_Configuration”,”Shore_to_shipDrone”,”ps:mandatory”,”Delivery Configuration”
“Engine_Configuration”,”Delivery_Configuration”,”ps:mandatory”,”Engine Configuration”
“Two_Engines”,”Engine_Configuration”,”ps:alternative”,”2 Engines”
“Four_Engines”,”Engine_Configuration”,”ps:alternative”,”4 Engines”
“Monitoring”,”Delivery_Configuration”,”ps:optional”,”Monitoring”
“Payload_Configuration”,”Delivery_Configuration”,”ps:mandatory”,”Payload Configuration”
“Payload_Capacity”,”Payload_Configuration”,”ps:mandatory”,”Payload Capacity”
“Payload_Security”,”Payload_Configuration”,”ps:mandatory”,”Payload Security”

The training results were unsatisfactory because features like “Delivery_Configuration,” “Payload_Configuration,” “Payload_Capacity,” and “Payload_Security” did not reflect any variability; they resembled a functional breakdown structure instead. After some trial and error, the second prompt was added to improve the results.

Prompt (after some shots):
(...) Very important: it is not allowed to have a ps:mandatory relation between a parent and child, when the child feature has no further children features at the level below.

The feature tree shown as CSV should only focus on those features that have variation and not covering all the requirements above.

For example: If the requirements have a form like “If required by “ create a ps:optional feature.
For example: “If equipped with” and “If equipped with” = Create two ps:alternative features for the requirement that have these two clauses.

Example of an invalid and not acceptable output generated below:

“Unique Name”,”Parent Unique Name”,”Variation Type”,”Visible Name”
“Shore_to_shipDrone”,”“,”“,”Shore to ship Drone”
“Delivery_Configuration”,”Shore_to_shipDrone”,”ps:mandatory”,”Delivery Configuration”
“Engine_Configuration”,”Delivery_Configuration”,”ps:mandatory”,”Engine Configuration”
“Two_Engines”,”Engine_Configuration”,”ps:alternative”,”2 Engines”
“Four_Engines”,”Engine_Configuration”,”ps:alternative”,”4 Engines”
“Monitoring”,”Delivery_Configuration”,”ps:optional”,”Monitoring”
“Payload_Configuration”,”Delivery_Configuration”,”ps:mandatory”,”Payload Configuration”
“Payload_Capacity”,”Payload_Configuration”,”ps:mandatory”,”Payload Capacity”
“Payload_Security”,”Payload_Configuration”,”ps:mandatory”,”Payload Security”
The output above is invalid because it does not focus on the features that have variation and it does not respect the following rule: “a ps:mandatory relation between a parent and child, when the child feature has no further children features at the level below is not allowed.

For example, the following pattern is wrong according to the rule above:

“Payload_Configuration”,”Delivery_Configuration”,”ps:mandatory”,”Payload Configuration”
“Payload_Capacity”,”Payload_Configuration”,”ps:mandatory”,”Payload Capacity”
“Payload_Security”,”Payload_Configuration”,”ps:mandatory”,”Payload Security”<|start_header_id|>assistant<|end_header_id|>

In the new prompt, rules are better specified, and the previous unsatisfactory output of the feature model is added as an invalid example.

Use Case Part 1: How to create an initial feature model from an existing specification of a legacy product that contains some variability but was not originally intended to serve a product line?

After refining the prompt, in Step 2, the PDF document containing the requirements from Section 20.5.1 is imported (Figure 20.2). Based on the content of the uploaded specification, the feature model is then generated in CSV format.

Figure 20.3 shows a correct formulation of the feature model based on the rules provided and document specification of the drone. At this stage, the feature model is ready to be exported as a CSV file (Step 3).

The CSV file is then imported in pure::variants and visualized in the tool-specific feature modeling notation as illustrated in Figure 20.4 and described in Step 4.

Use Case Part 2: How to add new features, necessary to develop the product line?

To complete Step 5, an additional prompt must first be given to the LLM. This prompt should specify the need to add new features to the existing feature model and revise the content as shown below.

Prompt:

(...) The user would like to add new features into the existing CSV output. Based on the user input, add the feature into the CSV.
<|eot_id|>

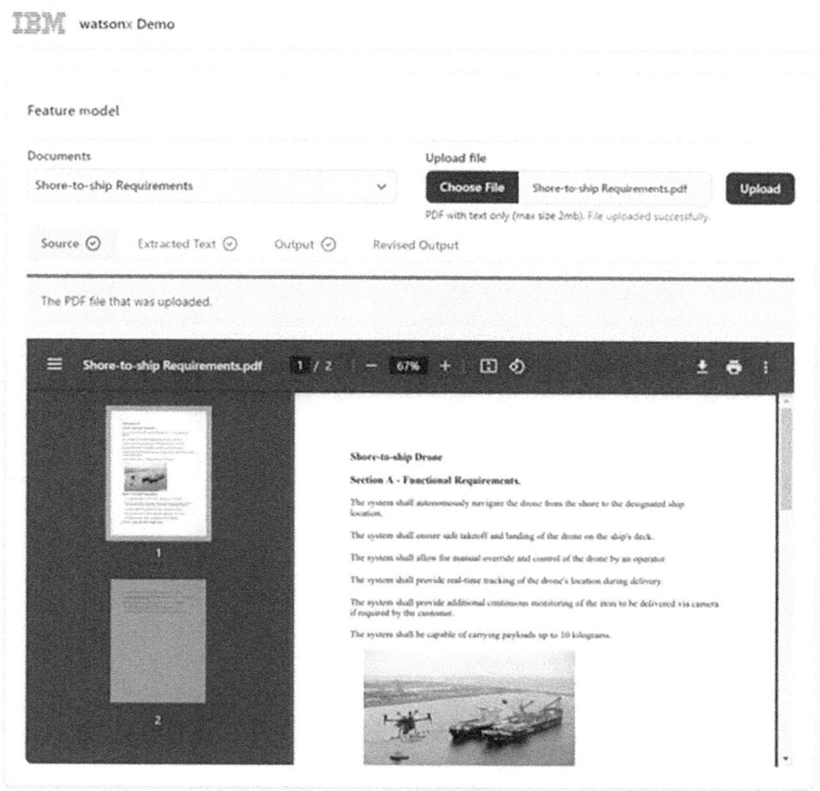

Figure 20.2 Import of the legacy specification pdf in the IBM watsonx application.

1) Provide alternative capability to support 4 round trips based on existing capability already available in the requirements;
2) Provide alternative capability to support a payload of 15 kg.
Provide as additional output also the requirements that are impacted by these changes.
<|start_header_id|>assistant<|end_header_id|>

The result, in this case, is satisfactory on the first attempt, as illustrated in Figure 20.5.

The revised feature model is imported again in PTC pure::variants, and the previous feature model is updated (Step 6), as shown in Figure 20.6.

Use Case Part 3: How to identify the existing requirements impacted by the new features and new requirements to be added or changed in the original specification?

To perform Step 7, it is also necessary to add an additional prompt that asks the LLM to provide information about the requirements impacted by the introduction of new features. This is a key step to understand the impact of changes on an existing asset and relate the requirement to the correspondent feature. It helps the identification of variation points in the requirements set.

Prompt:
<|eot_id|>
Provide as additional output the requirements that are impacted by the change, that consists of the introduction of new features.

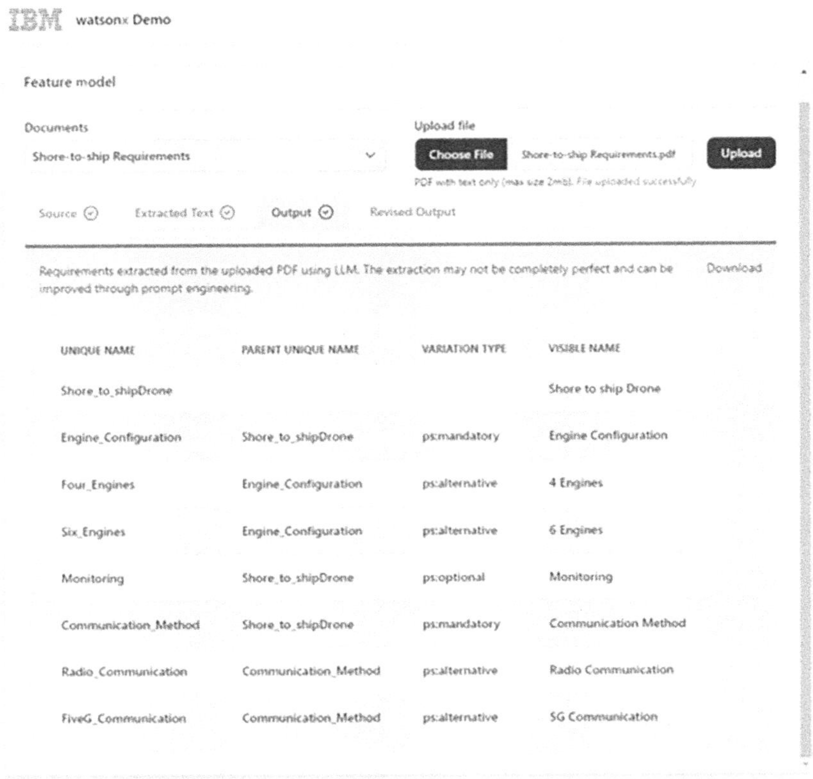

Figure 20.3 Feature model output in the IBM watsonx application.

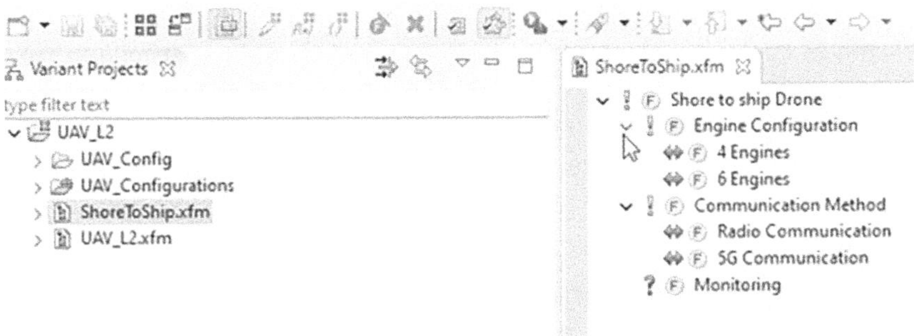

Figure 20.4 Feature model imported in PTC pure::variants.

Highlight which new feature is related to which requirement and what is the change. The focus shall be only on those requirements that are impacted by the new features.
<|start_header_id|>assistant<|end_header_id|>.

The final result provides the requirements that are impacted by the change of adding new features (Step 7), as depicted in Figure 20.7.

Nota bene: The full use case presented here can also be applied to the "evolution of a product line" that has not been developed following a feature-based PLE approach. In that case, the document

IBM watsonx Demo

UNIQUE NAME	PARENT UNIQUE NAME	VARIATION TYPE	VISIBLE NAME
Shore_to_shipDrone			Shore to ship Drone
Engine_Configuration	Shore_to_shipDrone	ps:mandatory	Engine Configuration
Four_Engines	Engine_Configuration	ps:alternative	4 Engines
Six_Engines	Engine_Configuration	ps:alternative	6 Engines
Monitoring	Shore_to_shipDrone	ps:optional	Monitoring
Communication_Method	Shore_to_shipDrone	ps:mandatory	Communication Method
Radio_Communication	Communication_Method	ps:alternative	Radio Communication
FiveG_Communication	Communication_Method	ps:alternative	5G Communication
Trip_Capability	Shore_to_shipDrone	ps:mandatory	Trip Capability
Single_Trip	Trip_Capability	ps:alternative	Single Trip
Four_Round_Trips	Trip_Capability	ps:alternative	4 Round Trips
Payload_Capability	Shore_to_shipDrone	ps:mandatory	Payload Capability
Ten_kg_Payload	Payload_Capability	ps:alternative	10 kg Payload
Fifteen_kg_Payload	Payload_Capability	ps:alternative	15 kg Payload

Figure 20.5 Revised feature model output in the IBM watsonx application.

specification or requirements set is part of the shared assets of an existing product line, where new features are added to it.

20.6 AI4MBPLE Opportunities and Threats: Hasta la Vista, Baby!

The previous examples demonstrate how LLMs can be trained to become the domain expert and methodology expert assistants of your team. These examples are just a few of the many potential use cases that could be developed in the MBPLE domain.

For instance, an AI can become "the Terminator" of the unused features, eliminating unutilized feature configurations in your product line (to avoid the cost of their maintenance), or it can define the best combinations of features (feature configurations) to meet new customer requirements. It can also help determine the right balance of variability and commonality within your product line and add variation points automatically to your shared assets superset.

Just like in the movie "Terminator," where John Connor teaches the intelligent humanoid to behave more human-like – famous is the line "No, no, no, no. You gotta listen to the way people talk. You don't say 'affirmative' or something like that. (...) And if you want to shine them on, it's 'hasta la vista, baby'" – an LLM, when properly trained, can become your secret weapon in product line development.

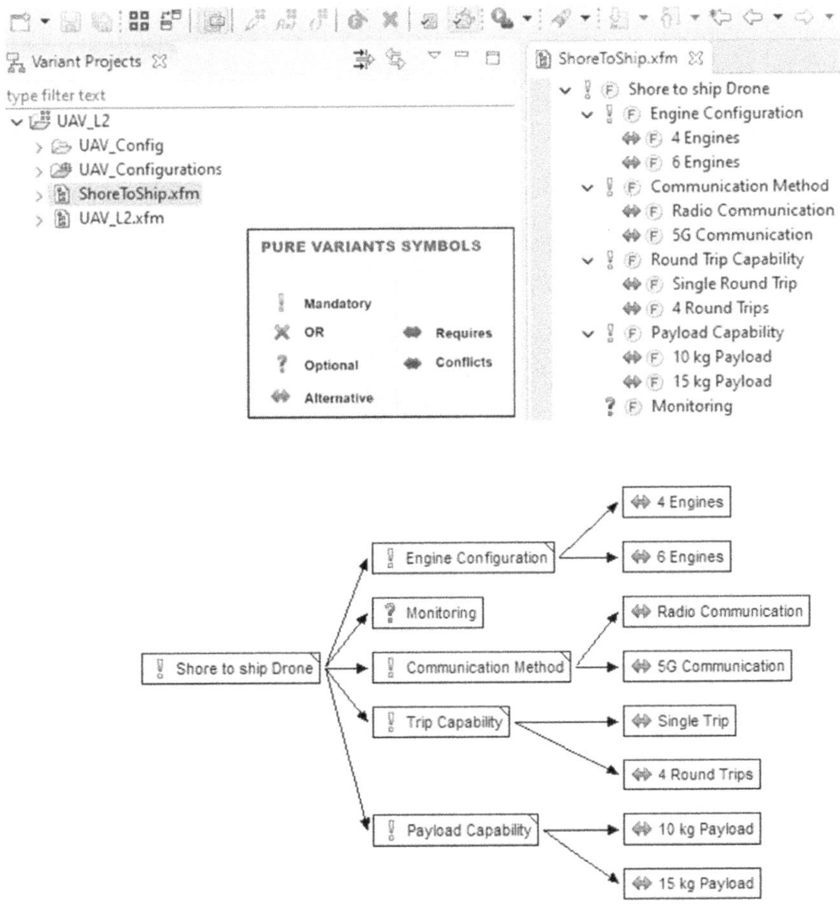

Figure 20.6 Feature model updated in PTC pure::variants.

However, while AI can be a valuable companion in developing product lines, it is important to be aware of potential threats. For example, relying too much on AI might lead to a loss of understanding of the system variability during feature model building, a typically creative process that can spark new features. Another challenge is the risk of AI hallucinations, where the model might provide false information if no governance mechanisms are in place, which an inexperienced engineer might mistakenly accept as valid.

Like any other technology, AI is not inherently good or bad; its impact depends on how it is used. Do not let your MBPLE AI assistant turn into the "bad" Terminator!

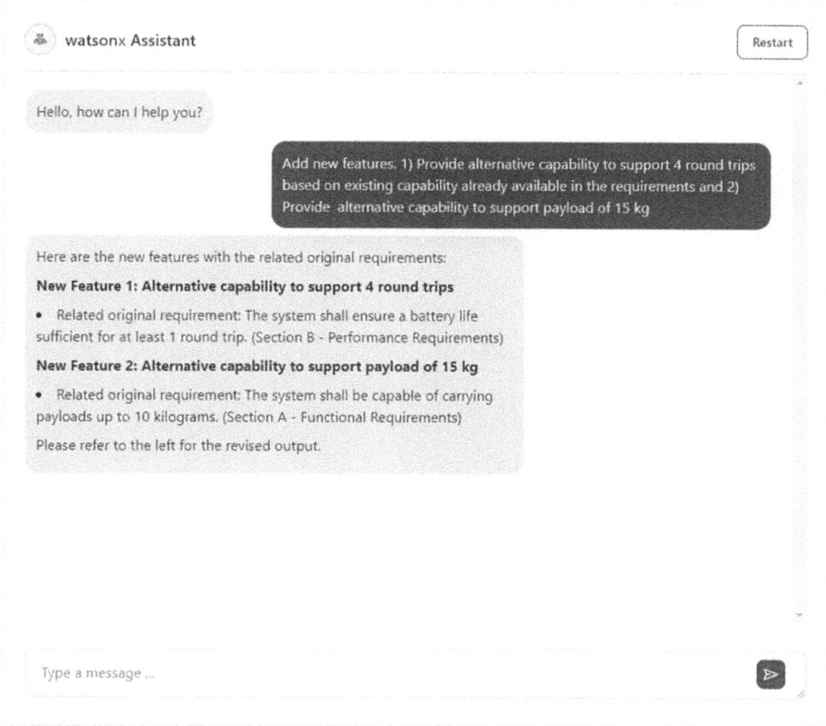

Figure 20.7 Requirements impacted by the new features in the IBM watsonx application.

References

Essoussi, M.H., Vivot, P., Deloye, L. et al. (2024). Large legacy systems design maintainability through modeling. ERTS 2024, June 2024, Toulouse, France. ffhal04614391f.

IBM watsonx (2024). IBM watsonx Introduction. https://www.ibm.com/watsonx?utm_content=SRCWW&p1=Search&p4=43700077029996461&p5=e&p9=58700008463302546&gclid=Cj0KCQjw-uK0BhC0ARIsANQtgGP933faAXTQsea3nrKAgmnSzt_ypaeGcwF9IaooIwKxfG5XsVWC9NAaAtmbEALw_wcB&gclsrc=aw.ds (accessed 19 July 2024).

Minsky, M. (1988). *The Society of Mind*. New York: Simon & Schuster.

OpenAI (2024). Prompt Engineering. https://platform.openai.com/docs/guides/prompt-engineering/prompt-engineering (accessed 17 June 2024).

PTC pure::variants (2024). pure::variants. https://www.ptc.com/en/products/pure-variants (accessed 10 May 2024).

Rosenberg, D., Weilkiens, T., and Moberley, B. (2024). *AI Assisted MBSE with SysML*. MBSE4U.

Russell, S. and Norvig, P. (2020). *Artificial Intelligence: A Modern Approach*, 4e. London: Pearson.

Turing, A. (1950). Computing machinery and intelligence. *Mind*, 59:433–460.

Part IV

Adoption of MBPLE

The next-to-last part of this book proposes different aspects to be considered for the adoption of Model-Based Product Line Engineering (MBPLE) in organizations. These aspects include the purpose and business value of MBPLE, an adoption framework and process, the setup and improvement of methods and tools, an information model, requirements for end-to-end tool chains, as well as general principles to set up an MBPLE organization.

Chapter 21 opens Part IV by presenting the elements that can be used to build a compelling business case for MBPLE based on its value proposition: cost-effectiveness, lead time reduction, quality improvement, and return on investment. The chapter demonstrates how MBPLE can enhance business profitability by leveraging the reuse of digital assets to improve product and service delivery.

Chapters 22 and 23 are dedicated to the adoption of MBPLE. The former chapter presents the MBPLE adoption quadrant (MBPLEAQ) tool, which is useful for identifying the MBPLE adoption route an organization can take based on its current maturity. The latter chapter complements the MBPLEAQ with an adoption framework that includes considerations about processes, methods, information models, tool chains, and organization. Chapter 23 further stresses the importance of upfront planning and clear goal definitions when making use of the framework.

Chapter 24 highlights the necessity of tailoring the approach presented in Chapter 12 to specific organizational contexts, customer requirements and project needs. Each stage of the approach is mapped to the technical processes of ISO/IEC 15288 (ISO/IEC 2023). To support the previous approach, Chapter 25 explores the development and continuous improvement of organization- and tool-specific methods, highlighting the importance of adapting standardized approaches to meet the needs of an organization.

Chapters 26 and 27 are respectively dedicated to the MBPLE Information Model and to an examination of the MBPLE tool chain that should support it. Using Systems Modeling Language (SysML) as the primary language, Chapter 26 details the abstract syntax and semantics of MBPLE concepts. The notion of information modeling is briefly introduced before the information models of the feature model, shared assets superset, and product portfolio concepts are defined. Chapter 27 presents what an MBPLE tool chain should be in terms of its key components and importance for the successful adoption of MBPLE in an organization.

Chapter 28 pulls together the concepts presented throughout Section IV and proposes general principles to set up an MBPLE organization. As an example of how these principles can be incarnated, the chapter proposes two generic organizational patterns. The chapter concludes with an analysis of the application of agile principles in the context of MBPLE, the setup of an MBPLE adoption team, and a clarification on the concept of "product lines-of-product lines".

Part IV concludes with a cross-interview of Dr. Danilo Beuche and Dr. Charles Krueger, two of the pioneers of the PLE world.

21

A Business Case for MBPLE

21.1 Introduction

From what has been exposed throughout this book, the reader can probably draw a logical conclusion about the purpose of model-based product line engineering (MBPLE): it should first and foremost be regarded as a way to improve the profitability of a business. This is achieved by maximizing the benefits of applying smart reuse strategies on digital assets to enhance the delivery of products and services. The path to fulfilling this goal requires conferring to an organization a clear vision of customer needs in given target markets and the capabilities to efficiently adapt its products to these needs. This should naturally lead organizations to higher overall performances and more successful and sustainable results in the long term.

While the previous arguments might be enticing and sound like sheer common sense (in particular, and without a doubt, to product line engineering (PLE) and MBPLE practitioners), they are usually insufficient to convince decision-makers and drive the transformation of the delivery approach of an organization. The objective of this chapter is to provide elements that can help to build an appealing business case for MBPLE. Whilst Section 21.2 presents the problem of clone-and-own approaches and the opportunity to shift to MBPLE (by analyzing scalability and maintenance as well as development cost and lead time), Section 21.3 presents a value proposition of MBPLE adoption that includes cost-effectiveness, lead time improvement, quality improvement, and return on investment. The reader must bear in mind, however, that the curves presented in the rest of this chapter to support the value proposition have been anonymized for confidentiality reasons.

21.2 The Problem and Opportunity Space

In today's competitive and global marketplace, it is increasingly difficult to find organizations and customers who are fully satisfied with the business performance of traditional reuse approaches to deliver bespoke solutions. In addition, fast-evolving, disruptive technologies can impose the need for new system architectures and thus, according to Conway's law, the need for a new organization (a huge challenge for many companies). However, still today, the most frequent reuse approach consists of delivering product variants that are custom-fit to match the specific needs of individual customers using "clone-and-own" procedures (see Chapter 3), which impede more agile and faster delivery of products, in particular, large-scale products.

Model-Based Product Line Engineering (MBPLE): The Feature-Based Path to Product Lines Success, First Edition.
Marco Forlingieri et al.

In order to keep pace with competition and changing operational contexts, customers in many sectors are indeed demanding frequent and modular upgrades, lower development costs, and faster delivery time. Even in the world of aerospace and defense, customers are now asking for faster, recurrent modular upgrades, which provide the system capabilities that are required on the field (INCOSE 2019). These new rules of the game, along with the growing complexity of systems and business contexts (as explained in Chapters 2 and 3), have pushed traditional clone-and-own reuse methods to their limits.

21.2.1 Scalability and Maintenance

Probably the most visible problem of traditional clone-and-own reuse methods is a well-known difficulty in the software development domain, usually referred to as "branching hell." Branching hell arises when an organization decides to allow for multiple customer-specific developments or fixes, which are dealt with in separate development "branches." In a nutshell, the problem is: "the more branching a product does, the more overhead for maintenance, validation, and configuration management," as discussed in Chapter 19. This state of affairs can become a big issue in the software world. When transposed to the development of large-scale complex systems, it can quickly reach gigantic proportions.

Let us take the example of error correction or debugging, an activity where branching can really become pure hell. First of all, let us assume (and this is a big conjecture) that when the clone-and-own mechanism is operated to create a new branch, engineers are able to clearly identify and keep track of the version that "best suits" their problem among the existing branches of the product. Since many large-scale systems will remain in operation for 20–40 years, the first issue concerns maintenance over the life cycle of these systems (debugging notwithstanding). If you are running a successful business, you may have *N* operational systems on the field (remember, these are all independent in a clone-and-own reuse approach). This means you will have to provide separate maintenance for the N individual systems over a long period of time.

Now, imagine that at one point in time, a bug is found in one of the systems in operation. The second issue that arises is that, to perform a proper job, one would most probably need to have all the customer-specific versions available (or have *N* digital twins of the *N* systems in operation) to reproduce the error. This brings along a third issue: finding out where the bug came from in the first place. In which branch was the bug introduced? Did it exist in the version that was cloned to create the branch in which the bug was found? This brings, in turn, the fourth and most costly issue: correcting the error. In the best case, this correction is conducted in a point-to-point scheme (i.e. between only two branches), meaning that the cost of correcting errors in a clone-and-own approach is proportional to 2^N (Figure 21.1). It might also happen that every branch conducts specific correction actions on its own. For more details about this matter, see Chapter 18, where we explore the topic of configuration management.

Finally, at some other point in time, the organization may decide that the best option would be to redevelop the product "from scratch" because the current branches have become utterly unmaintainable. This again implies huge new investments for the organization and higher costs for its customers.

As previously explained in Chapter 3, clone-and-own approaches might be suitable in certain limited cases (like when trying to penetrate a new market for the first time with a breakthrough solution derived from a previous product) or for certain types of industries in which a new product instance is delivered only every other lustrum or decade. But even in those situations, starting from scratch might be a more effective solution than clone-and-own. Indeed, three *sine qua non* prerequisites must be in place for such an approach to have a chance to succeed. First, teams involved in the development and delivery of the product must be black belt and eighth dan in configuration

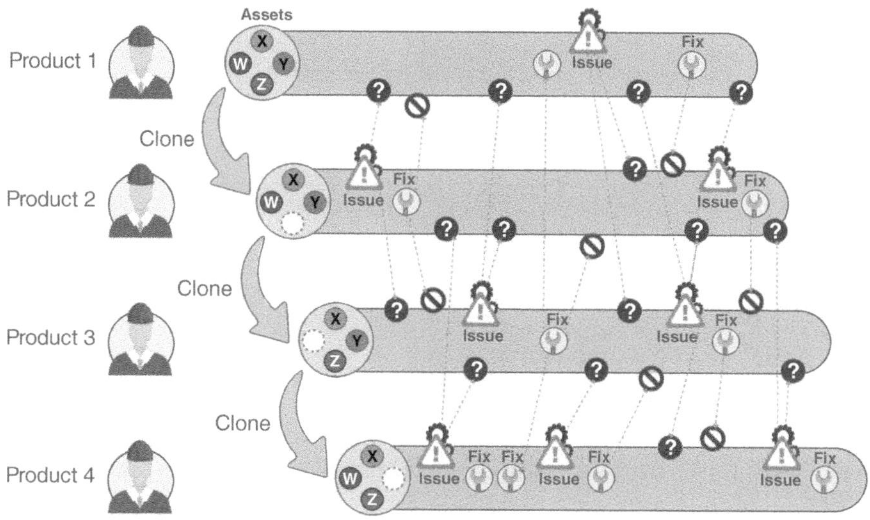

Figure 21.1 Correcting errors in a clone-and-own approach (without MBPLE).

management. Second, the technical debt of the product that will be used to create the new clone must be estimated and thoroughly documented. Third, an up-to-date architecture description document along with its justification file must be properly formalized and available.

Note: Throughout their careers, the authors of this book have very (very) rarely come across teams that met such high standards.

21.2.2 Development Costs and Lead Time

While the previous section was devoted to maintenance and debugging costs, we will mainly focus on development costs in the present section. Figure 21.2 shows a typical evolution of cumulative development costs in a clone-and-own approach as a function of delivered product instances. As we can see, cumulated development costs are proportional to the number of product instances N in a clone-and-own approach (continuous line in Figure 21.2). For completeness sake, Figure 21.2 also shows the total cumulated costs, including debugging costs, as exposed in the previous section (dotted line).

The curves in Figure 21.2 can be explained by several factors. On one hand, verification and validation costs and delays are usually incompressible in a clone-and-own approach. The reason for this is that, since teams that "own the clone" do not have, in general, a precise estimation of the technical debt of the product being cloned, they all tend to perform full verification and validation campaigns independently of what has been carried out on the product being cloned or in previous product instances. This is just a normal human reaction by which teams try to reassure themselves with some level of confidence in the delivered cloned product.

On the other hand, even though teams are supposed to reuse an existing product, the modifications that they must perform to adapt the clone to the specific needs of a given customer usually translate into the development of fixes, additional debugging activities, and integration work that are very often underestimated (as explained in the previous section). This unanticipated work, which naturally translates into higher costs and longer lead times regarding original project goals, tends to grow exponentially when the product that is cloned is poorly documented in terms of architecture, justification of design choices, or technical debt.

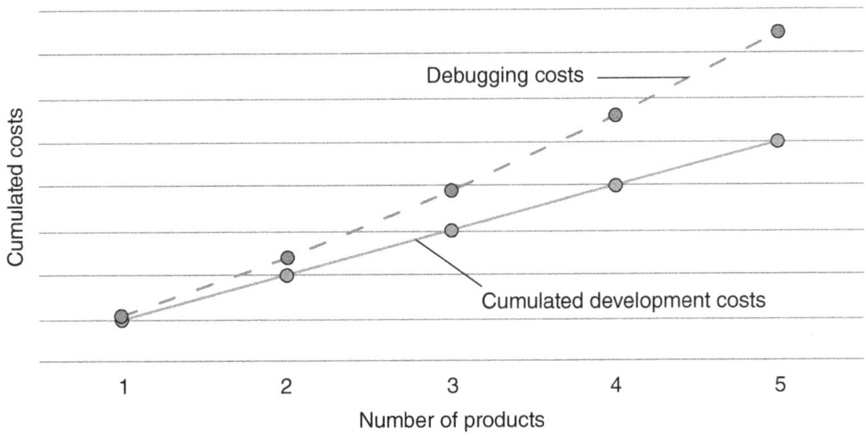

Figure 21.2 Cumulated development costs in a clone-and-own approach (without MBPLE).

21.3 MBPLE Value Proposition

The value proposition of MBPLE is based on a very simple principle: Transitioning from the management of many independent products, built through relatively large and siloed development projects, to a single endeavor (aka Product Line Program) that delivers product instances via smaller, more cost-effective developments (Navas et al. 2023).

MBPLE enables the management of the resulting portfolio of related products as one single entity instead of having to manage separately many single entities. The relations among the shared asset supersets of the product line, and among those and all of their product models, are indeed formalized, explicit, tracked, and maintained over time. The MBPLE digital thread provides a solid foundation for effective decision-making by enabling, for instance, impact analyses, sensitivity analyses, and multidisciplinary analyses (see Chapter 18). Once again, to be successful, this new way of working must become the common delivery approach of the entire organization as introduced in Chapter 5.

As stated in previous chapters, models also contribute to the cost-effectiveness improvement brought by MBPLE, thanks to the formal or semi-formal languages in which models are described. These languages not only support communication among teams or facilitate interoperability, but they also support advanced verification activities. Examples of these activities include checking that assets possess the expected properties or verifying that assets are correct, complete, and consistent with regard to other assets.

In the following paragraphs, the benefits of MBPLE are further developed. They are proposed as different components to build a business case for MBPLE.

21.3.1 Cost-effectiveness Improvement

The most visible benefit of MBPLE is undoubtedly the cost-effectiveness of the approach. In this section, we focus on cost avoidance and lead-time improvements. Section 21.3.3 further dwells on required investments and the overall return of investments.

Let us start by comparing the cumulated development costs of a given number of products developed with a clone-and-own approach and with an MBPLE approach (Figure 21.3). The light gray

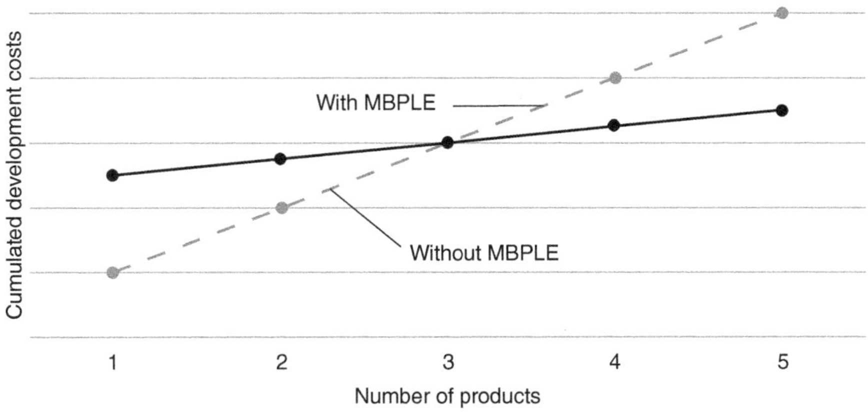

Figure 21.3 Comparison of cumulated development costs with and without MBPLE (theoretical).

line in Figure 21.3 represents the cumulated costs in the former approach as a function of the number of member products, as presented in Section 21.2.2. The dark gray line represents the cumulated costs in an MBPLE approach for the same number of member products.

As we can see in the figure, the initial cumulated costs of the MBPLE approach are higher because of the initial investments required to implement the approach. Up to the third member product, the cumulated costs of the MBPLE approach are higher than those of the clone-and-own approach (i.e. without MBPLE). The point where the two lines cross represents the payoff point of the MBPLE approach. By experience, this point is typically reached between the second and fourth member products. From that point on, the cumulated costs of the clone-and-own approach become higher than those of the MBPLE approach.

The area between the two lines to the right of the payoff point represents the benefits obtained with the MBPLE approach. Of course, the higher the number of member products, the higher the benefits obtained with an MBPLE approach. The theoretical representation in Figure 21.4 suggests that the required investments to implement MBPLE are available from the start, including the first member product. This is not the case for many large-scale systems or within large organizations, in which investments are granted gradually on a multi-year basis (we elaborate further on this aspect in Section 21.3.3).

One way of evaluating the cost-effectiveness of MBPLE is to consider the engineering efforts (thus, engineering costs) that are avoided when implementing the approach. Figure 21.4 shows the effort avoidance to perform a *development task* in an MBPLE approach for a given number of impacted member products. A development task represents any activity, work package, or work product that has a clearly defined scope, whose execution is required to deliver a member product, and whose associated effort (or workload) can be measured. Examples include issuing a validation plan, writing product brochures or issuing cost estimations for calls for tenders, writing a system requirement specification document, correcting a bug, writing an interface control document, producing the code of a software module, or drawing mechanical or electrical design diagrams.

Each bar in Figure 21.4 is associated with a given number of member products that are impacted by the task. The black zone of each bar represents the "unitary effort" to execute the task (i.e. perform an activity or produce the expected work product). The dashed zone represents the effort required to implement MBPLE for the given task (like transforming artifacts required to execute the task into shareable, reusable assets, setting up tools, or instantiating assets), which

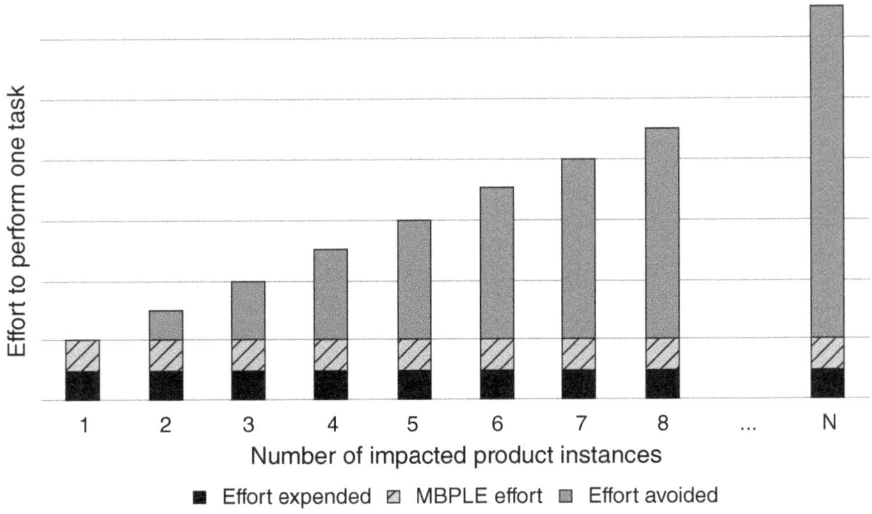

Figure 21.4 Effort avoidance to perform a task, thanks to MBPLE. *Source:* Adapted from INCOSE 2019.

is independent of the number of impacted member products. The light gray zone represents the effort that would be required to execute the task for each of the impacted member products in a clone-and-own approach. For example, the effort required to execute the task for two member products would be two times the unitary effort (i.e. the task would be executed once for each member product); the effort required to execute the task for three product instances would be three times the unitary effort, and so on and so forth.

The efforts represented by the light gray zones are thus the efforts that do not need to be provided in an MBPLE approach. Indeed, the efforts to implement MBPLE for a given task and to execute the task are only provided once for the benefit of all member products, whatever their number. If we go back to the example of bug detection and correction exposed in the previous section, let us assume that an error has been detected and needs to be corrected. In an MBPLE approach, the correction would only be performed once on the shared asset supersets of the product line, then deployed to the member products (this would be done by deriving the new version of the assets thanks to the automation capabilities of MBPLE). Of course, the decision to deploy the correction on the derived products must be done on a member product-by-member product basis, taking into consideration the criticality of the defect found, the development stage, and original configuration of each derived member product.

21.3.2 Lead Time Improvement

To establish a relation between engineering efforts and lead time, one needs to have an estimation of the available workforce in the organization. In our example, if the organization has enough workforce to parallelize the correction of each product instance, then the impact on lead time would be neglectable. However, if that is not the case, the correction of the product instances would rather occur in a serial mode (i.e. one, two, or three member products at a time, depending on the available workforce). The impact on lead time would then be proportional to the number of derived products.

It is worth underlining that MBPLE also provides the capabilities to perform quick impact analysis and provide useful information for decision-making before performing the correction.

On the one hand, impact analysis enabled by the MBPLE digital thread will point out what assets (and what parts of those assets) would need to be upgraded. Then, automated non-regression tests would be performed only once, all configurations of the member products being known. On the other hand, if the results of the impact analysis show that only a reduced number of member products are concerned, the correction would only be deployed on those member products.

Finally, it is easy to imagine that teams that perform their work in a clone-and-own approach and without the analysis and automation capabilities provided by MBPLE do so in highly stressful conditions. Such working environments are naturally more error-prone and have negative impacts on productivity, thus on lead time. One could thus argue that the inherent characteristics of MBPLE have a liberating effect on teams and organizations that adopt it.

21.3.3 Quality Improvement

Figures 21.3 and 21.4 (in addition to Figures 21.5 and 21.6) point to a simple MBPLE principle: "the more member products you derive, the more you gain." This same principle applies to the quality of a product line or, to be more precise, to the quality of the derived products of the product line.

Integration, verification, validation, and qualification (IVVQ) are the first activities for which gains are obtained when implementing MBPLE in an organization. These are mainly performed on the derived products of a product line. When a member product goes through an IVVQ campaign, the product configuration that was used for its derivation earns what we may call validation or qualification "credits." Therefore, the more a product configuration is used to derive similar products, the higher the credits of this configuration will be. In some industries, it is even possible to qualify a product (or parts of a product) via "demonstration" or "certificate" in order to avoid performing full IVVQ campaigns, as long as it can be proven that the product configuration and the context in which the product will operate remain unchanged with respect to previously qualified products.

Figure 21.5 shows the evolution of the volume of IVVQ activities as a function of the number of derived products. This figure shows that the more a given product configuration is used, the more it becomes "mature" in terms of validation and qualification. As a consequence, the volume of IVVQ activities tends to decrease as the number of instantiated products issued from the same product configuration grows.

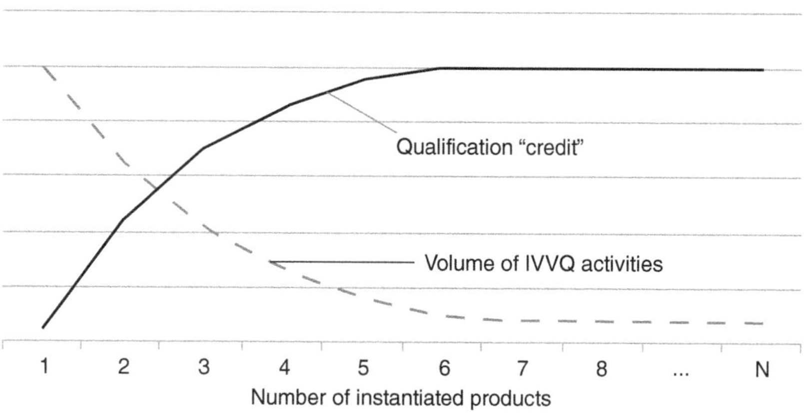

Figure 21.5 Volume of IVVQ activities and qualification credit as a function of the number of derived products issued from the same product configuration.

Figure 21.5 also shows that the volume of IVVQ activities eventually reaches an asymptote, which means that there will always remain a certain volume of IVVQ activities to be performed. This is particularly true for safety-critical and mission-critical systems, as detailed in Chapter 24.

As different feature configurations are used to derive different member products over time, the full scope of a product line is gradually covered. While performing the IVVQ of the 150% product line is practically impossible, the more different member products are validated and qualified, the higher the "credits" of the product line as a whole will be. Finally, it is worth underlining that validating and qualifying all unconstrained potential member products of a product line is neither feasible nor desirable. In this case, defining a reduced number of planned member products that meet the needs of targeted markets, market segments, or even categories of customers, as explained in the previous chapters, looks like good practice. These allowed configurations contribute to reducing the qualification space and to obtaining the qualification of the product line as a whole at a faster pace.

21.3.4 The Return on Investment of MBPLE

Challengers of MBPLE and PLE usually advance the arguments of the "huge" initial investment that is required to set up a product line approach compared to the traditional clone-and-own approach and the "long" period of time that is required to reach the payoff point and start obtaining benefits. This short-sighted view puts aside the fact that, like the money one would invest in a financial product, MBPLE is indeed an investment. Just like the money one would put in an investment plan, MBPLE provides higher dividends in the mid- to long term. If a person decides to go for the immediate quick win or withdraw the money from the bank before the investment plan reaches its term, chances are this person will either lose money or not obtain the maximum benefits in the long term (which in the end accounts for the same). But the person has indeed the choice.

As stated in Section 21.3.1, the required investments to set up a product line are not usually granted in their entirety right at the program kick-off. Investments are more commonly granted gradually on a year-to-year basis and usually follow some sort of "stairway-shaped" curve, as shown in Figure 21.6.

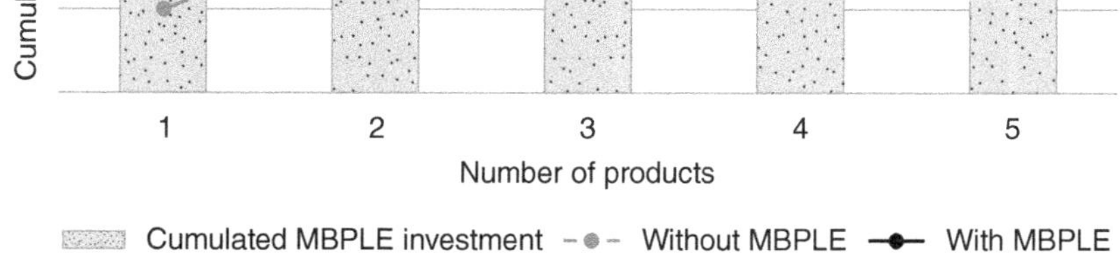

Figure 21.6 Cumulated development costs with and without MBPLE considering a gradual investment scheme.

There are two notable differences between this figure and the theoretical curve shown in Figure 21.3. First, we can observe that the payoff point can be reached "sooner" when investments are done gradually (which is quite logical because the initial investments are smaller). Second, we can also observe that, compared to the theoretical curve, cumulated costs for MBPLE are slightly higher in this type of investment scheme. This is due to the fact that the cost of instantiation tends to be slightly higher in the latter case because setting up the "product line factory" would require some additional preparation work for every instance as the scope of the product line grows with newly developed features or shared assets of different nature. Still, the area between the light and dark gray lines to the right of the payoff point (which, as stated before, represents the benefits obtained with the MBPLE approach) is worth considering.

In a purely analytical approach, the return on investment of MBPLE could be estimated as the ratio of the initial investment and the obtained benefits (savings or avoided costs). A more pertinent estimation of the value and the return on investment of MBPLE could be obtained by calculating the ratio of the areas between the two lines to the right (i.e. the benefits of MBPLE with respect to traditional clone-and-own approaches) and to the left (i.e. the investment cost of MBPLE with respect to clone-and-own approaches) of the payoff point in Figure 21.3 or 21.6. Without dwelling further into numbers, let us just insist on the fact that the higher the number of derived products, the higher this ratio will be (thus, the higher the return on investment of MBPLE).

Figure 21.7 shows a comparison of typical nonrecurring costs (NRC) curves associated with three different delivery approaches: clone-and-own, delivery using modeling and simulation, and MBPLE-based delivery. The NRC shown in Figure 21.7 only includes costs related to design, development, implementation, and initial investments.

As stated earlier, the initial cost required to set up the MBPLE approach usually requires a higher initial investment, which explains why the set of curves related to a first member product derivation is very similar among the different approaches (we made the assumption that setting up modeling and simulation capabilities also requires a higher initial investment compared to clone-and-own approaches). The curves on the right of Figure 21.7 represent the cumulated nonrecurring costs for a given number of member products over a period of time (the same number

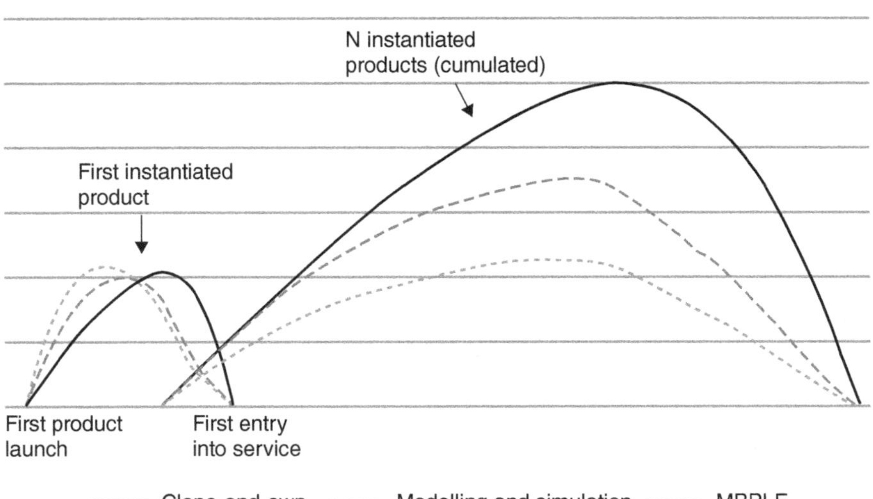

Figure 21.7 Nonrecurring cost comparison between three different approaches (clone-and-own, modeling and simulation alone, MBPLE).

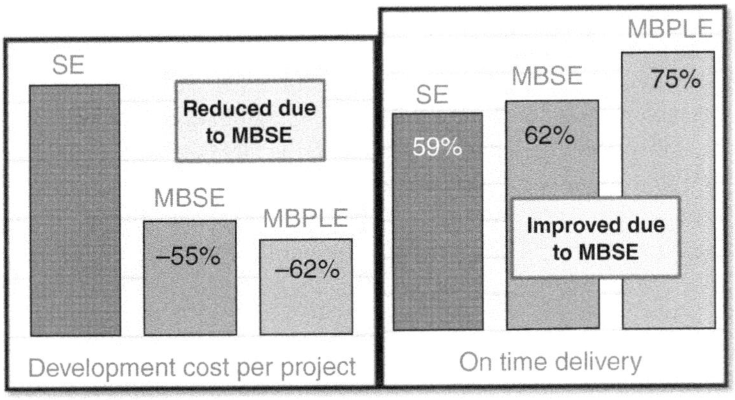

Figure 21.8 Comparison of development costs and on-time delivery obtained with SE, MBSE, and MBPLE. *Source:* Adapted from Carroll and Malins, 2016 / U.S. Department of Energy / Public domain.

for the three approaches). This figure provides an example of the type of decision tools that can be used by a company to simulate different cases and decide on the level of investments to be allocated to a product line based on risk-to-benefit estimations.

An interesting literature review of the justification of MBSE is provided in (Carroll and Malins 2016). Among the many sources analyzed by the review is a study that drew a comparison between the results obtained by projects using MBSE, MBPLE, and traditional SE based on the analysis of several hundreds of projects (Figure 21.8). This work revealed that projects using an MBSE approach cost 55% less than projects applying traditional SE. In addition, projects using MBSE deliver on time 62% of the time, compared to 59% for traditional SE. Finally, it appears that applying MBPLE translates into even higher benefits: 62% cost reduction and 75% on-time delivery.

Beyond the numbers, the value of MBPLE relies on its capacity to act as an enabler of profitable growth for an organization (see Chapter 28). When engineering teams improve their performance by executing engineering tasks only once (instead of many times for a plethora of different products) and are relieved from performing manual, repetitive tasks through automation, they are enabled to "do more." The budget and resources that are made available, thanks to MBPLE, can now be used, for instance, to explore other business opportunities or work on innovative features to grow the business.

Therefore, probably the right question a top manager, CTO, or CEO should ask themselves when trying to decide whether implementing MBPLE is pertinent or not for the business is not about the return on investment, but rather, "What should I ask my engineering teams do when they have finished their week's job by Wednesday afternoon?"

References

Carroll, E.R. and Malins, J.R. (2016). *Systematic Literature Review: How is Model-Based Systems Engineering Justified.* https://doi.org/10.2172/1561164.

INCOSE (2019). *Feature-Based System and Software Product Line Engineering: A Primer.* San Diego: INCOSE.

Navas, J., Bonnet, S., Voirin J.L. and Chalé Gongora, H.G. (2023). A value-driven, integrated approach to model-based product line engineering. *INCOSE 2023 International Symposium.* (Hawaii, USA), San Diego: INCOSE.

22

The MBPLE Adoption Quadrant

22.1 Introduction

It is emphasized throughout this book that adopting model-based product line engineering (MBPLE) is not an "overnight" effort; it requires time to be implemented and accepted within a corporate context. Its adoption depends on several factors, but two main drivers justify its implementation: the increasing level of system complexity and the variability experienced by the organization, as introduced in Chapter 2. In theory, a company could transition from predominantly document-based (single) systems engineering to model-based development of product lines and their derived products. However, the practice shows that other transitional development approaches are usually encountered before MBPLE can be fully adopted.

To simplify and visualize the transition from one stage to another, we developed the "MBPLE adoption quadrant" (MBPLEAQ), illustrated in Figure 22.1.

On the vertical axis, we see the degree of complexity of the system under development, while on the horizontal axis, we see the degree of variability.

We identified four incremental development approaches depending on the degree of both variables. The lower-left quadrant is where systems with relatively low levels of complexity and variability can be found. In this case, a traditional document-based system engineering approach with a single-system development scope might not be the best approach for the company, but it is still sufficient. The upper-left quadrant is associated with systems that present a higher level of complexity but low variability. An MBSE approach is the most suitable here. In the lower-right quadrant, we observe systems with relatively low levels of complexity but a higher degree of variability. In this case, a system family engineering approach (aka feature-based product line engineering [PLE]) is sufficient and may not justify the investment in a model-based approach. Finally, in the upper-right quadrant, we position systems that present both high degrees of complexity and variability. These systems will benefit the most from the MBPLE adoption.

The adoption quadrant also serves to explain the different patterns of the MBPLE adoption. The transition phases from one quadrant to another are also important and are the main focus of this chapter. The MBPLEAQ is a useful tool for companies to understand where they stand and whether the level of complexity and variability experienced by their products necessitates an MBPLE approach.

Section 22.2 briefly covers the transition from document-based (single) systems engineering to model-based systems engineering. Section 22.3 shows the pattern from a document-based (single)

Model-Based Product Line Engineering (MBPLE): The Feature-Based Path to Product Lines Success, First Edition.
Marco Forlingieri et al.

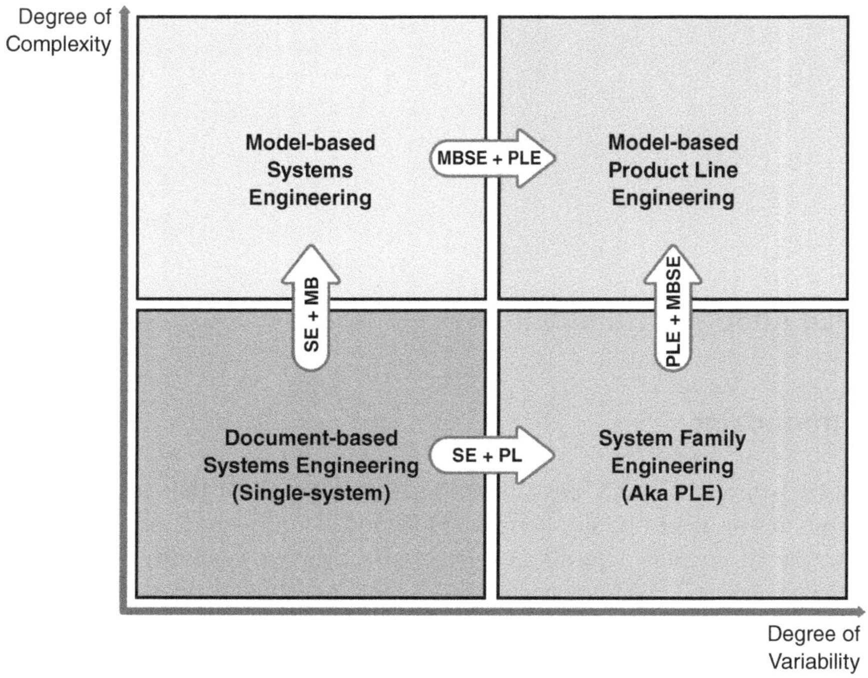

Figure 22.1 MBPLE adoption quadrant (MBPLEAQ).

system development to a system family engineering (aka feature-based PLE) approach. Sections 22.4 and 22.5 present the transition to MBPLE from MBSE and from system family engineering (aka feature-based PLE), respectively.

22.2 From Document-based Systems Engineering to Model-based Systems Engineering

The topic of this section is the center of gravity of Chapter 8, where the key aspects of such transitions are discussed. However, it is important to focus on the intermediate step that companies adopt while shifting to MBSE. The transition is well explained by "the evolution of MBSE" represented in the book *Systems Engineering Demystified* (Holt 2022).

Companies usually first experience a model-enhanced stage, where textual requirements are still central but models are linked to them to establish traceability and enhance their understanding (see arrow "SE + MB" in Figure 22.1). Only after the stage has reached its limits in dealing with increasing complexity, the company can implement an MBSE approach (both approaches model-centric and model-based are considered part of MBSE).

22.3 From Document-based Systems Engineering to System Family Engineering (Aka PLE)

Once the product portfolio of a company increases in variety, the variability of the systems developed tends also to rise, becoming with the time hard to manage and control. At this stage, companies start to look at approaches, such as reuse, modularization, architecture composability, and clone-and-own (see Chapter 3). The latest technique is usually the most natural and adopted, even when the organization announces to benefit from a product line-based approach (see "SE + PL" arrow in Figure 22.1). This trend is well documented in the literature (Clements et al. 2014; Chalé Góngora et al. 2014) and it is part of the historical evolution of PLE as a discipline (see the "Dolly Era" in Chapter 7). We experienced such a transition in the early phases of our involvement at Renault, Alstom. Bombardier, Thales, and Airbus as well as the numerous organizations consulted along our professional careers.

22.4 From Model-based Systems Engineering to Model-based Product Line Engineering

In industrial contexts, we often encounter the false myth or misunderstanding that MBPLE is only centered on the modeling of variability with systems modeling language (SysML) assets. This is a wrong statement as discussed already in Chapter 8, when we introduced the definition of MBPLE as: "the application of feature-based PLE in combination with MBSE where architecture models are central but not exclusive for realizing the product line and its member products." However, in the transition phase from MBSE to MBPLE, it is often the case that the PLE approach will be exclusively focused on the SysML assets, especially when the team or division adopting it has a strong focus on the model-based discipline (see "MBSE + PLE" arrow in Figure 22.1). In this way, the other domain models do not benefit from the feature-based PLE approach and variability inconsistencies may arise. Soon it becomes evident the need to extend the feature-based PLE approach to other domains, such as requirements, MCAD, ECAD, etc., and integrate them within an MBPLE framework. A similar pattern is exemplified by the MBPLE adoption at Airbus (Madeira et al. 2023).

22.5 From System Family Engineering (Aka PLE) to Model-based Product Line Engineering

Several companies managed to successfully implement a PLE approach. However, in some cases, they do not have MBSE models as central assets of the PLE factory. This is often the case when organizations migrate from systems family engineering (not model based) to an MBPLE approach.

In the transition phase, the MBSE domain will be treated as any other domain to be included within a feature-based approach. However, in this way, the MBSE models will act as standalone models with low interdependencies with other assets such as textual requirements, MCAD, ECAD, SW architecture, test models etc. (see "PLE + MBSE" in Figure 22.1). Soon it will become evident that there is a need to create an MBSE framework (or even better, an MBPLE framework) that holds the parts together and brings consistency. This is when the organization transitions completely to the upper right quadrant (Figure 22.1).

22.6 The MBPLEAQ Applied in the Industrial Cases

The MBPLEAQ is a simplified "tool" that is primarily used to:

- Understand the differences between different systems engineering approaches when dealing with increasing complexity and variability;
- Assess where the organization is in the adoption of MBPLE;
- Identify the pattern undertaken in the MBPLE adoption.

In the last part of this book (Part V), we use the MBPLEAQ to visualize the paths toward the MBPLE adoption of the five organizations featured in the industrial cases.

References

Chalé Góngora, H.G., Ferrogalini, M. and Moreau, C. (2014). How to boost PLE by using MBSE – a case study of a rolling stock product line. *Proceedings of the 5th International Conference on Complex Systems Design and Management* (CSDM, Paris, FR). Springer.

Clements, P., Gregg, S.P., Krueger C. et al. (2014). *Second Generation Product Line Engineering Takes Hold in the DoD.* 27, 12–18.

Holt, J. (2023). *Systems Engineering Demystified: A Practitioners Handbook for Developing Complex Systems Using a Model-Based Approach,* 2e. Packt Publishing, Limited, UK.

Madeira, R.H., de Sousa Pinto, D.H. and Forlingieri, M. (2023). *Variability on System Architecture using Airbus MBPLE for MOFLT Framework.* Seville, Spain: INCOSE International Symposium, 33, 601–615.

23

The MBPLE Adoption Framework

23.1 Introduction

For most organizations, key advantages such as reducing development costs and time-to-market, enhancing the quality of design artifacts, managing complexity, and boosting reusability are central to evaluating the return on investment. These benefits also serve as fundamental principles that underscore the utility of model-based product line engineering (MBPLE). As indicated in Chapter 21, constructing a robust business case for adopting MBPLE is an essential initial step before proceeding with further activities. Although the literature extensively details the benefits of MBPLE (Chalé Góngora and Greugny 2017), each organization must identify specific advantages that motivate its adoption of MBPLE.

Similar to model-based systems engineering (MBSE), the adoption of MBPLE necessitates careful planning and clear definition of its essential pillars and enablers. As demonstrated by the MBPLE mission at Airbus, adopting the MBPLE approach requires adherence to standards and an incremental strategy to address product line development challenges while securing validation from key stakeholders (Forlingieri 2022). This adoption is not an "overnight" process and demands a deep understanding of the organizational context. Therefore, there is no universal formula; however, several critical components can be pinpointed. Reflecting on similarities with MBSE adoption, organization-driven MBSE methodologies and frameworks typically comprise three major parts: language, method, and tool (Delligatti 2013). Yet, the D3 MBSE Adoption Toolbox proposed by Chami et al. (2018) includes additional components, such as the "personnel." According to the MBPLE adoption framework at Airbus, the key dimensions of the MBPLE framework include process, methods, information model, tools, and environment.

These examples, among others discussed in the final section of this book as industrial cases, demonstrate that implementing a digital transformation where MBPLE is a key pillar necessitates a holistic approach. The MBPLE approach, in the context of digital transformation, extends beyond mere technology implementation and considers broader impacts on processes, people, and the organizational culture or environment (Straub et al. 2021). Building on these premises, a recommended adoption framework is introduced here, encompassing the following: process (Section 23.2), methods (Section 23.3), information model (Section 23.4), tool chain (Section 23.5), and organization (Section 23.6).

Analogous to the MBSE D3 Adoption Toolbox (Chami et al. 2018), these pillars are constructed and validated during the definition and development phases, and then rolled out within the organization and product programs during the deployment phase (that is why the D3 stands for). While the MBPLE team plays a critical role in the definition and development phases, during the

Model-Based Product Line Engineering (MBPLE): The Feature-Based Path to Product Lines Success, First Edition.
Marco Forlingieri et al.

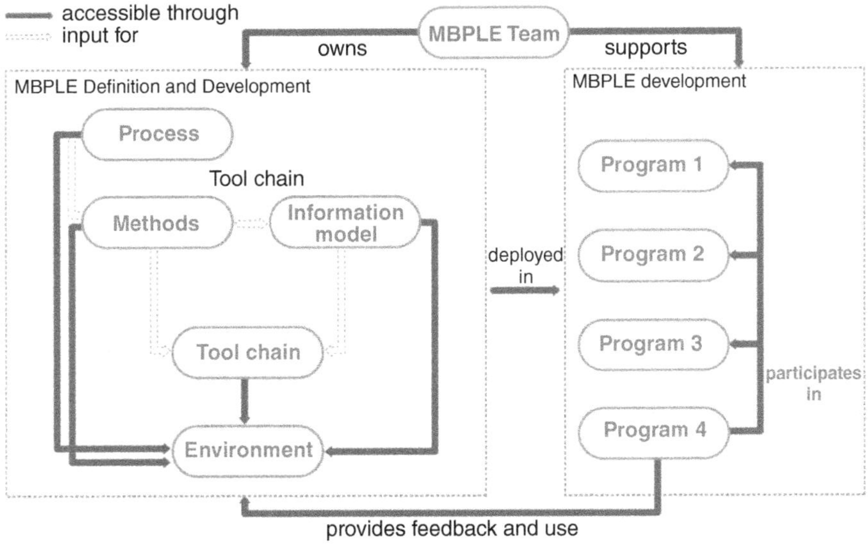

Figure 23.1 Overview of the MBPLE adoption framework and the three adoption phases.

deployment phase, programs begin to assume ownership of the framework. Figure 23.1 summarizes the adoption framework and its relationship to the three phases.

23.2 MBPLE Process

Companies that develop complex systems typically maintain extensive process landscapes to ensure efficient and effective operations. Those adhering to systems engineering principles, as specified in ISO/IEC 15288 (ISO/IEC/IEEE 2023a), already incorporate these processes as a fundamental part of their Product Development Process (PDP) (Ulrich and Eppinger 2004). ISO/IEC 15288 (ISO/IEC/IEEE 2023a) establishes standards for system lifecycle processes and provides guidance on integrating these processes into an organization's workflow. This is based on the necessity of aligning technical and management processes with the overarching business strategy.

MBPLE introduces a sophisticated approach to product development, concentrating on the creation and management of a product line and its member products. Within the PDP framework, it is crucial that MBPLE processes align with existing processes to ensure unified and effective operations.

Integrating MBPLE processes within the existing PDP requires a thoughtful adaptation of the current process landscape. This adaptation is essential to preserve the PDP's flexibility and responsiveness while meeting the unique demands and objectives of MBPLE. For example, adopting this approach enables more strategic resource allocation, moving from the single-product responsibility to the product line scope, enhanced cross-functional collaboration, and reduced duplications of responsibilities in development.

MBPLE significantly impacts a broad range of processes within an organization. From the technical management processes and technical processes (focus of Chapter 24) outlined by ISO/IEC 15288 (ISO/IEC/IEEE 2023a), to the broader business and procurement processes, the influence of MBPLE is comprehensive. For example, consider the configuration management processes. The focus here extends beyond a single system to include a product line and all its member products. This expansion adds complexity to configuration management practices as the scope of configuration becomes broader. More details about the role of configuration management in MBPLE are provided in Chapter 19, while Chapter 24 covers the process topic in depth.

23.3 MBPLE Methods

Methods are extensively utilized in systems engineering. They delineate the "How" for the "What" established by the process, detailing the steps while remaining independent of specific tools. It is not accurate to refer to a single MBPLE method; rather, it is more appropriate to discuss various MBPLE methods. Indeed, although the method for defining a feature model and linking features to those parts of the assets that represent a variation should be one and consistent, multiple methods can be formulated to manage the variability in each specific domain (e.g. requirements, SysML models, CADs, etc.). Given the impracticality of developing a standardized, universal method for MBPLE applicable across multiple domains, we have identified six takeaways, based primarily on our experience and public references, to assist methodologists in defining MBPLE methods.

Takeaway 1: The feature model shall be a distinct asset, serving as the sole source of variability across various domains

Initially, implementing feature models across diverse digital assets such as requirements, design models, and CADs is crucial for a comprehensive MBPLE approach. This practice facilitates uniform variability management across multiple types of assets, highlighting the significance of an integrated approach to managing variability. As stipulated by the most recent feature-based PLE standard ISO/IEC 26580 (ISO/IEC 2021), when the product line development lifecycle generates multiple assets, it is highly beneficial to develop and maintain the feature model as an independent source of variability, separate from any other assets (Malone et al. 2018).

Takeaway 2: MBPLE shall not solely concentrate on MBSE assets, yet these assets are central in ensuring consistent implementation of variability

MBSE Architecture frameworks like CAF at Continental (Seidel and Forlingieri 2023), and R-MOFLT at Airbus (Madeira et al. 2023), which are examples well known to us authors of this book, incorporate variability modeling into more traditional system modeling. Due to SysML v1's recognized limitations in supporting variability modeling, the representation of variability and product lines is often neglected in MBSE methods and frameworks (Madeira et al. 2023). When PLE mechanisms are integrated with MBSE, the shared assets superset is modeled, and the variation point is only connected to those model elements that are variable, as they do not appear in every product of the product line. However, one significant challenge of this approach is modeling a product line architecture that is both valid in SysML and conceptually robust according to the system semantics (Forlingieri and Weilkiens 2022). Since SysML models can encompass interdependencies ranging from requirements to CAD models, they help maintain consistency across different assets. For example, a logical architecture can meet system requirements and form the basis for a structure that is further developed into a Feature-oriented MCAD model. In this context, the SysML model ensures consistency among these various assets. When introducing variability into requirements, SysML models, MCADs, and so forth, the feature model acts as the single source of variability to be implemented across the assets, and the SysML model ensures a consistent implementation across these assets. This principle forms the fundamental assumption of MBPLE: it does not imply focusing exclusively on SysML models, but rather on the model-based approach to ensure a consistent implementation of variability.

Takeaway 3: Variability is inherently multidimensional, and this characteristic should be reflected in the definition of MBPLE methods

Chapter 17 of this book introduces and develops the four dimensions of variability: co-variability in product, manufacturing, and services; variability in development lifecycle; variability in layers of abstraction; and variability in system hierarchy levels. These dimensions, initially identified at Airbus (Forlingieri 2022), provided the organization with crucial insights for developing MBPLE methods. For example, considering an aircraft, the variability of the system of interest (SoI) – the aircraft in the Airbus case – must account for variability inputs from the final assembly line (FAL) and vice versa, if the SoI is the FAL. The second dimension emphasizes that variability must be addressed throughout the entire lifecycle, from concept design to after-delivery customization. Variability then cascades hierarchically along systems levels top-down from the market but can also be infused bottom-up by legacy solutions and suppliers. Last but not least, variability may be pertinent at one abstraction layer (e.g. the physical layer) but irrelevant at another (e.g., the functional layer). This multidimensionality of variability in complex systems makes the model-based approach more necessary than a choice, when implementing feature-based PLE.

Takeaway 4: MBPLE methods should be developed incrementally while maintaining a focus on the broader picture

Given that MBPLE methods are applicable to all domains involved in a product line's development, it is impractical to comprehensively cover all domains at once before beginning to implement and deploy MBPLE methods. This statement should not be misinterpreted. It is essential to develop an information model that captures all assets within the scope and their interdependencies, but this does not necessitate having a fully detailed method developed for each asset. Capitalizing from lessons learned at Alstom (Chalé Góngora et al. 2014), Airbus (Madeira et al. 2023), and Continental (Seidel and Forlingieri 2023) across three distinct industries, a practical starting point for defining methods is to initially focus on textual requirements and SysML models. Given the complexity of such systems, it is advisable to first establish a method that might involve modeling variation in a SysML model or defining a feature model, initially at one hierarchical level before expanding to multiple levels. Another example, limited to the SysML model, is to start with modeling variation in SysML by focusing on structural views before progressing to behavioral ones, once sufficient experience has been gained.

Takeaway 5: Tools and tool chains shall not dictate the definition of MBPLE methods

This statement does not imply that tools are unnecessary or irrelevant. Rather, it stresses the importance of defining methods independently of any specific tool or tool chain initially (Forlingieri and Weilkiens 2022). It is crucial, after establishing this foundation, to assess how the methods align with what existing tools can provide and identify any discrepancies. Tools are designed to help organizations address challenges and should not dictate the standards or direction of method development activities. This principle applies not only to the development of MBPLE methods but also to any methodological definition.

Takeaway 6: MBPLE methods shall consistently serve and facilitate the needs of the end-users
A fundamental objective of MBPLE methods is to enhance the modeling process and the end-user experience by minimizing effort and potential discrepancies. It is essential to collaborate closely with principal end-users to pinpoint their specific needs for variability management and to implement the methods across diverse domains, while welcoming feedback for enhancements. This focus on the user ensures that MBPLE methods remain effective and flexible in various organizational environments (Madeira et al. 2023).

Chapter 25 covers this topic more extensively, providing some more examples of methods.

23.4 MBPLE Information Model

In Chapter 7, we revisit the historical development of feature modeling languages and the creation of SysML. While SysML benefits from a standardized language (ISO/IEC 2017), this is not the case for feature modeling or variability languages. The common variability language (Haugen et al. 2012) represented the most significant effort to define a standard for variability modeling, drawing from the Feature oriented domain analysis language (Kang et al. 1990). However, it ultimately failed, and not due to technical reasons alone!

Instead of focusing solely on the language, it is more appropriate to discuss the information model. This is because MBPLE encompasses more than just the modeling language; it requires an information model that spans all the domains involved in MBPLE. Such an information model enables the mapping of elements to method outputs and maintains tool independence across methods. A notable example is the Systems Engineering Common Architecture Model (SECAM) from Airbus (Wirtz and Bouffaron, 2020), which also incorporates the variability aspect. Ideally, an information model should address the components of a feature model and their connections to other assets. Chapter 26 digs deeper into this subject.

23.5 MBPLE Tool Chain

In the preceding section, we emphasize an essential principle for defining MBPLE methods: "Tools and tool chains should not determine the definition of MBPLE methods." There should be a clear separation between method formalization and its implementation using a specific tool or tool chain. MBPLE methods should be supported by an information model, as previously mentioned, to facilitate the mapping of method activities to different tools. This approach is crucial as it helps mitigate lock-in effects and enhances the interoperability of assets among various internal and external stakeholders.

A definition of an MBPLE tool chain, like any tool chain, needs to incorporate an As-Is topology that reflects the existing tools based on current methods and a To-be topology that plans for the future integration of tools in a subsequent phase. This strategy should be paired with a roadmap,

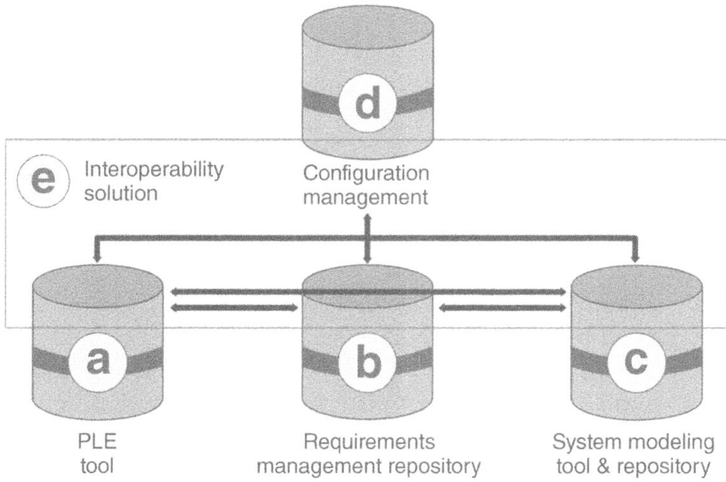

Figure 23.2 Simplified basic MBPLE tool chain.

providing visibility into what tools will be available and when, which assists the MBPLE team in prioritizing their solutions' definition and development. It is unrealistic to initially define a comprehensive MBPLE tool chain and then implement it.

Figure 23.2 displays a basic MBPLE tool chain (Chalé Góngora et al. 2014), which includes:

(a) PLE tool
(b) Requirements management repository
(c) System modeling tool and repository
(d) Overarching configuration management
(e) Interoperability solution for tools to exchange data, queries

The diagram illustrates the PLE tool (a) as a distinct entity, not integrated within other solutions. It facilitates the definition and management of feature models and configurations, linking variable assets to features, and enabling the transformation of assets from other domain-specific tools. The requirements management repository (b) contains sets of textual requirements with variations and interfaces with the PLE tool. Similarly, the system modeling tool and repository (c) should also connect with the PLE tool. A configuration management solution (d) sits atop the other domain applications, managing and controlling the configuration of assets. The interoperability (e) among the applications in scope shall be built on existing standards such as OSLC (OSLC 2021) and MoSSEC (ISO 2021). Such a basic tool chain already offers robust MBPLE capabilities and supports its initial deployment.

However, the MBPLE team should also envision a more extensive solution by outlining and working towards the definition and deployment of a broader tool chain (Chalé Góngora et al. 2014), as depicted in Figure 23.3, which might include:

(f) Software repository
(g) Test repository
(h) BOM tool and repository
(i) CAD tool and repository
(j) Others

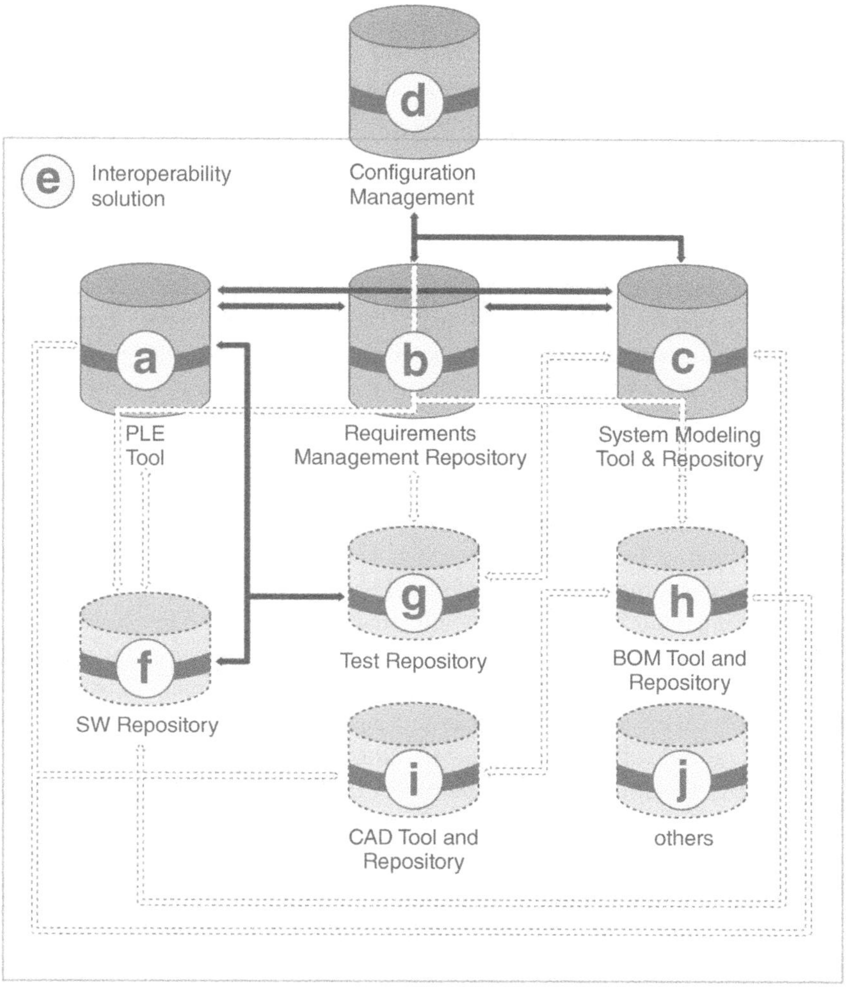

Figure 23.3 More comprehensive MBPLE tool chain.

We advise that the additional applications shown in light gray in Figure 23.3 be implemented in a second phase, following a successful initial deployment of the basic MBPLE tool chain.

Additional considerations during the tool chain definition are summarized as follows:

PLE transformation mechanism: While primary PLE tools enable asset transformation within several domains, this process typically occurs separately within each tool.

ALM and PLM integration: The PLE tool shall facilitate communication with both application lifecycle management (ALM) and product lifecycle management (PLM) domains, though significant integration challenges remain, particularly regarding configuration management.

Feature-assets linking: This capability is vital for filtering and transforming variability across different domain assets, but each link should be maintained carefully to avoid duplications. For instance, if a system requirement and a SysML model element are already linked, should the feature also link to both asset types for the same purpose?

Interoperability standards: It is essential to rely on interoperability standards rather than isolated API solutions or tool-specific options. This will promote the adoption of MBPLE and the inclusion of tools from various vendors or open-source solutions.

Chapter 27 will explore this topic in greater detail.

23.6 MBPLE Organization

In large-scale or high-tech systems, developing a product line typically involves multiple customer projects, unlike mass-market commercial products. This process begins with comprehensive risk and opportunity analyses, which consider factors such as leveraging knowledge from past projects, evaluating technical scope similarities, identifying competitive advantages, securing funding, and addressing knowledge gaps.

In an MBPLE approach, a company's business strategy is outlined in strategic plans and roadmaps for its product lines. These roadmaps define market requirements, target positioning, expected features, investments, revenues, and sales opportunities, and are regularly reviewed by strategic teams and product line heads. The roadmap is reflected in the product line's architecture and supported by technical roadmaps of its subsystems and components.

Supporting a product line's development and maintenance often involves hybrid funding schemes that combine self-funded and external budgets. Initial funding might come from major customers or self-funding stages, evolving over time to include customer contributions and centralized financial flows managed by the product line development program.

A best practice in the industry is to manage the product line as a single entity, allowing flexibility in development plans. Organizing the product line strategy and roadmap within a coordinated development program ensures consistent strategic planning, governance, and operations. This programmatic approach helps balance long-term strategic objectives with short-term financial goals, effectively aligning company strategy, product policy, management, engineering, and financial aspects.

Understanding the relationship between agile methodologies and product line development is also crucial within the organization, being the two practices complementary as explained in Chapter 28.

Successfully adopting MBPLE requires a dedicated team that goes beyond the organization's traditional structure. This includes the core MBPLE team responsible for defining and developing MBPLE, the MBPLE personnel outside the core team who validate and use the MBPLE framework in various projects and programs, and the MBPLE environment where the framework can be developed and validated independently of development programs. Chapter 28 explores these aspects to provide readers with a clearer understanding of MBPLE's role within an organization.

References

Chalé Góngora, H.G., Ferrogalini, M. and Moreau, C. (2014). How to boost PLE by using MBSE – a case study of a rolling stock product line, *Proceedings of the 5th International Conference on Complex Systems Design and Management* (CSDM, Paris, FR). Springer.

Chalé Góngora, H.G. and Greugny, F. (2017). Where the big bucks (will) come from – implementing product line engineering for railway rolling stock. *INCOSE 2017 International Symposium* (Adelaide, Australia). San Diego: INCOSE.

Chami, M., Aleksandraviciene, A., Morkevicius, A. and Bruel, J.M. (2018).Towards solving MBSE adoption challenges: The D3 MBSE adoption toolbox. In: *INCOSE International Symposium*, Washington DC, USA, (7–12 July 2018). San Francisco, CA: Wiley. 28(1): 1463–1477.

Delligatti, L. (2013). *SysML Distilled: A Brief Guide to the Systems Modeling Language*. 1e. Addison-Wesley Professional.

Forlingieri, M. (2022). The four dimensions of variability and their impact on MBPLE: how to approach variability in the development of aircraft product lines at Airbus. *Proceedings of the 16th International Working Conference on Variability Modelling of Software-Intensive Systems* (VAMOS '22, 23–25 February 2022), Florence, Italy. ACM, VaMoS.

Forlingieri, M. and Weilkiens, T. (2022). Two variant modelling methods for MBPLE at Airbus. *INCOSE International Symposium*, 32(1): 1097–1113.

Haugen, Ø., Wąsowski, A. and Czarnecki, K. (2012). CVL: common variability language. *Proceedings of the 16th International Software Product Line Conference – Volume 2 (SPLC '12)*. New York, NY: Association for Computing Machinery, 266–267.

ISO/IEC (2017). Information technology – object management group systems modeling language (OMG SysML). (ISO/IEC 19514: 2017).

ISO (2021). Industrial automation systems and integration – product data representation and exchange – application protocol: For modelling and simulation information in a collaborative systems engineering context (MoSSEC). (ISO 10303-243: 2021).

ISO/IEC (2021). Software and systems engineering – methods and tools for the feature-based approach to software and systems product line engineering. (ISO/IEC/IEEE 26580: 2021).

ISO/IEC/IEEE (2023). Systems and software engineering – system life cycle processes. (ISO/IEC/IEEE 15288: 2023).

ISO/IEC (2023). Systems and software engineering – methods and tools for model-based systems and software engineering. (ISO/IEC/IEEE 24641: 2023).

Kang, K., Cohen, S., Hess, J. et al. (1990). Feature oriented domain analysis (FODA) feasibility study. *Technical Report CMU/SEI-90-TR-21*. Pittsburgh, USA: Software Engineering Institute, Carnegie Mellon University.

Madeira, R., Pinto, D. and Forlingieri, M. (2023). Variability on system architecture using Airbus MBPLE for MOFLT framework. *INCOSE International Symposium*, 33(1): 601–615.

Malone, R., Friedland, B., Herrold, J. et al. (2018). Incorporating variability and reuse into system architecture models – principles and challenges. *INCOSE International Symposium*, 28(1): 1–15.

OSLC Core Version 3.0. (2021) *Part 1: Overview*. (ed. J. Amsden and A. Berezovskyi). OASIS Project Specification 02.

Seidel, E. and Forlingieri, M. (2023). Moving towards a server-zone vehicle architecture with MBSE at continental. *INCOSE International Symposium*, 33(1): 1509–1523.

Straub, F., Weking, J., Kowalkiewicz, M. et al. (2021) Understanding digital transformation from a holistic perspective, *PACIS 2021 Proceedings. 23.* https://aisel.aisnet.org/pacis2021/23 (accessed 13 June 2023).

Ulrich, K. and Eppinger, S. (2004). *Product Design & Development*, 3e. New York: McGraw-Hill.

24

MBPLE Process

24.1 Introduction

There are various ways to address process tailoring and adaptation when implementing model-based product line engineering (MBPLE). Although MBPLE does not fundamentally alter the engineering processes in an organization, it does extend them in specific ways. For instance, requirements engineers will continue to work on requirements as usual, but now they will handle a superset and create variation points. This also applies to software engineers, test engineers, architects who build design models, and others. Governance remains crucial, with change control boards continuing to function as before. However, changes now involve shared asset supersets and feature models, which are reviewed and vetted from the perspective of the entire product line. These and other changes must be reflected into the organization's processes.

This chapter extends the four MBPLE steps from Chapter 12, highlighting the need to tailor the approach for real-world MBPLE execution, as well as specific organizational and systems engineering processes. Each section of the chapter, from 24.2 to 24.12, presents one of the 11 MBPLE extended steps and their mapping to the technical processes of ISO/IEC 15288 (ISO/IEC 2023). The final Section 24.13, briefly covers the nontechnical processes (ISO/IEC 2023) and emphasizes their importance in rolling out MBPLE successfully.

While familiarity with ISO 15288 (ISO/IEC 2023) aids in understanding the content presented here, we do not cover all possible mappings between MBPLE steps and the system life cycle processes. Instead, we highlight their key interdependencies, particularly between MBPLE and the technical processes (ISO/IEC 15288).

The Matrix 24.1 shows the mapping of MBPLE extended steps with the systems life cycle processes.

24.2 Define the Product Line Scoping

The step precedes the MBPLE four-step approach and contributes to the definition of feature models, feature configurations, shared assets, and product models. It describes which member products and shared assets shall be part of the product line, including the identification of their commonality and variability. This requires as inputs market analysis, stakeholder needs analysis, legacy specifications and models and the identification of the main drivers of variability for the product line. The Product Line Scoping activity is well described in the ISO/IEC 26550 (ISO/IEC 2015) and adapted in ISO/IEC 26580 (ISO/IEC 2021).

Model-Based Product Line Engineering (MBPLE): The Feature-Based Path to Product Lines Success, First Edition.
Marco Forlingieri et al.

Matrix 24.1 Mapping of MBPLE extended steps with the systems life cycle processes.

Mapping of MBPLE extended steps with the related system life cycle processes ISO/IEC 15288	**Define the product line scoping**	**Define feature models**	**Define feature configurations**	**Define shared assets**	**Derive product models**	**Verify the product line**	**Customize the product models**	**Verify the member products**	**Produce the member products**	**Validate the member products**	**Evolve and decommission the product line**
Business or mission analysis	X	X	X								X
Stakeholder needs and requirements definition	X	X	X	X	X		X				X
System requirements definition	X	X	X	X	X		X				X
System architecture definition		X	X	X	X		X				X
System design		X		X	X		X				X
Verification						X	X	X			X
Implementation									X		X
Integration									X		X
Validation										X	X

Examples of questions that shall be answered during this phase are:

1. *Which products shall the product line support?*
   For instance, based on market needs and enterprise objectives, the products to be developed are identified.
2. *Who are the stakeholders?*
   The key stakeholders for the product line development and those that benefit from its derived member products are identified here.
3. *What are the market's needs?*
   These are essential inputs to define the product line and member products to be developed.
4. *What are the legacy products to be used as a references?*
   Usually, new products have resemblance to previous ones, which can be used as reference.
5. *What assets are common and variable among the member products?*
   Identification of those shared assets that shall be kept variable and those that should be kept common across the member products.

Those questions help the definition of a feasible product line, avoiding overstretching of the member products, requirements and cost. Planning must start with a clear definition of the product line and its scope that is a joint effort of product line management, PLE teams, marketing, and other key functions.

Mapping to the ISO/IEC 15288 Systems Life Cycle Processes: Define product line scoping is a step that necessitates several inputs coming from nontechnical life cycle processes. However, here we focus on the technical processes of ISO/IEC 15288 (2023). The most important process for this process step is the "business or mission analysis," since a product line scoping consists of a mix of business inputs and technical inputs. The product line scoping can also be further refined in the "stakeholder needs and requirements definition." While these steps are usually applied to the single-system life cycle, with the introduction of MBPLE, the focus shifts to the product line life cycle and the member products life cycle, once derived.

24.3 Define Feature Models

An entire chapter is dedicated to this process step (Chapter 13) so we do not cover it here further. What it is important to highlight is that feature models are an output of the product line scoping and serve to capture the variability in a formalized way.

Mapping to the ISO/IEC 15288 Systems Life Cycle Processes: "Define feature models" is an iterative activity that starts in the "business or analysis mission" process and continues until the "design definition." Market-related features and high-level features are likely to be identified in the early life cycle process, including also the "stakeholder needs and requirements definition" and "systems requirements definition." More detailed features such as technical features and domain-specific features are defined in the later "system architecture definition" and "design definition" processes. The definition of features is done in parallel with the traditional activities of the life cycle process (e.g. requirements elicitation and definition, architecture definition etc.), but the focus is here centered on the product line system and not on the single system.

24.4 Define Feature Configurations

Chapter 14 covers this process step. Similarly, for the previous step, they are an output of the product line scoping. The focus here is on the mapping with the system life cycle process.

Mapping to the ISO/IEC 15288 Systems Life Cycle Processes: Feature Configurations follow the same definition pattern of the feature models (see Section 24.3). The most important aspects (features) for the market and customer are taken into account in the early process, while the selection of technical features, which are hidden to the customers, are usually defined in the later processes.

24.5 Define Shared Assets

Chapter 15 covers this process step. Similarly for the previous steps, the initial stage of the identification of shared assets is also an output of the product line scoping. This section focuses on the mapping with the system life cycle process.

Mapping to the ISO/IEC 15288 Systems Life Cycle Processes: The definition of the shared assets, including the modeling of variation and linking with the features, starts with the "stakeholder needs and requirements definition" and continues until the "design definition," where the activity is performed in the specific domains. For instance, the definition of requirements as shared assets is mainly defined in the "stakeholder needs and requirements definition" and "system requirements definition." The definition of variation in the system architectures and related architecture models are defined in the "system architecture definition," while SW models or CAD models in the "design definition" process.

24.6 Define Product Models

Like for Sections 24.3–24.5, this step is discussed in a dedicated chapter (Chapter 16). We stress here the fact that this step together with "define feature configurations" consist of the bridge between the product line development and the member products derivation. While feature configurations and product models are defined during the development of a product line, they are used along the derivation of member products. They are the main inputs and references for the development of member products.

Mapping to the ISO/IEC 15288 Systems Life Cycle Processes: "Define product models" start with derivation of requirements assets ("stakeholder needs and requirements definition" and "system requirements definition"). It continues with the derivation of system architecture models ("system architecture definition") and the domain-specific models such as SW, MCAD, ECAD, etc. ("design definition").

24.7 Verify the Product Line

This is the first process step that follows the four-step approach. According to the definition of the ISO/IEC 15288, *"the purpose of the Verification process is to provide objective evidence that a system, system element, or artifact fulfills its specified requirements and characteristics"* (ISO/IEC 2023). In our case, we refer to a system product line, and we apply the process to features, feature configurations and shared assets developed for the product line.

Verification artifacts and their traceability with requirements can be developed in the previous step for the product line and used in this process. As the variability expressed by the product line may (potentially) fulfill an infinitive number of configurations, it is only possible to verify the system product line for the feature configurations in scope. This process step is also iterative and can start as early as the first shared assets are defined.

Mapping to the ISO/IEC 15288 Systems Life Cycle Processes: Although verification assets are typically established early in the life cycle, concurrent with the requirements definition, this step is predominantly aligned with the ISO/IEC 15288 "Verification" process. It is important to note that while the system product line can be verified for member products in scope (based on feature configurations and related product models) using the shared assets available, validation cannot be performed. This is because a product line, as a final implemented system, does not exist. This aspect is further elaborated in Section 24.9.

24.8 Customize the Product Models (If Needed)

This step is directly related to "define product models" and has the primary scope to develop specificities and customizations to the derived product models. This happens because in the real world a product line hardly meets all the specific customer requirements. This is usually a management decision that opted for developing extra specific features that are not part of the product line. The project handles these features as customization and member product specificities, because it does not meet the business case elaborated for the product line (e.g. it is unlikely that other member products will require these features). Sometimes, in a second stage, those specific features are added within the product line scope, impacting its evolution (see Section 24.11). A good strategy in handling these member product-specific adaptations is to limit them to part of the system, where their impact is contained in terms of changes and engineering re-work. A system modular architecture and building-block approach may facilitate the introduction of such specificities.

Mapping to the ISO/IEC 15288 Systems Life Cycle Processes: This step necessitates rework and modifications in the derived product models. Typically occurring after the product line is delivered, it involves rerunning the activities performed for the system product line, from "stakeholder needs and requirements definition" to "design definition," but only for the specific Δ (delta) added to the member product. Establishing digital continuity among the assets helps identify changes and minimize the re-work effort, as explained in Chapter 18.

24.9 Verify the Member Products

After the eventual product model specificities are developed in the "customize the product models," the new resulting product models should be verified for the Δ (delta) developed outside the product line scope.

Mapping to the ISO/IEC 15288 Systems Life Cycle Processes: The key life cycle process involved here is again the "verification" process, but only for the Δ (delta) developed for the member product (specificities).

24.10 Produce the Member Product

The production step only applies to the member products and not to the product line. It occurs when the system is finally integrated, and built. The variability here of the components is finally visible in the set of member products derived by the product line.

Mapping to the ISO/IEC 15288 Systems Life Cycle Processes: The process step is performed in both the life cycle process "implementation" and "integration" as defined by the ISO/IEC 15288 (ISO/IEC 2023).

24.11 Validate the Member Products

Once the member product is produced, either partially or completely, the “validation” process must be fully executed for each individual member product derived from the product line. According to ISO/IEC 15288, *“the purpose of the Validation process is to provide objective evidence that the system, when in use, fulfills its business or mission objectives and stakeholder needs and requirements, achieving its intended use in its operational environment”* (ISO/IEC 2023). Since a product line, being an abstract concept rather than a finite product, cannot be observed “achieving its intended use in its operational environment,” it is impossible to validate the product line itself. Validation is only possible for the derived member products. Therefore, the product line can be considered validated only for the in-scope member products that have been validated.

Mapping to the ISO/IEC 15288 Systems Life Cycle Processes: After discussing the application of verification and validation activities for both the product line and its derived member products, it may initially seem like redundant effort, but it actually results in a significant reduction of overall effort. Validation assets, similar to verification assets, are often predefined as part of shared asset supersets for the product line, but they are only executed during this step and in the “verify the product line” phase. Specifically, the “verification” step occurs once, not for each member product. Only changes (Δ delta) resulting from adaptations in the product models require additional verification. This approach translates to lower nonrecurring engineering costs for the organization, improved system quality due to early detection and resolution of defects across all member products, and shorter program development times, thanks to reduced time spent on redundant activities.

24.12 Evolve and Decommission the Product Line

In Chapter 18, we explored the evolution of product lines, particularly when new features necessitate changes in the existing product line. Product lines commonly evolve over time and eventually become obsolete. It is possible for member products to be phased out while the product line continues to be maintained and used for deriving new member products. Conversely, a product line may be decommissioned even before its derived member products are phased out.

When discussing concepts like maintenance and decommissioning of product lines, we are not referring to the operational maintenance or retirement of a specific system. Product lines are not finite products; therefore, our focus is on managing all assets that contribute to the development and sustainability of a product line.

Mapping to the ISO/IEC 15288 Systems Life Cycle Processes: In ISO/IEC 15288 (ISO/IEC 2023), we encounter the “maintenance” and “disposal” processes, which may seem similar to the idea of maintaining (and evolving) and disposing of a product line. However, it is crucial to distinguish that these processes are intended for systems that are in operation, which is not the case for a product line. It is more appropriate to align this process step with all the technical processes described earlier in ISO/IEC 15288 (ISO/IEC 2023). This is because the evolution of a product line involves revising various assets, but only for the delta (changes) that are implemented.

24.13 MBPLE Mapping with the Non-Technical Processes

The preceding sections outline the mapping of MBPLE steps with the technical processes detailed in ISO/IEC 15288 (ISO/IEC 2023). This chapter does not aim to comprehensively document all interdependencies between MBPLE extended steps and the processes outlined in the standard. Instead, it emphasizes the most critical relationships. Furthermore, it does not provide a complete adaptation of the MBPLE approach to a specific enterprise context, as systems engineering processes must be tailored to meet the unique requirements of each organization.

Given the focus on the technical aspects of the life cycle processes, detailed coverage of the linkages with organizational project-enabling processes and technical management processes has not been included. The next paragraphs provide a short discussion on the impact of MBPLE on nontechnical processes.

Organizational Project-enabling Processes: This process category enables the technical management processes and technical processes. The MBPLE implementation shall also consider their adaptation within the enterprise. For instance, the "life cycle model management" process should be adapted to describe the life cycle models for both the product line and its member products. Other processes in this category, such as "infrastructure management," "portfolio management," "human resources management," "Quality Management," and "knowledge management," do not require specific adaptation of the steps to be performed but should be expanded in scope to cover the product line and its member products. For example, "human resources management" must supply key personnel with MBPLE competencies for product line development, "quality management" ensures adherence to internal guidelines and quality standards, "portfolio management" provides inputs to the product line scoping, "infrastructure management" provides the MBPLE tool chain, and "knowledge management" facilitates the reuse of feature models, feature configurations, and shared assets, as well as the collection and sharing of learning materials and lessons learned for the product line development.

Technical Management Processes: This category covers the management aspects of the technical processes, which are also impacted by MBPLE. For example, "project planning" must distinguish between planning for a product line project and its member products. Similarly, "project assessment and control," "measurement," "risk management," and "quality assurance" must differentiate between the product line and its derived member products. The "measurement" process shall define new KPIs specific to product line development, such as the percentage of commonality across member products. The most impacted processes by MBPLE are "information management" – distinguishing between shared assets information and product model information- "configuration management" – impacting all technical processes through the management of changes and configurations of features, feature configurations, shared assets, and product models- and "decision making" – applied in all MBPLE steps, such as deciding the best product line architecture, whether to develop specificities for member products, or when to phase out the product line.

If you are reading this book with the goal of adapting your enterprise processes to an MBPLE approach, we strongly suggest the readers first to determine whether your organization has already implemented system life cycle processes. Then, proceed with the guidance provided here, tailoring it to your specific enterprise context. For those who have not done it yet, we highly recommend reading ISO 15288 (ISO/IEC 2023) and the *International Council on Systems Engineering* Handbook

(Walden et al. 2023) to gain a comprehensive understanding. As a famous model-based systems engineering (MBSE) podcast acknowledges at the end of each episode: "Trust us, we are systems engineers!" (The MBSE Podcast 2024).

References

ISO/IEC (26550: 2015). Software and systems engineering – reference model for product line engineering and management.

ISO/IEC (26580: 2021). Software and systems engineering – methods and tools for the feature-based approach to software and systems product line engineering.

ISO/IEC/IEEE (15288: 2023). Systems and software engineering – system life cycle processes.

The MBSE Podcast (2024). Podcast webpage. https://mbse-podcast.rocks/ (accessed 17 July 2024).

Walden, D.D., G.J. RoedLer, K. J. Forsberg, et al. (eds.) (2023). *Systems Engineering Handbook: A Guide for System Life Cycle Processes and Activities*, Version 5. San Diego, CA (US): INCOSE.

25

MBPLE Methods

25.1 Introduction

Chapter 23 has already addressed the topic of model-based product line engineering (MBPLE) methods and presented takeaways. In this chapter, we will explore the topic in more depth.

First, Section 25.2 defines the concept of method as it is understood in this book and distinguishes it from other concepts such as process and methodology. The following Section 25.3 introduces the distinction between general and specific methods based on OMG's model-driven architecture (MDA) (OMG 2014). Finally, Section 25.4 shows how organization- and tool-specific methods can be developed using an MBPLE method's task example.

25.2 Methodology, Process, Method, and Tool

Methods describe how to perform a task. For example, a description of how to model a feature tree. They should not be confused with processes that describe "what" needs to be done but not "how." For instance, an MBPLE process can describe that a feature model shall be developed to specify the variability of the product line but not how the feature model is defined. Tools help to carry out the methods efficiently. While you could draw the feature tree on a piece of paper, being considered a sort of "tools," they are probably not the best choice for this engineering task. You should use a feature modeling tool that is much more effective, particularly in managing features and connecting them with shared assets.

Methodologies are collections of processes, methods, and tools. The definitions of the terms process, method, tool, and methodology are based on Estefan and Weilkiens (2020), illustrated in the concept model in Figure 25.1. Not shown, but not to be forgotten, are the "actors" who execute the process methods and use the tools. A methodology references one to many processes. Each process references one to many methods and a method is linked with one to many tools. While processes are rather independent of methodologies, and methods are rather independent of processes, tool can be specific for methods. Therefore, the relationship between method and tool is bidirectional.

25.3 Independent and Specific Methods

This book describes the MBPLE process and methods, particularly in Part III. Of course, this is helpful, but it is insufficient to implement in a concrete organization or project. Part V presents various industrial MBPLE cases from different organizations. As you read, you will revisit many

Model-Based Product Line Engineering (MBPLE): The Feature-Based Path to Product Lines Success, First Edition.
Marco Forlingieri et al.

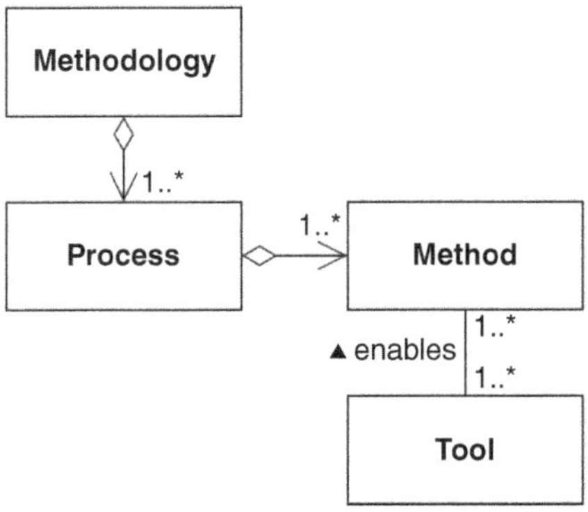

Figure 25.1 Concept model methodology, process, method, and tool.

concepts covered in other book chapters. However, these concepts have been adapted and supplemented, with some parts omitted. The book, along with many other publications, remains independent of any specific organization's needs or tool features.

In line with the MDA (OMG 2014), methods can be divided into organization-independent methods (OIM) and organization-specific methods (OSM), as well as tool-independent methods (TIM), and tool-specific methods (TSM).

Figure 25.2 provides an overview and lists the combinations of method kinds. OIM and TIM are found in this book and other books and standards. OIM and TSM are, for example, described in handbooks provided by (MB)PLE tool vendors. They are tool-specific but organization-independent methods.

In some organizations, OSMs are defined in cross-organizational method descriptions and developed and maintained, most of the time, by engineering methodology departments. Besides expertise, this type of organization unit also needs the power to define cross-organizational methods. They are typically responsible for the organization's processes and tools landscape to ensure their harmonization and governance within the organization. It is a balancing act between standardization, individual needs, and freedom for the engineers and projects.

Organizations should customize the processes and methods from books, standards, and other sources to their specific needs. The primary goal of an organization is not to perfectly implement the published methods but to develop successful products. The adaptation affects the methods rather than the processes. The how (methods) varies more in organizations than the what (processes).

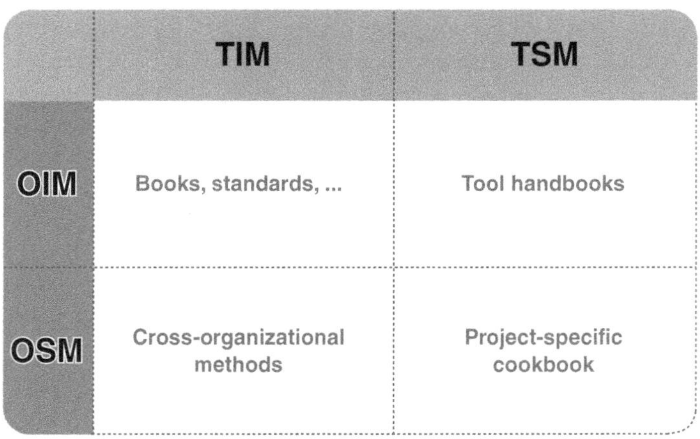

Figure 25.2 Independent and specific methods.

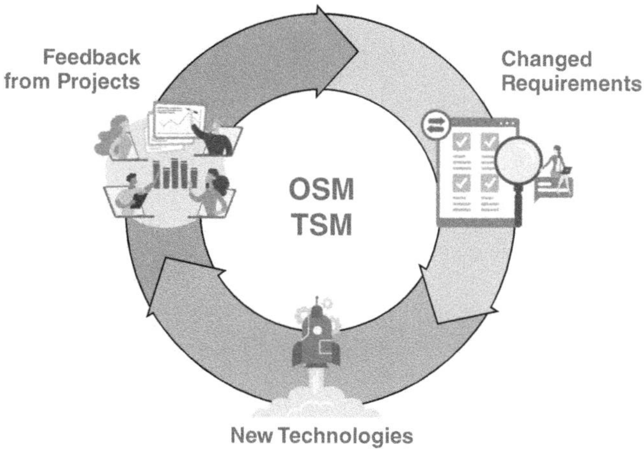

Figure 25.3 Continuous methods improvement.

Developing OSMs and TSMs is not a one-off task but a continuous process. Changes in requirements triggered by various entities such as organizations, markets, new technologies, and project feedback must be regularly incorporated into the OSMs/TSMs (Figure 25.3). If necessary, variants of the methods shall also be considered in different areas of the organization. The MBPLE concepts can also be used here to implement a "method product line." For example, the specific "member methods" can be documented in a project cookbook. This is where the OSMs and TSMs come together (Figure 25.2). Of course, it is not a clear-cut distinction, and TSMs can also be developed organization-wide.

25.4 Method Development

Methods can be developed similarly to a systems engineering project: there are, besides others, requirements, a number of external stakeholders, use cases with inputs and outputs, and a solution architecture or collection of methods derived from these. The OIM, as described in this book, is a reference architecture to which the solution architecture is aligned. The required tools can then be derived, and the TSMs can be developed based on the OSMs. However, the tools are often available in practice before the OSMs are developed.

Figure 25.4 shows a context diagram providing some sketches as an example for OSM/TSMs for MBPLE. Of course, many more roles and external systems should have been listed, but the scope is kept short for the sake of simplicity.

Based on the identified actors in the context, the use cases of the actors can now be identified and described. This is typically an iterative process. The use case analysis leads to further actors, who in turn lead to further use cases, and so on.

The actor "product management" has the use case "show impact of a feature change," among others (Figure 25.5). In the interview with product management, the following is outlined: the feature model is displayed in the web-based PLE dashboard. The product management marks a feature that is to be changed, which can also mean adding a new sub-feature or deleting a feature. The product management then receives a list of all affected shared assets, including their status, to estimate the scope of the change and see which departments should be involved in the planning.

The scenario implies that the engineering models and the modeling environment are set in a way that the question of impact can also be answered. As described in Part III, the features are linked

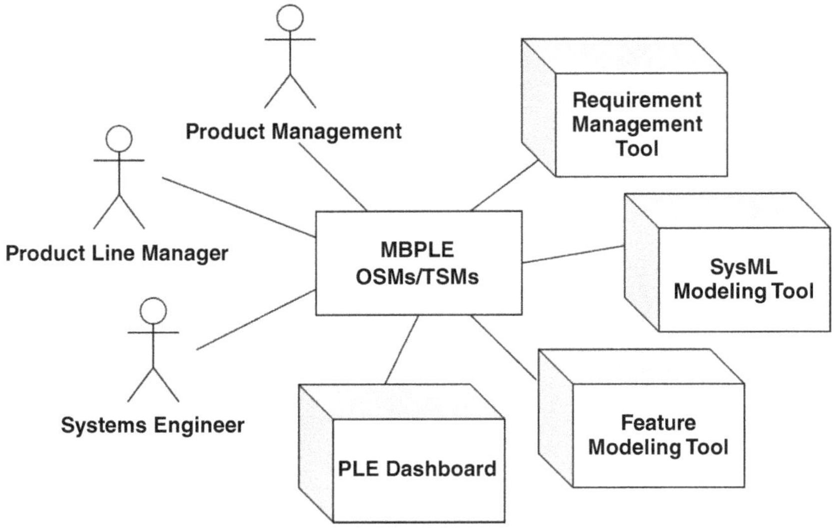

Figure 25.4 MBPLE OSMs/TSMs context.

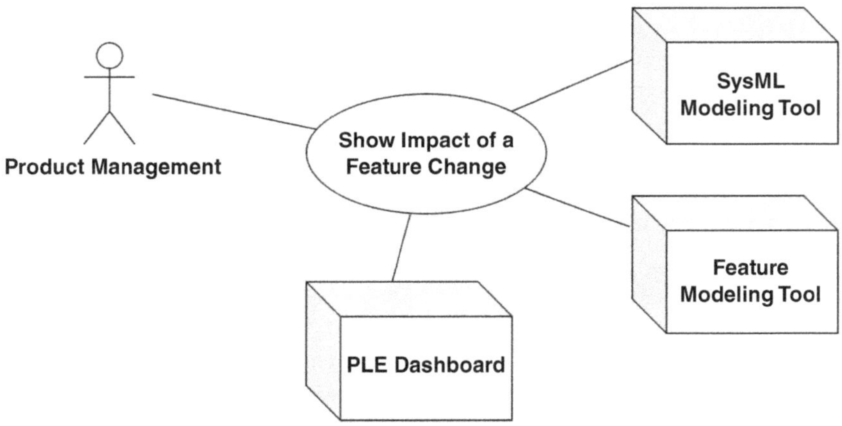

Figure 25.5 MBPLE use case "show impact of a feature change."

to shared assets, including systems modeling language (SysML) models. One SysML model represents the backbone of the product line and specifies how all the assets are linked together, including the references to more specific engineering tools like Mechanical Computer-Aided Design (MCAD), Electronic Computer-Aided Design (ECAD), or software engineering tools.

The product management request can be addressed as follows: the feature in question is linked to shared assets in the backbone SysML model. From there, further linked shared assets, including references in other models, can be identified. The devil is then in the details, requiring clarification of which traceability paths to follow and to what extent.

This primarily concerns OSMs. TSMs describe how the features and shared assets in different modeling tools are technically connected with each other.

The output of the impact analysis is a list of impacted assets. The organization-specific description of the output includes properties like name, location, responsible organization unit, and status. This implies that methods exist to create this information. In particular, a shared asset must be linked with an organization unit and status. Shared assets are stored using different engineering tools, but all should use the same set of organization units and status kinds. You need an agreement across the organization on these sets and a technical solution to store them in a single location that all shared assets engineering tools can access.

This simple example shows what is involved in a simple product management use case. It is important to specify the methods well and to master their implementation, as they minimize the many small hurdles of day-to-day project work and make the processes more effective. Otherwise, improvisation occurs, many meetings are called to overcome the hurdles, things are done twice, misunderstandings lead to conflicts, and so on.

References

Estefan, J.A. and Weilkiens, T. (2020). MBSE methodologies. In: *Handbook of Model-Based Systems Engineering* (eds. A.M. Madni, N. Augustine and M. Sievers). Cham: Springer International Publishing. 1–40. Available at: doi: 10.1007/978-3-030-27486-3_12-1.

OMG (2014). 'Model Driven Architecture (MDA) MDA Guide rev. 20.0, ormsc/2014-06-01'. Object Management Group.

26

MBPLE Information Model

26.1 Introduction

This chapter dives into the detailed structure and semantics of variability concepts within the model-based product line engineering (MBPLE) context. Building on the concepts presented in Chapter 9, the abstract syntax of these concepts is formulated in this chapter. It is intended for advanced users who want to dive deeper into the definition of the concepts, for example, to implement them themselves in modeling languages or tools. The information model is defined by using a subset of Systems Modeling Language (SysML) v1 modeling of blocks. Other modeling languages (e.g. UML) can also be used to specify concepts. As we primarily use SysML in this book, we also use it for the information model.

The chapter begins with an introduction to information modeling in Section 26.2, explaining the model elements used to define the semantics and abstract syntax of domain-specific terms. It then aligns its structure with the one presented in Chapter 9, illustrating the MBPLE information model coherently and sequentially (from Sections 26.2 to 26.10).

Key elements include detailed explanations and visual representations of the MBPLE information model, encompassing feature models and the details of features, including their identifiers, descriptions, and binding times. It explores feature constraints, explaining how they govern the relationships and conditions among features within a model.

Additionally, this chapter specifies the concept of feature configurations, emphasizing their role in ensuring compliance with feature constraints within a selected feature set. It also explores the use of the Object Constraint Language (OCL) for the formal expression and validation of these constraints (OMG 2014).

The chapter discusses shared assets within the MBPLE information model, outlining their roles and classifications and differentiating between core elements, variants, and variations. It also addresses the concept of variant configurations, highlighting them as a unique type of shared asset.

Finally, the information model covers the product portfolio and member products of a product line.

Model-Based Product Line Engineering (MBPLE): The Feature-Based Path to Product Lines Success, First Edition.
Marco Forlingieri et al.

26.2 How to Read an Information Model with SysML

An information model – also known as a domain, concept, or domain knowledge model (Weilkiens 2020) – defines the semantics and abstract syntax of terms in a specific domain. For example, the *Systems Engineering Book of Knowledge* provides an example of a systems engineering concept model (SECM) about high-level systems engineering concepts (SEBoK Authors 2021).

If you are already familiar with SysML, you can skip this section. The following briefly explains some SysML basics used for the information model.

The semantics of a term is typically informally specified by text in natural language. The information model specifies the structure of a term and its relationships to other terms. Figure 26.1 uses a subset of SysML v1 block model elements with a simple example. A concept is represented by a SysML block. The properties of the concept, if any, are modeled by value properties and listed in a separate compartment with the textual syntax "name: Type," whereby the type specification is optional. The type is a value type like Boolean, string, or an enumeration.

In SysML, a "generalization relationship" describes a connection between a more detailed, specific concept and a broad, general concept. The specific concept inherits all the characteristics of the general concept and may also have its own or change some of the inherited ones. The generalization relationship is noted as an arrow with a closed arrowhead.

In SysML, a composite relationship means that a concept consists of several parts that are defined by another concept. In contrast, a reference relationship is similar but implies a reference to another concept rather than ownership of it. At the end of this relationship is a property name, and the number of objects involved is specified by a range, written as [lowerBound..upperBound], which defines the minimum and maximum number of objects that can be contained in this relationship. The composite relationship is an arrow with an open tip and a black diamond at the other end. If it is a reference relationship, the diamond is missing.

You can read the information model in Figure 26.1 as follows:

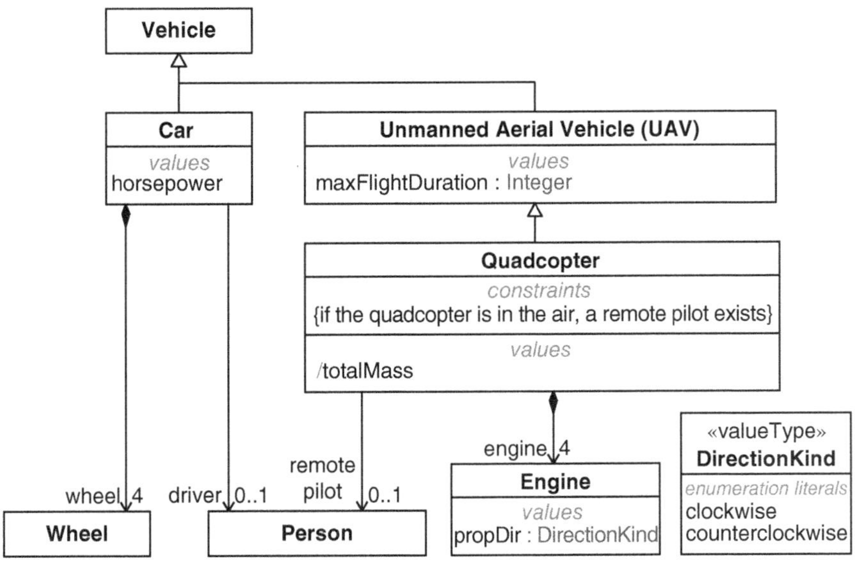

Figure 26.1 Example information model.

- A Car and an unmanned aerial vehicle (UAV) are kinds of a vehicle.
- The Car owns four wheels specified by the concept Wheel and has a horsepower value property.
- The Car also references an optional driver specified by the concept Person.
- The UAV has a value property maxFlightDuration typed by the value type Integer.
- The Quadcopter is a special kind of UAV. It owns four engines defined by the concept Engine.
- The Engine has a value property specifying the rotating direction of the propeller. The type of the value property is an enumeration.
- The Quadcopter also references an optional remote pilot defined by the Person concept.
- The Quadcopter has a constraint that ensures the remote pilot is present if the quadcopter is in the air. The constraint is specified using a natural language expression. It can also be specified more formally with the OCL (OMG 2014).
- The Quadcopter's value property totalMass has a "/" prefix, which tags it as a derived property. Its value can be derived from other information in the model, which is not shown here.

In the following section, we will use this kind of modeling to specify the MBPLE information model.

26.3 Product Line

The product line is the overarching element representing a family of products, which includes a variability model, shared assets supersets, product models, and member products (within a product portfolio; Figure 26.2).

26.4 Variability Model

The variability model is the overarching concept containing a feature model and a set of feature configurations (Figure 26.3). It, therefore, contains all the information about variability in the product line, including the feature selections for the planned member products of the product portfolio.

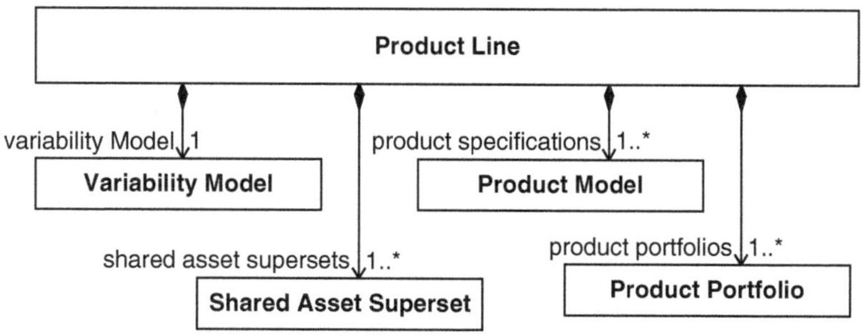

Figure 26.2 Information model: product line.

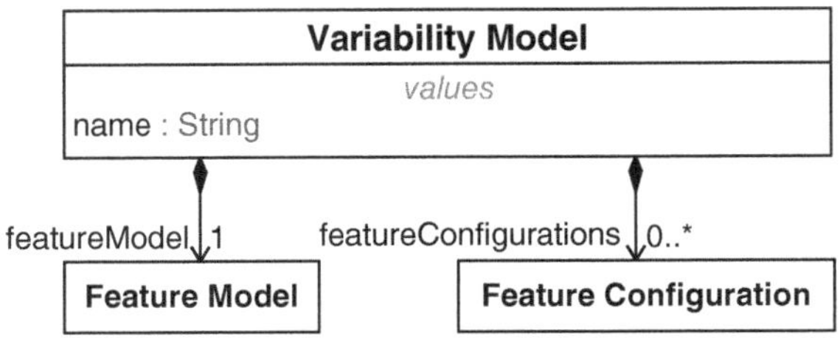

Figure 26.3 Information model: variability model.

26.5 Feature Model

The feature model specifies a product line's variability. It has a name and owns the root feature of the set of features, which is also referenced as a derived union (Figure 26.4). The features are organized in a hierarchical tree structure. The root feature is the feature from which the tree spans the subfeatures. The derived property "features" is the set of all features contained in the feature tree. It is derived from the subfeature relationships explained further as follows.

Feature models are also often called feature trees. The terms can be used synonymously. Strictly speaking, the feature model is the repository (i.e. the model data), and the feature tree is a view of the model.

A feature is a product's characteristic that differentiates it from other products within the same product line. It has an identifier, a name, a description, and a binding time. The identifier shall be unique within the feature model. The binding time is a value from the enumeration value type "LifeCycleKind."

A feature can reference another feature. It can bind features about the same variability in different areas of a feature tree or reuse a feature in another context. The referenced feature can also be a feature or the complete tree of a different feature model.

A feature can have subfeatures specified by a subfeature relationship in the information model (Figure 26.5). The derived Boolean property "isEnd" indicates if subfeatures are defined or if this feature is a leaf.

The subfeature relationship connects a feature (the master) with one subfeature. The property "subFeature" is derived and represents an owned or referenced subfeature. Exactly one of these

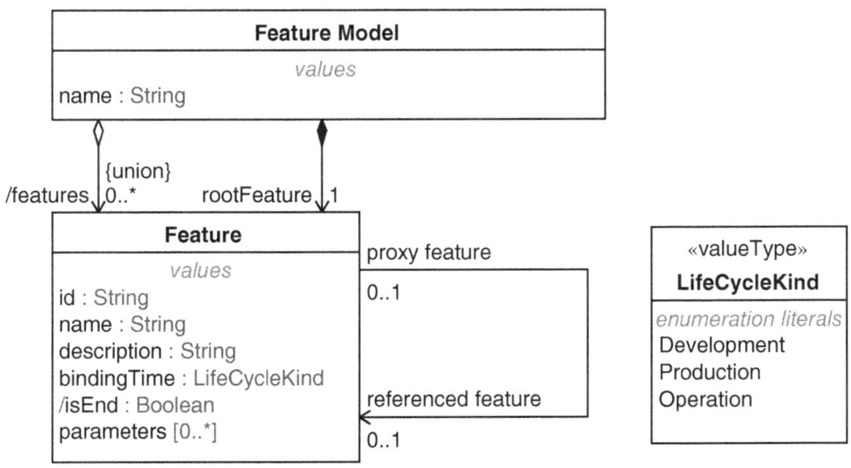

Figure 26.4 Information model: feature model.

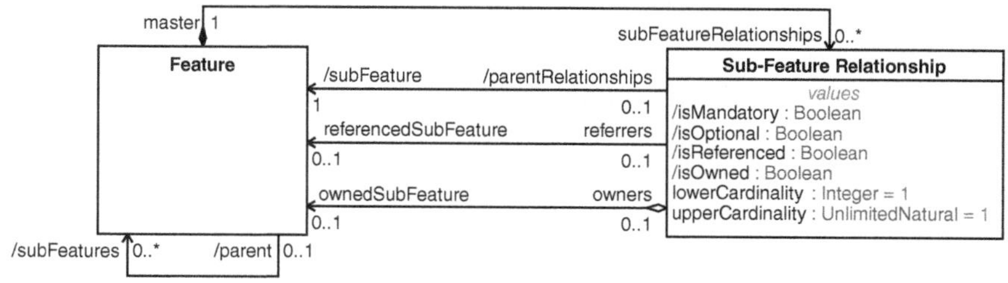

Figure 26.5 Information model: subfeatures.

two kinds must be set. The derived properties "isOwned" and "isReferenced" directly show the kind of subfeature relationship. A feature can have many subfeature relationships.

The relationship specifies the lower and upper cardinality of the subfeature. The default is a lower and upper cardinality of 1. If the lower cardinality is zero, the subfeature is optional. If it is greater than zero, the subfeature is mandatory. The properties "isOptional" and "isMandatory" are derived from the cardinality values. If the upper cardinality is greater than 1, more than one of the subfeatures can be selected by a feature configuration.

The derived properties "subFeatures" and "parent" are derived from the property "subFeatureRelationships."

26.6 Feature Constraint

A feature constraint specifies an expression about features that must always be true in the context of a feature configuration. The expression is specified by the operation "constraintExpression()," which returns true if the expression is true for a given feature configuration (Figure 26.6). The feature constraint involves at least two features whereby one could be specified as the source element if the expression is directed. The source element is the first feature in the ordered set of referenced features.

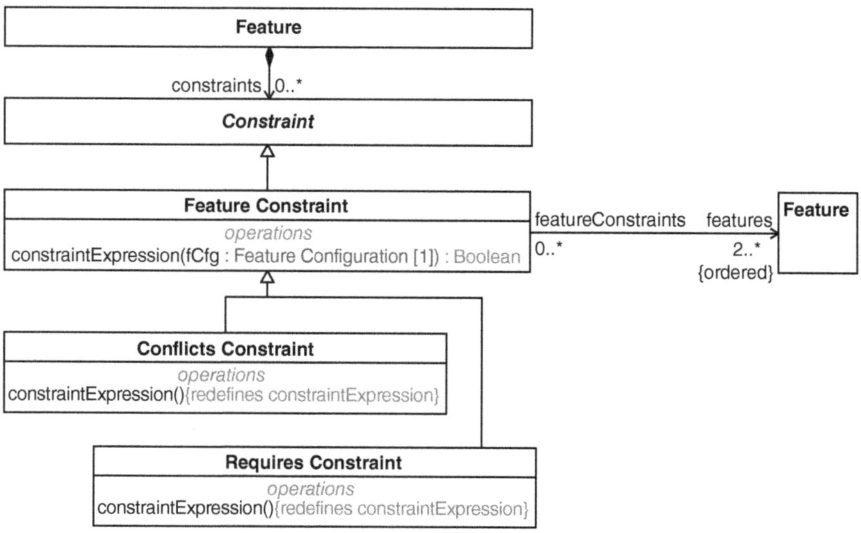

Figure 26.6 Information model: feature constraint.

The "conflicts" constraint is a special feature constraint that redefines the operation "constraintExpression()." It specifies that the features are in conflict with each other and that only one of them can be a member of the given feature configuration. The constraint is specified by using the OCL (OCL v2.4, 2014). OCL is a formal language used to describe expressions on models. The OCL expression for the conflict feature constraint is as follows.

```
features->select( f | fCfg.selectedFeatures->includes(f) )->size() <= 1
```

In natural language, the expression means checking all features in the set "features" and selecting those features that are a member of the set "selectedFeatures" of the given feature configuration. There may be only zero or one feature in the selection.

The "requires" constraint is a special feature constraint that also redefines the operation "constraintExpression()," specifying that a feature configuration must select all other features if the source feature is part of the feature configuration. The OCL statement is as follows:

```
if fCfg.selectedFeatures->includes(features->first()) then
        fCfg->includesAll(features)
else
        false
Endif
```

26.7 Feature Group

A feature can have a group of alternative subfeatures. The feature group constrains the cardinality of subfeatures (Figure 26.7). The feature group specifies a lower and upper cardinality. The OCL statement of the constraintExpression() operation is defined as follows.

```
lowerCardinality <= subFeatureRelationships->collect(feature | subFeature)->select( f |
fCfg.selectedFeatures->includes(f))->size() <= upperCardinality
```

If the upper cardinality is 1, it is an XOR group – also known as an alternative. That means exactly one of the group's features can be selected. If the upper cardinality is unlimited, it is an OR group. That means you can select any of the features. The lower cardinality controls that at least one and the maximum allowed number of features are selected within the group.

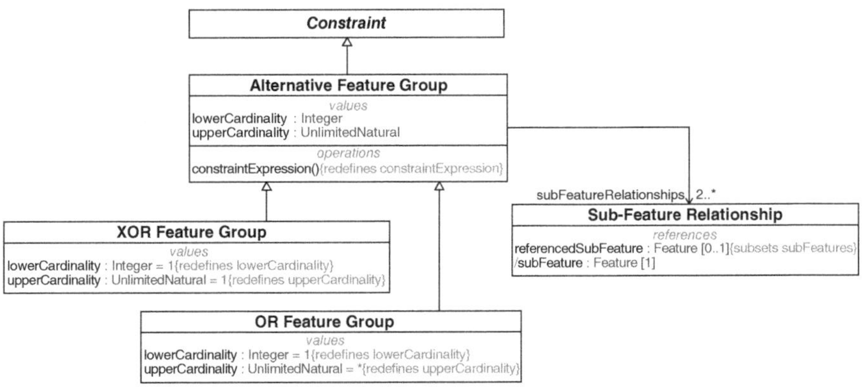

Figure 26.7 Information model: alternative feature group.

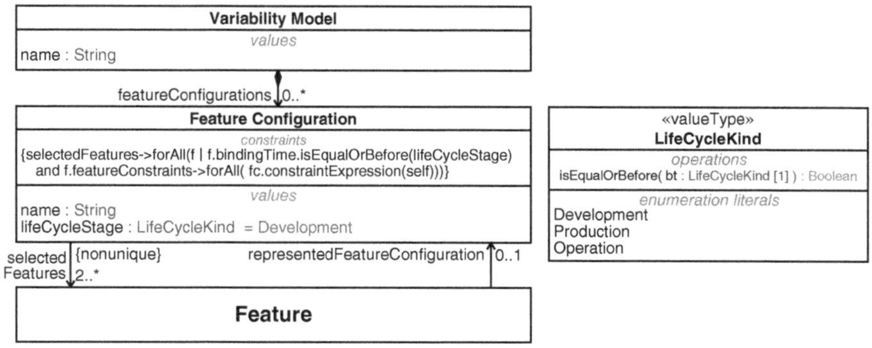

Figure 26.8 Information model: feature configuration.

26.8 Feature Configuration

A feature configuration is part of a variability model and specifies a valid set of selected features of a feature model for a member product. A feature configuration has a name and references a set of selected features (Figure 26.8). The constraint of the feature configuration assures that all feature constraints that cover selected features are met.

The constraint expression given in OCL is as follows.

```
selectedFeatures->forAll( f |
        f.bindingTime.isEqualOrBefore(lifeCycleStage) and f.featureConstraints-
        >forAll(fc.constraintExpression(self)) and
        f.parentRelationships->forAll( sfr | sfr.lowerCardinality <=
                                             selectedFeatures->including(f)->size()
                                             <= sfr.upperCardinality)))
```

26.9 Shared Assets

A shared asset is a digital artifact that contributes to the architecting, design, fabrication, operation, maintenance, and retirement of a product (and its components). It can be a member of one or more shared assets supersets.

The shared assets superset can have a name and own shared assets that specify the products (Figure 26.9).

A shared asset can also have a name. All other properties are outside the scope of MBPLE and are defined by the specific engineering language of the shared asset, such as SysML, CAD, and so forth.

The shared assets are distinguished between core elements and variants. A core element is used for all product line products, whereas a variant is only used for specific products.

Variation is a special core element, also known as a variation point. It is where variability happens in the system. The nature of this variation is inherently abstract, requiring a specific design decision to be made concrete. The design decisions are represented by the variants related to the variation (Figure 26.9).

A variation implements the feature that specifies the variability, and the variants implement the appropriate subfeatures (Figure 26.10). This scenario is also depicted in Chapter 9 in Figure 9.7.

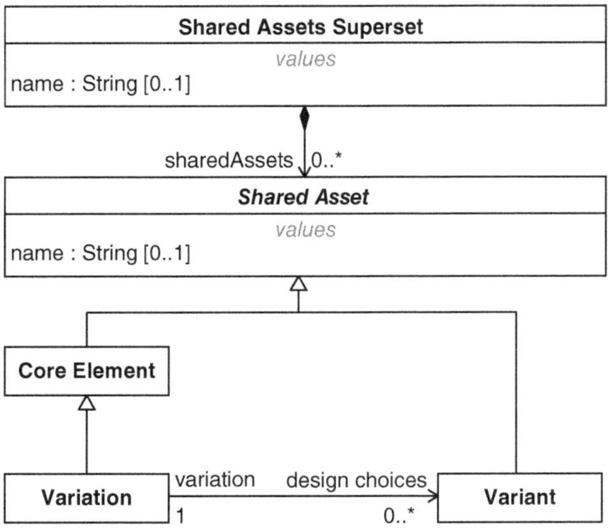

Figure 26.9 Information model: shared assets superset.

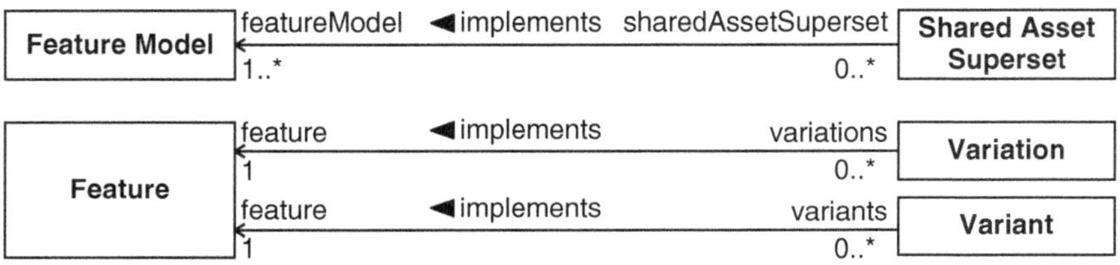

Figure 26.10 Information model: shared assets/features relationships.

26.10 Product Model and Member Product

A product model is a specification of a member product. It refers to the corresponding feature configuration. It is derived from shared assets, including the core elements and the variation and variant elements, which can be derived from the relationship to the feature configuration. The product model can still contain variability. Variations with binding time "Production" or "Operation" have not yet been resolved. Therefore, many member products can refer to a product model (also known as product asset instance [ISO/IEC 2021]).

A member product is a concrete physical product specified by a product model that is part of an organization's product portfolio. Figure 26.11 shows the definition of the "Product Model" concept.

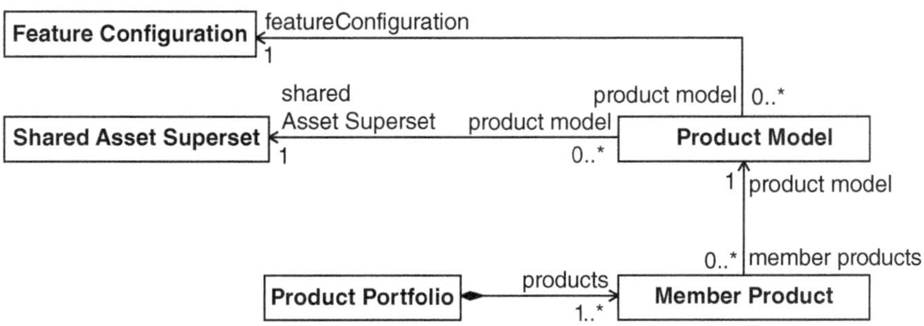

Figure 26.11 Information model: member product.

References

ISO/IEC (2021). ISO/IEC 26580: 2021 Software and systems engineering – methods and tools for the feature-based approach to software and systems product line engineering. ISO/IEC: https://www.iso.org/standard/43139.html.

Object Management Group (OMG) (2014). *Object Constraint Language Version 2.4, formal/2014-02-03*. Object Management Group.

SEBoK Authors (2021). Systems engineering core concepts: https://sebokwiki.org/w/index.php?title=Systems_Engineering_Core_Concepts&oldid=67939 (accessed 15 June 2023).

27

MBPLE Tool Chain

27.1 Introduction

In this chapter, we explore the concept of model-based product line engineering tool chain, focusing on its various components and their roles in the adoption of MBPLE. Figure 27.1 illustrates five distinct categories of MBPLE tool chain components, providing clarity, particularly for those new to this subject. Additionally, for each solution category, the key capabilities related to MBPLE, the existing commercial and open-source tools, as well as the gaps, are presented.

In Section 27.2, we begin with the product line engineering (PLE) solution, a cornerstone of any MBPLE tool chain. This component allows teams to define and manage feature models and configurations, ensuring consistency across the many variations of a member product. It acts as the "engine" of the MBPLE tool chain.

Next, in Section 27.3, we shift our attention to the model-based systems engineering (MBSE) solution, particularly highlighting SysML v2 (Object Management Group [OMG] 2024). This transformative standard introduces enhanced variability modeling capabilities into system modeling. While the full transition to SysML v2 is ongoing, it is important to discuss the current implementation of SysML, its integration, and its limitations concerning MBPLE.

In Section 27.4, our discussion then moves to the application lifecycle management (ALM) solution, detailing how it has evolved to integrate with both PLE and MBSE tools across different tool vendors. This integration is crucial for managing the life cycle of software-intensive components within product lines, covering everything from initial design to their continuous evolution.

In Section 27.5, we explore the product lifecycle management (PLM) solution, which is central to the digital transformation of engineering and manufacturing. Integrating PLE solutions into the PLM domain facilitates the management and continuity of complex product data and variability. However, there are still overlaps with legacy variant management solutions that are embedded in PLM systems.

In Section 27.6, the conversation turns to the configuration management (CM) solution, which plays a vital role in tracking and managing changes and variations across the product line. This segment highlights the necessity of a unified configuration management strategy to ensure coherence and integrity across all product line components.

We conclude the chapter with Section 27.7 by looking forward to the future evolution of the MBPLE tool chain and its landscape, anticipating how current trends and new solutions might shape its development.

Model-Based Product Line Engineering (MBPLE): The Feature-Based Path to Product Lines Success, First Edition.
Marco Forlingieri et al.

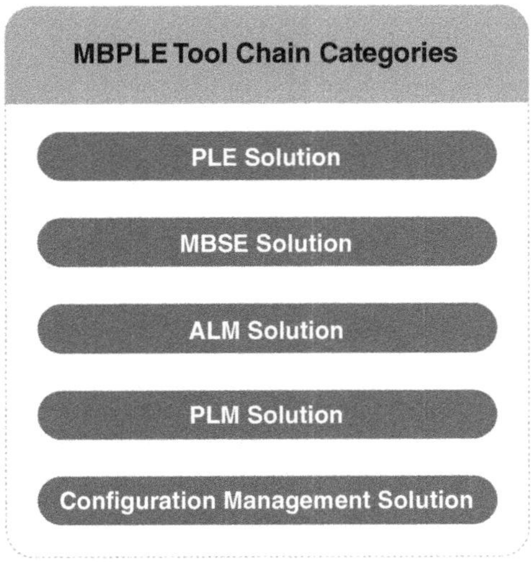

Figure 27.1 MBPLE tool chain categories.

27.2 PLE Solution

The PLE solution is the "engine" of an MBPLE tool chain since without it there will not be an MBPLE approach. It shall provide four main basic capabilities to the users:

1. Defining and managing feature models.
2. Defining and managing feature configurations.
3. Linking mechanism between variable assets and features.
4. Transforming the shared assets consistently in the domain-specific tools.

A PLE tool usually distinguishes between feature models and shared assets. Since the definition of variability and its capture into feature models is an iterative process and includes multiple system hierarchy levels, PLE tools also offer two additional capabilities:

5. Creating partial feature configurations, assuming that the user has not chosen all features at a specific development stage but only part of them.
6. Structuring and managing feature models and configurations at different hierarchy levels (e.g. system, subsystem, components, etc.)

PLE solutions automatically check if the chosen features are allowed in the feature configurations. This means checking if the selected features meet all the required relationships and constraints defined in the feature model.

Since PLE tools shall be accessed by all the stakeholders who contribute into the development of the product line, going from the marketing team to the system developers, it is beneficial to provide a web interface with limited functionalities and a client interface for those that are working hand-on with features and shared assets.

Finally, the integration with other engineering domains shall be facilitated by open API or support of standards like OSLC (OSLC 2021) and MoSSEC (ISO 2021). This is a prerequisite for the realization of an end-to-end MBPLE tool chain.

PLE tools: Today there are mainly two PLE alternative commercial solutions in the market, pure::variants (PTC pure::variants 2024), recently acquired by PTC and Gears (BigLever 2024) by

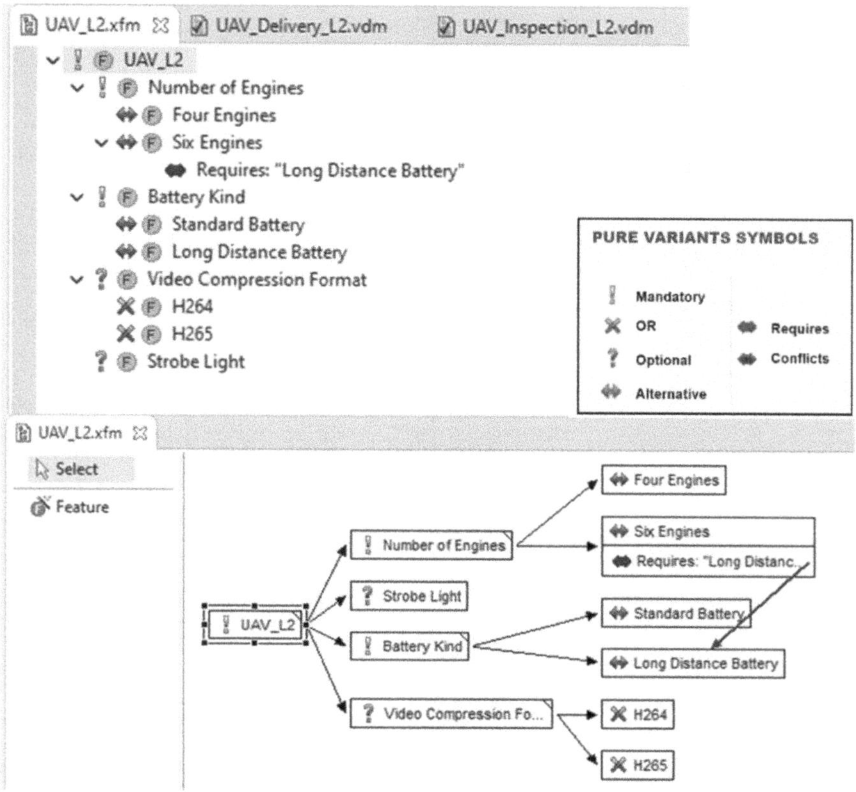

Figure 27.2 Example of feature model in PTC pure::variants.

BigLever Software. Due to the lack of a standard variability language and variability exchange language, those two solutions set their own standards and guidelines to adopt a PLE approach within several industries. While Figure 27.2 shows an example of a feature model in PTC pure::variants, Figure 27.3 shows the same example in Gears. In Chapter 13, the open-source solution called FeatureIDE (METOP 2020) was introduced. Similar to pure::variants, which is based on Eclipse, FeatureIDE offers capabilities more oriented toward research usage rather than full-scale organizational adoption. More information about these tools can be found on their websites or in several existing publications.

Gaps: PLE tools are advanced and set the standard for the discipline. Without them we would have not probably had the industrial application of PLE. However, one of the gaps that those solutions have is the lack of a full modeling experience. This does not mean that feature models are not models, since they resemble the three main characteristics highlighted in Chapter 10 (*MBEML-1, MBEML-2, and MBEML-3)* and provide the capability to link feature and model elements, including the generation of a product model from the shared assets supersets. The gap mainly concerns, for instance, the act of modeling features similarly to SysML or CAD tools as well as the possibility to create different views of the same feature model.

This is probably due to the fact that those solutions were conceived to support PLE mainly in software development and still strongly rely on their original technology. What they provide is more a graphical representation of the feature model with limited modeling capability.

This gap was first identified by Chami et al. (2017) in their work "Model-based variability solution with SysML" where they used SysML and a specific profile extension to model the features and their configurations.

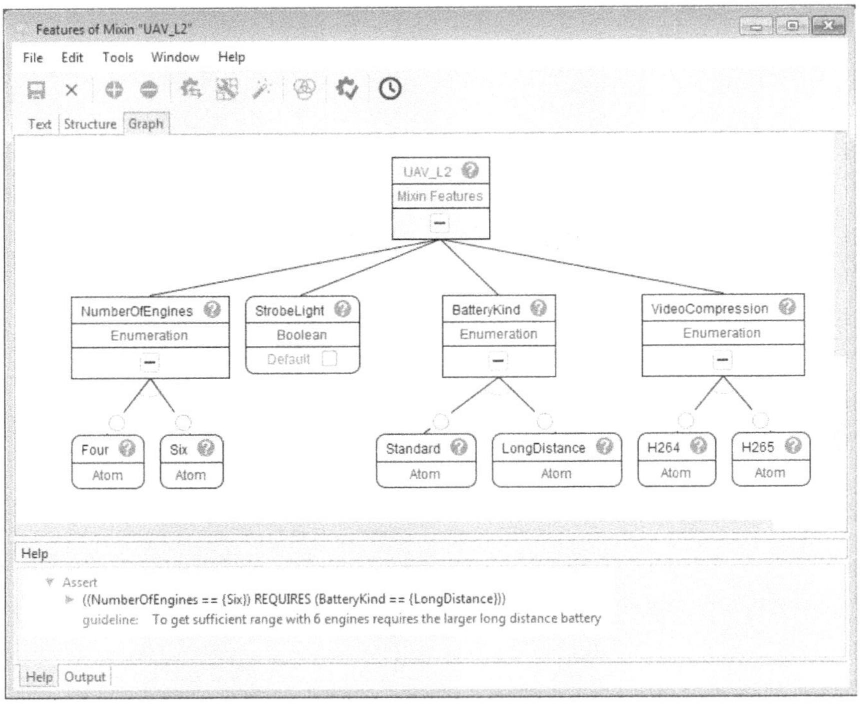

Figure 27.3 Example of feature model in Gears BigLever Software.

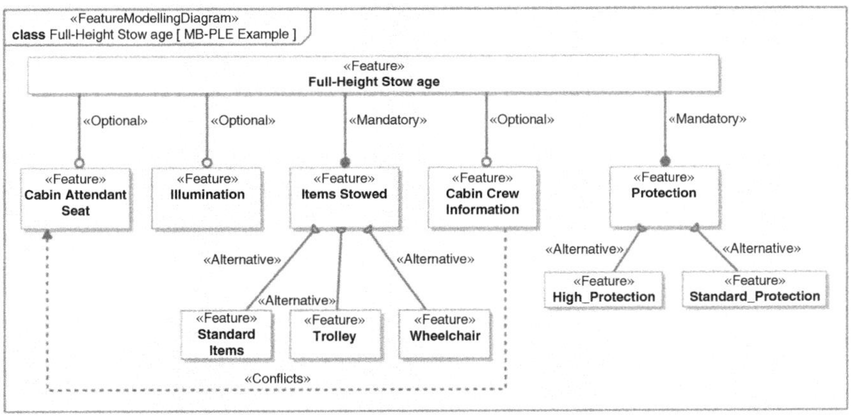

Figure 27.4 SysFM example with SysML. *Source:* Adapted from Forlingieri et al., 2022 / John Wiley & Sons.

Forlingieri and Weilkiens (2022) proposed a similar approach, named System Feature Modeling (SysFM) illustrated in Figure 27.4, in continuation with the approach started by Forlingieri at Bombardier Transportation, but exploring its coexistence with the main PLE tools. It is important to highlight, once more, that SysML tools are not PLE tools. We strongly recommend limiting the usage of SysML only for capturing the variability in feature models and defining the feature configurations in those organizations where MBSE is predominant to facilitate user acceptance. Those organizations shall enable in a second stage the critical capability to import or, even better, synchronize the feature models and configurations in a PLE tool. In fact, in both Bombardier

Transportation and Airbus's cases, feature models and configuration, after being defined in the SysML tool, were imported into a dedicated PLE tool.

Another gap is more on the consistency and management of the transformation from the shared assed into the product model across different domains. Due to the multiple commercial solutions that can integrate with PLE tools, it is hard to achieve a consistent and standard way to manage the transformation. This challenge can be partially addressed by implementing integration solutions based on interoperability standards rather than open or proprietary APIs, as discussed in Chapters 6 and 18.

27.3 MBSE Solution

Without an MBSE approach, the "MB" part of MBPLE is unachievable. As noted, MBPLE does not only handle variations in system models; it integrates a broad range of engineering assets holistically. Yet, SysML models are crucial for ensuring the consistent implementation of variability across different engineering domains. These models essentially define how variability is structured across shared assets. An MBSE solution for MBPLE should at least include:

1. Establishing dependencies and constraints between Feature-SysML models.
2. Linking with PLE tools to display feature models and their configurations.
3. Filtering and previewing the outcomes of feature configurations in the SysML model.
4. Transforming SysML shared assets into specific product models.

Such capabilities are also mentioned for the PLE solution. However, the MBSE solution should be able to mirror these capabilities to allow the interoperability on the MBSE side, such as, for instance, creating dependencies from the MBSE between a model element and a feature. A key additional capabilities that is not only relevant to MBPLE is:

5. Versioning and control of the SysML models (also part of the CM solution)

It is important to note that SysML was not designed for modeling product lines but for systems, which makes it unsuitable for direct application to product lines without adaptations. Although SysML v1 supports a wide array of systems engineering tasks, it lacks elements for modeling the product lines, such as features (Forlingieri and Weilkiens 2022). SysML v2 Notation (OMG 2024) bridges this gap.

MBSE tools: Since the advent of SysML, SysML v1 tools like Rhapsody by IBM (IBM Rhapsody 2024), MagicDraw (also known as Cameo System Modeler) by Dassault Systemes (Cameo 2024), Enterprise Architect by Sparx Systems (Sparx 2024), and Integrity Modeller (now PTC Modeller) by PTC (PTC Modeler 2024) have added SysML capabilities to their UML modeling features. Except for Enterprise Architect, the other three are also embedded as part of the ALM solution of IBM and PTC and the PLM solution of Dassault Systemes and PTC, respectively. All the presented MBSE solutions are connected with PLE tools and allow the synergy between PLE and MBSE. Several documents and publications about each solution and their SysML-specific capabilities exist, so this is not the place to further detail them (tool examples are not shown on purpose). The open-source scene is mainly dominated by Capella by Obeo (Capella 2024), which is not based on the SysML language. It also includes other tools like Papyrus (Papyrus 2024), which is SysML-based.

Gaps: As mentioned in the previous paragraph, SysML v1 and its tools were not developed with the intention of modeling variability, which presents challenges such as creating a product line architecture that is both valid in SysML and conceptually well-formed according to system semantics (Forlingieri and Weilkiens 2022). However, to address this challenge, the latest version of

SysML, SysML v2, introduces specific concepts for modeling variability, as shown in Chapter 15. This provides a consistent foundation for developing tools and methods to model variability in the system model.

In Section 27.2, an important gap is identified: the lack of a full modeling experience for feature and configuration definition. This has pushed some MBSE tool vendors to integrate PLE functionalities within their system modeling tools. While this may appear as a solution for projects with a limited scope and few engineering assets, it is difficult to scale for large organizations where the PLE tool should not depend on other domains, but rather being holistic. We should avoid the paradox where MBSE, intended to break down silos in engineering and enhance collaboration, instead creates a silo for MBPLE!

27.4 ALM Solution

PLE solutions started to be used in software development already at the beginning of the 2000s. This means that since their birth, they had to be integrated with ALM solutions, originally used only in developing software. This includes, but it is not limited to, requirements management, test management, and source code management disciplines.

As mentioned before, MBSE solutions can be also considered as part of an ALM solution if integrated. Interoperability standards like OSLC support primarily the links between the solutions that are part of the ALM domain and also the connection with the PLE solution.

The ALM solution shall provide the following minimal capabilities to support MBPLE:

1. Linking with PLE tools to display feature models and their configurations.
2. Filtering and previewing the outcomes of feature configurations in the ALM assets such as requirements, test cases, and source codes.
3. Transforming ALM shared assets into specific product models consistently.

Additional capabilities that are not only relevant to MBPLE are:

4. Integrating with an MBSE solution
5. Integration with PLM tool chain
6. Versioning and control of the ALM assets (also part of the CM solution).

ALM tool chains: In the last decades, several solutions entered the ALM arena; however, for simplicity we mention here just the most popular that, we believe, cover around 90% of the market. The Engineering Lifecycle Management by IBM (IBM ELM 2024) offers traditional ALM capabilities and integration with the main PLE solutions. The same for Codebeamer by PTC (PTC Codebeamer 2024), which since 2022 owns one of the two PLE solutions, pure::variants, and provides similar capabilities. Polarion by Siemens (Siemens Polarion 2024) also covers the same capability span. All three ALM tool chains also have integration with one or multiple MBSE solutions and provide similar version and control functionalities. As an open-source solution, it is worth mentioning the combination of the Atlassian family (Atlassian 2024) with Jira, Confluence, XRay, and the GitHub (GitHub 2024) flavors that offer "light" ALM capabilities. We do not show any examples of the mentioned tools since the specific ALM tools are not central to this book.

Gaps: Common gaps are usually related to the limited model-based capabilities and the complexity of their usage. For instance, even if they integrate with MBSE solutions, their integration is often based on heavy synchronization approaches between the MBSE assets and other ALM assets, or it is not as smooth as linking a requirement element with a system element inside a SysML tool, being both part of the same model. Even when the integration is built on OSLC, it is not always fluid and user-friendly. Surprisingly the ALM integration is often more straightforward and functional with the PLE solutions, even if provided by other vendors. The main limitation for both ALM and PLM solutions, as it will be discussed in the next paragraph, consists of the tool vendor lock-in effects. In fact, due to the complex architecture and integration challenges among ALM tool chains, it is in theory possible to have ALM tools from different vendors, but in practice hard to realize.

27.5 PLM Solution

PLM tool chains have rapidly become a fundamental pillar of engineering and manufacturing as well as a central component of digital transformation across various industries. Serving as the critical collaboration platform, PLM ensures digital continuity and links all related product data, including MCAD, ECAD, BOMs, simulations, and more.

With the integration of PLE solutions into the PLM domain, it has become easier to define and manage the variability of bills of materials, MCAD models, and ECAD models.

Historically, PLM systems typically utilize built-in variant management solutions that are not feature-based or PLE-based.

The modern PLM solution shall provide the following minimal capabilities to support MBPLE:

1. Linking with PLE tools to display feature models and their configurations, similar to the ALM solution.
2. Filtering and previewing the outcomes of feature configurations in the PLM assets such as MCAD, ECAD, and BOMs.
3. Transforming PLM shared assets into specific product models consistently, similar to the ALM solution.

Additional capabilities that are not only relevant to MBPLE are:

4. Integrating with an MBSE solution
5. Integration with PLM tool chain.
6. Versioning and control of the PLM assets (also part of the CM solution).

PLM tool chains: It is possible to list three main commercial tool chains that, we believe, cover a big part of the PLM market. These are Windchill by PTC (PTC Windchill 2024), Teamcenter by Siemens (Siemens Teamcenter 2024), and 3DExperience (Dassault Systemes 2024) by Dassault Systemes. All three platforms provide the aforementioned PLM capabilities and have integration with the main PLE tools. As mentioned before, sometimes they provide overlapping or conflicting functionalities with the PLE tools, but except for a few cases this trend is changing since the main vendors support more and more the PLE-based approach to develop product lines. A clear example of it is the recent acquisition of pure::variants by PTC. Due to the complexity of PLM tool chains and the capability to scale to full enterprise, no open-source holistic PLM solutions exist. In line with the previous sections, we do not display any examples of the mentioned tools.

Gaps: Two main gaps are worth mentioning here. The first is the lack of PLM and ALM tool chain integration. Even if more and more organizations aim at achieving digital continuity along the entire development lifecycle, the definition and management of variability for a product line that includes ALM and PLM assets still remains a challenge. Sometimes partial integration exists.

Alternatively, companies can still organize their shared assets in the two distinctive tool chains. Having the PLE solution and the MBSE solution as integration points between the two.

The second main gap is related to the overlapping variant management legacy capabilities of PLM solutions that sometimes conflict with the PLE mechanism. In fact, having variant management capability in the PLE solution does not mean that the solution follows a PLE-based approach guided by the IS0 26580 (ISO/IEC 2021).

27.6 Configuration Management Solution

As shown in Chapter 19, CM provides the capability to reuse engineering assets of different domains with different lifecycles status. All engineering assets, ALM or PLM, can be reused as well as configured from a single source of truth for different versions and variants. Each of these information sources possesses its own configuration identification specific to its domain and lifecycle. One of the primary challenges is integrating all these different assets of the product line into common and consistent shared assets configurations. This is the consequence of the coexistence of several domain-specific CM systems.

A CM solution shall support MBPLE with the following capabilities:

1. Integrating with a PLE solution and working in synergy with it.
2. Accessing the repositories where the MBSE, ALM, and PLM shared assets are stored and querying the data in the configurations, keeping the authoring tools responsible for changes in the assets.
3. Identifying which is the common and variant part of the product model within the configuration of each member product.
4. Creating product models from the shared assets that are consistent and in line with the feature configurations and model transformation.

A CM solution is not limited to the capabilities mentioned earlier, but these are key for the implementation of the MBPLE tool chain.

Gaps: Configuration management solutions, often referred to as version control solutions, commonly utilize a method known as branching. This involves creating a copy of a set of assets that then evolves independently from the original. While branching has several appropriate uses, it is unsuitable as the primary method for managing variations within a set of reusable assets (known as variation in space, see Chapter 19 for more details).

When variations are managed by initially creating branches, it usually results in unnecessary workload, because the branched asset (e.g. consider a requirement set) is not entirely modified; a significant portion often remains unchanged between the original and the branched copy. Unless the granularity of the versioned assets closely matches the granularity of the variations, branching in version management is not effective alone for MBPLE. In fact, version and control management, essential for tracking changes to the shared assets throughout their lifecycle, should not be confused with variability and variant management. Hence, often a configuration management solution is proposed by tool vendors as a way to manage variability. This is usually due to the lack of understanding of the MBPLE approach and to the lack of synergies and integration with the PLE tools that are often seen by organizations as unnecessary if a configuration and control management solution is already in place. It is key to stress the fact that product lines similarly to single products require a configuration management approach, and one is not a substitute for the other. Chapter 19 focuses entirely on the CM topic.

27.7 The Future of the MBPLE Tool Chain

On one hand, it is challenging to predict how companies will embrace the MBPLE too lchain in the future, as the inherent "variability" makes predictions nearly impossible. On the other hand, we can identify some critical factors that will significantly influence the adoption of the MBPLE tool chain.

First, in recent years, we have observed two main trends that are somewhat contradictory. There has been the development of more interoperability standards to facilitate collaboration across tools from different vendors, such as OSLC and MoSSEC. Concurrently, several acquisitions by large PLM or ALM vendors of independent PLE and MBSE solutions occurred. This can lead to a "crossroads" where companies must choose whether to adopt a multi-vendor approach and focus on integration or to opt for a single-vendor solution. In an ideal world, the multi-vendor approach would likely be more advantageous for organizations wanting to implement MBPLE, but in practice, it can be challenging to execute. We already see companies opting for a "third way," where they depend on a primary tool-vendor platform but maintain some flexibility to integrate third-party solutions.

Secondly, SysML v2 is considered to be a game-changer not only for MBSE but also for MBPLE. This is not only because it introduces variability elements into its language, but primarily due to its open API, which facilitates the easier integration of the SysML model with variability. If all vendors adhere to the API specified by the new standard, achieving digital end-to-end continuity will be simpler. However, due to the novelty of the language, several open points remain. For instance, it is not yet clear how SysML v2 asset transformation will be supported by PLE tools after the introduction of the variant notation. The INCOSE PLE Working Group (INCOSE PLE WG 2024) is coordinating the establishment of a common understanding among PLE and MBSE tool vendors for the implementation of important SysML v2 aspects related to PLE.

Lastly, we hope that the PLE community of experts, driven by the INCOSE PLE Working Group, will establish a standard language for defining and exchanging variability data. Similar to SysML v2, a standardized variability language would enhance the current integration landscape and lead to greater flexibility in selecting PLE tools within a company's existing tool chain.

References

Atlassian. (2024). Atlassian products. https://www.atlassian.com/software (accessed 11 May 2024).

BigLever (2024). BigLever software gears. https://biglever.com/solution/gears/ (accessed 10 May 2024).

Cameo (2024). Cameo system modeller. https://www.3ds.Com/products/catia/no-magic/cameo-systems-modeler (accessed 11 May 2024).

Capella (2024). MBSE capella. https://mbse-capella.org/ (accessed 11 May 2024).

Chami, M., Forlingieri, M. and Oggier, P. (2017). Model-based variability management solution with SysML. *Prostep Journal* 2017 (1): 38–41.

Dassault Systèmes. (2024). 3DExperience platform. https://www.3ds.com/3dexperience (accessed 11 May 2024).

Forlingieri, M. and Weilkiens, T. (2022). Two variant modeling methods for MBPLE at Airbus. *INCOSE International Symposium* 32 (1): 1097–1113.

GitHub (2024). GitHub. https://github.com/ (accessed 11 May 2024).

IBM ELM (2024). IBM engineering lifecycle management, https://www.ibm.Com/products/engineering-lifecycle-management (accessed 11 May 2024).

IBM Rhapsody (2024). IBM engineering systems design rhapsody. http://www.ibm.com/products/systems-design-rhapsody (accessed 11 May 2024).
INCOSE PLE WG (2024). INCOSE PLE Working Group. https://www.incose.org/Communities/working-groups-initiatives/product-lines (accessed 12 July 2024).
ISO (2021). Industrial automation systems and integration – product data representation and exchange – application protocol: for modeling and simulation information in a collaborative systems engineering context (MoSSEC). *(ISO* 10303–243: *2021*). ISO.
ISO/IEC 26580:2021 (2012). Software and systems engineering – methods and tools for the feature-based approach to software and systems product line engineering.
METOP (2020). FeatureIDE, https://www.metop.org/featureide (accessed 1 October 2023).
Object Management Group (OMG) (2024). OMG system modeling language version 2.0, ad/2023–02–11. Object Management Group.
OSLC Core Version 3.0. (2021). *Part 1: Overview 23 April 2021*. (eds A. Jim and B. Andrii). OASIS Project Specification 02.
Papyrus (2024). Eclipse papyrus, https://projects.eclipse.org/projects/modeling.mdt.papyrus (accessed 11 May 2024).
PTC. Codebeamer. (2024). PTC codebeamer. https://www.ptc.com/en/products/codebeamer (accessed 11 May 2024).
PTC. Modeler. (2024). PTC modeler. https://www.ptc.com/en/products/ptc-modeler (accessed 12 July 2024).
PTC Pure::Variants. (2024). Pure::Variants. https://www.ptc.com/en/products/pure-variants (accessed 10 May 2024).
PTC Windchill. (2024). PTC windchill PLM software. https://www.ptc.com/en/products/windchill (accessed 11 May 2024).
Siemens Polarion (2024). Polarion ALM software. https://plm.sw.siemens.com/en-US/polarion/ (accessed 11 May 2024).
Siemens Teamcenter (2024). Teamcenter PLM software. https://plm.sw.siemens.com/en-US/teamcenter/ (accessed 11 May 2024).
Sparx (2024). Enterprise architect. https://sparxsystems.com/products/ea/ (accessed 11 May 2024).

28

MBPLE Organization

28.1 Introduction

As stated throughout this book, implementing model-based product line engineering (MBPLE) in an organization entails aligning all sectors, divisions, and functions around a common delivery approach. While Chapter 23 presents an overall adoption framework for MBPLE, and Chapter 24 explains the necessity of adapting the organization to the "MBPLE way of working" and the need to tailor MBPLE processes to the context and needs of the organization, this chapter details key organizational aspects. Section 28.2 presents guidelines to set up and operate the organization supporting an MBPLE approach. Section 28.3 provides two examples of generic organizational patterns to operate the model-based product line in different contexts.

The organizational patterns presented below should be considered as implementation models. In most cases, the organizational changes required to reach a specific target must be planned and be considered as, or integrated into, an enterprise transformation program. As a reminder, a commonsensical approach would be to align the organization and the architecting approach of the product line, which in turn should be dictated by the business context and constraints (INCOSE 2019). The chapter closes with brief presentations of the synergies between agile principles and MBPLE (Section 28.4) and of the MBPLE adoption team (Section 28.5) and concludes with an important clarification of the concept of product line of product lines in Section 28.6.

28.2 Guidelines for Setting Up and Operating an MBPLE Enterprise

The birth of a product line: In the field of large-scale or high-tech systems, the development of a product line is generally not performed through a single customer project, but rather through the execution of several customer projects (AFIS 2015). The situation is quite different for commercial products in mass markets, of course. But, in fact, how is a product line born?

In the general case, the decision to develop a product line is taken after a series of opportunities versus risks analyses that take into consideration several aspects, such as:

- The feasibility of accessing and capitalizing knowledge from past customer projects or from customer projects being enforced.
- The technical scope covered by these projects to evaluate the similarity of the delivered solutions.

Model-Based Product Line Engineering (MBPLE): The Feature-Based Path to Product Lines Success, First Edition.
Marco Forlingieri et al.

- The identification of achievable competitive advantages or a groundbreaking concept from data obtained through market analyses and business intelligence.
- The possibility of allocating budget and resources to finance the development of the product line, which is generally segmented over time.
- The identification of "unknowns" or knowledge gaps in the current product offer.
- The possibility of gathering data and information to support key decisions.

Giving a reason to live to the product line: In a MBPLE approach, the business strategy of a company should be formalized in strategic plans and roadmaps of its product lines, or in similar documents. Roadmaps define what is required or expected from each product line, for what markets or customers, and at which point in time. These elements are usually defined by teams in charge of the strategy and the product policy of the company; they are reviewed regularly (at the pace of relevance) and are typically owned by the "head of the product line." Examples of information contained in product line strategic plans and roadmaps include the following:

- The current and target positioning of the products in specific markets.
- The expected features over time, differentiators to outplay the competition.
- The market segmentation.
- The required investments and expected revenues, and foreseeable volumes of sales and opportunities.

The roadmap of a product line is incarnated in its architecture, captured in great measure in the MBPLE digital assets (predominantly models). The roadmap is also supported by the technical roadmaps and policies of the subsystems and components that constitute the product line. These elements are usually defined by the architects or the technical authorities of the product line, and must be managed in a coordinated way.

Feeding the product line: To support the development, deployment, evolution, and maintenance of the product line, most companies put in place hybrid funding schemes that combine self-funded and external budgets in a staged approach. External budgets come from customers that buy (or intend to buy) products issued from the product line. Even in fully self-funded developments, investments are generally granted in several stages. So, the development of the product line is performed thanks to a series of customer projects and self-funding stages that must be managed in a coordinated way (that is, within a program). These schemes are very common in market-pull sectors that are driven by call-for-tender mechanisms.

It must be pointed out that funding mechanisms can evolve over time. The initial funding sources to launch the development of the product line may differ from those that will eventually be in place at later life cycle stages. Typical funding mechanisms include the following:

- Initial funding (product line launch):
  - Full or gradual self-funding for upfront development of the product line.
  - Funding by a major customer within a product line "launch" project.
  - Joint self- and customer-funded development.
- Maintenance and upgrade funding (product line "run" mode)
  - Pro-rata contribution by customer projects to the evolution and maintenance of the product line.
  - One single financial flow centralized and managed by the product line development program.

Raising the product line: Whatever the organizational pattern, one of the best practices in the industry is to organize the development of the product line as a whole, as if it were a single entity, despite the fact that the product line roadmap might contain unknown aspects, and to provide enough degrees of freedom to allow the evolution of the development plan over time. For this, it is highly appropriate to organize the implementation of the strategy of the product line and the execution of the product line roadmap within a coordinated, single endeavor. This endeavor is usually referred to as the "product line development program," which is accountable for the overall profit and loss statements of the product line (in the mid- and long terms) and is usually managed by the "head of the product line program."

Such a programmatic approach is paramount for managing the life cycle of the product line and for coordinating in a consistent manner the delivery of the products of the product line.

It provides indeed a consistent framework for strategic planning, organizational setup, governance, and day-to-day operations.

A product line development program is the most appropriate structure to address diligently the potential conflicts between long-term strategic objectives (i.e. the expected profitability achieved through the realization of the roadmap of the product line) and short-term objectives (i.e. the revenues, cash, and profit and loss achieved through the execution of customer contracts). In fact, this programmatic approach allows to align and connect in an effective manner a company's strategy, product policy, program management, offers and projects management, architecting and engineering, as well as the financial aspects of the product line, as covered in Chapter 21.

28.3 Examples of Organizational Patterns

The guidelines exposed above should allow a company to define the principles that will frame the definition and governance of its MBPLE-based enterprise. However, since the number of different possible MBPLE organizations can be huge, in this section we propose two generic organizational patterns to which the reader can refer to, depending on the reader's particular business context.

In order to better understand the organizational patterns presented below, let us first take a slightly different look at an MBPLE enterprise based on the principles exposed in the previous section. Figure 28.1 shows the dependencies of different categories of actors in the MBPLE enterprise.

Actors at the business level can be considered as a circle of investors who have an interest in the product line; they are the internal customers of the product line program. Actors in the product line program and in the development teams coordinated by the program can be considered as the entrepreneurs of the product line; they develop, promote, and require sponsorship and financing from internal customers. Finally, the development of the product line must be supported by capabilities provided by an MBPLE adoption team, like the one presented in Section 28.5 hereafter.

Figure 28.2 below shows the first generic organizational pattern for rather vertical businesses and highly integrated product line teams. This figure covers only the highest level of the product line. In this pattern, the overall authority of the product line is in the hands of the "head of the product line," who is supported by the "chief architect of the product line" and the head of the product line program. This line of business is accountable for the overall profit and loss of the product line and reports directly to the business authorities, normally at the level of the executive committee of the company.

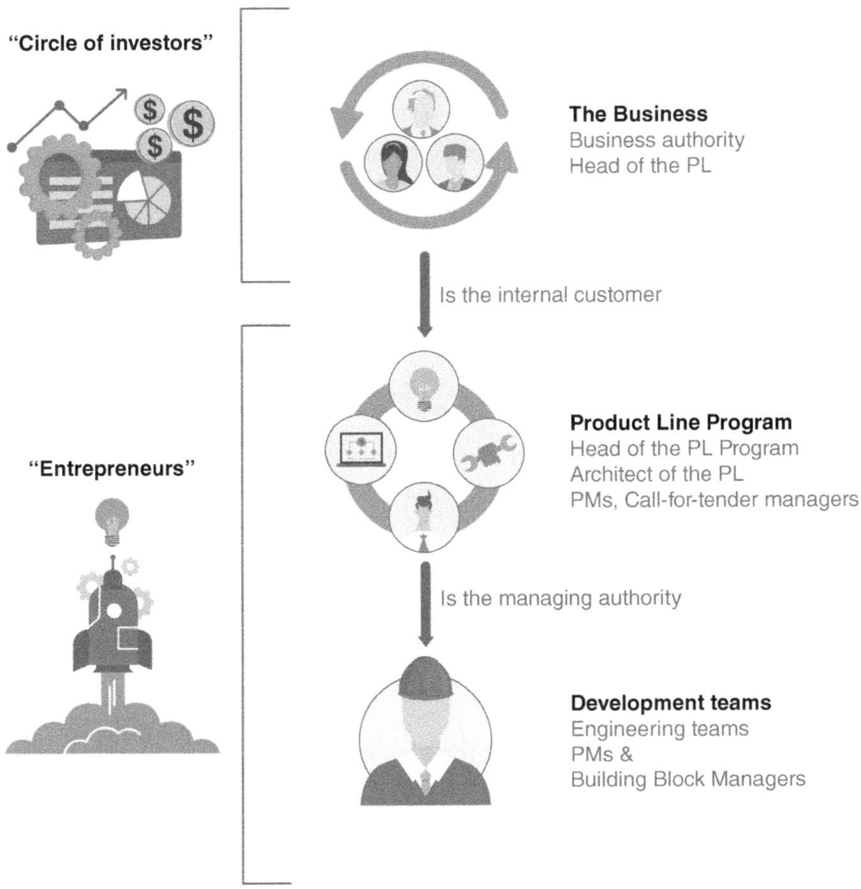

Figure 28.1 A different look at an MBPLE-oriented enterprise.

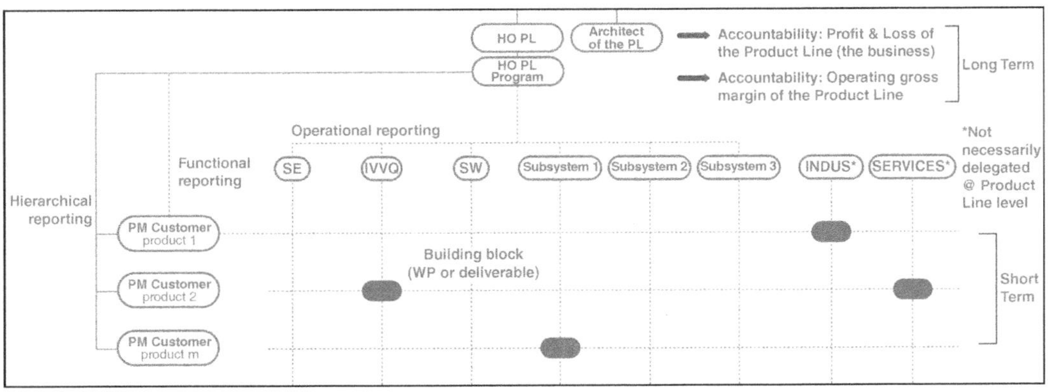

Figure 28.2 Organizational pattern at product line level.

The "head of the product line program" oversees the different disciplines that work within customer projects to deliver products. He also supervises customer project managers and coordinates the deliveries expected by customer projects. The head of the product line program is accountable for the operating gross margin of the product line, which can be seen as the integration or consolidation of the operating margin of each customer project.

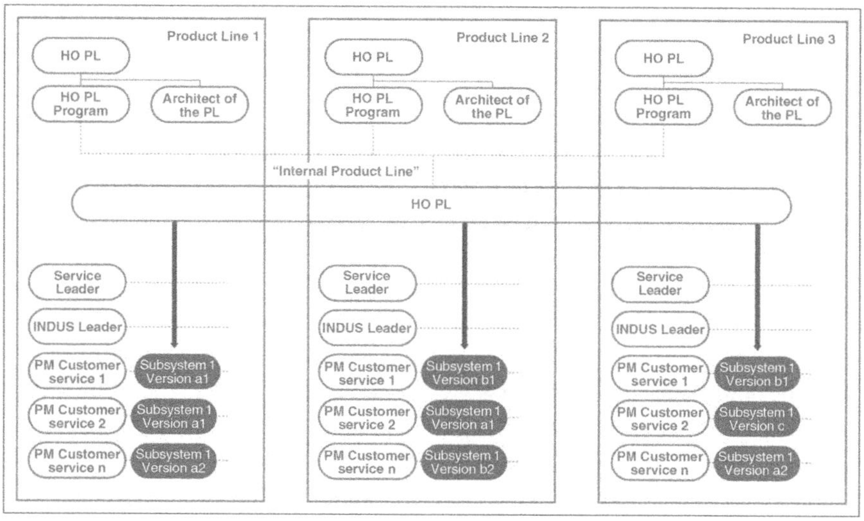

Figure 28.3 Organizational pattern at the subsystem level.

The second generic organizational pattern shown in Figure 28.3 below concerns those businesses that put in place a "composable" approach to deliver the products (or building blocks) of the product line (the approach is explained in Chapter 3). The figure represents only one of the subsystems of the product line. In this pattern, "subsystem 1" contributes to three different product lines and can be seen as an "internal" product line.

The head of Subsystem 1 is accountable for the delivery of the expected versions of Subsystem 1 (including all necessary assets and documentation) to the different customer projects within each product line. To compose a product, the other subsystems of the product line would follow the same principle and provide the deliveries required by customer projects. In this pattern, the role of the "product line architects" is paramount to guarantee that the composed products will possess the emergent properties expected by the customers. In certain cases, a "chief product line architect" might be necessary to carry out this work consistently across the different product lines.

In order to guarantee the consistency of the overall product line configuration, the MBPLE enterprise requires managing variability at different levels, across domains, and across disciplines, whatever the organizational pattern. The deployment of MBPLE into different levels of the system breakdown structure must be planned carefully and its implementation must be carried out consistently. The methods and concepts presented in Chapters 13–16 provide the capabilities to manage multilevel/multilayer variability in a consistent manner.

28.4 So, What About Agile?

To explain how agile principles can be applied in an MBPLE organization, we first attempt to draw a simplified picture of the different elements that allow the MBPLE enterprise to conduct and operate its business.

The application of agile methods is particularly appropriate for the early stages of the product line life cycle (setting up the scope and architecting the product line). Agile methods can be applied to define and review the product line plan and the product line roadmap. Methods and tools dedicated to value identification and tracking (like value canvasses, empathy maps, value-pulled developments or key decisions and knowledge gaps) are extremely useful to identify product line differentiators, rank architecture concepts of the product line, prioritize product line features and support arbitration and decision-making.

Agile methods can also be applied during the early design activities of the product line, like architecture definition or operational analysis (Gregg et al. 2016). But most importantly, agile methods can (should!) be applied to conduct the development of the very first member products of the product line. Besides the methods and tools mentioned above, approaches like iterative developments (not necessarily incremental), product backlog and sprints, and integrated product teams – in which Integration verification validation and qualification teams are integrated from the very beginning – are particularly effective to develop the first member products of the product line in a consistent manner. The application of agile methods in this context is also instrumental in "rolling out" and fine-tuning the MBPLE organization's methods, tools and way-of-working, and anchoring healthy agile practices in the genes of MBPLE teams.

At later stages, once the product line is established, agile methods can be applied to operate the product line in an effective and efficient way. As explained earlier in the book, in MBPLE product models are "derived" from the shared asset supersets greatly improving the speed (and quality) of the development. Here again, value-based agile methods can be used to perform very efficient gap analyses between new customer needs and the feature model of the product line, and define the appropriate member product configuration. Agile methods can of course be used for product line upgrades or the development of a new product line if required.

There are, however, some points that require particular attention when applying agile methods in an MBPLE context. First, for well-established product lines, the emphasis of agile methods should be more on supporting smart reuse and regular reviews of the value proposition of the product line, so there is practically no need to do agile "from scratch." Second, the term feature must be clarified from the beginning: features have different meanings in agile development (features are related to services of functionalities that drive business value and are implemented in sprints) and in MBPLE (features are differentiating characteristics of a product that are used to formalize variability).

28.5 MBPLE Adoption Team Setup

One of the best practices in industry to support the adoption of MBPLE (and later the operation of the MBPLE enterprise) is setting up an MBPLE adoption team. This adoption team is composed of the following elements:

1. MBPLE team, that is responsible for the definition and development of MBPLE.
2. MBPLE personnel that are outside the MBPLE team and validates the MBPLE framework. Personnel include engineers and managers.
3. MBPLE environment, as a space where the MBPLE framework can be defined, developed and validated outside the development programs.

MBPLE Team: The MBPLE team owns the definition and development of the overall MBPLE framework and supports the deployment in the product line development program (see Figure 28.4). The MBPLE team can be part of a digital transformation program, like (Digital Design, Manufacture and Services (DDMS) in Airbus (Forlingieri and Weilkiens 2022), if its adoption is an enabler of the transformation. Alternatively, the MBPLE team can be included within the Method and Tool department of the organization or as part of a Center of Competencies (CoC). While the MBPLE team should work synergistically with the model-based systems engineering (MBSE) team, we recommend

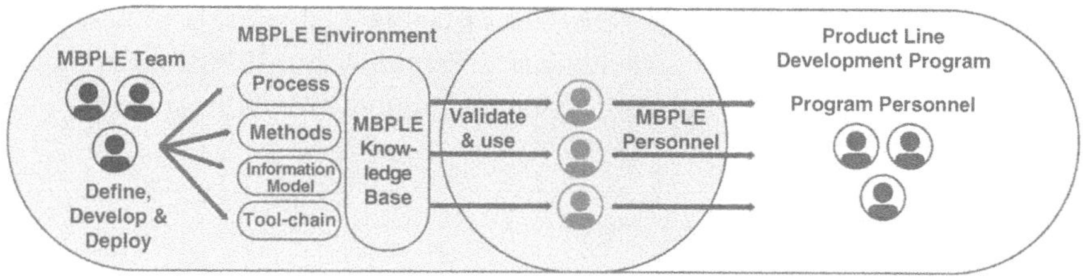

Figure 28.4 Interdependencies among MBPLE team, personnel and environment.

that it remains a separate entity rather than an extension of MBSE. This is because MBSE is just one of several domains with which MBPLE interfaces. The teams shall include the following:

Process experts, method experts, responsible also for the information model, tool experts, and coaches that have experience in deployment and can support the MBPLE personnel in validating the solution as well as in deploying it. MBPLE coaches and the MBPLE personnel guide the transition of the organization in deploying MBPLE within product line programs. For instance, the MBPLE team can vary from a few members of three or four people up to a bigger team of 15 or 20 people depending on the scope of the adoption and the size of the organization.

MBPLE Personnel: As illustrated in Figure 28.4, it serves as the bridges between the MBPLE team and the programs, facilitating the implementation of MBPLE within an organization. Often referred to as MBPLE champions, their role involves validating components such as processes, methods, the information model, and the tool chain, while also providing essential feedback. Their insights are invaluable due to their development experience.

This validation ensures that the MBPLE framework does not remain theoretical – an "ivory tower" development – and does not suffer from low user acceptance upon its rollout. The MBPLE personnel also play a key role in identifying early adopter programs willing to implement the solution with the support of both the MBPLE personnel and the MBPLE team.

It is paramount to recognize that the "human factor" is pivotal in any adoption process. Organizational motivation is important, but individual motivation is equally vital. For example, engineers need to understand how MBPLE can improve their daily tasks. Clear answers to such questions should be provided to them. Awareness needs to be raised among managers and engineers, with managers also needing to see a compelling business case to back the initiative as sponsors, as explained in Chapter 21. Regular training and coaching sessions are essential to facilitate this process.

Adopting new methodologies often faces significant resistance, making one of the greatest challenges not technical, but related to people's acceptance of change. It's crucial to tailor the understanding of MBPLE to different levels within the organization. While managers need to grasp the aspects relevant to their roles, engineers require a more in-depth knowledge. Not everyone needs to understand every detail, but clear, role-specific communication is essential for successful adoption.

MBPLE Environment: The core concept of the MBPLE environment is to establish a "safe" space where the comprehensive MBPLE framework can be defined, developed, and validated prior to the deployment in programs (see Figure 28.4). This environment also facilitates the understanding of the future organizational structure needed to develop the product line with MBPLE. It incorporates all resources and feedback from proofs of concept and early adopters, as well as lessons learned, contributing to the MBPLE "knowledge base." This knowledge base includes detailed descriptions of processes, norms, training materials, demonstrators, tool guidelines, and access to a pre-production tool environment, among other resources.

MBPLE knowledge should be readily accessible, user-friendly, and actively promoted by the MBPLE team to progressively engage more stakeholders. Essentially, the MBPLE environment acts as a rehearsal for the actual MBPLE deployment, laying the groundwork for its success.

28.6 Product Lines-of-product Lines

We conclude this chapter with a short clarification note, with the intention of helping readers who might come across the barbaric term of "product lines-of-product lines," often introduced in the discussion about the product line's organization. Let us set aside right away two of the more common misunderstandings associated with this concept. First, product lines-of-product lines have nothing to do with systems of systems. Second, the term product lines-of-product lines is often erroneously used to refer to multilevel or multilayer feature models.

Having made these clarifications, let us come back to the basic definition of a product line as the group of products that a company sells to sustain its business. Strictly speaking, very few examples of product lines-of-product lines exist in the industry – see, for example, Gregg et al. (2016). This practice is present in companies that sell products issued from a product line (*pl*) to external customers while integrating these same products into a higher-level product line (*PL*) whose products are also sold to external customers. The governance of both product lines, *pl* and *PL*, lies within the scope of the same company, albeit probably allocated to different teams. Examples of this type of business include airspace surveillance systems, earth observation systems, or combat management systems, which might integrate products (e.g. radars, satellites, ground stations) that can be sold separately to other customers.

Let us consider now an original equipment manufacturer (OEM) who buys components from providers that apply a product line approach to deliver their products to different customers (as typically done in automotive, aerospace, or railway). The OEM integrates these sourced components into the higher-level products of its own product lines. Here, however, there is no overarching instance that governs the product lines of the OEM and its providers. Even though they are closely related, these are two different businesses.

It is also important to note that a company can adopt a product line approach not only to deliver the products it sells but it can also apply product line principles to develop all or some of the components of its products. These components can implement different reuse strategies and apply specific MBPLE techniques. In general, though, the business cases of these components are justified by the business case of the product lines to which they contribute. In the end, all the investments and resources required to operate the MBPLE enterprise are financed by the income generated by the sale of the member products of its product lines.

References

AFIS (2015). *Systems Product Line Engineering Handbook*. Cepaduès. France.

Gregg, S., Scharadin, R., and Clements, P.C. (2016). The best of both worlds: agile development meets product line engineering at Lockheed Martin, *INCOSE 2016 International Symposium* (Edinburgh, Scotland). INCOSE: San Diego (US).26 (1): 951–965.

INCOSE (2019) *Feature-based system and Software Product Line Engineering: A Primer*. INCOSE, San Diego.

29

PLE Pioneers' Perspectives: Beyond Tools and Tool Vendors

29.1 Introduction

The authors of this book have been dealing with product line engineering (PLE) and more recently with model-based product line engineering (MBPLE) from the late 2000s, however, as covered in Chapter 7, the PLE discipline sees its birth at least a decade before. This is mainly thanks to two of the pioneers of the discipline, Dr. Charles Krueger and Dr. Danilo Beuche. Both, one in the United States and the other in Germany, had the intuition to work on a more structured and efficient way to develop software by introducing the concept of software product lines, that then evolved in feature-based PLE. The key aspect of how everything stated is that, in both cases the idea of developing software product lines came with the intent to solve their daily academic projects that required extensive coding.

Differently than in the other chapters, this is structured as dialog between one of the authors, Marco Forlingieri, and the two eminent guests. To avoid repetitions and facilitate a smooth read, some questions are repeated for both of our guests; some others are not. It is worth highlighting that, while the answers and definitions given in the interview do not always align with our perspectives as the authors, the fundamental principles and essence of PLE are widely accepted and shared. Let's get started!

29.2 Presentation of the PLE Pioneers

Marco Forlingieri: *Welcome Charlie and Danilo to this open dialog among PLE experts. Tim, Guillermo and I are grateful to have you here, since we strongly believe that no book about PLE could be written without your contribution. How would you like to introduce yourself to our readers?*

Dr. Charles Krueger: *Thanks Marco! I am the founder and CEO of BigLever Software (BigLever 2024), which for over two decades has helped organizations adopt and benefit from feature-based PLE. With more than 30 years of experience in systems and software engineering practice, I am an acknowledged leader in the PLE arena, with many publications in the field of PLE. I am passionate to bring innovative PLE concepts, state-of-the-art methodologies, and success stories to the forefront of the systems engineering community. Aside from the leading role at BigLever, I was the lead editor for the ISO/IEC 26580 (ISO/IEC 2021) standard on feature-based*

Model-Based Product Line Engineering (MBPLE): The Feature-Based Path to Product Lines Success, First Edition.
Marco Forlingieri et al.
 Companion Website: www.wiley.com/go/forlingieri/mbple1e

PLE and past co-chair for the INCOSE PLE International Working Group. I am also a current member of the Forbes Business Council. Everything started back in the days, when I received my PhD in computer science from Carnegie Mellon University and helped to pioneer the field of systems and software product lines.

Dr. Danilo Beuche: *I am Vice President of Strategy and Go-to-Market at PTC, former CEO and co-founder of pure systems. The software company created pure::variants (PTC pure::variants 2024), a tool developed for the implementation of product line technologies in embedded software systems. Puresystems was acquired by PTC in 2023. I began my career in the field of embedded operating systems and software families in the mid-90s. The research on tool development for feature-based software development at the University of Magdeburg ultimately led to the establishment of pure systems in 2001. Additionally, since 2016, I have served as an honorary professor at the Institute for Information Systems at the University of Leipzig.*

29.3 The Early Encounter with the PLE Discipline

Marco Forlingieri: *I would say you are both an authority in the PLE field. Now let's go back to the beginning. Could you share the story of your first encounter with PLE or variant management? What captured your interest in this field?*

Dr. Charles Krueger: *My Master's project at Carnegie Mellon was to author the ACM Computing Surveys issue in June 1992, simply titled Software Reuse, which became the most widely referenced publication in the field of software reuse. The taxonomy used there identified application generators that automatically produce large-scale software systems from high-level abstractions. This was the most effective and promising form of software reuse out of the seven different approaches being explored at the time.*

The powerful and inspirational implications from that study led to my 1997 PhD thesis at Carnegie Mellon, entitled "Modeling and Simulating a Software Architecture Design Space" (Krueger 1997), which further elaborated how generative reuse could be applied to large-scale software architectures rather than just small-scale software components.

In my first commercial job, I and another engineer spent several months putting together "Pearl scripts" that allowed a team of 120 engineers to build eight different "flavors" of a complex mulmillion-line telecommunications software system from a shared collection of software files, without any clone-and-own. With less than a year worth of effort invested, we measurably tripled the output of the team of 120 engineers. Insights from this inspirational experience provided the seeds of the feature-based PLE field as we know it today.

Dr. Danilo Beuche: *I was first exposed to the challenges and benefits of product lines in a university course on object-oriented design of high-performance operating system families – based on the ideas of David Parnas about program families from the 70's (Parnas 1976) for massively parallel computers by Schröder-Preikschat in 1994 (*Schröder-Preikschat 1994*).*

I joined his research group the following year and began working on porting the project to a new embedded platform. Initially, the idea of having a highly configurable operating system with numerous C++ defines seemed promising, as it allowed for various configurations. However, in practice, creating new working configurations was challenging due to the extensive C++

preprocessor defines that needed to be set and the significant background knowledge required about dependencies and code structure. This complexity deterred frequent configuration changes. To address this issue, we aimed to simplify the process and improve the usability of program families, also known as product lines. This goal garnered the interest of several research group members, including myself.

However, this work on configuration approaches was intended to be only the "tool" to gain more time for the fancy stuff, i.e. developing highly customizable operating systems for special-purpose applications. Only a couple of years later, it turned into being the subject of main research with embedded operating systems as the "demonstrator" application. Working with the automotive industry in Germany in the late 90's in joint research projects, we learned that the software in this domain was becoming the perfect application for these ideas, and no off-the-shelf industry solution was available at that point in time.

Doing what good researchers do, when they see that their ideas can turn into a commercially "exploitable" solution, we (Holger Papajewski, Friedrich Schön, Wolfgang Schröder-Preikschat, and I) decided to create a start-up to do so under the name "pure::systems." The rest is history.

29.4 The Primary Benefit of PLE

Marco Forlingieri: *Charlie, Danilo, I can see that for both of you the benefits of PLE were the drivers for deepening the topic and making it at the center of your professional life. However, if you could select one primary benefit to emphasize for PLE, what would it be, and why is it significant?*

Dr. Charles Krueger: *Modern feature-based PLE has one simple opus of magic. It allows the full lifecycle of systems engineering assets to be automatically generated from clear and concise high-level feature-based abstractions for a family of products or systems, thereby eliminating the conventional approaches of clone-and-own and tool-specific variant management, as well as the associated manual inefficiencies. This mechanism enables engineers to shift away from the low-value, labor-intensive, replicative, error-prone engineering effort that deprives them of the time and energy better spent on high-value innovative work that advances business objectives.*

Dr. Danilo Beuche: *The efficiency gains (i.e. the time of engineers not spent on repeating work others already have done before) when developing and maintaining a product line. These efficiency gains are so pervasively embedded in the PLE practice. For instance, a reduced asset base and size to maintain saves time in its maintenance; the typically better test coverage leads to better quality, resulting in less time spent on issue fixing. This often turns into better revenue opportunities by having new product features delivered to multiple products more easily. It must not be overlooked that building a product line is inherently more complex compared to building a single product instance. But all statistics and our own experience show that it already starts paying off with a few product instances to be built and maintained.*

29.5 Differences in PLE Application Between Software, Systems, and Across Industries

Marco Forlingieri: *Now I have a question only for Charlie, since I know your strong statement on the following matter, which some of the readers may disagree with. Do any notable disparities exist in applying PLE principles to software development versus system development?*

Dr. Charles Krueger: *In 2006, I noticed that the same feature-based PLE principles applied to software could be applied equally well to model-based systems engineering (MBSE) and other systems engineering assets and disciplines. We filed for US patents on this concept in 2007 and released the industry's first commercial "PLE bridge" integrations into Systems Engineering tools shortly after that, specifically for IBM Rhapsody (IBM Rhapsody 2024).*

From the ISO/IEC 26580 perspective and from my industry experience, there are no meaningful differences in the principles and strategies for implementing and deploying feature-based PLE to software engineering versus systems development.

Marco Forlingieri: *For you, Danilo, I have another question, always focusing on differences. What are the differences in applying PLE in various industries such as automotive, railway, aerospace, and consumer goods? How do these industries differ in their approach and challenges faced in adopting PLE?*

Dr. Danilo Beuche: *Clearly, certain industries are far ahead in MBSE adoption than others, and that also relates to the use of PLE. Aviation and Defense are leading industries in those disciplines. There are clear differences among systems of various nature. Obviously, a home appliance, like a dishwasher, is not as complex as a car or an airplane. And this impacts the specific PLE approach like many other factors: number of variations, number of product variants, product line lifecycle duration vs. product lifecycle duration, regulations, to name a few. However, I am not able to pinpoint major differences when it comes specifically to the PLE approach across industries. The approach is quite straightforward and industry-independent.*

29.6 PLE Standards and Their Development

Marco Forlingieri: *From your previous answers, it is clear that you strongly support the application of feature-based PLE across software, systems, and heterogeneous industries. PLE standards become essential to regulate the discipline and set shared guidelines. What role did you play in the development of norms such as ISO/IEC 26550 (ISO/IEC 2015) 26580, Variability Exchange Language (VEL) (OASIS 2018)– still not published – etc.? Could you provide some insights into your contributions to these standards?*

Dr. Charles Krueger: *In 2015, the INCOSE standards group asked me to become their liaison in the ISO/IEC Software and Systems Tools and Methods working group. At my first meeting with the working group, I saw a clear opportunity to create a new standard on the modern feature-based PLE tools and methods since the existing early-generation academic PLE standard at the time – ISO/IEC 26550 – did not adequately reflect the commercial advances in the field.*

This led to the ISO/IEC 26580 on the feature-based approach to PLE. I was the lead editor on that effort and recruited Paul Clements, another of the PLE pioneers, to be the co-editor. At that time, I leveraged my role as co-chair on the INCOSE PLE working group (INCOSE PLE WG 2024) to collaborate with both INCOSE membership and ISO membership to gain a broad industry consensus on ISO/IEC 26580.

When the OMG SysML v2 (OMG 2024) standard initiative began to work on the variant modeling portion of that standard, the initiative leader, Sanford Friedenthal, asked me to lead the variant modeling working group to assure that SysML v2 and ISO/IEC 26580 were mutually aligned and compliant. Their plan at the time was to embed a full PLE solution into SysML v2, but this would have been an

MBSE-only PLE solution rather than an orthogonal PLE solution for the full systems engineering life cycle and therefore not ISO/IEC 26580 compliant. Furthermore, this would have been an enormous undertaking by the SysML v2 team, having a scope of effort that they did not yet fully appreciate.

I helped them separate the two concerns of MBSE and feature-based PLE, showing how the addition of a concise variation point construct into the SysML v2 language would be sufficient for an ISO/IEC 26580 compliant MBSE solution that allowed the feature-based PLE concern to be managed by a separate ISO/IEC 26580 feature-based PLE compliant tool, with the PLE feature catalog, Bill-of-Features, and PLE Factory Configurator all outside of the SysML v2 scope.

Dr. Danilo Beuche: *I am a member of the ISO working group, which is responsible for the ISO 265xx family of standards. While not being the main editor of ISO/IEC 26580 (credits must go to Charles Krueger and Paul Clements), I was part of the core team who worked on this standard for a couple of years. And I am quite happy with the impact this standard has been able to achieve. As part of the ISO WG, I am also reviewing other related PLE standards, namely some of the newer members of the 2655x/2656x family standards.*

The VEL is an "indirect" result of a larger publicly funded industry research project my company pure systems participated in. The core idea and language prototypes for this language came out of this project, and pure systems with other interested parties started the standardization effort by establishing a dedicated technical committee in OASIS (OASIS 2018). Personally, I would consider myself rather the business sponsor of pure systems' VEL activities. The main work was done by other pure systems folks – Michael Schulze and Uwe Ryssel – on the language side; the development team built libraries to make this language an integral part of pure::variants. Today, we use this language actively in our product to communicate with other products, such as Catia Magic (Cameo 2024). Nevertheless, it is not yet a final standard out of OASIS. But there is more, pure systems also contributed to AUTOSAR's effort to include variability into their standards (AUTOSAR 2024).

And, not to forget, about a decade ago I was working together with many contributors from other companies and organizations on the OMG CVL – Common Variability Language (Øystein et al. 2013) concept, which sadly was never finalized. Even earlier we initiated an Eclipse project around building a feature modeling language, but this never got enough traction, so we stopped it many years ago.

29.7 Synergies and Challenges of the Liaison PLE and MBSE

Marco Forlingieri: *As you know, all three authors of this book have been promoting the adoption of PLE in combination with MBSE (aka MBPLE). How do MBSE and PLE complement each other? Can you elaborate on the synergies they offer and the challenges they pose when integrated?*

Dr. Charles Krueger: *MBSE and PLE are fully complementary and orthogonal concerns. MBSE's concern is on the structures and behaviors of a system. PLE's concern is on the distinguishing characteristics among the members of a family of similar systems. At the intersection of the MBSE and PLE concerns is the variation point, which allows the crosscutting concern of PLE to be reflected as feature-based PLE variability within the concern of MBSE model elements.*

By applying feature-based PLE to MBSE, a single MBSE superset model with variation points can represent the model for an entire system family portfolio. While managing the superset MBSE model and feature-based PLE model is more complex than managing the MBSE model for a single system, it is much simpler and more efficient than managing a collection of clone-and-own copies of the MBSE model for each member of the system family portfolio.

Dr. Danilo Beuche: *Before answering these questions, let me point out that I (and not only I, see the INCOSE Handbooks statements on PLE and systems engineering) consider SE (without MB prefix) and PLE as having a symbiotic relationship. The concept of describing variability through variation points is a mandatory part of the SE when being applied to families of systems (which many complex systems to which "proper" SE is applied to, are).*

With that being said, the relation between MBSE and PLE is quite interesting. Theoretically, a perfect match, as in most approaches for PLE, some kind of variability model(s) is an essential element. However, before the advent of SysML v2, none of the OMG standards, such as SysML (v1) or UML, had any construct to support high-level variability modeling and, even more critically, supported variation points in their languages out of the box, which in turn meant that expressing variations in models was difficult without building individual extensions. This lack of direct support was and is, in my opinion a showstopper. Especially the representation of shared superset assets can cause grief when tools or languages have no native understanding of the concept of a product configuration.

Therefore, it has always been necessary to develop language and tool extensions to effectively integrate these aspects. Notable examples include Tim Weilkiens' VAMOS approach (Weilkiens 2016) and the integration of the orthogonal variability model, based on Klaus Pohl's ideas (Pohl, Böckle, and Linden 2005), into PTC Modeler (PTC Modeler 2024). Both approaches are fully implemented within the respective modeling language meta-models. To address this challenge, some MBSE tools have developed proprietary language extensions and tool integrations. These extensions, for example, connect to feature-based PLE tools such as Gears or pure::variants.

29.8 The Protagonist Role of the Feature Model in PLE

Marco Forlingieri: *As illustrated extensively in this book, feature models play a crucial role in PLE. Why are feature models essential in PLE, and how do they facilitate the management of product variability?*

Dr. Charles Krueger: *Feature models (or the feature catalog) are orthogonal to MBSE models and other models in other engineering artifacts such as mechanical BOMs. For example, MBSE models describe structures and behaviors for the system(s) of interest, whereas the PLE Feature Catalog describes the high-level abstractions for the distinguishing characteristics among the different products in a product line.*

Abstraction is the key to the value of feature models. There will likely be two or three orders of magnitude fewer elements in a feature model than there are variation points in the engineering assets across the engineering lifecycle. For example, a feature in a feature model might be the optional capability for pedestrian detection in a car that comes in four different flavors: (1) none, (2) pedestrian warning that sounds a warning alarm, (3) pedestrian braking that automatically applies brakes, and (4) pedestrian avoidance that applies brakes and steering. These four abstract variants in the feature model will control thousands of complex and interdependent variation points in requirements, architecture, design, mechanical BOMs, electrical controllers, software, calibration data, user manual documentation, test cases, certification documents, manufacturing plans, service documents, sales brochures, and much more. Having concise high-level abstractions in the feature models that drive the precise, repeatable, automated behaviors of variation points provides powerful benefits such as engineering complexity reduction, reduction in errors compared to manual approaches, and overall reduction in engineering effort.

Dr. Danilo Beuche: *Let me rephrase the question: Why is a dedicated variability model essential in PLE, and why are feature models, in my opinion, a particularly good choice for variability modeling?*

When we look at the variability model, it is at the heart of a product line, it allows one to focus on what differentiates products without having to understand how the system achieves that differentiation technically. As variability is a main driver; before even building the solution, it must be representable in a solution-independent way. In many cases, PLE variability must be referenced when working on various other assets, such as source code and test plans. Therefore, it should be easy to use and free from excessive "unnecessary noise" from the perspective of most users, of which we have many in product lines. A clear separation of concerns is crucial here. There are many ways to model variability explicitly, such as decision diagrams, orthogonal variability models, and propositional logic. Feature models are just one approach. Now, let's discuss why feature models are the "perfect" choice for this purpose.

As someone who fell in love with feature models almost three decades ago, I have a fairly biased view here. Around 1998, when I was trying to find a solution to the problem of making complex configuration logic easily accessible to (software) engineers, I came across an article from Kryzsztof Czarnecki. In this chapter, he introduced the idea of feature models, and it immediately clicked in my brain. This combination of a few language constructs was immensely powerful yet easy to explain and remember. The original FODA (Kang et al. 1990) ideas were in many aspects an inspiration yet not sufficient for real-world modeling when I tried to capture the logic of the operating system product line we were working at that time. So, I built a "new" feature modeling language, which is now manifested in pure::variants. All the enhancements and developments done were intended to preserve key properties of the nature of feature models. Easy to grasp and use even for the "casual" user when writing and configuring, yet powerful enough to cover a majority of PLE use cases.

Due to the many stakeholders being exposed to the PLE variability, having an easy to read and learn language is paramount for acceptance and usability. This is the "superpower" of feature models; they just have the right balance. If we look at it from a "mathematical" perspective, for instance, the OVM language is basically identical to what you can express with feature models, yet, to me, reading and grasping the relationship of multiple OVM variation points is much harder, at least for my brain, than reading the equivalent feature model. Similarly, if we look over the fence into the world of PLM tools such as Siemens Teamcenter (Siemens Teamcenter 2024), PTC Windchill (PTC Windchill 2024), or Dassault Enovia (Dassault Systèmes 2024), to name a few, there is configuration logic usually expressed in "flat" lists of variation points connected via logic rules in the background. This is almost identical to the OVM approach. But as refinement relationships must be expressed through "invisible" rules. These complex dependencies are much more difficult to grasp for the casual user.

29.9 Common Misconceptions About PLE and Usage of a PLE Tool

Marco Forlingieri: *There are several myths or misunderstandings about MBSE, such as the fact that "MBSE wants to replace SE" or that "it wants to eliminate requirements." Regarding PLE, Charlie, what are, according to your experience, some prevalent misconceptions that people have about PLE, and how do these misunderstandings impact its adoption and implementation?*

Dr. Charles Krueger: *Early-generation PLE methods focused on reuse, where reusable artifacts in a reuse library could be leveraged to create member products in a product line of similar systems. Unfortunately, this simple reuse concept is the "obvious" one that people intuitively gravitate to. Sadly, the recommended methodology in books, papers, and even in standards like ISO/IEC 26550 has clone-and-own style reuse at the foundation.*

Many organizations have gone down this "obvious" path, only to be overwhelmed by the complexity of managing all the nearly identical but distinct clones in their portfolio. These organizations tend to abandon their PLE initiative and then spread the message that PLE doesn't work. I characterize this phenomenon as "the things about PLE that are obvious do not work and the things about PLE that do work (i.e. ISO/IEC 2680) are not obvious." This is why in ISO/IEC 26580 we use the term "sharing" rather than "reuse." The common meaning of reuse is a cloning event, whereas sharing connotes joining together for a long-term collaborative journey with supersets.

Another prevalent misconception is that adding a PLE tool into an engineering practice will provide the desired benefits of efficiency, quality, cost reduction, complexity reduction, and scale. However, feature-based PLE requires organizational change and engineering workflow change to be successful. This is articulated in ISO/IEC 26580, but organizations sometimes believe they can ignore this reality and still be successful by installing a modern PLE tool while avoiding the more challenging people-oriented issues of modernizing organization structures and processes. I characterize this phenomenon as changing technology is easy, but hanging people is hard.

Marco Forlingieri: *I often hear the statement: "Why do we need a PLE tool if we can do everything in the systems modeling tool?" Why is there a need for specialized tools to manage variability in product lines? What limitations exist in relying solely on system modeling tools for this purpose?*

Dr. Danilo Beuche: *The answer to this question is kind of a summary of what I already expressed before: There is a need for an explicit dedicated variability modeling language with properties making it easy to use for specifically that purpose. The variability model is at the core of PLE and referenced from many other data assets throughout the engineering flow. If this kind of model is being defined in a dedicated tool like pure::variants or in a systems modeling tool makes no difference from a theoretical point of view.*

Practically speaking, with MBSE not being as widespread as it could and should be, for a lot of users, a dedicated tool without the "overhead" of MBSE is quite attractive. It also helps to get started with PLE without having to introduce MBSE, too, to benefit from this. And with no formally defined variability language built into SysML, all approaches are currently "proprietary." Whereas there is a solid offering for dedicated product line factory configurators (as tools like pure::variants or Gears are classified according to ISO 26580) for commercial customers as well as open-source research tools like FeatureIDE with similar capabilities.

This picture may (or may not) change with the success of SysML v2, as the approach does not preclude anyone from building explicit variability modeling into their SysML v2 approach as a language extension and/or to add this to a revised standard at some point in time.

As a side note, one practical limitation of many MBSE tools available today is the challenge of collaboration and evolution of models. Graphical notations are inherently difficult to compare and nicely merge when concurrent changes are made in different branches. This limits the use of models in software-development-like workflows (e.g. using feature branches). However, this kind of workflow is paramount for modern, agile development (and not only there). We designed and built pure::variants in a way that things like three-way compare and merge are nicely supported by the modeling approach and in the tools UI. This was not an easy task for feature models, but it is so much harder for MBSE languages.

29.10 SysML v2 as Potential "Game-Changer" for MBPLE

Marco Forlingieri: *Along this book and ultimately in the last answer of Danilo, we heard about the advent of SysML v2. As PLE pioneers and tool vendors, do you perceive SysML v2 primarily as a threat or an opportunity for PLE? How do you think it will influence the landscape of PLE methodologies?*

Dr. Charles Krueger: *Variant modeling in SysML v2 was intentionally designed to be compliant with ISO/IEC 26580 and aligned to industry best practices in feature-based PLE. The synergy between these two highly visible standards validates the role of PLE in the future of MBSE and systems engineering. The key to success will be how well MBSE tool vendors comply with both ISO/IEC 26580 and SysML v2. If these vendors do not understand or do not comply with the good guidance provided in these standards, then they might do more damage than good to the landscape of PLE and MBSE.*

Dr. Danilo Beuche: *SysML v2 introduces embedded variation and variants as native elements of the language, which is a significant improvement and will greatly facilitate the integration of MBSE and PLE. In my opinion, the separation of concerns is well managed. This approach allows SysML v2 to seamlessly connect with both existing and newly developed PLE variability modeling concepts and tools, reflecting the orthogonality of the driving variability models in PLE. I believe this will make MBSE in combination with PLE much more attractive. I also think that it is a huge opportunity for MBSE to become more accessible and integrated in companies' engineering approaches beyond those domains where the use of MBSE is kind of mandated. And thus, it will be a relevant element of PLE methodologies of the future.*

Yet, I see SysML v2 only as one element of many in the successful PLE/SE approach. I don't see all product lines being built using SysML v2, while being appropriate for many. It also depends on how the SysML v2 tool vendors will implement the integration of the SysML v2 variability concepts into their tools. We have some interesting times ahead of us with SysML v2. Looking forward to them!

29.11 The Key Absent in the PLE Arena: a Variability Modeling Standard

Marco Forlingieri: *While we see SysML already advancing to a second new life with SysML v2, why is there not a widely adopted standard for feature modeling or variability modeling languages? What challenges do you foresee in establishing such a standard?*

Dr. Charles Krueger: *The feature ontology required for an effective feature-based PLE feature catalog in complex, commercial, large-scale system families is very sophisticated, with modularity, hierarchical composition, layers of abstraction, mixing instantiation with generalization, and more. Early efforts to specify PLE feature modeling standards were mostly academic and suitable for small-scale demonstrations but not suitable for large-scale commercial experience. Creating a standard requires a lot of time, money, and effort. While feature-based PLE has been in the early stages of the technology adoption curve, PLE vendors have been laser focused on creating the tools and methods that enable repeatable success stories. As feature-based PLE "crosses the chasm" into the broader adoption by the mainstream, pressures to create industry standards will increase and benefit those involved.*

Dr. Danilo Beuche: *As a tool vendor, one has always a very ambivalent relationship to standards. On one hand, good standards create better understanding and accessibility of concepts, but you are always concerned about commoditizing away your competitive advantage by making it easier for others to build similar tools based on your know-how being exposed through good standards. And even worse, bad and/or too restrictive standards may kill innovation. From a user's point of view, this is different; here, interoperability and choice of multiple tools for the same purpose are key benefits. From my point of view, standards like VEL and SysML V2 are balancing this nicely. Over time, with growing knowledge and expertise, with feature-based product lines being a widely accepted PLE approach supported by multiple tools, we will probably see more formal language standards emerge.*

29.12 The Future of MBPLE with the Rise of AI and Large End-to-End Proprietary Solutions

Marco Forlingieri: *We are heading to the last part of our discussion, and I would like to have your opinion, Charlie, on a "hot" topic nowadays: What are the potential advantages and disadvantages of integrating artificial intelligence (AI) technologies into (MB) PLE processes? How might AI enhance or disrupt current practices?*

Dr. Charles Krueger: *The combinatorics in PLE is staggering. With only 33 independent optional feature choices, you can specify a unique product configuration for every human on planet Earth. With only 280 independent optional feature choices, you can specify a unique product configuration for every atom in the known universe. Complex product lines may have thousands of unique feature choices. Although advanced PLE tools provide capabilities to dramatically reduce combinatorics, the numbers can still remain astronomical. Product portfolio managers face the challenge of guessing how many products for how many feature combinations will be economically desirable and optimal to the market and their corporate bottom line. A good role for AI is to explore market trends and projections with the PLE feature combinations to plan the perfect product line portfolio.*

Marco Forlingieri: Danilo, in 2023 we assisted in the acquisition of pure systems by the ALM and PLM vendor PTC (PTC News 2024). *How do you envision the future of PLE tools? Will they evolve to become tool chain independent, or will they remain closely tied to specific PLM or ALM tool vendors?*

Dr. Danilo Beuche: *That is a good question to which I have no definitive answer. Let me break it down into areas where I am certain and areas where the future remains uncertain.*

I strongly believe that PLE will become more widespread in many industries. For companies and teams deciding about tools, it will become a critical point to see with which tools PLE can be done in an efficient manner. For instance, PLE integration is already part of many RfP (requests for proposals) of customers, addressing ALM and MBSE vendors. I believe we will see a new wave of competing approaches and solutions coming to the market in the near future. But for customers, the main challenge is how to integrate this in their entire tool chain. Fully closed one-vendor ecosystems will only have limited acceptance. Hence now, tools with the special focus on PLE like pure::variants are quite an attractive choice. If enough tool vendors decide or are forced (e.g. by the way of industry standards) to integrate standard APIs in a nice way, then tools like pure::variants can become more tool chain independent. But based on our experience, there is one critical element: Easy access to variability models in all connected tools; for instance, when working with test plans, engineers must be able to interact seamlessly with PLE models from within the test plan. They should be able to review the test plan for a specific product instance easily and add variations to a test case or test plan without being forced to switch tools and contexts. Future PLE tools must deliver this capability to remain appealing for most use cases.

For now, where basically each combination of a PLE tool and engineering authoring tools requires some kind of proprietary work to achieve this level of integration, it is not possible for a PLE tool to be tool chain independent. A wide adoption of VEL would be a step closer to tool-independence and more choice for the users, but VEL is not sufficient as it does not cover the technology to directly expose variability models to the users in the authoring tools. Here surely, a widely accepted standard for PLE variability models and the availability of rendering components could make the job easier.

To summarize, sooner or later, PLE concepts will be pervasive. But I do not know if this will be through an open collaborating ecosystem of engineering tools, including a standalone PLE factory configurator with a standardized API or through many point-to-point integrations. Or if MBSE and SysML v2++ will take over the world and become the hub for PLE.

29.13 Conclusion

During this friendly talk, Dr. Charles Krueger and Dr. Danilo Beuche gave us insightful and not obvious answers on the PLE topic, including its often troublesome "marriage" with MBSE. What fascinates us, the authors of this book, is their passion and entire professional life dedicated to PLE. After almost 30 years, they are still at the forefront of this powerful formula and the magic of sharing commonality and managing variability to deliver customer satisfaction. This is ultimately the essence of feature-based PLE.

References

Autosar (2024). Automotive open system architecture. https://www.autosar.org (accessed 4 July 2024).

BigLever (2024). BigLever software gears. https://biglever.com/solution/gears/ (accessed 10 May 2024).

Cameo (2024). Cameo system modeller. https://www.3ds.com/products/catia/no-magic/cameo-systems-modeler (accessed 11 May 2024).

Dassault Systèmes (2024). 3DExperience platform. https://www.3ds.com/3dexperience (accessed 11 May 2024).

IBM Rhapsody (2024). IBM engineering systems design rhapsody. https://www.ibm.com/products/systems-design-rhapsody (accessed 11 May 2024).

INCOSE PLE WG (2024). INCOSE PLE Working Group. https://www.incose.org/communities/working-groups-initiatives (accessed 12 July 2024).

ISO/IEC (2015). Software and systems engineering – reference model for product line engineering and management (ISO/IEC/IEEE 26550:2015).

ISO/IEC (2021). Software and systems engineering – reference model for product line engineering and management (ISO/IEC/IEEE 26580:2021).

Kang, K., Cohen, S., Hess, J. et al. (1990). Feature oriented domain analysis (FODA) feasibility study, *Technical Report CMU/SEI-90-TR-21*, Software Engineering Institute, November, 1990, Carnegie Mellon University, Pittsburgh, USA.

Krueger, C.W. (1997). *Modeling and Simulating a Software Architecture Design Space*. School of Computer Science, Computer Science Department, Carnegie Mellon University, Pittsburgh, PA.

OASIS (2018). OASIS variability exchange language (VEL). https://www.oasis-open.org/committees/tc_home.php?wg_abbrev=vel (accessed 23 July 2023).

Object Management Group (OMG) (2024). OMG system modeling language version 2.0, ad/2023–02–11. Object Management Group.

Øystein, H., Wąsowski, A., and Czarnecki, K. (2013), CVL: common variability language. In: *Proceedings of the 17th International Software Product Line Conference* (SPLC 13), 277. New York, NY, USA.

Parnas, D. (1976). On the design and development of program families. *IEEE Transactions on Software Engineering*, vol. SE-2, pp. 1-9. https://doi.org/10.1109/TSE.1976.233797.

Pohl, K., Böckle, G., and Linden, F. (2005). *Software Product Line Engineering: Foundations, Principles and Techniques.*

PTC Modeler (2024). PTC modeler. https://www.ptc.com/en/products/ptc-modeler (accessed 12 July 2024).

PTC News (2024). PTC alm. https://www.ptc.com/en/news/2023/ptc-acquires-pure-systems (accessed 26 February 2024).

PTC pure::variants (2024). Pure::variants. https://www.ptc.com/en/products/pure-variants (accessed 10 May 2024).

PTC Windchill (2024). PTC windchill plm software. https://www.ptc.com/en/products/windchill (accessed 11 May 2024).

Siemens Teamcenter (2024). Teamcenter plm software. https://plm.sw.siemens.com/en-US/teamcenter / (accessed 11 May 2024).

Schröder-Preikschat, W. (1994). PEACE-A software backplane for parallel computing. *Parallel Computing* 20: 1471–1485.

Weilkiens, T. (2016). *Variant Modeling with SysML*. MBSE4U.

Part V

MBPLE Industrial Cases

To close this book, five real-world cases of model-based product line engineering (MBPLE) adoption in three different industries are proposed: aviation, defense and heat, ventilation and air-conditioning (HVAC) equipment, represented by Airbus, MBDA, Thales, Raytheon and Belimo.

To select the industrial cases, different criteria were identified. These criteria are independent of the modeling language and tools used by the different contributors:

- Adoption of systems engineering processes as defined by ISO/IEC 15288.
- Implementation of product line-based development.
- Application of ISO/IEC 25550 and 25580 standards.
- Use of features to represent and manage variability.
- The approach to implement MBPLE can be mapped to the 4 key steps of Chapter 12.
- Adoption of a model-based approach.
- At least two types of assets are controlled by the feature model (e.g. requirements, MBSE, CAD).

While there might certainly be more than five cases that comply with those criteria –like some of the works referenced throughout the book– the intention of this last part is to provide a "fresh picture" of the current state of adoption and deployment of MBPLE conscious (and hoping) that this picture is fast evolving in today's world.

Each case presented in Part V proposes an overview of the adoption of MBPLE and zooms in on a specific topic of interest. The case presented by Airbus focuses on the unique characteristics of the aviation industry and explores the concept of "variability cascading" across several levels of the system hierarchy and across different abstraction layers (the reader can refer to Chapter 18 for key concepts).

The case presented by MBDA is centered on the implementation of a model-based approach with Systems Modeling Language (SysML) and its integration with feature-based product line engineering and provides detailed examples of feature models and other shared assets, such as electrical design artifacts.

Taking a different point of view, the case presented by Thales reflects on a 15-year journey of product line development, evolving from document-based and clone-and-own approaches to a very mature, organization-wide delivery approach based on MBPLE.

Raytheon's case, the sole non-European example, highlights the US Department of Defense's (DoD) concept of the "digital trinity." It demonstrates how modern system family engineering enhances this concept, enabling the DoD and its defense contractors to innovate rapidly and maintain relevance. This approach extends beyond the traditional model-based application of PLE by integrating DevOps practices and a Modular Open Systems Approach (MOSA) architecture.

In the last industrial case, Belimo highlights the market-driven context that prompted the company to adopt MBPLE. The case focuses on variability management, stressing the differentiated application of variability during two phases: an early development stage, which includes concept and system architecture definition, and a later stage, including system design.

Part V concludes with a brief analysis of the five industrial cases, highlighting the similarities and differences in MBPLE adoption among the cases.

30

Airbus: MBPLE in Commercial Aviation

Davi Henrique de Sousa Pinto

30.1 Introduction

Digital era: The digital and artificial intelligence (AI) era brings challenges to all industries, who need to adapt to survive the increasing competition and quick change of environment (Knaster and Leffingwell 2020). The challenges go across all layers of an enterprise, from business to technology, manufacturing, operations, and services. The aerospace industry, historically spearheading innovation and driving changes due to its complex needs and products (Walden et al. 2023), has been facing the growing and fast needs to digitalize itself to remain competitive.

Rise of product line engineering: In this environment, the product line engineering (PLE) discipline rose from highly variable and customizable software products in the nineties, which required more sophisticated techniques to manage the variability and reuse (Kang et al. 2009). Thousands of features, driving both static and dynamic perspectives of software source code and runtime, meant more sophisticated and formal descriptions of variability, processes, and techniques to harvest, understand, and automate development.

Requirements and systems engineering at Airbus: At the same time, systems engineering penetration increased in all stages of the life cycle of aircraft development. The perceived need to tackle more complex aircraft from manufacturers, such as Airbus, and certification authorities enforced standards such as the ARP 4754A (Society of Automotive Engineers Aerospace 2010). Although focusing mostly on requirements engineering, it functioned as a crucial step in shaping both processes and culture to systems engineering, laying the foundations which enable the current top–down push from the enterprise of model-based approaches, data-centric processes, digital continuity, and PLE.

Next generation of Airbus aircraft: These advances are mandatory for the next generation of aircraft, such as the zero-emission, which aims at targeting not only business but also societal demands regarding sustainability. Recent technologies, such as AI and future iterations, also rely on strong digitalization and change readiness efforts to be implemented in a timely manner. They are enablers for more optimized products in both development, manufacturing, and operations.

Increasing complexity: One of the ways to measure complexity is the amount of source lines of code (SLOC) within a system. Airbus and Boeing data shows that the SLOC is doubling roughly every four years (Feiler et al. 2009). SLOC cannot grow indefinitely, as it impacts affordability

Model-Based Product Line Engineering (MBPLE): The Feature-Based Path to Product Lines Success, First Edition.
Marco Forlingieri et al.

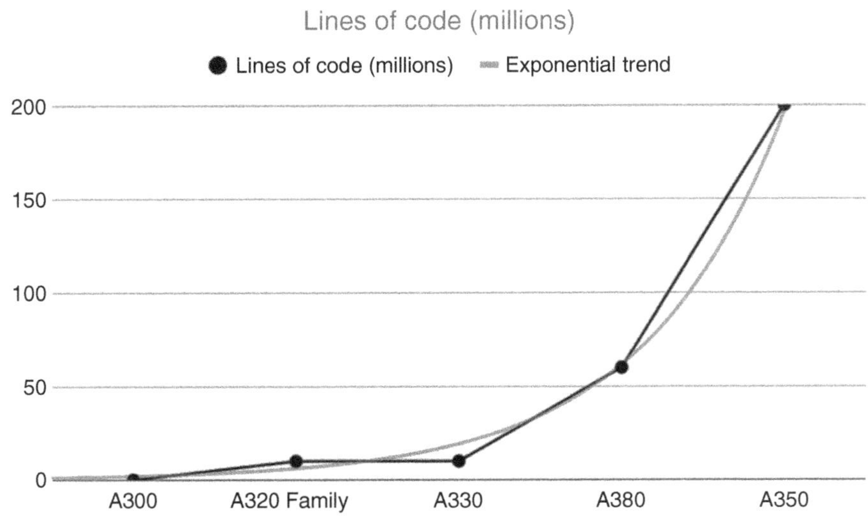

Figure 30.1 Software complexity in Airbus' commercial aircraft.

(Feiler et al. 2009). Approaches such as PLE help reduce the costs of such extensive source code by better managing variability and reuse. Figure 30.1 shows the exponential growth in Airbus aircraft lines of code.

30.2 MBPLE at Airbus

Digital design, manufacturing and services: To tackle the previously described challenges, Airbus has launched in 2019 a group-wide program, called Digital Design, Manufacturing and Services (DDMS) (Ferrogalini 2019). This program, with its significant budget and resources, aims at preparing the whole enterprise for the next generation of products while upskilling, capitalizing, maturing, and battle-hardening key capabilities on current successful product iterations.

Capitalizing on existing aircraft: The A220, A320, A330, and A350 families are still thriving in the current market (Airbus 2024a,b), with huge backlogs and constantly submitted to new updates and modernizations. This is a perfect playground and environment for ironing new capabilities and processes.

30.2.1 Model-Based Systems Engineering

Complex environment: Deploying wide group changes in complex environments such as the Airbus Group is not simple. Solid foundations in systems engineering are necessary before any attempt at widening the scope to proposed initiatives such as model-based systems engineering (MBSE), multidisciplinary analysis and optimization (MDAO), or PLE.

Requirements-based engineering: The transition to a requirements-based engineering approach was the first step taken. The sheer volume of requirements that needed to be formalized in a complex configuration management environment, while having to remain robust and airworthy, made the transition take its time. A cultural change was also vital to achieve, along with the development and maturation of IT tools that supported this effort.

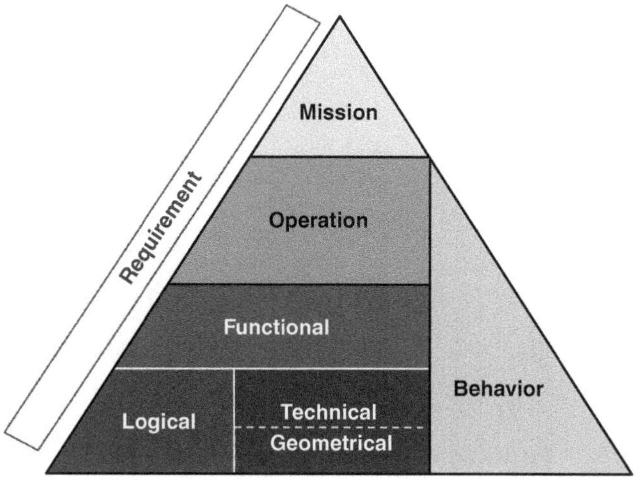

Figure 30.2 Airbus R-MOFLT architecture framework.

Expansion to systems engineering: The next logical step was the adoption of a broader systems engineering processes scope. Changes of this caliber are fundamentally distinct amongst Airbus Divisions. The business size, airworthiness, and certification requirements make Airbus commercial adoption slower and denser than the Airbus helicopters (AH) and Airbus Defence and Space (ADS). On the other hand, faster advances from AH and ADS bring much-needed development and feedback to any group-wide transformation, such as DDMS's envisioned systems engineering transformation. Nevertheless, initiatives in the Commercial Aircraft Systems department go back to almost a decade.

R-MOFLT architecture framework: Several initiatives within the group in the last two decades, along with MBSE academic and industrial developments, led to the creation of a group-wide MBSE architecture framework based on the Systems Modeling Language (SysML): Requirements, Mission, Operational, Functional, Logical, Technical Analysis (R-MOFLT) (Ducamp et al. 2022). As seen in Figure 30.2, the R-MOFLT framework covers both problem and solution spaces, supporting the Airbus Systems Engineering Referential processes.

30.2.2 Product Line Engineering

Origins at Airbus: Although several decentralized initiatives were taken within the group, the first more organized PLE developments were in the Airbus Defence and Space division. It started by focusing on requirements management and applicability. Later, MBSE assets were included, and a formal model-based product line engineering (MBPLE) was established within DDMS, expanding to all Airbus divisions.

Local optimum: Product lines are one of the pillars of the DDMS program. The principles of reusability and overall optimization are core to the DNA of the Airbus organization. Due to the sensitivity of product profitability related to its performance, localized techniques, along with several successful programs spanning for decades, created several "silos" of local processes. Those share many of the important concepts seen in product lines, although not standardized or managed as such. Those include modularization, reusability (from cross-program in clone-and-own styles, to jointly managed, such as in lower-level components).

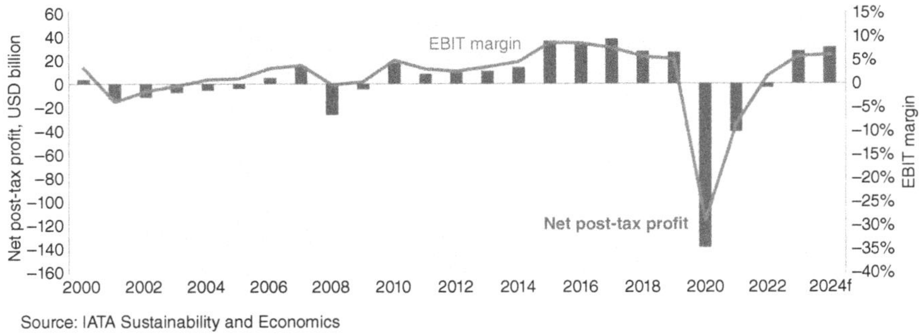

Figure 30.3 Global airline net profit and EBIT margin.

30.2.3 Focusing on Aviation

Safety first: For civil aircraft, the main driver for the development and operation is safety (ICAO 2023), as a single accident can profoundly harm the manufacturer's trust and cost millions or billions in financial damage, on top of the human cost in injuries and deaths.

Slim profit margin (IATA 2024): Aviation's profitability is fragile and low (Figure 30.3). Jet fuel, with its volatile price linked to oil prices, makes up around 30% of aviation operating costs. On top, the increasing costs of climate change and decarbonization put increasing pressure on the industry's already slim margin. With alternative sustainable aviation fuel costing more than twice as much as aviation fuel, existing solutions to reduce dependency on fossil energy are not economically viable yet.

To optimize operational profitability and retain a strong market position, Airbus has historically invested large amounts of cash on weight reduction, manufacturing efficiency, and other initiatives.

Role of PLE: In this environment, PLE is one of the levers to increase performance on all axes of development (products, manufacturing, and services) and operation. Although the applied approach might not be the same as the ones used for other industries, the core principles remain the mastering of variability and reuse while increasing quality.

PLE is also a key element in optimizing the production ramping up, which has been highlighting inefficiencies and bottlenecks on processes.

30.2.4 Model-Based Product Line Engineering

Beyond product lines: Airbus has chosen to integrate into its DDMS transformation project, a MBPLE initiative. Its mission is to cover not only product line development but also variability management and trade-off analysis. The scope spans across business units, and it aims at implementing, tailoring, and expanding the ISO 26550:2015 (ISO/IEC 2015) family.

Feature-based approach: The Airbus MBPLE framework has its foundations in the feature-based approach described in the ISO 26580:2021 (ISO/IEC 2021). As previously mentioned, the framework emphasis is not only on product lines, which has its own organization within DDMS. The focus lies on variability management, and how variability models and PLE configurators can be used in different disciplines.

Modeling approaches: From a SysML modeling perspective, the framework is versatile and covers both "direct and clean" modeling approaches described by Forlingieri and Weilkiens (2022).

Configuration management: The product line life cycle added a considerable complexity to configuration management, as both phases (domain and application engineering) shall be managed in tandem, with traceability not only within but also between them. The Airbus implementation targets at performing configuration management in the variability models. The other asset classes are in general covered by their own domain (requirements, MBSE models, etc.).

Customization: From offer to delivery, variability is a key aspect for customization. Here the challenge is a transversal variability management approach to maximize profitability through quicker anticipation of market needs, and faster feasibility studies and time to market.

Trades: Variability management is at the heart of trades. From a technical perspective, a trade can be seen as a provisional product line, with the trades' candidates seen as product line variants. Provisional here means an architectural trade that can be run in hours but also a longer pre-program phases spanning for years, while concepts and studies are performed before architectural freeze. From that point, development can go back to a single product or remain a product line covering a family of products.

Feature-based variability on trades: The end-to-end trade flowchart below (Figure 30.4) exemplifies this principle, which uses the powerful PLE techniques of variability management to manage not only architecture and parameters, but also the simulation model.

Powering multidisciplinary analysis and optimization: Many of the existing trades are already performed with effective and specialized tools, which are not meant to be replaced by PLE techniques. Where PLE can place a fundamental role is on MDAO, where the multimodel, multidisciplinary nature of the analysis benefits from having a more standard variability description and possibly configurators on model instantiation.

30.3 Challenges for MBPLE Implementation

Heterogeneity of variability management: Without the existence nor the application of standards, variability has been historically managed in diverse ways: spreadsheets, scripts, macros, matrices, templates, filters, and customized systems. This means that processes and organizations have invested and adapted themselves to variability management and not all have pain points related to it.

Obstacles to a holistic approach: This heterogeneity is a barrier to achieving a more holistic view and management of variability, a pillar of product lines. It requires strong sponsorship and business case to prove the benefits on wider scope outside of existing silos.

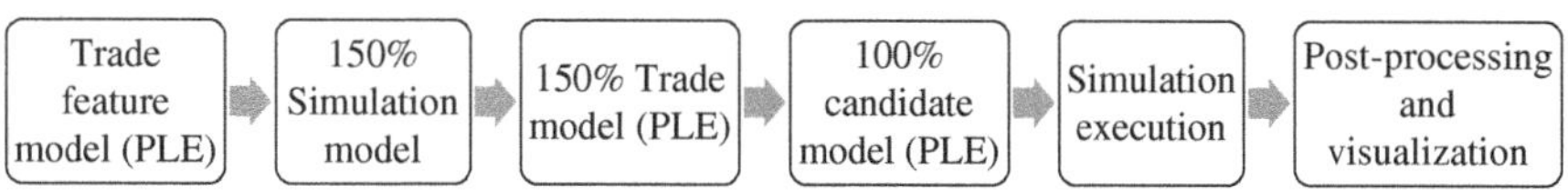

Figure 30.4 Simplified trade flow using PLE techniques.

30.4 Variability Cascading

This section presents and discusses valuable principles related to variability cascading. Although focusing on SysML (Object Management Group [OMG] 2024) models and textual requirements, the principles can be extended to other similar languages, such as UML (OMG 2017), and other classes of assets, such as 3D elements.

At Airbus, pure::variants (PTC pure::variants 2024) is mainly used for feature modeling and as a PLE configurator. For SysML modeling, Cameo Systems Modeler (Cameo 2024) is the tool used. Pure::variants has a direct connector to Cameo Systems Modeler, and these tools are used in this section to illustrate the concepts. Figure 30.5 shows the current tool chain. Airbus tooling never dictate the framework, but it is the opposite. The principles are centered at a holistic and agnostic framework, based on data products, ontology formalization and data continuity.

30.4.1 Dimensions of Variability

The principles and techniques here can be applied to any of the four dimensions of variability Figure 30.6 (Forlingieri 2022).

From a technical perspective, though, the four dimensions can be split into two categories:

1. **SysML variability cascading (requirements and MBSE) – intra-system**, mainly covering the "variability in layers of abstraction" dimension. This focuses on how to cascade variability in a consistent manner along the system engineering processes (ISO/IEC/IEEE 15288 2023). In our context, this means cascading variability in textual requirements and MBSE models for a given system of interest (SOI). The MOFLT systems architecture framework has been expanded to include variability and support PLE architecting through the MBPLE4MOFLT method (Madeira et al. 2023).

Figure 30.5 Airbus MBPLE tool chain.

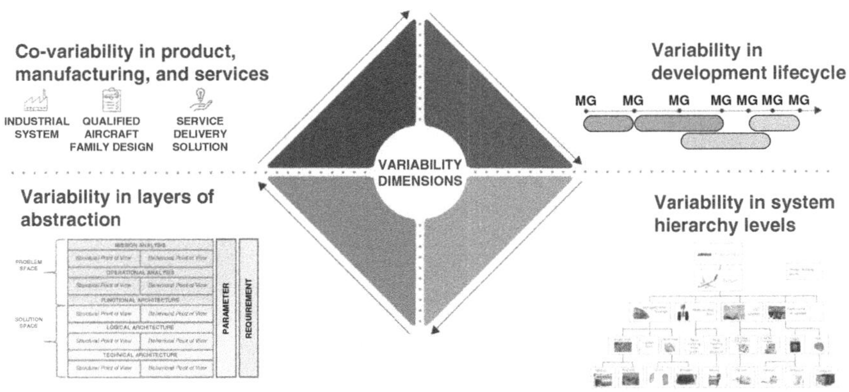

Figure 30.6 Four dimensions of variability.

2. **Variability model (feature models) cascading – inter-system**, mainly covering the "co-variability in product, manufacturing, and services," "variability in development lifecycle," and "variability in system hierarchy levels" dimensions. The focus here is on cascading variability between different SoI. Most of this consists of multimodel and multilevel feature models. If different SOI models are linked, the techniques from "intra system" can be applied.

Figure 30.7 illustrates how both kinds of cascading ("intra-system" and "inter-system") work together in a "co-variability in product, manufacturing, and services" context.

SysML: Figure 30.8 illustrates how the SysML covers both structural and behavioral views from a system while supported by requirements. Moreover, all views are linked together, maintaining continuity and consistency. Naturally, variability can impact all those views, and cascading of variability both inside the same views and cross-views needs to be taken into consideration.

In this section we consider the cascading in the following SysML diagrams:

1. **Structural**: Block definition diagrams (BDD) and internal block diagrams (IBD).
2. **Behavior**: Activity diagrams (ACT) and state machine diagrams.
3. **Requirements:** Requirements diagrams.

30.4.2 Variability Cascading Main Principles

The cascading principles are illustrated by a simplified aircraft example, which proposes a new optional capability to improve fuel consumption and reduce emissions. This capability aims at delaying engine start by using a wheel powered engine in the landing gear for ground operations. The example is inspired by the e-Taxi aircraft concept (Madeira et al. 2023), with its feature model described in Figure 30.9.

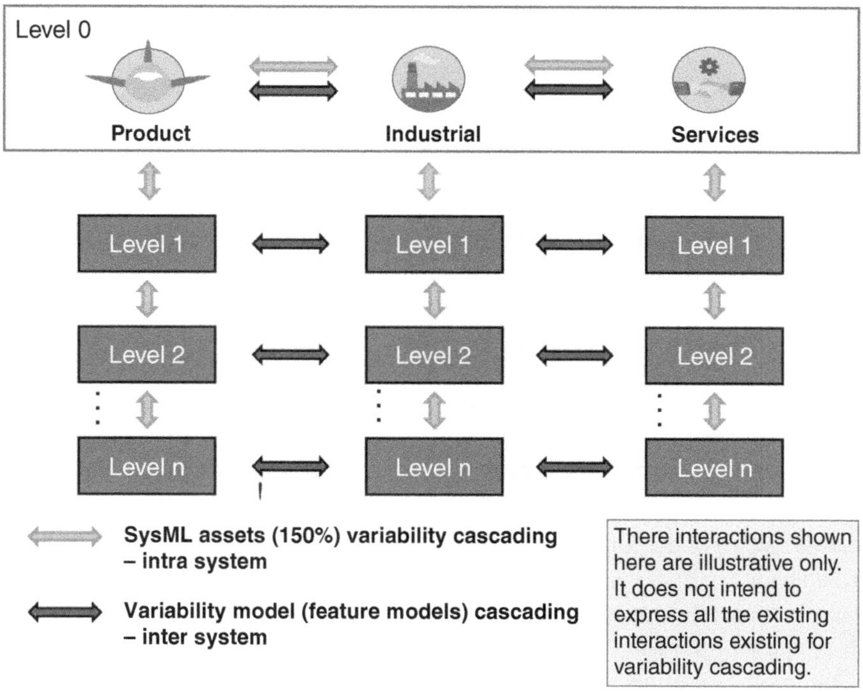

Figure 30.7 Variability cascading overview.

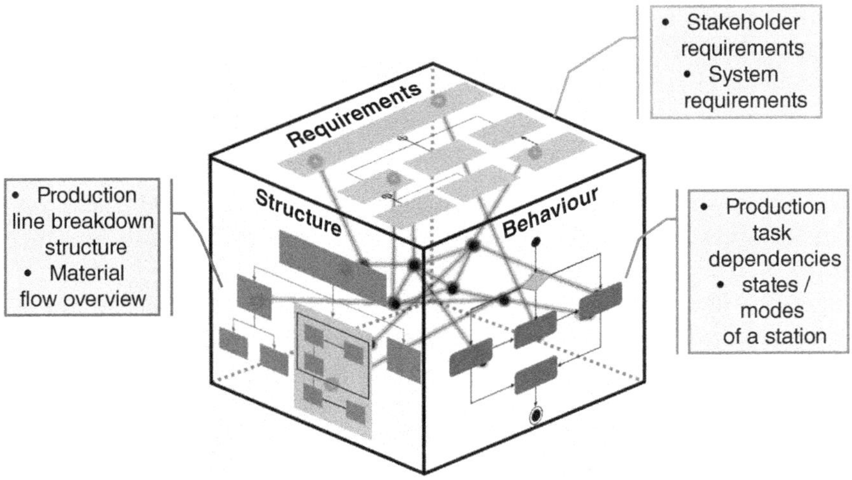

Figure 30.8 MBSE model views.

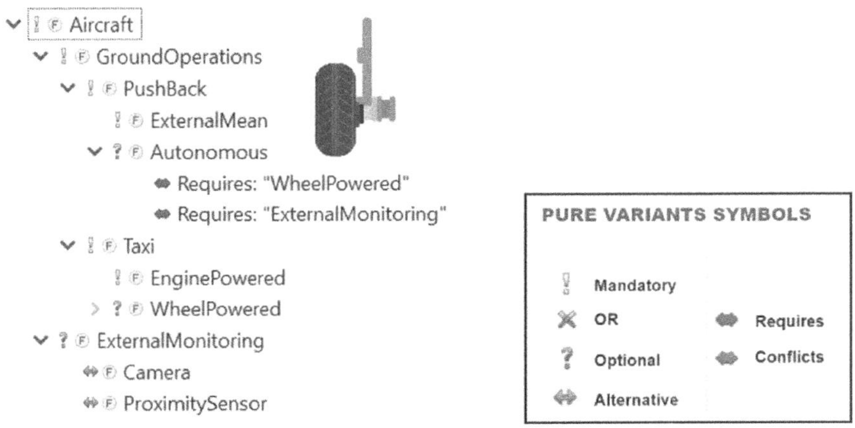

Figure 30.9 e-Taxi simplified feature model.

Focus on core elements driving variability: The use of variation points by constraining assets to features shall be the minimum possible and reserved for core and root elements driving variability. Usage of variation points for cleaning of models or convenience shall be avoided. Remember that variation points are expensive to maintain from a consistency and semantic perspective.

Example: One of the functions used by the system to perform an electric wheel-powered taxi is called "Produce AC Movement on LG from electric power." Figure 30.10 shows the function represented by a SysML block and its owned elements. This is a variable function linked to the feature "Electric."

This function is part of the functional architecture (as a SysML part), as shown in Figure 30.11. Also, its behavior is part of an activity diagram, as shown in Figure 30.12.

This example shows the power of analyzing and identifying the true root elements driving the variability. By applying a single variation point in the block representing the function, all its owned elements inherit it (meaning they also get deleted together with its owner during a model

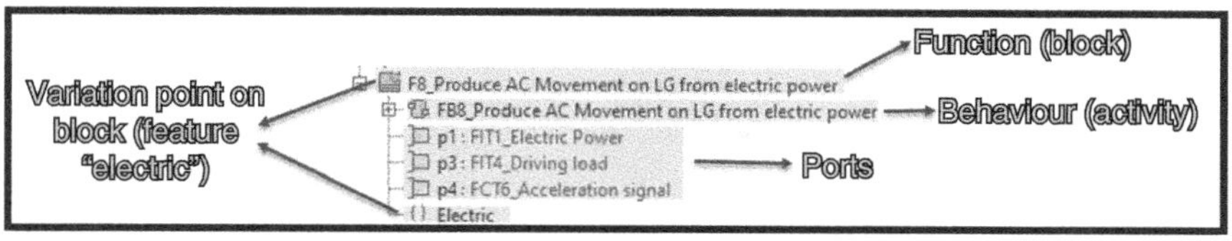

Figure 30.10 Function "Produce AC Movement on LG from electric power."

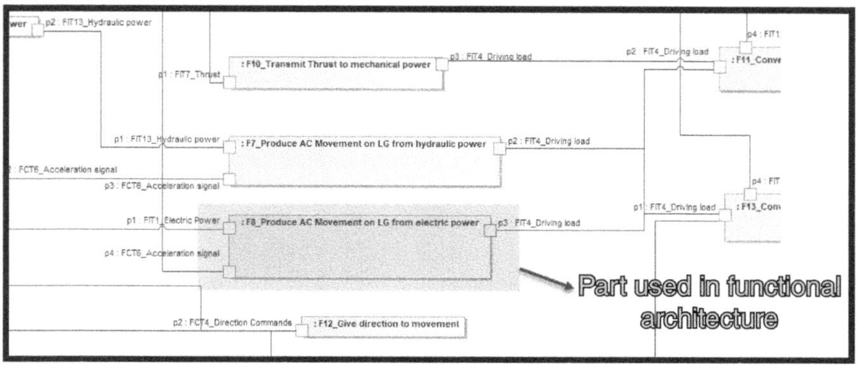

Figure 30.11 Extract of the functional architecture highlighting the studied function usage as a SysML Part.

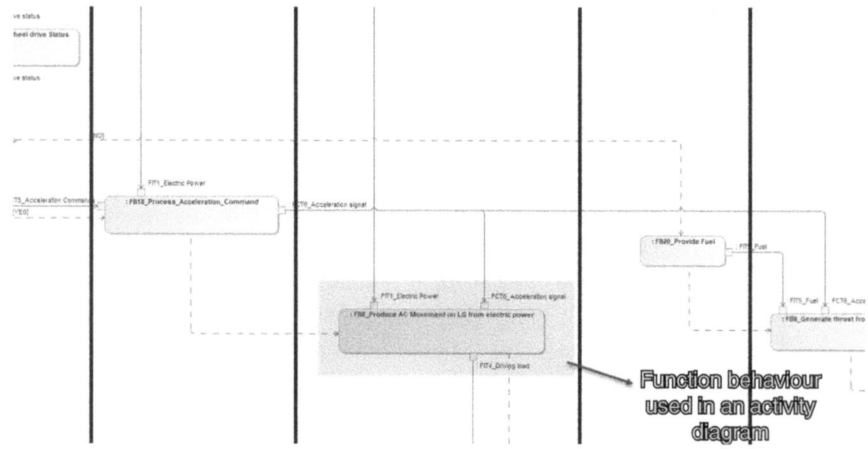

Figure 30.12 Extract of an activity highlighting the behavior of the studied function within the context of Taxiing-In.

transformation). Not only that, but most tools will cascade by default the removal of elements to their usages in diagrams (for example, all parts of the aforementioned block also get removed from BDDs and IBDs, as well as the activity from ACT diagrams).

The result of this minimalistic approach to variation points will not always result in clean models and leaving hanging elements, such as diagram ports (Figure 30.13). This cleaning can be either done manually or automatically. The temptation here shall be resisted, as creating nonessential variation points can create a nightmare later, when trying to manage their consistency.

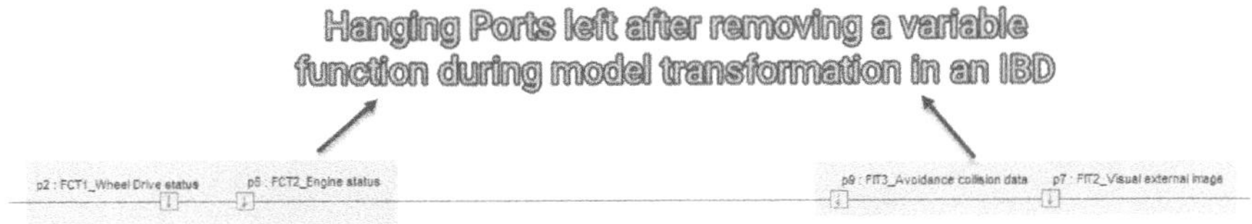

Figure 30.13 Port left hanging after model transformation which removed a function. Clean-up is required in this case.

30.4.3 Integrate Local and Global Variability

The variability being defined in a system element rarely lives on its own. External interactions normally exist and can impact the definition of variation points. External variability can come in the form of other variability models driving variation point's definition (aka using features from other feature models) or existing variation points in other models/assets, which should be cascaded to the working model – for example, a variation point in a system being cascaded to a subsystem.

Example: During the definition of an industrial process (behavior view) on a SysML model, several variation points are needed. Some of them derived from variability in the product definition (structural view). In this case, the product structure variability, including requirements, is cascaded to the industrial behavior variability.

30.4.4 Use Validation Rules and Automation

To achieve the full potential of variability cascading, automation and validation checks are essential. They are responsible for the integrity of complex models and interactions between different elements.

Example: A variable requirement is created to fulfill the feature "wheel powered" (Figure 30.14). At the functional level, two different functions were defined to satisfy this requirement, fulfilling the two alternative features "hydraulic" and "electric." After the model transformation, if either "electric" or "hydraulic" were selected, a function would still have a requirement to satisfy, as the "Wheel Powered" feature will be selected in either case. This means that those variation points are compatible, and no inconsistency will be created in this case.

Moreover, the "satisfy" link could be used by an automation to automatically cascade variation points. In fact, Airbus has developed a plugin to support MBPLE SysML model variation points cascading and validation checks to guarantee consistency as described.

30.4.5 Master Variability Path

One of the challenges of variability cascading is the consistency. This is even harder when working in multimodal environments. In those scenarios, the variability path shall be mastered. What is meant here is that variability should be identified at its root, and all the branches of cascading shall be identified, and the best technique to manage this cascading selected.

30.5 Conclusion: Ready for Take-Off?

Not everything that shines is gold: There is no "silver bullet" when it comes to larger changes like the ones of PLE and MBPLE. It requires investments not only in PMT (process, method, tool), but also in organizational changes. Several pillars are required, such as solid requirements

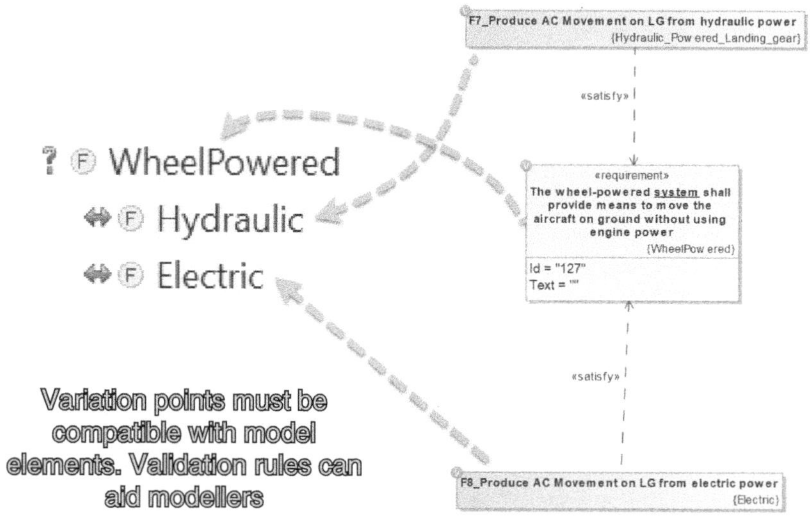

Figure 30.14 Variation points must be created in a consistent manner. Automation and validation rules are essential to manage this complexity.

management, systems engineering, digitalization, and data management, among others. While the principles of PLE are universal, aviation has its own specificities.

Variability management: It is at the heart of PLE. It is an extra layer of information that can be attached to any digital asset. Its traceability shall be mastered. Consistency here remains the primary challenge.

Variability cascading: It is key to achieving consistency in 150% models. Cascading is not only applicable to a single context (like an MBSE model or a 3D model), but also between them. Automation is key here.

Cascading principles: Focus on the core of variability, the correct level of abstraction, while mastering the cascading path. All of that by using the minimum amount of variation points, which should not be used for cleaning or convenience only. Remember that variation point consistency management can be very hard.

Keeping ahead of the pack: Airbus is a market leader in commercial aviation. Keeping itself ahead of the pack is no simple task. Maintaining the current fleet efficiently while innovating for future aircraft is a big challenge that requires strong digitalization efforts. Initiatives focused on reuse/optimization, such as MBPLE, are essential to achieving future business and societal objectives.

References

Airbus (2024a). ZEROe – towards the world's first zero-emission commercial aircraft, viewed 6 June 2024. https://www.airbus.com/en/innovation/low-carbon-aviation/hydrogen/zeroe (accessed 6 June 2024).

Airbus (2024b). Orders and deliveries – commercial aircraft. https://www.airbus.com/en/products-services/commercial-aircraft/market/orders-and-deliveries (accessed 6 June 2024).

Cameo (2024). Cameo system modeler. https://www.3ds.com/products/catia/no-magic/cameo-systems-modeler (accessed 11 May 2024).

Ducamp, C., Bouffaron, F., Ernadote, D. et al. (2022). MBSE approach for complex industrial organization program. In: *INCOSE International Symposium* 32 (1): 839–856.

Feiler, P.H., Hansson, J., De Niz, D. et al. (2009). System architecture virtual integration: an industrial case study. *Software Engineering Institute Technical Report* (CMU/SEI-2009-TR-017).

Ferrogalini, M. (2019). Modelling and Simulation @Airbus: A fundamental digital transformation axis across product, manufacturing and support in service. Presentation at MODELS Conference, Industry Day, Munich, Germany (18 September 2019).

Forlingieri, M. (2022). The four dimensions of variability and their impact on MBPLE: how to approach variability in the development of aircraft product lines at airbus. In: *Proceedings of the 16th International Working Conference on Variability Modelling of Software-Intensive Systems,* pp. 1–4.

Forlingieri, M. and Weilkiens, T. (2022). Two variant modelling methods for MBPLE at Airbus. In: *INCOSE International Symposium* 32 (1): 1097–1113.

Hummell, J. and Hause, M. (2015). Model-based product line engineering: enabling product families with variants. In: *2015 IEEE Aerospace Conference,* 1–8.

IATA (2024). Global outlook for air transport – deep change. https://iata.org/en/iata-repository/publications/economic-reports/global-outlook-for-air-transport-june-2024-report/ (accessed 8 June 2024).

ICAO (2023). Safety report (2023 edition). https://www.icao.int/safety/Documents/ICAO_SR_2023_20230823.pdf (accessed 8 June 2024).

ISO/IEC (2015). Software and systems engineering – reference model for product line engineering and management (ISO/IEC 2655 0: 2015).

ISO/IEC (2021). Software and systems engineering – method and tools for the feature-based approach to software and systems product line engineering (ISO/IEC 26580:2021).

ISO/IEC/IEEE (2023). Systems and software engineering – system life cycle processes (ISO/IEC/IEEE 1528 8: 2023).

Kang, K.C., Sugumaran, V., and Park, S. (eds.) (2009). *Applied Software Product Line Engineering.* Boca Raton: CRC Press.

Knaster, R. and Leffingwell, D. (2020). *SAFE 5.0 Distilled: Achieving Business Agility With The Scaled Agile Framework.* Boston: Addison-Wesley Professional.

Madeira, R.H., de Sousa Pinto, D.H., and Forlingieri, M. (2023). Variability on system architecture using airbus MBPLE for MOFLT framework. In: *INCOSE International Symposium* 33 (1): 601–615.

Object Management Group (OMG) (2017). Unified Modelling Language (UML). Version 2.5.1.

Object Management Group (OMG) (2024). OMG Systems Modelling Language (OMG SysML). Version 1.7.

Prieto-Diaz, R. (1990). Domain analysis: an introduction. *ACM SIGSOFT Software Engineering Notes* 15 (2): 47–54.

PTC pure::variants (2024). *pure::variants*' https://www.ptc.com/en/products/pure-variants (accessed 10 May 2024).

Society of Automotive Engineers Aerospace (2010). *Guidelines for Development of Civil Aircraft and Systems:* SAE ARP 4754 Rev. A. SAE.

Walden, D.D, G.J. RoedLer, K. J. Forsberg, et al. (eds.) (2023). *Systems Engineering Handbook: A Guide for System Life Cycle Processes and Activities.* Version 5. San Diego, CA, USA: INCOSE.

31

MBDA: Building an End-to-end Model-based Framework for Product Lines

Dieter Wagner

31.1 Introduction

This chapter introduces how model-based product line engineering (MBPLE) has been implemented at MBDA. Given the high complexity of MBDA's products, their development typically requires more than a decade of time. An instance of this complexity can be seen in the Command-and-Control Tactical Operation Center, which is partially covered in the next sections. Higher complexity, if not properly managed, leads to higher development costs and time. Consequently, MBDA has initiated an improvement program with the objective of halving the lead time and reducing nonrecurring costs by 25%.

As part of the program, a model-based end-to-end development process known as the "end-to-end model-based engineering (E2EMBE)" process has been launched. A crucial component of this novel E2EMBE process is feature-based product line engineering (PLE) in line with the ISO/IEC 26580 (ISO/IEC 2021).

The primary focus of this chapter is "the conjunction" between PLE and MBSE. To illustrate it, the "Command-and-Control International Product Line (C2IntlPL)" is used as an example.

31.2 MBDA Motivation for MBPLE's Adoption

The MBDA Group, a European defense organization, is one of the world's three leading missile systems companies and has a significant presence in Germany, France, England, and Italy. In 2022, MBDA had an employee base of over 14 000 employees, generating a significant turnover of 4.2 billion euros (MBDA 2024). MBDA's aim always revolves around developing products that aptly meet the requirements expressed by MBDA's customers. At the same time, the main concern is to produce systems that meet the different requirements of different military areas, which differ significantly in terms of their practical application. The MBDA's product portfolio includes missiles for applications such as "Meteor," an air-to-air missile; "Taurus," an air-to-ground missile; and "Enforcer," a hand-held surface-to-surface missile.

As MBDA's systems grow increasingly complex, development times have correspondingly lengthened, often exceeding 10 years on average. In light of recent geopolitical changes, the urgency for faster product development has become paramount. Despite this, MBDA's development process remains rooted in a document-centric and waterfall approach until 2022.

Model-Based Product Line Engineering (MBPLE): The Feature-Based Path to Product Lines Success, First Edition. Marco Forlingieri et al.

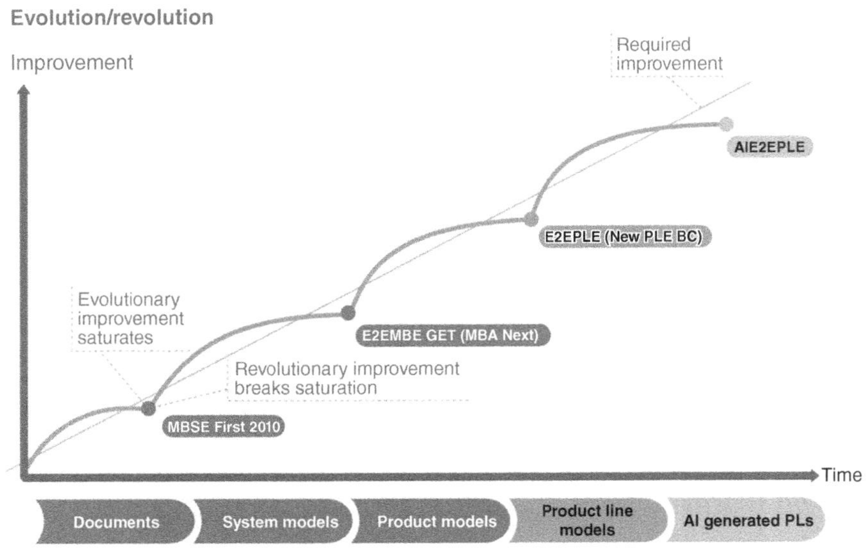

Figure 31.1 MBDA evolution/revolution.

In fact, in 2010, MBSE was introduced in the company as a revolutionary improvement since the document-based approach reached saturation, as illustrated in Figure 31.1. Unfortunately, the MBSE adoption without top–down sponsorship and support quickly reached its limits. As a result, a new transformation program was launched in the MBDA in 2022 with the aim of finally introducing consistent model-based development. E2EMBE approach lays the foundation of the subsequent model-based product line introduction, the end-to-end product line engineering ([E2EPLE] is the MBDA name for MBPLE).

The E2EMBE approach focuses on the key following objectives:

(1) **Enabling digital continuity:** The methodology E2EMBE is based on different engineering models. The end-to-end indicates that the method includes the entire product development lifecycle process. SysML models are predominantly used for MBSE, while UML models are for software development, MCAD (Dassault Systèms 3DEXPERIENCE 2024) for mechanical designs, ECAD (Siemens 2024) for electrical and electronic circuit diagrams, and an assortment of other models created using specialized tools in their respective domains. To ensure that those individual models are not managed in silos, they interoperate with each other, thereby establishing what is commonly referred to as a digital thread. A prominent example of suitable interoperability standards used at MBDA for this purpose is the Open Services for Lifecycle Collaboration (OSLC 2023). The connection of all models through a digital thread enhances the overall coherence and integration of the product line development process, fostering better communication and collaboration among the various domains involved in the project.
(2) **Enabling a single source of truth:** The fundamental principle of establishing a single source of truth holds outstanding importance within the E2EMBE methodology, embracing digital continuity. This procedure is based on the consistent use of the latest references to assets located in the E2EMBE information model.
(3) **Enabling controlled reuse:** Enabling controlled reuse is a necessity at MBDA. New programs should be constructed with modular and reusable frameworks, ensuring flexibility and efficiency in development. In order to proficiently supervise the reuse process and monitor the utilization of particular modules across various projects and iterations, the adoption of a tool-supported methodology becomes imperative. The emergence of E2EPLE presents itself as a practical and

effective solution for overseeing and regulating controlled reuse within the organizational framework. E2EPLE offers a comprehensive approach to managing and enforcing the reuse of modules, thereby enhancing the overall sustainability and scalability of projects within the MBDA.

(4) **Enabling variability:** When reusing development resources, a significant challenge is the need to comply with customer requirements, which are not fully met by existing implementations. To tackle this particular challenge effectively, it is key to deploy a well-thought-out strategy that focuses on enabling variability within the development process. This method involves adapting existing functionality by introducing a new variant that is specifically designed to meet a customer's individual needs. The efficient management of these diverse variants is governed by the use of the E2EPLE method.

(5) **Managing configuration:** E2EPLE emerges as a central component in facilitating the administration of different models and versions, guaranteeing a structured and effective configuration process. By leveraging E2EPLE, organizations can enhance their ability to manage the complexity inherent in E2EMBE, thus optimizing operational efficiency and ensuring consistency and integration of diverse models and versions.

31.3 The MBSE Framework as MBDA Foundation for MBPLE

All the above principles were considered when the E2EPLE methodology was defined and integrated into the E2EMBE process. To understand how the MBPLE approach works, it is important to first review the MBSE portion of the E2EMBE.

Figure 31.2 shows the structure of the MBDA's MBSE framework. In the following section, a brief description of the rows and columns of Figure 31.2 is introduced.

Operational architecture: It explains the system from the perspective of the end user. Essentially, it describes how operators interact with the system by presenting various use cases. It represents the system as a black box whose external interfaces serve as points of interaction with the outside world. It provides a comprehensive understanding of the operational aspects of the system and how users interact with it.

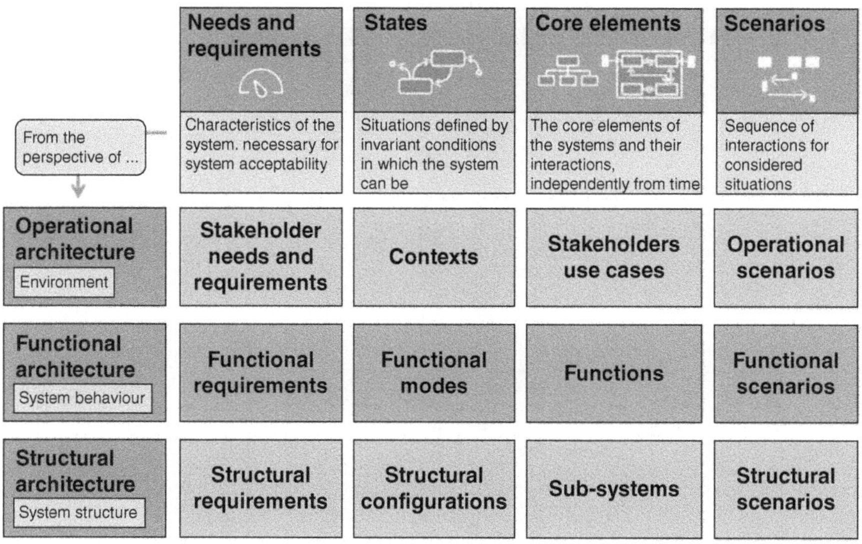

Figure 31.2 MBDA MBSE framework.

Functional architecture: It outlines the system's functions in a manner that is agnostic to any solution within the boundary of the product context. This approach ensures that there are no constraints imposed by specific solutions or design parameters. This architectural blueprint also illustrates the interplay of functions through functional chains, depicting how they collaborate to achieve desired outcomes. The functions are linked to the corresponding use cases, creating a cohesive structure that guides the system's behavior.

Structural architecture: It covers the realization of one or multiple possible configurations that meet the requirements set forth by the functional architecture. This layer presents a spectrum of physical architectures that can manifest the envisioned functionalities. The functions outlined in the functional architecture are assigned to specific elements within the physical architecture, which serve as the building blocks for implementing the desired functionalities. This allocation ensures a clear mapping between the abstract functions and their concrete realizations within the system.

Needs and requirements: They consist of the essential specifications for each architectural component, guiding the assignment of model elements to ensure alignment with stakeholder expectations and project objectives.

States: They hold varying significance across the three different architectural structures due to the unique ways in which data is processed and interpreted within each system. Each architecture brings forth distinct methods and algorithms that influence the interpretation and utilization of the statistics presented in the column.

Core elements: They include a comprehensive list of essential components tailored to each specific type of architecture, serving as a key reference point for understanding the fundamental building blocks required for the development and implementation of the corresponding architectural structure.

Scenarios: They provide a detailed representation of the chronological sequence of activities and functions required to implement the various activities derived from use cases and functional chains, thus offering a comprehensive overview of the temporal progression within the system architecture.

The above-described MBDA MBSE framework can be applied recursively on any level of the system, as shown in Figure 31.3. This means that the system-level model is decomposed into subsystems, and, in turn, the subsystem-level models are broken down into equipment.

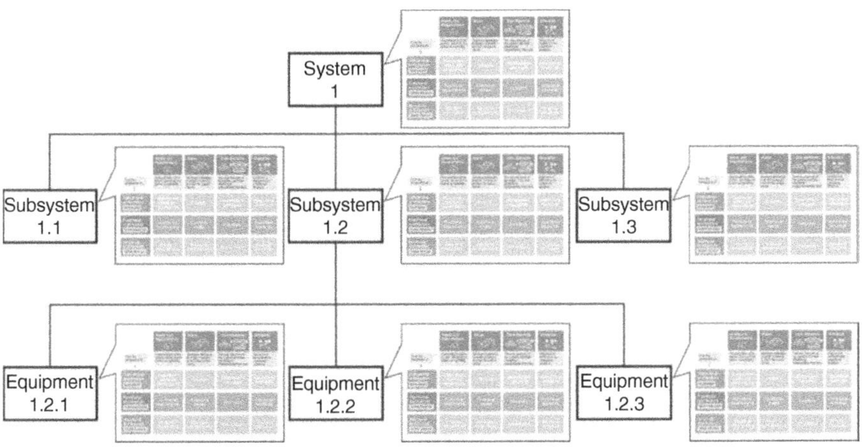

Figure 31.3 MBDA MBSE framework hierarchy.

31.4 The E2EPLE Methodology

To facilitate the implementation of the PLE combined with MBSE, it is important to establish a precise scope for the product line. An illustrative example of this implementation is demonstrated in the upcoming sections, through a simplified subset of the "C2IntlPL."

Figure 31.4 shows the hierarchical structure of the product lines, showcasing a collection of distinct product lines that are interconnected and interdependent. As each product line offers a range of products, these member products are used as "building blocks" for the parent product line.

The product line model, realized with PTC pure::variants (PTC pure::variants 2024) shown in Figure 31.5 is organized into folders to make navigation within the model easier. The structure of the model is designed per level to facilitate the exploration of the product line model, and it is explained below.

Assets folder: It contains references to the E2E models. These references indicate the exact location of the shared asset superset and unshareable asset in their respective versions.

Feature catalog folder: It contains at least one feature catalog (aka feature model). Depending on the project's needs, some features from the main feature catalog can also be outsourced to a separate feature catalog.

Feature catalog: The feature catalog in Figure 31.6 contains an additional semantic to support the MBDA MBSE framework.

The additional semantic is based on specialized features, which are described in the following section.

Package feature: The inclusion of a package feature is essential for enhancing the organization of models within a product line. The package feature serves the purpose of structuring models in

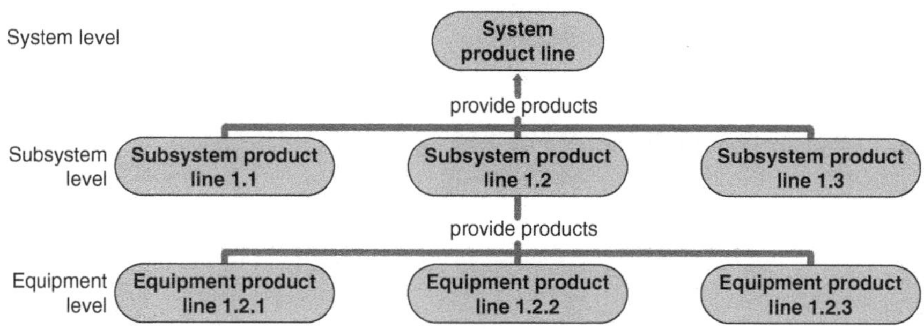

Figure 31.4 Product line hierarchy.

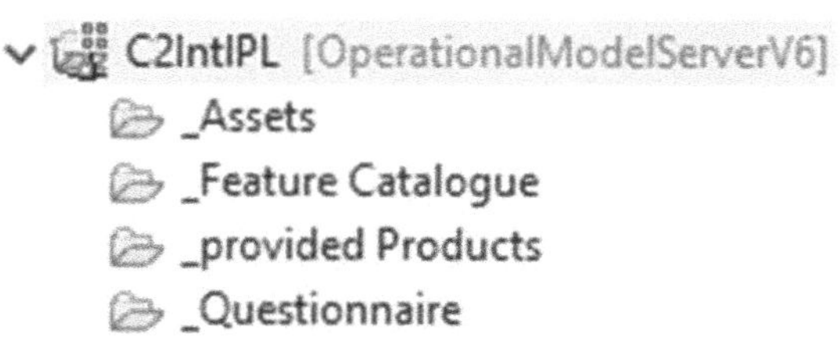

Figure 31.5 Product line model.

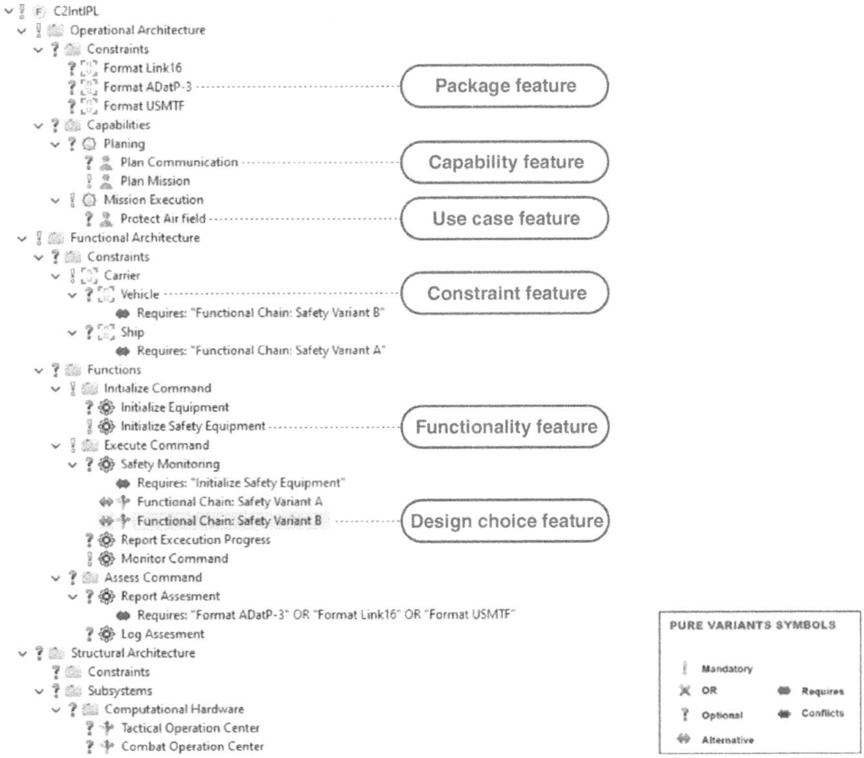

Figure 31.6 MBDA feature catalog.

a more efficient manner. It is important to note that package features are assigned to any shared assets superset elements. Therefore, the recommendation is to align the MBDA MBSE framework model with the feature catalog structure as closely as possible. This alignment facilitates a more coherent and systematic approach to model organization, thereby enhancing the overall orientation within the system.

Capability feature: It plays a crucial role in capturing the diverse capabilities of the system. These capabilities are essentially the fundamental building blocks of the system's functionalities. The primary objective here is to develop a set of capabilities owned by MBDA, enabling reusability across various projects. However, it is also important to highlight that there are customer-specific capabilities that are not intended to be shared across different projects.

Use case feature: Within the MBDA MBSE framework, the use case feature represents a traditional method of delineating the system's usage capabilities from the user's perspective. For each capability, at least a use case is provided to articulate MBDA's intended utilization of the capabilities. In practice, customers often have unique requirements regarding how they utilize these capabilities, leading to multiple use cases associated with each capability. This results in a diverse collection of use cases, with some owned by MBDA and others by the customers, showcasing a high level of variability in the system.

Constraint feature: It serves the purpose of capturing various constraints originating from customers, national legislation, standards, or MBDA's product strategy. These constraints play a criti-

Table 31.1 Cross-reference feature type versus architecture layer.

Architecture	Operational	Functional	Structural
Feature type			
Package feature	X	X	X
Capability feature	X		
Use case feature	X		
Constraint feature	X	X	X
Functionality feature		X	
Design choice feature		X	X

cal role in narrowing down the solution space within the system. For instance, the feature catalog example showcases a constraint from MBDA's product strategy, limiting the supported communication formats to three options (Link15, ADatP-3, USMTF) for any given product.

Functionality feature: It comprises the atomic building blocks that form the basis for constructing capabilities within the system. These functionalities are interconnected to define the behavior of capabilities, forming functional chains that start with an incoming event and conclude with an outgoing event.

Design choice feature: To cater to the varying needs of different customers, functional chains may exhibit differences in functionality or fidelity levels. As a result, the design choice feature is introduced to capture the variability present in functions and functional chains.

Table 31.1 indicates which specialized feature type is used in the different architectures.

The selection is based on best practices resulting from various internal proof-of-concepts.

In addition to the elements described above, it is key to mention other components that form the so-called product line model. These are:

Provided products folder: It contains the product portfolio of the product line. Each product in the portfolio is defined by its own bill of features.

Bill of features: It contains product specifications for this product. The bill of features (aka feature configuration) is the selection of features needed to fulfill the customer's needs.

Questionnaire folder: It contains an optional questionnaire designed to capture customer needs and preferences, fostering a customer-centric approach to product development. The questionnaire aims to gather valuable insights and feedback from customers. The answers to the questionnaire are integrated into the corresponding Bill of Features for further analysis and decision-making processes. The inclusion of customer feedback in the product line development cycle enhances customer satisfaction and ensures that products align with market demands and preferences.

It is important to note that, due to contractual obligations, not all assets within the model are shareable, highlighting the need for secure and controlled access to certain elements of the product line model. This restriction ensures compliance with contractual agreements for handling sensitive information within the product line model and highlights the importance of data security and confidentiality in PLE.

To implement the variability described above in the product line model, two additional elements that are at the core of the MBPLE approach are introduced as follows:

Shared assets superset: It contains all development assets needed during the product development cycle. The MBSE model is part of the shared assets superset. All assets need to be connected to the features or their variations. These connection points are called variation points.

- Variation points: To enable PLE for MBSE models, it is essential to incorporate variability as an integral part of the MBSE model. The specific location within the MBSE model where variability is implemented and referred to as the "variation point." Each variation point is precisely linked to the corresponding feature of a feature model, ensuring a systematic approach to managing variability.
- At MBDA we defined three distinct types of variation points: "atomic," marked as (1), "starting," marked as (2), and "propagated," marked as (V) variation point, as illustrated in Figure 31.7.

The figure illustrates a simplified (collapsed hierarchy) perspective of the different variation points within the MBSE framework. This visual representation aids in understanding the strategic placement and relationship of variation points in the overall model structure. By categorizing variation points into specific types, such as atomic, starting, and propagated, modelers can effectively capture and represent the variability. Leveraging these variation points facilitates the creation of adaptable and customizable MBSE framework models that can accommodate diverse requirements and configurations. Understanding the nuances of each variation point type is essential for implementing PLE successfully in MBSE models and ensuring the efficient management of variability throughout the system development process.

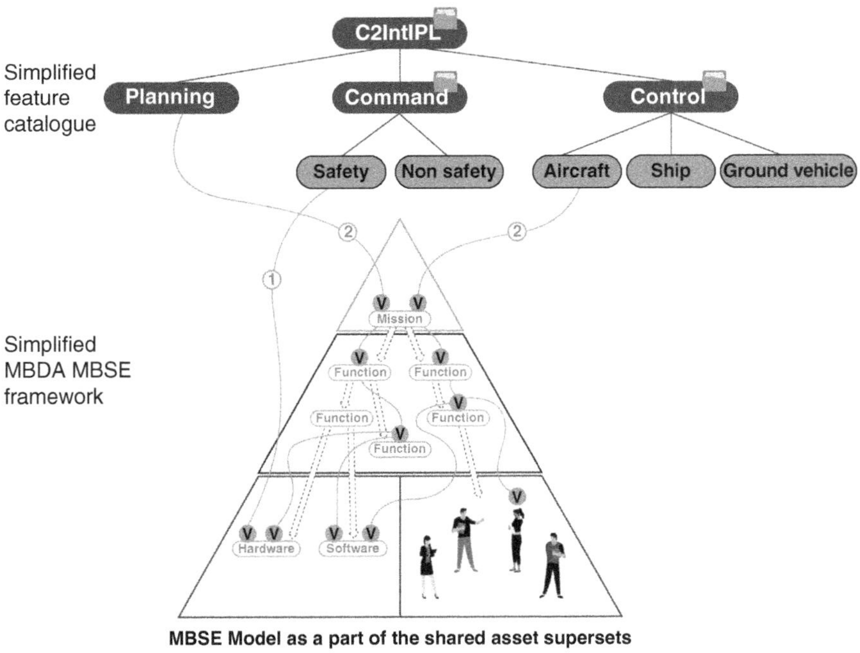

Figure 31.7 "Atomic," "starting" and "propagated" variation points.

Atomic variation point: The utilization of the atomic variation point is specifically targeted toward the management of variability for functional and structural architecture exclusively. The term "atomic" signifies the absence of any dependent child model elements, a characteristic that is uniquely viable within the structural architecture domain. This concept holds significance because the structural architecture will be populated by the resulting products of the child product, thus making the "atomic" variation point a crucial design decision in constructing the building blocks of the system. As illustrated in Figure 31.7, the "safety" feature is explicitly linked to a hardware element in the structural architecture, serving as a prime illustration of a design choice feature within the architecture. The design choice feature and constraint feature are effectively implemented through the utilization of "atomic" variation points, highlighting a sophisticated approach to architectural design and decision-making.

Starting variation point: The variation point, known as starting, consists of a model element that is linked to other model elements and is either within the same architectural level or spans the hierarchical structure of architectural levels.

The starting variation point is strategically positioned within the MBSE model, typically associated with other elements like capabilities, use cases, or functional chains. This strategic placement ensures that the foundational aspects of the variations are well-defined and aligned with the overarching objectives of the project.

In the illustrative scenario shown in Figure 31.7, the presence of two distinct "starting" variation points (marked as 2) is highlighted, each linked to specific features within the operational architecture. One use case is linked to the feature "planning," while the other use case is linked to the feature "aircraft," a feature variant of the feature "control."

Essential to the insertion of the starting variation point is the absence of any break in the model dependency, the meta-model, which extends from the operational architecture to the structural architecture. This crucial aspect ensures that a capability or use case can be easily extracted from a 150% MBSE model. By conducting a model transformation (extraction), it is a prerequisite that all model elements essential for the advancement of a capability or use case are retained.

Propagated variation points: To facilitate the PLE factory in identifying the appropriate elements, the concept of "propagated" variation points is assigned to all associated model elements pertaining to a capability or use case. This strategy ensures that the necessary components are effectively transmitted and preserved throughout the transformation process.

31.5 Not Only MBSE Assets: The ECAD Variability Management Within MBPLE

In the E2EMBE method, the models for software, mechanical, electrical, and electronic domains also contribute to the E2EMBE information model. As already mentioned, the MBDA framework focuses on the realization of a central MBSE model with connections to the other engineering models. It should be noted that the MBDA framework model contains equipment-level software and hardware that are modeled as low-level components in the structural architecture. These low-level blocks must be then replaced with other domain-specific engineering models. For this purpose, the MBDA E2EMBE method offers a collection of connectors that enable this interchange.

To enable the reuse of software and hardware, variability management is required. The E2EPLE method offers two different approaches based on the availability of PLE connectors:

- If a PLE connector (e.g., E3Cabel) is available, the management of variability within the ECAD tools is done by adding the variation points directly in the corresponding models. The structural architecture is populated from the ECAD using the MBDA E2EMBE interchange functions.
- If no PLE connector (e.g., Mentor and Matlab/Simulink) is available, the management of variability is done by adding the variation points directly in the structure architecture. The engineering domain models are populated with the contents of the structural architecture using the MBDA E2EMBE exchange functions and not in the domain-specific model.

31.6 E2EPLE Tool Chain

In the MBDA environment, two MBSE tools, IBM Rhapsody (IBM 2024) and the open-source Capella (Capella 2024), are used for system analysis and design. The application of the MBDA MBSE framework is the same for both tools, ensuring a consistent approach and methodology. PTC pure::variants is used as a PLE tool to realize the MBDA E2EPLE method. PTC pure::variants support both IBM Rhapsody and Capella, enabling a similar application of the same PLE techniques and strategies. PTC Pure::variants linked to the MBSE tools via individual bridges. The bridge provides functions for adding features to model elements, previewing resulting models based on a concrete bill of features, and transforming or generating the final MBSE framework model.

While in Capella, feature propagation occurs automatically through an internal dependency tree that links elements from the higher-level model to those in the lower-level model; IBM Rhapsody does not support automatic feature propagation. To address this limitation, MBDA has developed an IBM Rhapsody "add-on" that enables feature propagation within the tool. Once a higher-level parent model element is linked to a feature, the add-on initiates the propagation process and assigns the same feature as "propagated variation points" to all lower-level dependent model elements.

31.7 A Real-Life Example for the E2EPLE

The following two figures show an example using both IBM Rhapsody and PTC pure::variants.

In Figure 31.8, two specific use cases, namely "Plan Mission" and "Plan Communication," are presented. Each of those individual use cases is linked to its respective constraints through the utilization of the "use case" features "PlanMission" and "PlanCommunication," which are shown in Figure 31.9. For the sake of clarity and simplicity in the illustration, the use cases have been associated with two generalized functions. The use case labeled as "Plan Mission" is connected to both "FunctionA" and "FunctionB." The other use case, "Plan Communication" is solely linked to "FunctionB." Upon the propagation of the use case "Plan Mission" using the IBM Rhapsody add-on, the resulting "propagated" variation point labeled as "PlanMission" is attached to both functions. Similarly, if the use case "Plan Communication" undergoes propagation, the function "FunctionB" will then acquire the "propagated" variation point associated with "PlanCommunication." It is important to note that the underlying logic here operates under the principle of logical disjunction, denoted by the OR operator. Consequently, the ultimate "propagated" variation point is determined

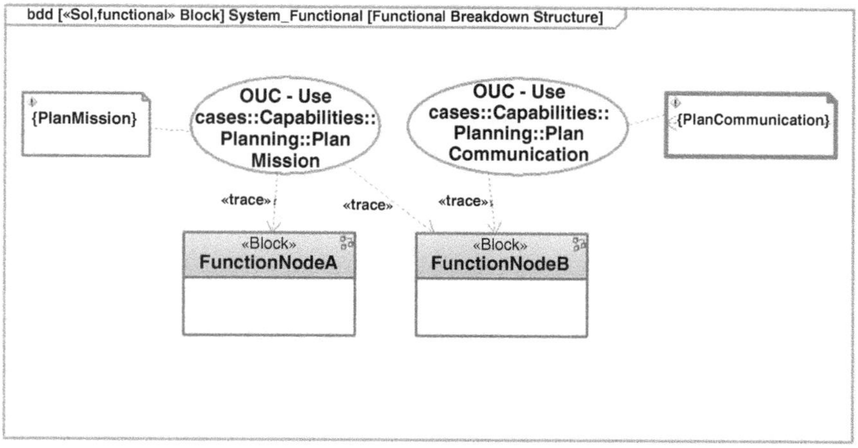

Figure 31.8 Propagation logic "starting" variation point.

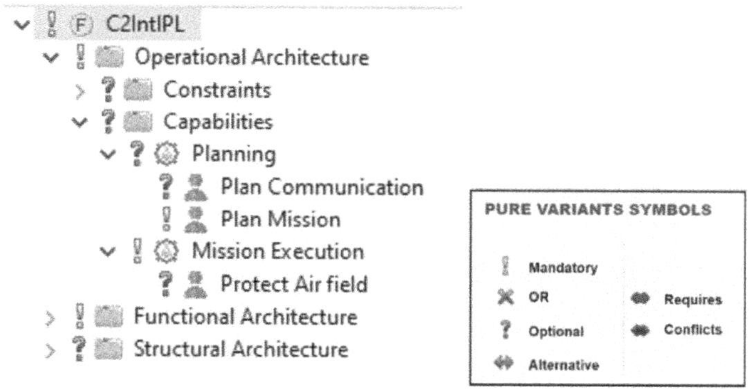

Figure 31.9 Propagation logic "starting" variation point.

as "(PlanMission) OR (PlanCommunication)." This implies that both use cases, being propagated, can use the inclusion of the corresponding variation point within the functions.

In Figure 31.10, there are two functional chains, namely "Functional Chain Variant A" and "Functional Chain Variant B," both linked to their respective design choice features, "SafetyVariantA" and "SafetyVariantB." Upon propagating the use case "Protect Air Field" to both functional chains, it exhibits a propagated variation point denoted as "ProtectAirField."

The add-on establishes a PTC pure::variants' constraint for "Functional Chain Variant A" as (ProtectAirField) AND (SafetyVariantA) and for "Functional Chain Variant B" as (ProtectAirField) AND (SafetyVariantB). This logical framework empowers PTC pure::variants to derive a MBSE model that exclusively incorporates one of the two functional chains.

Figure 31.11 provides a visual depiction of a product preview wherein the design choice feature selected is SafetyVariantB, resulting in the graying out of SafetyVariantA and its corresponding anchored constraint.

Since MBPLE does not focus only on MBSE assets, the following part shows a simple extension of the presented approach for an ECAD model.

To import an ECAD model into IBM Rhapsody, an additional IBM Rhapsody add-on was developed. It reads an XML file generated by Xpedition Designer, which describes the electrical hardware. The XML file is partitioned into three sections:

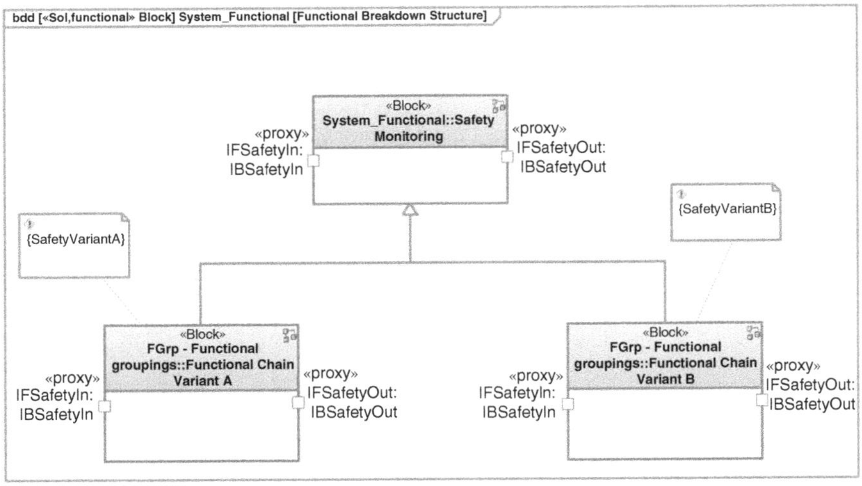

Figure 31.10 Propagation logic "atomic" variation point.

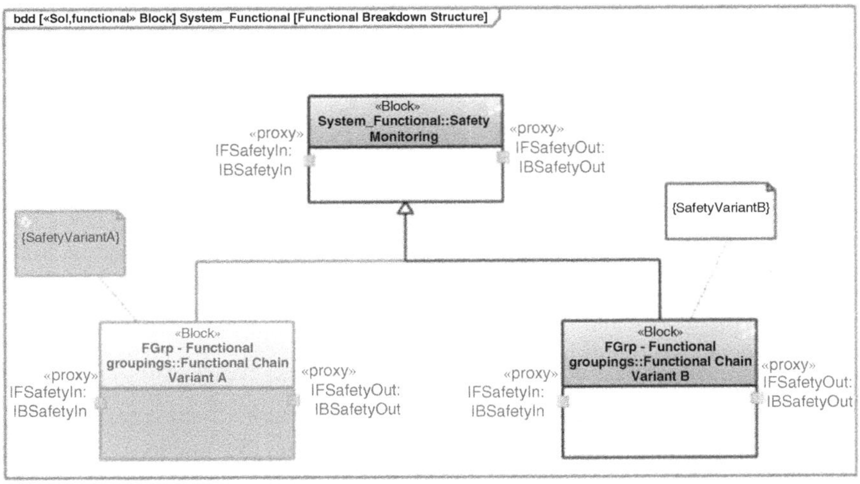

Figure 31.11 Preview of PLE factory configured MBSE framework model.

Signal group definition: It defines all relevant electrical signals used in the ECAD design. The RhGUID is an IBM Rhapsody unique identifier to recognize the corresponding MBSE model element. In addition, all signals may contain attributes such as tolerances to define the signal.

Here is an extraction of the XML file section:

```
<signalgroup RhGUID="GUID" name="Power">
      <signal RhGUID="GUID" name="V240" type="Power"/>
             <attribute  RhGUID="GUID" name="Tolerance" value="+-10V"
      <signal RhGUID="GUID" name="V400" type="Power"/>
      <signal RhGUID="GUID" name="V15" type="Power"/>
</signalgroup>
```

Assembly definition: It defines the collection of assemblies for the electrical boards.

In the example below, the device "TOC" contains two variations of mainboards and two variations of IOBoards. The device and each assembly contain their connectors called "ports."

The Ports are SysML proxy ports, which allow the nesting of other proxy ports.

Note: Due to the variability, the boards of the same type have the same set of connectors. The variability is based on signal groups and signals defined by the netlist.

Here is an extraction of the XML file section:

```
<device RhGUID="GUID" name="TOC">
<assembly RhGUID="GUID" name="MainboardA">
<port RhGUID="GUID" name="X1"/>
<port RhGUID="GUID" name="J1"/>
</assembly>
<assembly RhGUID="GUID" name="MainboardB">
<port RhGUID="GUID" name="X1"/>
<port RhGUID="GUID" name="J1"/>
</assembly>
<assembly RhGUID="GUID" name="IOBoradA">
<port RhGUID="GUID" name="J1"/>
<port RhGUID="GUID" name="X2"/>
</assembly>
<assembly RhGUID="GUID" name="IOBoradB">
<port RhGUID="GUID" name="J1"/>
<port RhGUID="GUID" name="X2"/>
</assembly>
<port RhGUID="GUID" name="X1"/>
<port RhGUID="GUID" name="X2"/>
</device>
```

Netlist: It contains the individual connections of signals between pins on connectors. In the example, the external connector of the device "TOC" has the variability of two different power signals, "V240 and V400". Depending on the capability of the mainboards, the power is connected to the right voltage signal.

Here is an extraction of the XML file section:

```
<netlist>
<net fromDevice="TOC" fromPin="1" fromPort="X1" signal="V240"
signalgroup="Power" toAssembly="MainboardA" toPin="1" toPort="X1"/>
<net fromDevice="TOC" fromPin="1" fromPort="X1" signal="V400"
signalgroup="Power" toAssembly="MainboardB" toPin="1" toPort="X1"/>
</netlist>
```

The import IBM Rhapsody add-on reads the XML and automatically creates the corresponding SysML elements for the structural architecture.

Figure 31.12 shows an ECAD-imported structural architecture model. The architecture was enriched by constraints that contain the relevant features of the feature catalog. For demonstration, the preview of PTC pure::variants is activated to show a product that contains only MotherboarsB and IOBoardA. After using the factory configurator of PTC pure::variants, all unused connectors and blocks are removed.

31.8 The Journey of E2EPLE at MBDA Continues

Since 2022, MBDA has embarked on a transformation toward establishing an E2EPLE and E2EMBE integrated approach to support the next generation of missiles and weapon systems. The presented approach based on MBPLE showed significant benefits, and it is a central pillar of

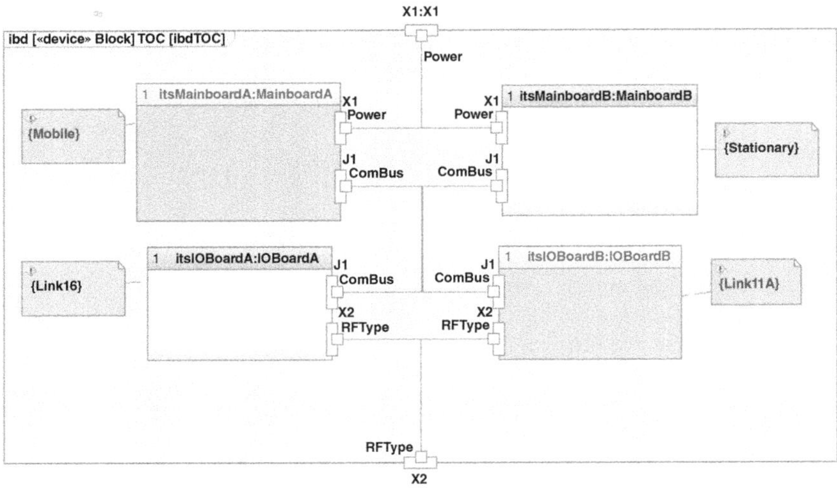

Figure 31.12 Preview of PLE factory configured ECAD imported structural architecture model.

MBDA's improvement program. Examples of capabilities developed within the E2EPLE framework, such as capturing and organizing consistently the variability within a product line model or connecting the feature catalog with the MBSE model and the ECAD model, are essential in developing multiple variants of MBDA's systems.

The MBPLE approach is currently in the rollout phase and has been recently adopted for the first products. Due to nondisclosure agreements between MBDA and its customers, no further information can be provided regarding its adoption.

Along with the successful outcomes of MBPLE at MBDA, three main challenges arose during its rollout and are highlighted as follows:

Introducing MBPLE to the folks: Introducing MBPLE into a non-PLE organization requires big efforts and leads to problems in the distribution of responsibility. For example, the project departments within MBDA have always acted as the end-to-end developers of finished products. Following this novel approach, their responsibility is mainly limited to the integration, verification, and validation of the products. To better address this challenge, MBDA is working on a new business case to transform MBDA into a PLE-enabled company in the long term. As part of the business case, other development areas such as electrical, electronic, mechanical, and software will be introduced to MBPLE.

Using variation in MBSE models: Understanding where and how a variation should be implemented in the MBSE model using the variation points presented with limited efforts.

Validating the product line model: The validation of a product line model can only be carried out on a transformed model (product model), which in turn means additional work. This area requires more investigation and necessitates better support from the existing tools landscape.

Annex 1: MBPLE Terms at MBDA.

Term	Description
Variation point	Location within the shared assed superset where the variation is located.
End-to-end model-based engineering	The end-to-end model-based engineering (E2EMBE) provides a digital continuity of a single source of truth development assets for the whole development lifecycle.
E2EMBE information model	The E2EMBE information is a set of connected models produced by different development domains.
Lower-level product line	A lower-level product line is a stand-alone product line that continues its product to the direct upper-level product line.
Upper-level product line Parent product line	Analysis on upper-level product line is a stand-alone product line that provides high-level features and consumes products of lower-level product lines as building blocks.

References

Capella (2024). Capella Webpage. https://mbse-capella.org/ (accessed 19 June 2024).

Dassault Systèmes (2024). Dassault systèmes webpage. https://www.3ds.com/de/3dexperience (accessed 20 May 2024).

IBM (2024). IBM Rhapsody. https://www.ibm.com/de-de/products/systems-design-rhapsody (accessed 20 February 2024).

ISO/IEC (2021). Software and systems engineering – methods and tools for the feature-based approach to software and systems product line engineering (ISO/IEC/IEEE 2658 0: 2021).

MBDA (2024). MBDA webpage. https://www.mbda-systems.com/ (accessed 20 May 2024).

OSLC (2023). OSLC webpage. https://www.open-services.net/ (accessed 19 December 2023).

PTC Pure::Variants. (2024). Pure::Variants. https://www.ptc.com/en/products/pure-variants (accessed 10 May 2024).

Siemens (2024). Xpedition Designer. https://eda.sw.siemens.com/en-US/pcb/xpedition-enterprise/ (accessed 10 April 2024).

32

Thales: A Long Road to MBPLE – from Initial Conception to Completion

Agnes Guiblin

32.1 Introduction

In 2023, Thales Group is present in 68 countries worldwide and employs 77 000 people. Thales Group is composed of three core business segments: aerospace and space, cybersecurity and digital identity, and defense and security. Thales surface radar (SRA) is part of the latter segment and is a global player in the naval, ground, and air radar surveillance domains. SRA has an internal footprint with nine sites in six countries. Our radar sensors provide our customers with the right information on all flying, driving, walking, or sailing objects, allowing them to take the right decision at any critical moment. From the ground and ocean surface to the stratosphere, we help our customers make the lives of their citizens and soldiers safer and ensure the protection of critical sites, borders, coastal areas, oceans, and airspace. More than 4000 Thales radars are in operation in over 30 countries worldwide (Thales 2024).

At SRA, product line engineering (PLE) has been deployed for over fifteen years on ground master radars (GMR). Our radars are military products designed mainly for air surveillance, but they can also be used for operational engagement. They detect and ensure the tracking of highly maneuverable targets (aircraft, helicopter, etc.) in order to provide an air situation to a remote or local command and control center. Our radars can be installed on a dedicated site or on mobile carriers (Thales 2024).

Using PLE concepts to implement a market-driven product policy and strategic reuse was both an opportunity and a challenge. PLE relies heavily on the development of shared elements, gradually adapted to new projects. It requires finding the right balance among operational capability, development complexity (e.g. processes, human interactions, architecture for reuse and implementation), radar quality, and increased productivity. A central role differentiating PLE engineering concepts from other reuse concepts is the explicit management of variability and product instances as an integral part of the approach. This aligns reuse with the reality that "as is" reuse is often very difficult. For instance, requirements for new products often result in additional or slightly different needs compared to previous products. Knowing and taking into account these new requirements from the start is almost impossible. The primary capability of PLE is to account for the variability of engineering elements that are subject to continuous evolution in the radar life cycle. This practice allows us to remain competitive in our market segment.

At the beginning of our PLE transformation, Thales decided to renew our product portfolio and invested in the development of a platform based on a composable product architecture using

Model-Based Product Line Engineering (MBPLE): The Feature-Based Path to Product Lines Success, First Edition.
Marco Forlingieri et al.

building blocks (BBs). One of the platform's objectives was to reduce nonrecurring costs by massively using software or hardware BBs in our radars and also reducing the number of development activities. The development of our radars is still realized today following this composable approach and shared across all military surface radars that have similar architectures. In 2011, the Ground Master 400 radar (GM 400) was already a commercial success with four large contracts. However, the team was still organized in "project mode." Ground Master 200 radar (GM 200) was in the development phase, and Ground Master 60 radar (GM 60) was in the prospect phase. At that time, the SRA economic results were not so good, leading to two main issues:

- "How to secure the reuse at the level of the Ground Master product line"?
- "How to ensure the qualification achievement when using a BBs platform for a radar with high variability and many parameters"?

32.2 Transitioning to PLE: Dealing with Different Reuse Approaches

To address those challenges, the team defined six "product reuse categories" (A–F) for the Thales Group as a means to describe the level of reuse of a product with respect to the related market needs. Categories A and B are more related to the project than to the product nature. Categories C and D are based on the product's characteristics and its modular design. Categories E and F are implemented with product variability to a managed set of features. These categories are described as follows:

A: **"Full-custom development."** It corresponds to developing each project as a new one, and it applies to markets with a single instance.

B: **"Copy and modify."** It corresponds to cloning an existing project baseline to create a new one (no relation is maintained between these two), dedicated to markets with few instances, mostly specific.

C: **"Reuse BBs."** It corresponds to defining a product baseline with a list of BBs (each having its own baseline). The project baseline implements a set of BBs. This is dedicated to markets with a medium number of instances with a combination of specificities and reuse.

D: **"Reference architecture and commonalities."** It corresponds to implementing at the project baseline the reference architecture and instantiating a set of BBs. This is dedicated to markets with a medium number of instances with a combination of specifics and reuse.

E: **"Managed variability and derivation process."** It corresponds to feature modeling implementation with explicit variability management and derivation process. This is dedicated to markets with a large number of instances marginally specific. It also allows customer-specific developments.

F: **"Managed variability and derivation process."** It corresponds to the direct reuse of products in project solutions. This is dedicated to rather stable markets with a large number of instances with no specific requirements. It does not allow any customer specifics.

The transition from reuse category C to D with the surface radar 3D (SR3D) Platform was difficult due to the flexibility required. The main objective was to develop a large, scalable product, but it ultimately led to an increase in the number of parameters in our radars. For GM radars, the increased complexity led to a radar setting with over 3000 parameters, complicating the SR3D platform qualification and reuse of generics BBs qualified was not efficient at the radar level.

At SRA, the positioning of the GM radar market segment was clear: "We needed to manage the product variabilities and allow specific developments." However, at that time, no "internal best practices" existed at Thales, so we looked at practices coming from the automotive industry, even if the GM radar production part was not comparable to a traditional car (e.g. over twenty different radars are produced per year). We were also interested in academic publications, especially from Carnegie Mellon University (Kang, Cohen, and Hess et al. 1990), and we started collaborating with other Thales units. The transition to product reuse category E was underway, and it generated important cultural and organizational changes, which affected several practices within our way of doing systems engineering. For instance, we developed a GM radar roadmap with a model-based approach and with a top–down thinking; we shared the models with all the stakeholders; we deployed the derivation process from product assets to projects. However, even if the model-based dimension was already there, we decided to focus first on the PLE implementation.

32.3 The Formalization of the Variability Management Approach

During the multistep transition to PLE, we worked on the formalization of the new engineering approach. We started by identifying the variation points of the GM400 surveillance radar with the product line manager, the product line architect, and the project engineering managers. We analyzed and refined the high-level feature descriptions of our product variability in order to obtain an engineering feature model able to express the variability impacts at the "domain engineering" level, according to the ISO/IEC 26550 (ISO/IEC 2015). For example, in the GM radar missions, we identified variability in the surveillance modes of air defense: "long range," "short range," and "extended air defense" for the detection of tactical missiles. For GM radar functions, we identified the functionalities related to mobility: a radar can be "fixed" or "mobile." We also identified and classified radar for aircraft types, such as IFF-type secondary antennas, which could be added to specific models only. At the interface level, we identified the functionalities related to communication with "remote," "local command," and "control centers," as well as the predisposition for the customer's equipment in the radar shelter. Proceeding this way allowed us to establish our first GM radar variability analysis. Figure 32.1 summarizes an example of the type of elements that were at the center of the variability analysis.

First, we formalized this analysis by collecting the so-called "variabilities." We introduced variability representations that allowed us to organize them – through parent-child relations-, characterize them – mandatory, alternative, option, OR features – and add dependencies between variabilities – requires, conflicts, and other constraints. This resulted in a GM radar feature tree.

In the second stage, following the internal product roadmap and the first customer contracts, we selected the variability for each project. At that stage, we had not adopted a specific PLE tool, so we focused on consolidating the approach and worked essentially with two types of representations (in table form in Excel and graphic form). Even if it was not tool-supported yet, such formalization produced several improvements.

For example, we used to spend a lot of time in meetings discussing the concepts of variability, mainly because people shared different points of view. By publishing the GM radar feature model, we shared the same reference with all the stakeholders, and communication became less conflictual. It brought consistency – same feature vocabulary, same roadmap, etc. – between the different stakeholders at offers, solutions, software, hardware development, industry, and service levels, as well as across projects. The feature model became a common reference to organize

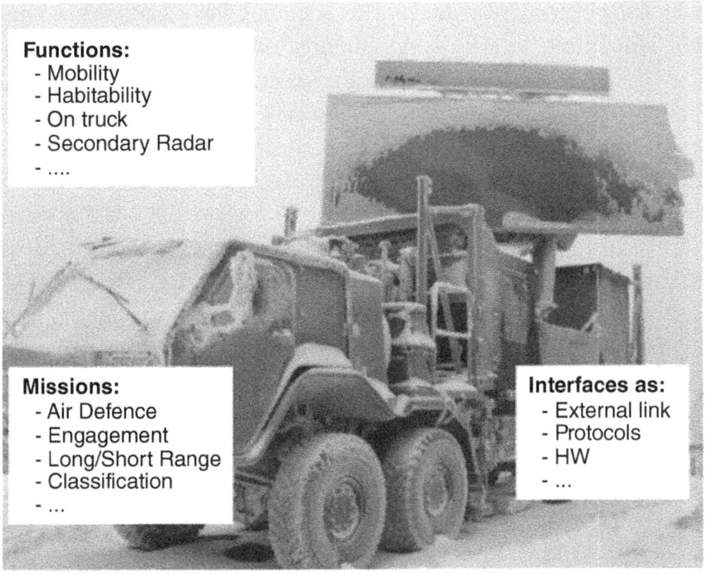

Figure 32.1 Partial scope of the variability analysis.

and monitor the GM product line, an engineering concept validated by the product line architect.

Before the new standard ISO/IEC 26580 (ISO/IEC 2021), the SRA team understood the key capability of a feature-based PLE approach. Since many variations simultaneously impact many assets and are subject to ongoing evolution, the feature model is an efficient way to share within the whole organization "what" the product line variability is and "how" it will or should evolve.

After introducing the foundation, it is time to have a look at the process we adopted. At the beginning of the transition, we were organized in what we call "reuse project mode." This means that when a new contract was signed, we looked for the project that best fitted the purpose of the contract specification and then proceeded by copying, pasting, and modifying the original (i.e. clone-and-own). This was often a source of error since the corrections on a project are rarely transferred to the others. This approach was "doing the job" with a few projects running in parallel, but it became unsustainable as soon as many more projects started running in parallel. The management part was also a challenge for the team. This led to the definition of a five-step variability management process. The process is summarized below.

Step 1: It consists of "the variability analysis." Features – equivalent to a functional characteristic of the product and that represents a viable unit of variability – are identified and organized hierarchically with variability types as mandatory, optional, alternative, OR, including feature dependencies as relations or constraints. This consists of the feature model, a visual representation of permissible variability amongst properties of a product within a product line.

Step 2: It consists of what we call "the project configuration." Features from the feature model are selected to specify a product variant.

Step 3: It consists of "variability mapping," which is where the variation points are identified into the product asset and linked to the related features with the support of logical equations and also calculations.

Step 4: It consists of the "derivation process." The derivation is triggered by applying the features selected for the project to the product assets to obtain the project instantiation results. Project-specific requests will be developed at the level of the project branch.

Step 5: It consists of the "specificity integration in the feature model." This means that if any specifics, developed within the customer project, present a potential for the product line then these will be integrated into the feature model after a favorable decision of the Configuration Control Board (CCB).

32.4 The Advent of a PLE-driven Organization

To implement the PLE approach described above, the "engineering development environments" should also be based on PLE principles. The PLE reference model emphasizes the key differences between product (aka product line) and project engineering and the need for two development cycles:

- First, the product engineering scope has the objective to define and implement commonalities and variability of the product line. This – domain engineering – is where the variability at the asset level is introduced (with feature model, requirements, modeling, radar standard configuration, etc.).
- Second, the project engineering scope has the purpose of meeting the customer's needs by exploiting the variability and assets of the product line via derivation – application engineering – as well as by creating specifics if necessary, as shown in Figure 32.2.

Based on the assets of the private configuration space at the domain level, a set of integrated tools, internally named "Orchestra suite," has been defined at Thales Group level to allow users to initiate the derivation process. A private system engineering data organization has been established to allow the teams to apply the rules of the SRA development "Orchestra suite," usage. Examples of the major documents and assets mapped in the PLE scope include:

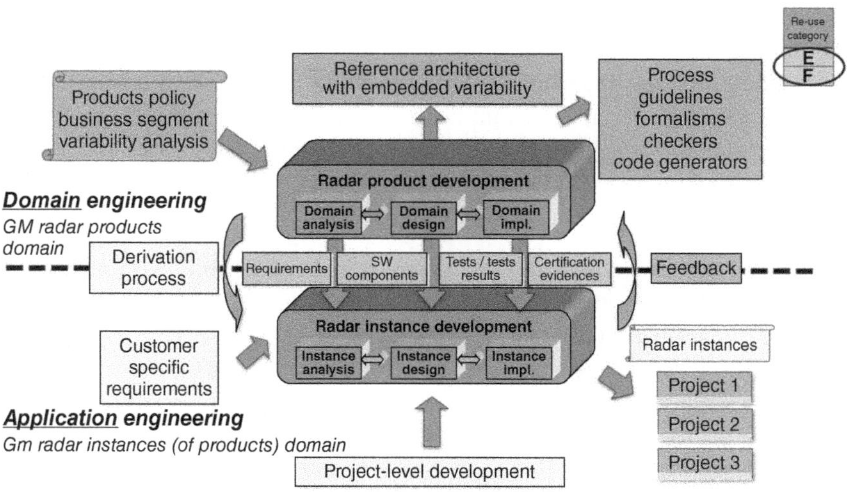

Figure 32.2 Thales SRA level orchestrated development environment.

- The technical description document is used by bid managers to frame the offer. If the customer requests a specific need in relation to the feature model, the bid manager identifies that there will be an additional cost in terms of development and/or qualification.
- The specification documents and the functional configuration audit, used by the engineering delivery manager frame the radar performances and control the impacts on the qualification of the product and projects.
- The definition breakdown structure, used by the industry, generates the applicable configuration of the project already in the early project phase.
- The test plan and test sheets, used by integration, verification, validation, and qualification management, generate the evidence that the requirement is met by the product – qualification done for a standard configuration in a radar state⇔versioning –if a specific requirement exists for the project a qualification complement must be done.

The implementation of variability management within the asset scope presented above has saved us time on the radar schedule. For instance, during the orientation review phase, the project documents are now automatically generated from the instantiated product documentation.

32.5 No PLE Exists Without a Solid Governance

In support of this new way of developing products, we also put in place the incremental standard configuration strategy. This allows us to validate perimeter and performance improvement, obsolescence management, and product financing from cumulative project taxes and self-funding budgets. The engineering team relies on the configuration produced by the derivation process to "freeze" the scope and perform the radar qualification. Consequently, the bid manager's act within a specific framework to come up with an increased reuse rate in the radar division. After several difficult years, we optimized the project lead time and finally realized savings, allowing also budget reduction in the call-for-tender phase. Nevertheless, competition has also come to our market segment, so this triggered the necessity to further improve the standard product and, at the same time, to limit the product options. This led to the introduction of the concept of "activable" options in standard product configuration for sales negotiation and export authorization. These are radar-integrated options that give the bid manager the flexibility to negotiate with the customer without impacting product development or qualification.

To enforce this new process, a new business line, the GMR, is created. Its primary responsibility is to establish a governance framework that can be synthesized with the following expression: "The anchorage to product leads the business, the standard configurations lead the radar qualification, and the projects follow."

Some of the governance rules are here summarized:

- The product line cannot be implemented without the support and involvement of the management whose objective is the product.
- One manager for products and projects is appointed.
- The product team leads the developments. New product features introduced into the feature model are approved in the CCB.
- The product team's budgets come from projects and self-funding.
- Communication and lobbying are necessary. A dedicated resource to deploy this PLE process is appointed to support engineering teams.
- Project teams focus on customer interface and specific deliveries.

32.6 Toward MBPLE: The Improvement of the PLE Approach Continues

During the transition to the PLE approach, we always sought to increase productivity. One enabler was to revise the existing radar parameterization scope. The complexity we faced consisted of managing over 3000 parameters that belonged to 40 – too large- software BBs. We applied PLE concepts and looked for variation points. One might think that the complexity of variability – the number of different product instances possible – grows more or less exponentially – each new optional element doubles the number of possible instances –, which quickly leads to a situation where testing all possible instances is impossible. Even the configuration of the variation points gets very complex due to all the dependencies to control. However, the misconception that variation points create additional complexity can be easily proved. A huge reduction in complexity can be achieved since several dozens of features may control thousands of technical variations. This reduced complexity, in our case, resulted in simpler parameterization, less complex testing of reusable BBs, and consequently simpler maintenance. We managed to control those 3000 parameters with only 70 key features that were part of the feature model. Radar's parameterization cost has been reduced from 120 to 4 hours, and consistency between projects has been increased, without mentioning that no dedicated radar experts are needed any longer to manage the right setting of parameters. This is a simple example of how a well-established PLE approach can make a difference.

We have also established a solid engineering data model structure, containing the specification reference, the PBS CI (configuration item structure of the product) and PBS FCH (functional chain structure), the IVV (integration, verification, and validation) reference, and the changes reference. This engineering data model is composed of different levels: system needs, logical architecture and physical architecture with embedded variability, and follows the Arcadia methodology (Voirin 2023). The increasing focus on the model-based approach – the shift toward (model-based product line engineering) MBPLE – and the introduction of a shared information model allow us to better control the changes of the functional chains and to better manage the technical debt. Since the GMR is a product line that has almost 15 years of existence, it is key to share the radar knowledge and to promote the development in co-engineering while being independent of the tools used at system, hardware, or software levels. A good publication that describes the synergy between PLE and MBSE at Thales is "A value-driven, integrated approach to model-based product line engineering" (Navas et al. 2021).

On the tools side, we also sought for improvements. For instance, we replaced Gears (BigLever 2024) with PTC pure::variants (PTC pure::variants 2024) to adhere to the decision taken by Thales Group and benefit from the one "Orchestra suite." Pure::variants, in fact, better meet the needs of Thales Group and secured the new GM AESA development while ensuring the delivery of parameter files for different GM radar products of GMR product lines.

This also involves setting up team coordination meetings to take into account the needs of the projects, the applicable versions of the BBs, and changes approved in the CCB. The feature model facilitates the entire collaboration process. To address the complex models of other engineering teams, we put in place the use of multiple interdependent and consistent feature models. For example, our radar solution is decomposed into several BBs, and some BBs have their own "local" feature model. As part of the composition of the radar, local feature models are connected to the higher-level radar feature model using dependencies and calculations. These reusable and configurable BBs are used in multiple product lines. In order to use a BB in a product line, the configuration of the BB is connected and linked at least to the radar-level feature model by some means. There are various approaches to achieve this outcome.

These include:

- The use of constraints and relations to connect features of different models.
- The use of preconfigured instances of the respective BB – providing a set of named alternative configurations or even just a single BB configuration – to be included in the product line assembly.
- A combination of both, by defining preconfigurations that provide a set of feature selections, etc. but are still leaving the final configuration of the BBs open to either manual selection or additional constraints and relations.

We also changed our product life cycle management tool and enterprise resources planner (ERP). We looked for variation points in the breakdown structures, and the feature model allowed us to define a standard applicable configuration as early as possible, not only to improve productivity but also to simplify the generic product definition breakdown structure.

The project's definition breakdown structure is now automatically generated from the product definition breakdown structure derivation. This is enabled by the connection of both product and asset lifecycle management (PALM) (Thales PALM 2024) and ERP-integrated tools with PTC pure::variants (PTC pure::variants 2024).

The final transition to an MBPLE approach allowed us to work on over 20 000 existing data modules.

We saw several improvements brought by the introduction of a feature-based PLE approach. However, it is worth mentioning that using feature models across product lines calls for proper change management and well-defined responsibilities regarding the evolution of the product line. The "price to pay" is the maintenance effort and potential duplication of features in different feature models, since independent reuse in multiple scenarios demands large amounts of independence of the configuration of the BBs.

On the organizational side, the main improvement focused on the interactions between the product engineering activities (aka PLE) and the Project engineering activities in line with their respective Lifecycles, which are usually not synchronized. Figure 32.3 outlines the respective contents of

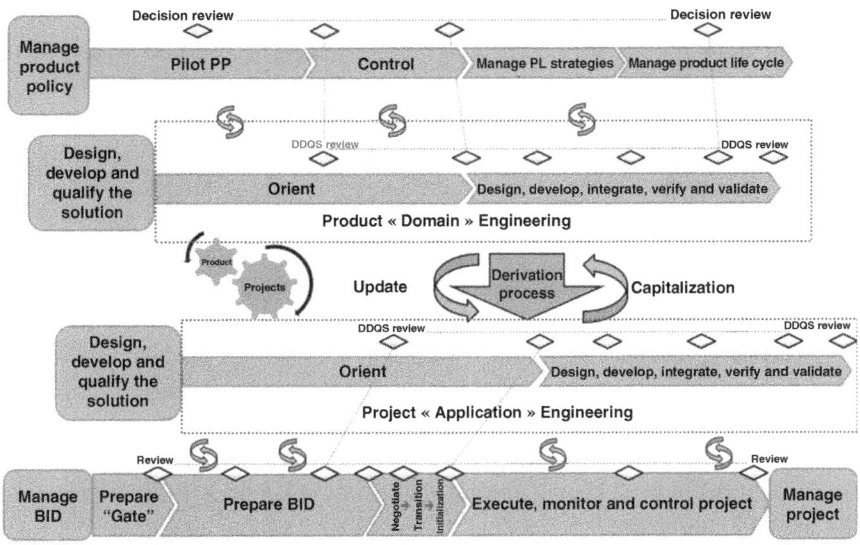

Figure 32.3 Product domain engineering and project application engineering.

product engineering ("domain") and project engineering ("application") in a dual DDQS (define, develop, qualify the solution) process representation. Each step (orient, design, etc...) refers to activities either within the product development lifecycle or within the project development lifecycle (like the derivation process). Those activities cover the PLE practices. We also leveraged the approach to support the "customer service," for instance, by linking the feature model to our customer service tool environment in order to automatically generate the customer's user documentation for the project.

32.7 (MB)PLE Benefits and Recommendations Based on SRA's Experience

The PLE and most recent MBPLE deployment's benefits and lessons learned on GMR are considerable and helped the SRA team to develop competitive, attractive, and sustainable radars. Some of the experienced benefits are listed as follows:

(1) Lead time reduction: This covers the proposals, the launch of the projects – automatic derivation of generic documents – and the radar manufacturing – thanks to the introduction of standard configurations.
(2) Quality improvement: Thanks to variability management, better coherence between projects exists and a reuse of qualified configurations is in place.
(3) Cost reduction: In both recurring costs – thanks to BBs and standard subassemblies reuse – and nonrecurring costs – thanks to variability management.
(4) Attractiveness improvement: Better features and higher performances at the product level and variability management allow to meet customer needs more easily – the engineering efforts of projects are mainly focused on customer specifics.

To achieve such benefits it is important to take into consideration some key recommendations that are grouped below for MBPLE adoption, feature models usage, product development vs project development, and architecture and BBs.

MBPLE adoption recommendations can be summarized as follows:

- Do not underestimate the weight of the architecture in the MBPLE success. For instance, choose mature architects and do not consider that architecting is only a matter of method or process; in fact, architecture models are not going to solve the project challenges alone.
- Do not consider MBPLE as an engineering issue only, moving from project development to product-based development involves the entire organization and requires cultural changes and reallocation of responsibilities and budget, as well as management support.
- Do not be too optimistic on actual skills and practices to jump from "no products" to "nothing but the product." It is a long journey!
- Do not believe that when the feature modeling is defined correctly and the architecture models are developed, then the product line is fully designed.

The feature models usage primary recommendations are:

- They shall be used to manage product lines over the entire product life cycle and not only in the initial stages.
- They are the result of an iterative process, but the product line design shall remain stable and sufficiently adaptable to meet changing market needs.
- They shall be used as the primary means of communication between all the project stakeholders.

- They shall be kept as an important knowledge source and preserved because almost no one can have a complete overview of complex systems like our GM radars. They can also be used to facilitate the training of new people.
- They shall include only variable features in order to remain simple and focus on variability and defined as a clear hierarchical structure for all stakeholders.
- They shall be reviewed by stakeholders regularly (e.g. obsolete feature removal, new feature introduction after product CCB's approval, bid and project configurations updating, generic assets impacts tracking, product line roadmap upgrading, etc..).
- They shall introduce an engineering concept that must be validated with project architects and the product line architect.

The key product development vs. project development recommendations are:

- A product line is not a project; a defect can spread to multiple applications in mass production. Hence, it is necessary to make in-depth qualifications of the product line before using it in projects; if possible, mature the product with long-lasting tests as soon as possible.
- Pay special attention to product configuration management and not only to the process. The permanent goal shall be to stick to the limited number of variants of the product decided by the product line manager.
- Avoid "wild and radical improvement." Once a product is stabilized, the major evolution costs are in the qualification; group and plan the improvements through batches at a low pace.

Finally, the major architecture and BBs recommendations are:

- Work for the technical success of the architecture. This happens when the reference architecture is reliable, resilient, and fully compliant with the technical challenge of the system under development; this is a real business differentiator. Consequently, some stable BBs can be used without change within multiple products, specifically hardware and low-level software BBs, on a larger perimeter than originally targeted.
- Harmonize, generalize and share modeling, simulation, IVV tools, test benches, and processes.
- Harmonize and generalize the product line and BBs architecture as the reference technical solution for the engineering community.
- Avoid the development of software BBs that are too large and require an excess usage of parameterization.
- Define clear roles between the BBs teams and product line teams (e.g. define who is responsible for the architecture implementation qualification).
- Increase awareness and establish a common terminology and semantics. For instance, in the GMR team since the beginning, there has been confusion and mix-up between variability and modularity/scalability/parameterization.

To conclude, the PLE and its consequent model-based deployment at GMR have been a long journey with many challenges that did not stop its adoption but, once solved, reinforced the necessity of establishing a consolidated model-based and improved version of it: the MBPLE approach. Thanks to the powerful feature-based PLE concepts and their adaptation to our context, we managed to show continuous improvement such as aligning bid data and project, engineering, and service phases, improving quality, reducing the cost and lead time of radars, and above all, remaining attractive in our competitive market segment. The GMR product line has succeeded in defining a "delivery" approach based on a product line that has become the common way of conducting business for all functions at Thales SRA.

References

BigLever (2024). Biglever software gears. https://biglever.com/solution/gears/ (accessed 10 May 2024).

ISO/IEC (2015). Software and systems engineering – reference model for product line engineering and management (*ISO/IEC/IEEE 26550: 2015*)

ISO/IEC (2021). Software and systems engineering – methods and tools for the feature-based approach to software and systems product line engineering *(ISO/IEC/IEEE 26580: 2021).*

Kang, K.C., Cohen, S., Hess, J. et al. (1990). *Feature-Oriented Domain Analysis* (FODA*) Feasibility Study.* CMU/SEI-90-TR-021. Software Engineering Institute, Carnegie Mellon University. http://resources.sei.cmu.edu/library/asset-view.cfm?AssetID=11231 (accessed 7 January 2023).

Navas, J., Bonnet, S., Voirin, J.L. et al. (2021). A value-driven, integrated approach to model-based product line engineering. *INCOSE International Symposium* 31, pp. 95–110.

PTC pure::variants (2024). *pure::variants.* https://www.ptc.com/en/products/pure-variants (accessed 10 May 2024).

Thales (2024). *Surface Radars Thales Group.* https://www.thalesgroup.com/en/markets/defence-and-security/air-forces/airspace-protection/surface-radars (accessed 20 July 2024).

Thales PALM (2024). *Product & Asset Lifecycle Management.* https://www.thalesgroup.com/en/worldwide/security/product-and-asset-lifecycle-management-palm (accessed 20 July 2024).

Voirin, J.L. (2023). *Arcadia Reference: Workflow and Activities, Thales.* https://mbse-capella.org/resources/arcadia-reference/Arcadia%20Reference%20-%20Activities.pdf.

33

Raytheon: System Family Engineering – Innovating at the Speed of Relevance

James Teaff

33.1 Introduction

At Raytheon, an RTX business, the foundation of everything we do is rooted in our values and a higher calling – to help our nation and allies defend freedoms and deter aggression. We bring the strength of more than 100 years of experience and renowned engineering expertise to meet the needs of today's mission and stay ahead of tomorrow's threat. Our team solves tough, meaningful problems that create a safer, more secure world (Raytheon 2024).In response to Department of Defense (DoD) Instruction 5000.97 digital engineering (DE) (DoD 2023), Raytheon is adopting the augmented system and method of systems family engineering (SFE), digital engineering, modeling and simulation (DEM&S) plus development operations (Dev*Ops) plus modular open systems approach (MOSA) open system architecture (OSA).

At Raytheon, the value of SFE using feature-based product line engineering (FbPLE) is compelling, with measured improvements across numerous key metrics including safety, security, quality, cost, time-to-field new features, technology upgrades, hardware and software maintenance deliveries, and similar. The use of FbPLE on US DoD contracts has resulted in aggregate superlinear cost avoidance for the DoD measured in hundreds of millions of US dollars and for the associated defense contracting teams equally impressive top and bottom-line improvement, enabling the DoD to move at the speed of relevance and contractors to innovate at the speed of relevance (Greg et al. 2015; Clements and Krueger 2019; Defense Innovation Board 2019; Clements and Krueger 2021). The ISO/IEC 265xx set of standards defines systems and software product line engineering as a general approach to engineer a family of technically similar systems in an efficient manner, taking advantage of the systems' similarities while respecting and managing their differences. ISO/IEC standard 26580:2021 *Software and systems engineering – methods and tools for the feature-based approach to software and systems product line engineering*, or more simply FbPLE, is a specific form of system family engineering that uses product feature models as the authoritative source of truth (ASoT) for defining and managing product variation across the system families of interest (SFoI) full life cycle; and automation in the form of a digital engineering ecosystem (DEE) comprising a daisy-chained product line engineering (PLE) factory and Dev*Ops software factory (ISO/IEC 2021; Defense Innovation Board 2019).

Model-Based Product Line Engineering (MBPLE): The Feature-Based Path to Product Lines Success, First Edition.
Marco Forlingieri et al.

Some benefits of the FbPLE can be measured using the following:

- Delivering 3x more capability within budget than non-FbPLE contracts
- Providing continuous delivery of value within weeks of contract award, and extending across the contract period of performance
  - New and modified software and hardware modules are securely delivered per contracted production and maintenance rhythm; including daily, weekly, monthly, and quarterly
- Enabling rule-based, automated, and semi-automated enforcement of International Traffic in Arms Regulations (ITAR) and similar, ensuring no product variant contains any content that is not allowed to be exported
- Significantly reducing contract execution risk
- Realizing an eightfold improvement in verification and validation time per production cycle

The key concepts of FbPLE are developed across this book and simplified in the INCOSE PLE Primer (INCOSE 2019).

In essence, engineers do not carry out development work on the product asset instances. Instead, they work on the shared asset supersets, the feature catalog, and the composition matrices – that is, they work in the digital asset factory. The automated factory configurator applies their work to each product variant instance that it affects. Change and evolution are handled systematically through well-defined governance processes. A factory rule base (not shown) automatically verifies the product asset instances are fit for use.

Feature-based PLE enables automated production of hardware with embedded software systems, software-only systems, or daisy-chained digital asset production lines integrated with hardware fabrication. It works in multiple security zones, enabling cost-efficient assembly of modules at differing classification levels, from unclassified through secret and top secret, efficiently leveraging an organization's global workforce (Teaff et al. 2019).

33.2 Introduction to the Digital Trinity

The digital trinity of DEM&S plus Dev*Ops plus MOSA OSA is depicted in Figure 33.1 (DoD 2018, 2020, 2022; Roper 2020, 2021). Let's take each concept of the digital trinity one at a time.

DE is defined as an integrated digital approach that uses authoritative sources of system data and models as a continuum across disciplines to support lifecycle activities from concept through disposal (DoD 2018). There is a lot going on in the definition, but the key concept is the use of digital models as

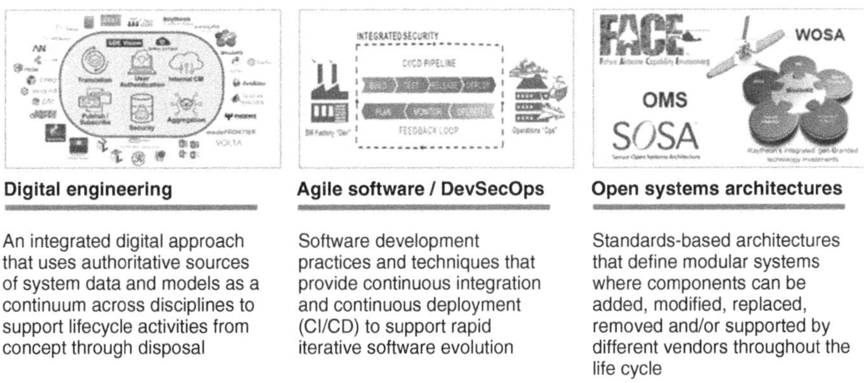

Figure 33.1 The digital trinity.

ASoTs. Take your vehicle's navigation system – you plug in your destination, analyze different routes to find the one you like, and start driving. The display shows your current location, when and in which direction to turn, and more. The navigation system uses a digital model – data that represents reality – that has been certified as accurate – it is a source of truth – by an authority – a company such as Google LLC. For the digital trinity, once you have certified digital models, you can do what-if analysis, high-fidelity simulations, and more. The Air Force calls this "simulate before you aviate" (DoD 2020).

Development-operations "plus" or Dev*Ops is defined as an agile method for fabricating, operating, and sustaining a family of systems that eliminates the historic divide between development (Dev) and operations (Ops), i.e. the infamous "push it over to operations each year and hope nothing breaks too bad" paradigm. The wildcard character "*" or star represents adding important system quality attributes to DevOps such as cybersecurity (DevSecOps); safety (DevSecSafetyOps); and more, resulting in Dev*Ops, sometimes referred to as DevStar (DoD 2022). Once you unpack Dev*Ops and abstract away the technical details, what appears is its key characteristic – the continuous delivery of value to the warfighter, with minimum viable product variants fielded in weeks to months after contract award and incrementally updated with new product features and technology day-by-day across the contract period of performance. Contrast this with the historic one-and-done program where a product is acquired and fielded years after contract award. As noted in the Defense Innovation Board's 2019 report, software is never done, and the internet of things (IoT) has demonstrated software is increasingly embedded in the physical devices – the hardware – we use daily (Defense Innovation Board 2019). Out of necessity, management practices at commercial companies have been transformed to product-based management rather than project-based management; that is, managing a family of products with continuous innovation, technology refresh, and similar.

The MOSA is the DoD's business and technology strategy for acquiring, operating, and sustaining families of systems composed of severable, reusable modules that are conformant to OSA (DoD 2020). An OSA is an architecture that separates the system into major functions and elements, which work together across interfaces in conformance with widely supported, consensus-based standards. Figure 33.2 depicts the key system quality attributes, of which severability, reusability, composability, and, of course, modularity are most frequently mentioned in literature.

Jargon aside, MOSA and OSAs enable the acquisition of assemble-to-order systems from best-of-breed system modules that, once fielded, can be effectively sustained throughout their life cycle, from installing new product features to swapping out system modules as part of a technology refresh – all in the operational environment.

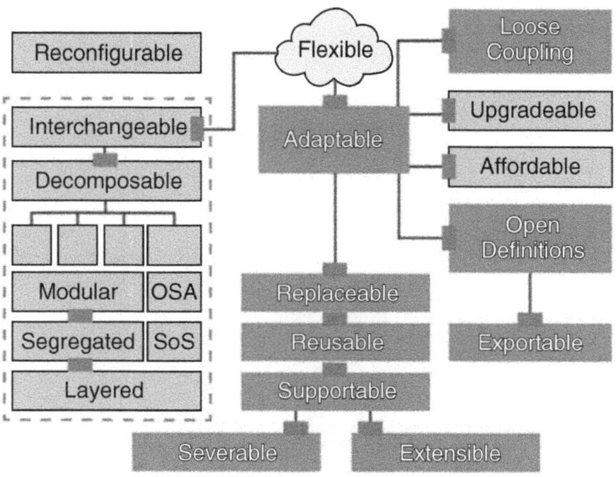

Figure 33.2 MOSA OSA key system quality attributes.

33.3 A SFE's Example: The Hypothetical Intelligence Gathering System

Using the hypothetical intelligence gathering system depicted in Figure 33.3, let's apply FbPLE plus DEM&S plus Dev*Ops plus MOSA OSAs, concentrating on the FbPLE aspects.

The H-IGN system's mission is to support the intelligence analyst via capturing and processing sensor data collected by sensor platforms. The H-IGN system comprises one or more unmanned vehicles (UxV), a ground control segment, and an intelligence analytics and dissemination segment. The H-IGN product portfolio supports three primary variations:

- Small area of interest (AOI): line of sight UxV control and one analyst such as covering a city block
- Medium AOI: less than 200 square miles and up to five analysts such as covering a city
- Large AOI: less than 125 000 square miles and up to 20 analysts

Simply stated, to apply FbPLE plus DEM&S plus Dev*Ops plus MOSA OSA, we take what we typically do for a product and add an engineering analysis step – feature-oriented scope, commonality, and variability analysis, or feature-oriented scope, commonality, and variability (FO-SCV), as depicted in Figure 33.4.

FO-SCV analysis begins with eliciting what product features are in scope for the product line, followed by determining what features can be common (invariant); and what features need to be variant (different form/fit/function) (Kang et al. 1990). The information from the FO-SCV analysis is captured in a product feature model and associated product feature profiles which together comprise the feature catalog (Clements and Krueger 2017). The product feature model and associated data from the digital engineering ASoT for the definition and management of product variation across the entire digital ecosystem. DE with FbPLE is continuous with stepwise refinement. Also known as top-down analysis, engineers iteratively create a set of architecture, design, and parametric analysis models at different levels of abstraction, and with different viewpoints and perspectives addressing the concerns of different categories of stakeholders and model consumers. The end result is a set of linked models comprising a digital thread.

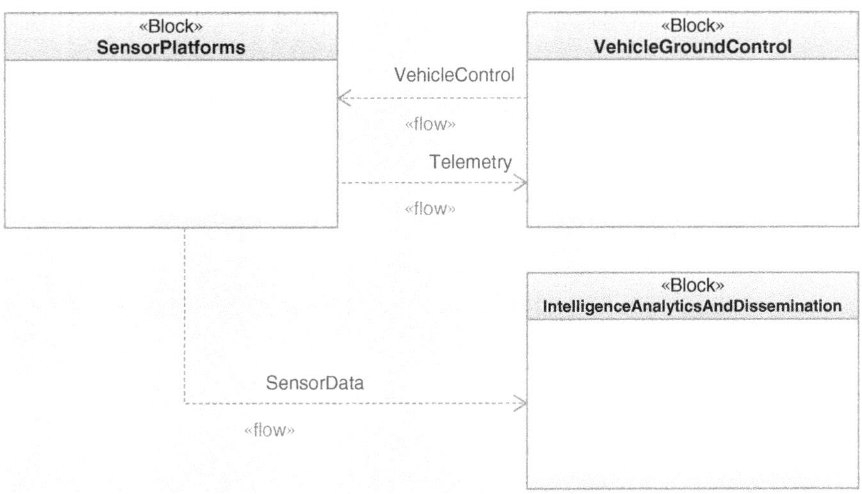

Figure 33.3 Hypothetical intelligence gathering network (H-IGN).

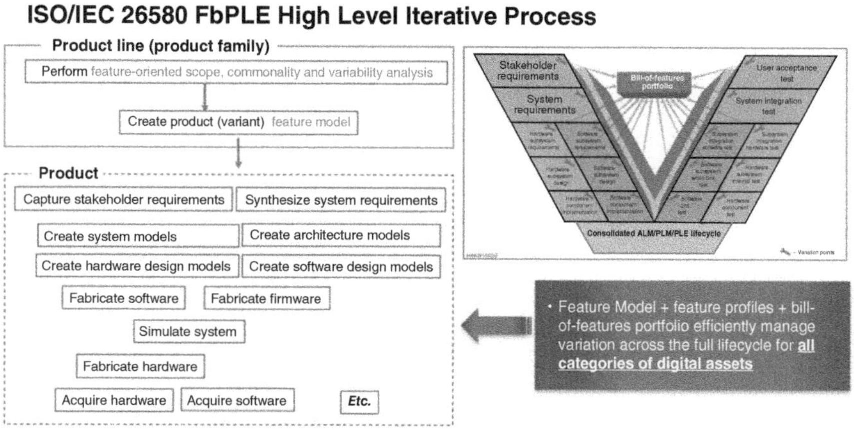

Figure 33.4 FO-SCV analysis:Part of digital engineering.

Let's do a quick technical deep dive into a small aspect of our H-IGN system to illustrate. First up is to identify variations, model them, and create a set of factory product rules forming the authoritative source of truth for variation across the SFoI.

The FO-SCV analysis identified the following variations in sensor platforms:

- One or more unmanned aerial vehicles
- One or more unmanned ground vehicles
- One or more maritime unmanned surface vehicles

The H-IGN system supports the following sensor platform control options:

- Continuous active ground control
- Autonomous vehicle control

Moreover, the system capabilities and total lifecycle cost for each product variant in the portfolio differ based on its product specification (its factory bill-of-features).

Time to capture the FO-SCV analysis in a feature mode. Product variant features are abstractions of the variant behaviors (behavioral features) and structure (structural features) – ultimately the form, fit, and function (FFF) – of system elements. A feature model represents the behavioral features and structural features in a hierarchical graph (Clements and Krueger 2017), which for our H-IGN sensor platform control modes results in the feature model in Figure 33.5.

For the security aspect of the digital trinity, the engineering analysis includes:

- Continuously analyzing the cyber-attack surface for each system variant in the product portfolio.
- Creating or amending cyber resiliency capabilities and cybersecurity controls for each system variant addressing each identified attack vector.
- Digitizing cyber resiliency and cybersecurity verification rules forming a living rule base.
- Using the factory's living rule base ensures each system variant automatically generated by the factory contains the requisite cyber resiliency capabilities and cybersecurity controls.

The cyber-attack surface analysis for the H-IGN system identifies the ground control of UxV communications system (COMMS) as an attack vector. Potential attacks include:

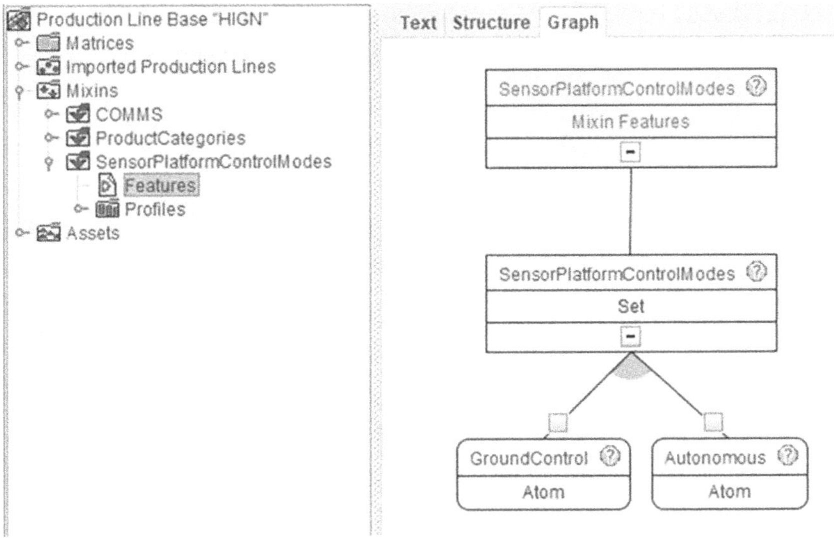

Figure 33.5 H-IGN sensor platform control modes feature model.

- Passive data interception
- Covert data modification
- COMMS disruption

The communications system feature's engineering ensures ongoing human and/or autonomous sensor platform control for each system variant, each differing in capabilities and cost. Features include:

- Wireless COMMS: radio frequency (RF) and microwave radio
  - Encryption algorithms
  - Frequency hopping algorithms
- Line of sight COMMS
- Wired COMMS: essentially the UxV is tethered to a ground operator

Modeling the COMMS capability set results in a variant feature model, depicted in Figure 33.6, comprising the wireless COMMS feature and the line of sight COMMS feature.

The H-IGN subject matter experts provide the following specifications:

- All product variants shall have redundant COMMS capabilities for greater cyber resiliency
- All product variants shall encrypt data to ensure cybersecurity
- RF COMMS shall use a frequency hopping algorithm to ensure cybersecurity

Additionally, for each AOI variant, the subject matter experts provide the following specifications:

- The small AOI variant
  - Shall have both wireless radio frequency and line of sight COMMS for greater cyber resiliency
  - Customers may additionally choose to add "basic" or "enhanced" wired COMMS, but not both (this drives capability and cost variation)
  - Shall not support autonomous vehicle control (this drives capability and cost variation)

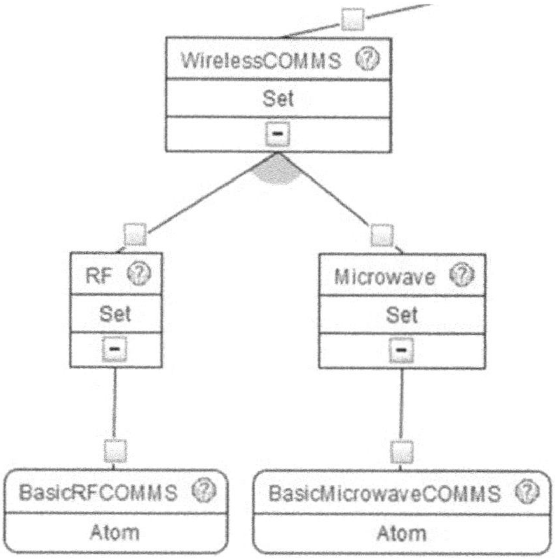

Figure 33.6 Subset of H-IGN COMMS capabilities.

- The medium AOI variant
  - Shall have both wireless radio frequency and microwave radio COMMS for greater cyber resiliency
  - Customers may additionally choose to add line of sight COMMS for greater cyber resiliency
  - Shall not support wired COMMS
  - Shall support autonomous vehicle control for greater cyber resiliency
- The large AOI variant
  - Shall have both wireless radio frequency and microwave radio COMMS for greater cyber resiliency
  - Shall not support line of sight COMMS
  - Shall not support wired COMMS
  - Shall support autonomous vehicle control for greater cyber resiliency

Each subject matter expert specification digitizes into a product rule. The product rules exist in the PLE factory rule base as assertions – Boolean expressions that evaluate to either true or false. For example, the subject matter expert specification *All product variants shall have redundant COMMS capabilities for greater resiliency* results in the product rule:

Assert ((COMMS.COMMSTypes > {WirelessCOMMS}) OR
((COMMS.COMMSTypes > {LineOfSightCOMMS}) OR
(COMMS.COMMSTypes > {WiredCOMMS})));

While the specifications *All product variants shall encrypt data*, and *RF COMMS shall use a frequency hopping algorithm*, results in the product rule set:

Assert ((COMMS.COMMSTypes.WirelessCOMMS.RF >=
{BasicRFCOMMS}) REQUIRES (COMMS.COMMSCybersecurity.
EncryptionAlgorithm == {EncryptionAlgo_Alpha}));
Assert ((COMMS.COMMSTypes.WirelessCOMMS.RF >= {BasicRFCOMMS})

REQUIRES (COMMS.COMMSCybersecurity.
FrequencyHoppingAlgorithm == {FreqHopAlgo_Bravo}));

Adding these assertions to the PLE factory's product rule base results in the initial rule base for COMMS (Figure 33.7).

Once the digitized product rules are in place, the PLE factory checks the assertions in the rule base and issues an error to the systems engineer for every rule violation as they work. For example, if a digital engineer attempts to design a system variant with basic RF COMMS without a frequency hopping algorithm, the factory throws an *assertion failed* when evaluating the product rule base:

Assertion failed: Assert ((COMMS.COMMSTypes.Wireless-
COMMS.RF >= {BasicRFCOMMS}) REQUIRES (COMMS.
COMMSCybersecurity.FrequencyHoppingAlgorithm ==
{FreqHopAlgo_Bravo}))

Just a couple of more steps, and we are done. Feature profiles are named selections of features in a feature model used by the factory configurator to tailor a digital asset – or more concisely, a feature profile is a *composition specification*. Figure 33.8 depicts a feature profile named *Medium AOI COMMS Variant Omega*. The checkmarks in the model indicate the set of features selected for the composition specification – *Basic RF Comms, encryption algorithm alpha*, etc. Boxes that are not checked indicate the set of features deselected for the composition specification.

The final step is to create digital assets, add variation points – planned for, controlled points of variability in assets to accommodate a specific operational context – and create the logic for the PLE factory configurator to exercise the variation points; that is, to compose the assets using one or more feature profiles in a bill-of-features. The Java snippet below depicts a simple software module that includes points of variability (sections of software code tagged with "///* BeginGearsBlock Java <tagName>") that the factory configurator will either include or exclude when tailoring the module (Figure 33.9).

And the accompanying asset logic for the factory configurator to delete tagged sections of the software module depending on the feature profiles in the composition specification:

When (true)
Select "NonsensicalCOMMSModule.java"
{
If (NOT (COMMS.COMMSTypes.WiredCOMMS >= {BasicWiredCOMMS})) {
DeleteBlock Java "FooTag";
}
If (NOT (COMMS.COMMSTypes.WiredCOMMS >= {EnhancedWiredCOMMS})) {
DeleteBlock Java "BarTag";
}
StripBlockDelimiters;
}

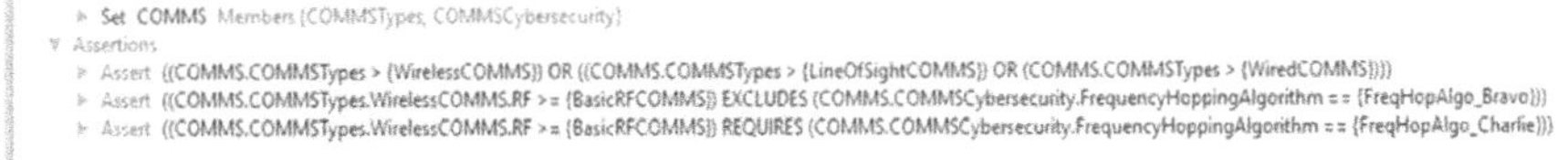

Figure 33.7 PLE factory's product rule base results.

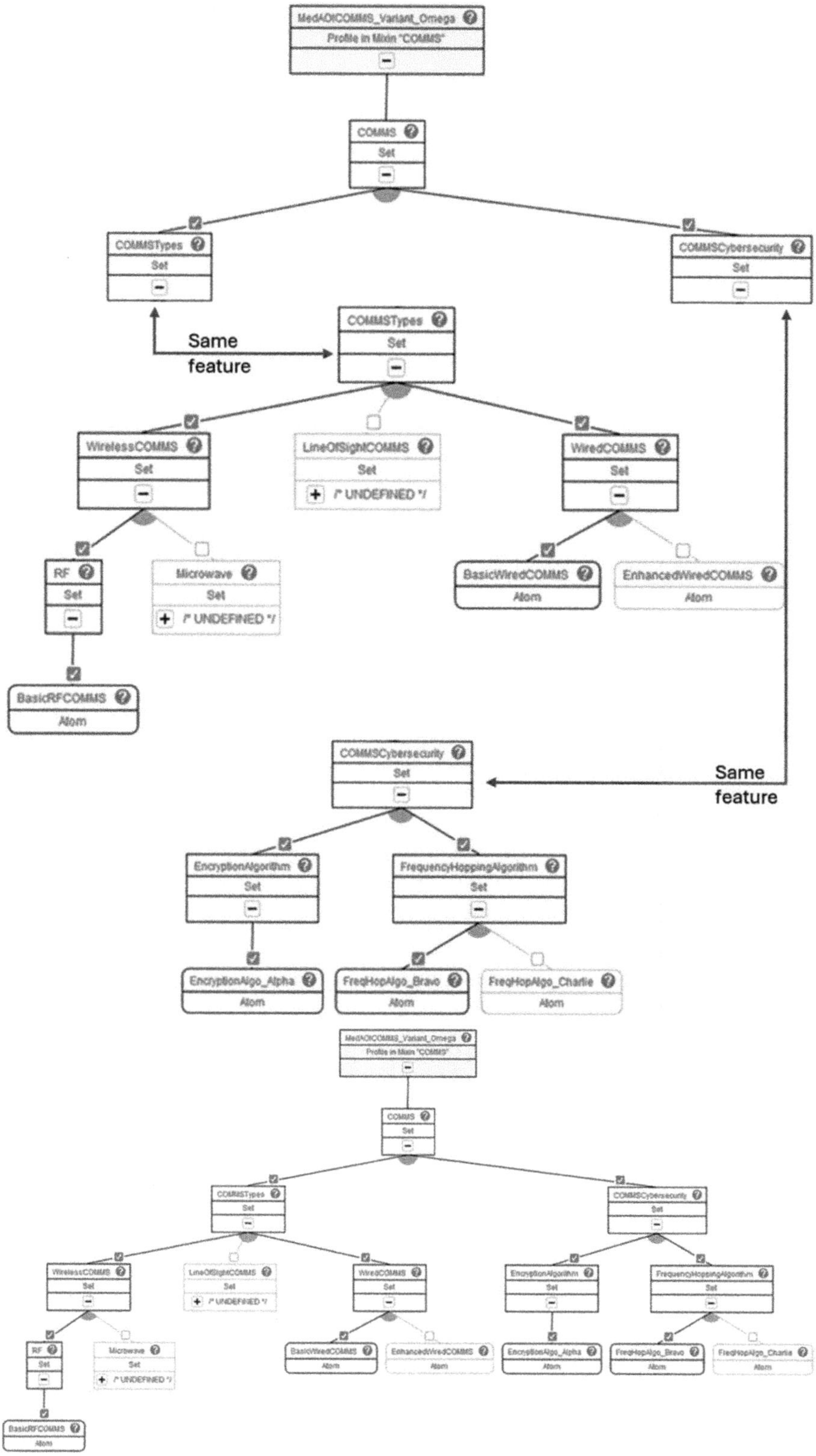

Figure 33.8 Example feature profile.

```java
package com.Raytheon;

public class NonsensicalCOMMSModule {

    public boolean doNothing () {

        ///* BeginGearsBlock Java FooTag
        System.out.println("Foo");
        ///* EndGearsBlock Java FooTag

        ///* BeginGearsBlock Java BarTag
        System.out.println("Bar");
        ///* EndGearsBlock Java BarTag

        return true;

    }

}

```

Figure 33.9 Simple Java SW module.

Returning from the depths of our analysis to our FbPLE plus digital trinity method, the increasingly rich feature model and digitized product rules are subsequently used to define and manage variations across all categories of models and associated digital assets, such as enterprise architecture models, system models, software modules, technical data packages used by hardware fabrication; bills-of-materials used by the supply chain to purchase commercial off-the-shelf hardware and software, and more. Finally, the resulting digital thread – linked models and data – is verified against the contractually requisite set of MOSA open system architectures (OSAs), referred to as a government reference architecture.

The digital ecosystem of engineering tools forming the PLE factory, the high-fidelity simulation environments, the analytics using digital twins reflecting the operational state of fielded systems, plus the hardware factories, comprise a factory-of-factories realizing a "Matrix movie"-like virtual environment. Adding a new variant to the system family is now as straightforward as creating a new bill-of-features that will assemble to order the system variant from the digital asset supersets. Innovation is as quick as adding variation points – or small sets of new digital assets – to the supersets of assets, reusing preexisting assets to automatically compose, certify, and field the new system variant in hours to days rather than months to years.

And there you have it – FbPLE plus DEM&S plus Dev*Ops plus MOSA OSAs applied to a hypothetical system family. At this point, you may be asking, where is the bang for the buck ... that comes during the operational lifespan of the system family when the digital asset factory (including the software factory), daisy-chained with the physical asset factory (hardware fabrication), daisy-chained with supply chains, and more, comprising a factory-of-factories spanning government and contractors created and certified to field the minimum viable product variants, is used hour-by-hour, day-by-day, to innovate and deliver value to the warfighter.

33.4 Challenges and Solutions

As with any paradigm change, adopting the FbPLE plus digital trinity method has a number of challenges, with the technical challenges relatively easy compared to the requisite organizational changes. Fortunately, industry, government, academia, and standards consortia have collaborated for 20+ years, culminating in a set of enablers in the form of standards and regulation-complying best practices to lower the risk of organizational change, including:

- Publication of ISO/IEC standard 26580
- Enhanced variation modeling mechanisms in the OMG SysML v2 standard
- Augmenting the systems engineering body of knowledge (SEBoK) with product line engineering addressing the engineering of SFoI
- Augmenting the INCOSE *Systems Engineering Handbook* addressing the engineering of SFoI
- Methods to pay for activities that benefit more than one program, using an approach that is compliant with federal acquisition regulations (FAR)
- Methods to enable export to countries where ITAR or export control restrictions apply, ensuring that no system variant contains any content that is not allowed to be exported
- Methods to enable secure and efficient production and maintenance where the system comprises unclassified and classified – at varying levels – content
- Model-based systems engineering best practices
- Two decades of software product line engineering best practices at the Software Engineering Institute
- Methods for efficient configuration management that scales to the small and the large
- Methods for verification and validation where human safety is involved; and/or where the fielded system cannot be easily maintained e.g. a satellite in orbit

Fiduciary due diligence requires we use two key enablers – a value forecast model and a set of metrics to measure achievement against the forecasted values. A number of publications are available addressing the metrics (Clements and Krueger 2019). For the value forecast model, we started with the structured intuitive model for product line economics (SIMPLE), amended with FbPLE concepts as described in Greg, Scharadin, and Clements (2015). Augmenting SIMPLE with value estimation techniques from agile DevOps resulted in a multivariable value forecast model we termed SIMPLE-plus-plus, or more simply SIMPLE++.

Historically, business value models for strategic reuse of digital assets were simple linear cost saving economic models. These economic models forecast savings – primarily as cost avoidance as a result of improved production efficiency – as a linear function of the number of products in the SFoI. These models have a number of characteristics, including:

- The models do not account for important customer and contractor value factors unrelated to cost avoidance, such as rapid adaptation to changing market or battlefield conditions (aka agility), and similar. Many of these are frequently referred to as intangible benefits, and their exclusion leads to incorrect, low valuations.
- The models do not adequately express near-term value gains vs. long-term value results.
- The models do not adequately handle aspects common to defense acquisitions, including varying, and at times lengthy acquisition cycles, low volume and periodicity of acquisitions, technology readiness level (TRL) requirements, and similar.
- The models do not account for the observed superlinear cost avoidance effect organizations – such as the US Navy – are experiencing as described in Greg, Scharadin, and Clements (2015).

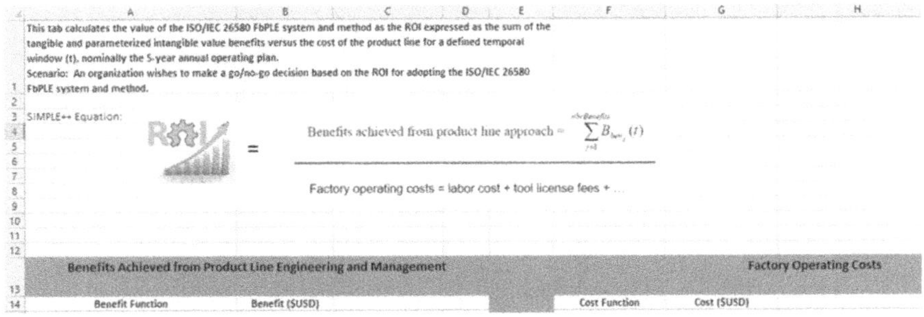

Figure 33.10 Multivariable tangible and parameterized intangible ROI calculation using SIMPLE++.

These characteristics led to SIMPLE++, a modern, comprehensive value-based model. Key characteristics of the SIMPLE++ model include:

- Inclusion of both cost avoidance and high-value customer and contractor benefits, including parameterized versions of benefits historically viewed as intangibles.
- Defense acquisitions aspects tailored into the model, e.g. export/import (EX/IM) compliance, US Federal Acquisition Requirement (FAR) compliance, MOSA conformance, and more.
- Inclusion of the superlinear cost avoidance effect.
- Fine-grained temporal view capable of expressing near-term value gains as well as long-term value gains.

SIMPLE++ extends the concept of value beyond solely monetary values to include other forms of value, including warfighter value, DoD acquisition value, defense contractor value, societal value, and more. The resultant enhanced value model uses a tailored *value language* to describe these facets. Business value points (BVPs) are used to quantify the intangibles as a reflection of their relative importance to decision-makers. Decisions are made using the BVPs, or the BVPs can be transformed into economic terms based on either industry-reported measures; or based on expert opinion. For example, values for end-user satisfaction can be gathered by an anonymous survey and then transformed into dollar amounts relevant to decision-makers, e.g. acquisition dollar spend versus value received, or for a contractor's positive top-line and bottom-line improvement. In combination with traditional economic parameters, the models provide a holistic return on investment (ROI) calculation as depicted in Figure 33.10.

33.5 Conclusions

This chapter explored the digital trinity plus modern system family engineering using FbPLE for SFoIs, a holistic solution enabling the DoD and defense contractors to innovate at the speed of relevance. Each aspect of the digital trinity – DEM&S plus Dev*Ops plus MOSA OSAs – was defined, and corresponding aspects of system family engineering as codified in ISO/IEC standard 26580:2021 feature-based PLE were defined.

A technical deep dive using a hypothetical system family described adding FO-SCV analysis to standard stepwise refinement engineering analysis. The output of the FO-SCV analysis was captured in a product feature model comprising the ASoT for product variation definition and management across the digital engineering ecosystem.

Cybersecurity and cyber resiliency system quality attributes of the digital trinity were analyzed, and a rule base was created and used by the factory-of-factories to continuously verify fielded system variants. Finally, common challenges and solutions were discussed, including the augmented structured intuitive model for product line economics-plus, plus (SIMPLE++) value forecast model.

The digital trinity plus modern PLE system and method has matured over the past 20+ years; is founded on numerous consortia-driven standards and regulation-compliant industry best practices; and has been successfully piloted in US DoD contracts, including the Navy's AEGIS product lines and the Army's live training transformation product lines. Application of this system and method has realized continuous delivery of value to the warfighter concurrent with superlinear cost avoidance for the US DoD.

References

Clements, P. and Krueger, C. (2017). A feature ontology to support feature-based product line engineering. In: *Proceedings of the 2017 INCOSE International Symposium.*Adelaide, Australia.

Clements, P. and Krueger, C. (2019). Measurements for product line engineering: what to measure and why. https://biglever.com/learn-more/white-papers-publications/ (accessed 10 April 2022).

Clements, P. and Krueger, C. (2021). Feature-based product line engineering in aerospace and defense. In: *Proceedings of the NDIA 2021 Virtual Systems & Mission Engineering Conference*. https://ndiastorage.blob.core.usgovcloudapi.net/ndia/2021/systems/Tue_23809_Krueger.pdf (accessed 07 April 2022).

Defense Innovation Board (2019). Software is never done, refactoring the acquisition code for competitive advantage. https://media.defense.gov/2019/May/01/2002126690/-1/-1/0/SWAP%20EXECUTIVE%20SUMMARY.PDF (accessed 08 April 2022).

DoD (2018). Department of defense digital engineering strategy. https://ac.cto.mil/wp-content/uploads/2019/06/2018-Digital-Engineering-Strategy_Approved_PrintVersion.pdf> (accessed 07 April 2022).

DoD (2020). Modular open systems approach (MOSA) reference frameworks in defense acquisitions programs. https://ac.cto.mil/wp-content/uploads/2020/06/MOSA-Ref-Frame-May2020.pdf (accessed 07 April 2022).

DoD (2020). US air force 2020 digital campaign virtual industry exchange day. https://www.afmc.af.mil/Portals/13/AF%20Digital%20Campaign%20Industry%20Exchange%20Day%20Combined%20Slides_Final%20v1.pdf (accessed 07 April 2022).

DoD (2022). Instruction 5000.02 operation of the adaptive acquisition framework (AAF). https://www.esd.whs.mil/Portals/54/Documents/DD/issuances/dodi/500002p.pdf (accessed 07 April 2022).

DoD (2022). *DoD enterprise DSOP initiative – DevStar definition*. https://software.af.mil/dsop/dsop-devstar/ (accessed 07 April 2022).

Greg, S., Scharadin, R., and Clements, P. (2015). The more you do, the more you save: The superlinear cost avoidance effect of systems and software product line engineering. In: *Proceedings of SPLC 2015. Nashville, USA*.

INCOSE (2019). Feature-based systems and software product line engineering: a primer. https://connect.incose.org/Pages/Product-Details.aspx?ProductCode=PLE_Primer_2019 (accessed 08 April 2022).

ISO/IEC (2021). ISO/IEC 26580:2021. Software and systems engineering – methods and tools for the feature-based approach to software and systems product line engineering. https://www.iso.org/standard/43139.html (accessed 08 April 2022).

Kang, K., Cohen, S., Hess, J. et al. (1990). Feature-oriented domain analysis (FODA) feasibility study. https://insights.sei.cmu.edu/library/feature-oriented-domain-analysis-foda-feasibility-study (accessed 07 April 2022).

Raytheon (2024). RTX corporate website. https://www.rtx.com/raytheon/who-we-are (accessed 28 July 2024).

Roper, W. (2020). There is no spoon: the new digital acquisition reality. https://software.af.mil/wp-content/uploads/2020/10/There-Is-No-Spoon-Digital-Acquisition-7-Oct-2020-digital-version.pdf (accessed 07 April 2022).

Roper, W. (2021). Bending the spoon: guidebook for digital engineering. https://www.af.mil/Portals/1/documents/2021SAF/01_Jan/Bending_the_Spoon.pdf (accessed 07 April 2022).

Teaff, J., Young, B., and Clements, P. (2019). Applying feature-based systems and software product line engineering in unclassified and classified environments. In: *Proceedings of the 2019 INCOSE International Symposium*. Orlando Florida, USA.

34

Belimo: Innovation in Comfort, Energy Efficiency, and Safety Solutions with Product Lines

Manuel Pijorr, Markus Hüppi, Daniel Messmer, Alba Pennisi, Mariana Reyes Perez, Mitko Tanevski, and Simon Hoffman

34.1 Introduction

Belimo is the global market leader in the development, production, and sales of field devices for the energy-efficient control of heating, ventilation, and air-conditioning systems. The focus of its core business is on damper actuators, control valves, sensors, and meters. Belimo values creativity and craftsmanship, continually setting market standards. Founded in 1975, the company employs over 2300 people, operates in over 80 countries, and has been listed on the Swiss Exchange (SIX) since 1995 (Belimo 2024).

Belimo's product portfolio has grown significantly over the years, driven by continuous innovation and market demands. Some of the key products are highlighted below.

Damper actuators: In 1976, Belimo made a significant breakthrough in the HVAC industry by introducing the first direct-coupled motorized damper actuator. This innovative technology was able to reduce installation time by two-thirds. With investments of approximately 7% of its revenue into research and development (R&D), Belimo has repeatedly achieved such breakthroughs. The advanced technology allows for seamless integration with building automation systems, providing precise control and optimization of airflows and meeting the growing demand for sustainability and energy efficiency.

Control valves: Since the beginning, Belimo has set new market standards with its control valves, for example, with its cutting-edge pressure-independent valves, the development of characterized control valves, or the energy valve, which maximizes energy usage within HVAC system.

Sensors and meters: Adding HVAC sensors and meters to its lineup allowed Belimo to offer comprehensive solutions to provide reliable and accurate measurement and monitoring with seamless building automation system integration.

Digital ecosystem: Belimo is dedicated to delivering superior products with the right digital connection now and in the future. The ecosystem of Belimo's smart devices enables flexible system integration through all common building automation communication protocols and Building IoT platforms. With the help of the additional internet of things (IoT) connection, buildings can be easily optimized, managed, and maintained.

Model-Based Product Line Engineering (MBPLE): The Feature-Based Path to Product Lines Success, First Edition.
Marco Forlingieri et al.

Belimo's success is rooted in its commitment to solution leadership and the creation of customer value. Significant investments in R&D have led to technological breakthroughs and proprietary technologies, anticipating market trends, and developing cutting-edge solutions.

As a key player in the HVAC sector, Belimo has experienced significant market growth, which brings substantial challenges in managing its wide products' portfolio while delivering customized products cost-effectively. To support this expansion and maintain high standards, Belimo is transitioning from product-oriented to product-line-oriented engineering. The main drivers behind this strategic shift are listed below.

Increased product's complexity: Belimo initially expanded its portfolio by transitioning from solely mechatronic devices with reduced complexity to embedded devices. Compared to mechatronic devices, an embedded device is more complex due to the integration of software with the hardware, which requires specialized knowledge in electronics and software development. Additional complexity arises from ensuring reliable communication, rigorous testing, regular software updates, and seamless system integration. In contrast, mechatronic devices do not involve these additional layers, making them simpler to design, manufacture, and maintain. Besides that, the dynamics of change regarding requirements and new technologies are higher in software development than in pure mechatronics development.

The introduction of IoT-enhanced products created new challenges: the increase of the level of "smart connectivity" through the IoT. This evolution has led to the development of more complex systems.

The integration of smart, connected devices requires advanced capabilities for interoperability and sophisticated control mechanisms, which further increase the complexity of both product development and deployment processes. Additionally, the dynamic of changing requirements and technologies keeps increasing.

Such a shift is also driven by new regulations in regard to cybersecurity compliance and by the increasing number of functional requirements as a response to limit the growing solution space caused by other interacting systems, e.g. smartphone applications or cloud infrastructure (see Figure 34.1).

Increased variability: Belimo operates in a highly variable context, as each building's HVAC system demands tailored solutions to meet specific requirements. With a product portfolio exceeding 15 000 items, managing this extensive range necessitates significant effort. To ensure a

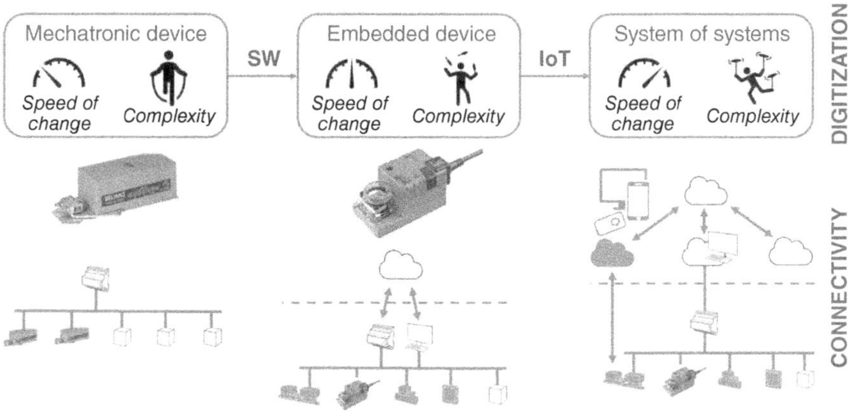

Figure 34.1 Increased product's complexity at Belimo.

homogenous portfolio and unique user experience, commonalities across different products need to be properly managed. Besides that, a significant amount of turnover is generated with customized solutions for an Original Equipment Manufacturer (OEM) market. Therefore, a certain speed and flexibility are needed to enhance our existing solutions.

Organizational growth: Due to a well-defined growth strategy, Belimo grew not just in revenue but in size as well. Its organizational growth asks for more systematic approaches, which can be scaled up globally to ensure seamless collaboration and solid know-how management. Belimo has recognized the limitations of a single product-oriented engineering approach in addressing these complexities. Key motivations for transitioning to a product line engineering (PLE) approach included:

- Enhanced reusability: By focusing on reusable engineering artifacts, PLE allows Belimo to leverage common components across multiple products, reducing development time and costs. Based on this, it allows to reduce the technical variance of the product portfolio keeping the market flexibility.
- Improved variability management: PLE provides a structured method to manage product variations systematically, ensuring that customization does not lead to inefficiencies. This is very important to enable proper configuration management across several product lines.
- Ensured consistency and quality: A product line approach ensures consistency in product design and quality, as standardized components and processes are used across the product portfolios.

Even though a PLE approach as such delivers more systematic possibilities to address the challenges mentioned, Belimo reached the limits regarding artifact handling, specifically in regard to reuse and configuration management across different products. Therefore, Belimo has decided to invest in a model-based product line engineering (MBPLE) approach. The basis for this improvement lies in the models, which describe the necessary information of a product line and can be referenced and maintained across their life cycle. Adopting such an MBPLE approach allows Belimo to effectively manage complexity, ensure consistency, improve efficiency, scale operations, and maintain robust documentation, all of which are crucial in implementing PLE.

However, transitioning from a product-oriented to a product-line-oriented approach supported by MBPLE presents several challenges, mainly related to organizational change management:

- Organizational resistance: Shifting to MBPLE requires significant changes in organizational culture and mindset. Employees accustomed to product-oriented methods may resist the new approach.
- Process overhaul: Implementing MBPLE necessitates a comprehensive overhaul of existing engineering processes, including the adoption of new tools and methodologies.
- Initial investment: The transition involves an initial investment in training, process development, and tool acquisition. This investment can be substantial, but the long-term benefits justify the costs.

34.2 Transitioning to MBPLE: Target and Definitions

The transition to MBPLE requires Belimo to adopt a more systematic approach to manage its extensive product portfolio. Following a feature-based PLE approach as described in the ISO/IEC 26580 (ISO/IEC 2021), Belimo is shifting to model-based and, therefore, to MBPLE to bring

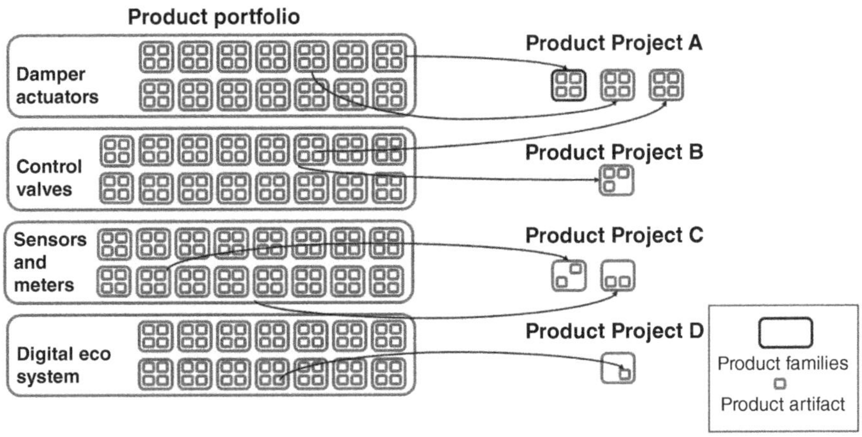

Figure 34.2 Portfolio mindset at Belimo.

consistency and a single source of truth along all the reused artifacts. This also includes a comprehensive configuration management for the necessary assets.

To keep certain flexibility regarding specific customer requests, the development projects at Belimo still focus on the development of single applications. Nevertheless, to be able to keep the product line definitions consistent and leverage them in the development projects, the modeling of artifacts (e.g. features, requirements, system elements) is always done in the context of the product portfolio, where the products under development belong to. By doing so, the overview across the whole portfolio is ensured, as well as reuse of artifacts is simplified.

This approach also allows comprehensive, up-to-date views about the used models across the whole portfolio. The project can be seen as a "vehicle" to create new versions of the product portfolio and of the product line-related models (see Figure 34.2).

In Belimo, the following concepts together with the related definitions have been introduced to ensure a common understanding within the organization.

Product family: A cluster of products sharing a common set of features, marketed similarly, and often sharing similar applications (see Figure 34.3).

Product line: A cluster of products and/or services sharing explicitly defined and managed system elements (both common and variable), built on the same core architecture, ensuring consistency and reuse inside. The same core architecture focuses here mainly on functional distribution on modules or system elements as well as the proper reuse of Belimo's core technology elements – e.g. the Application-Specific Integrated Circuit (ASIC), which consists of a custom-designed integrated circuit for a particular task or application. The product line and product family definition in Belimo diverges slightly from the definition of the ISO/IEC 26580 (ISO/IEC 2021).

Product platform: It consists of Belimo's core technology elements – system elements – which are shared across the majority of Belimo products, like an ASIC, the onboard software, or the smartphone application. Besides the core technology elements, features, feature options, and requirements are also reused for multiple products and are therefore considered elements of the product platform. The product platform shall ensure that the functional behavior of the devices is aligned and leads to a proper user experience across Belimo's complete product portfolio (see Figure 34.3).

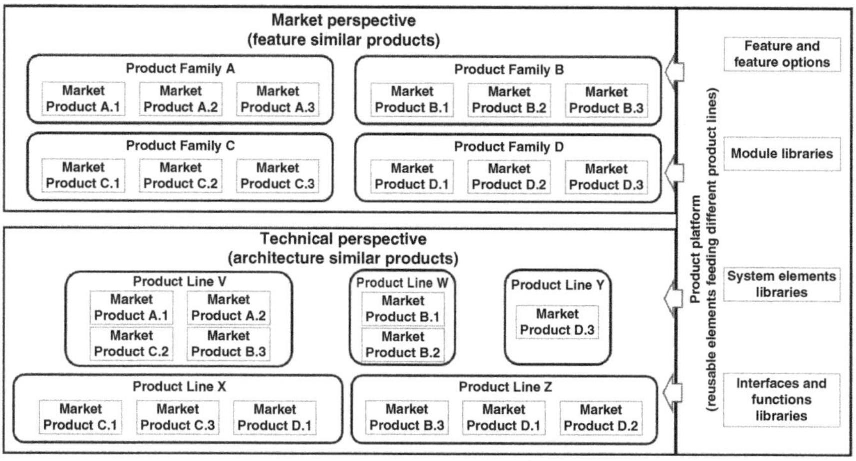

Figure 34.3 Market and technical perspective.

Feature: A specific aspect or capability of a product designed to meet a particular market or user need. Features are variant drivers, cluster requirements (stakeholder or system), and use cases.

Feature option: A specific refinement or setting available to the customer, providing additional functionality or personalization (e.g. color options or connectivity alternatives). The feature and feature options definition in Belimo also diverges from the feature definition of the ISO/IEC 26580 (ISO/IEC 2021).

System element: A discrete part of a system that realizes specified System Requirements, forming components, modules, products, or products of products.

By looking at its product portfolio, Belimo has identified two different perspectives, as illustrated in Figure 34.3: The "market perspective" and the "technical perspective."

Market perspective: Perspective on the product portfolio, focusing on product families. This perspective is related to the problem space. The market perspective shows commonalities across product families with elements from the product platform (e.g. features, feature options).

Technical perspective: Perspective on the product portfolio, focusing on product lines. This perspective is related to the solution space. The technical perspective shows commonalities across product lines with elements from the product platform (e.g. system elements).

Belimo's vision is to streamline the product creation process by simplifying product configuration from both market and technical perspectives. By examining both perspectives, Belimo identifies product families and product lines based on shared features and architectural commonalities. Belimo's approach recognizes the orthogonal nature of the feature-based and architectural-based portfolios (product families and product lines). The intersection of these portfolios is represented by so-called market products, which are abstract representations of real products from Belimo's product portfolio. Besides this, the split allows proper communication about the market products to different stakeholders with different perspectives.

34.3 A Glance of the MBPLE Approach: Asset's Definition Across Different Perspectives

As stated in ISO/IEC 26580 (ISO/IEC 2021), domain assets focus on reusable components and models that implement the commonalities and variabilities across a product line, while application assets are tailored from these domain assets to create specific products, incorporating customizations and specific configurations necessary to meet individual product requirements. Depending on the life cycle of the product, different assets are considered. The main domain asset, considered during the modeling definition in the "concept" phase of the product development are features, feature options, modules, and system elements (see Figure 34.4).

Features and feature options: Customizable aspects of the products that represent specific capabilities or characteristics desired by the customer specified with requirements (market perspective). Additionally, verification procedures are linked to the requirements so that they can be reused based on the features and their options. These assets are defined and managed in PTC Codebeamer (PTC 2024).

Modules and system elements: Discrete, reusable parts of the system fulfilling specific requirements and functions covered with MBSE models. These models are defined and managed in iQUAVIS (iQUAVIS 2024), a MBSE tool (not SysML-based).

Considering the product platform, domain assets can be shared across product lines instead of being specific to one product line. All domain assets are structured within libraries, enhancing their reusability and traceability in a modeling context across different product families and product lines.

The market products are considered "application assets" in Belimo's product portfolio. They are bridging the gap between customer needs and technical capabilities, providing a clear and coherent framework for product development as well as properly connecting the different perspectives. Within product-oriented development projects, additional product-specific application assets like feature and feature options or modules and system elements can be developed. Within these projects, it is possible as well to enrich the domain assets of the product families and product lines to increase the scope of their definition.

During the industrialization phase of the product development, additional domain assets are considered for reuse – e.g. mechanical CAD models for automated generation of product CAD models, BOMs for automated generation of product BOMs, SW source code, and parameterization

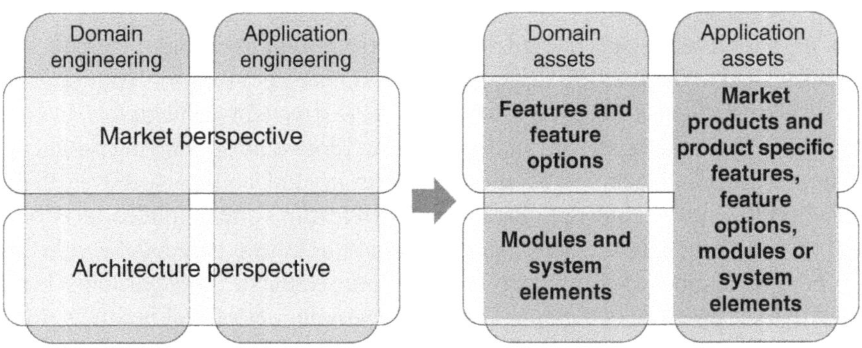

Figure 34.4 Domain and application assets across market and technical perspective.

files. All these assets, including their combinatorial and automated generation of applications, are handled in SAP VC (SAP 2024).

Depending on the phase, the assets can have different levels of abstraction. For example, during the concept phase of a development project, the following abstractions are considered:

- Features and feature options represent variance on the requirements level which are maintained in Codebeamer (PTC 2024).
- Modules and system elements describe the structure of a product on a more logical level of abstraction covered by MBSE models in iQUAVIS (iQUAVIS 2024).
- A market product is still configurable in a range that has no influence on the product's architecture. These market products are binding elements that are covered in Codebeamer and iQUAVIS.

Symmetrically, during the industrialization phase of a development project, the following abstractions are in focus:

- Features and feature options represent variance on the sales level, which is represented by sales characteristics in a product configurator (SAP VC).
- Modules and system elements describe the structure of a product on a physical level of abstraction considering mainly supply chain relevant aspects. This is represented in the BOM inside the PLM system.
- A market product is a so-called finished good that has no variance anymore. This is covered as a "material" in the PLM system.

Belimo's MBPLE journey is ongoing. In fact, the company is in the process of defining a streamlined and comprehensive methodology that would allow to integrate process and tool wise the more abstract view provided during the concept phase with the view on the assets created during the industrialization phase. This would allow an improved end-to-end workflow as well as traceability across the entire development. For instance, the current approach does not have a consistent 1:1 relationship between the features in different systems (e.g. Codebeamer and SAP VC).

34.4 Variability Management at the Core of MBPLE

Managing variability of the assets is crucial for Belimo to efficiently define customer-relevant products compared to the past, where highly specific projects were developing customized solutions with limited reuse capability across the portfolio. With this, diverse market needs of product families can be fulfilled while maintaining high standards of quality and performance within a product line.

Different key elements are defined to describe the valid combinatorial across the domain and application assets (see Figure 34.5).

Feature model: This consists of a feature-to-feature matrix that maps and defines the relationships between different features and their options. It identifies dependencies, conflicts, and synergies among features. Based on this matrix, a set of allowed feature-based product descriptions is derived.

Variant model: This consists of a system element-to-system element matrix that maps and defines the technical compatibility across different system elements. It identifies dependencies, conflicts, and synergies among system elements. Based on this matrix, a set of allowed system element-based product descriptions is derived.

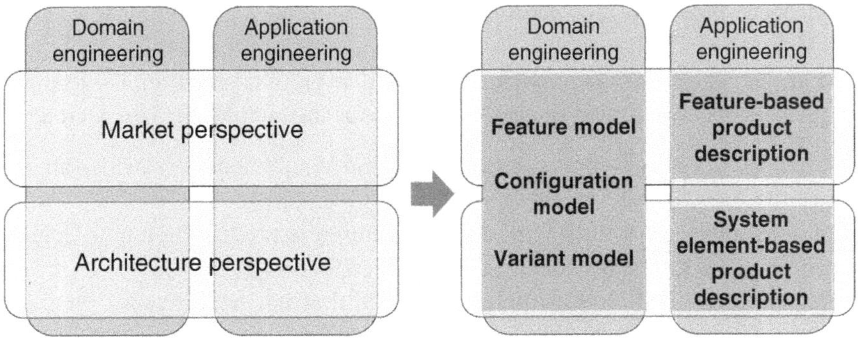

Figure 34.5 Conceptual model of Belimo's variability management.

Configuration model: This model maps features and feature options with system elements, showing which system element or combinations thereof can fulfill a specific feature. It is the basis for the definition of the system element-based product description based on feature or feature option inputs. For instance, when a customer selects a set of features for their product, the configuration matrix indicates the system element combinations that will meet those requirements. The final product results from assembling those system elements.

Feature-based product descriptions: This is a simplified representation of a product, based on the combination of feature options. In simple terms, a feature-based product description is a collection of feature options. These descriptions outline the combinations of features that can be offered to customers, ensuring that only marketable product configurations are developed – similar to the bill-of-features.

System element-based product descriptions: This is a simplified representation of a product, based on the combination of system elements. In simple terms, a system element-based product description is a collection of system elements. These descriptions specify products created using technical compatible combinations of system elements. This ensures that all product configurations offered to customers can be operated.

The elements are used, depending on the different levels of abstraction of the assets mentioned in Section 34.4 and the development phase of the project.

For instance, during the concept phase of a development project (see Figure 34.6):

- The feature model is created to clarify the proper scope of the development project, showing the requirements variance by reusing requirement assets based on features and options from the feature model.
- The feature-based product descriptions are created based on the feature model to define the necessary market products (application assets) and collect the requirement assets from the domain. Additionally, application-specific requirements assets might be added.
- The system element-based product descriptions are defined for the market products based on the MBSE model assets from the domain, which consider reusable architectures, system elements, and module models from the domain.
- A variant model and configuration model are not explicitly defined during the concept phase. The logic is implicitly modeled with the other three models. This simplification is used because the scope of the market variance described with the feature-based product descriptions is considered the same as the technical variance described with the system element-based product descriptions.

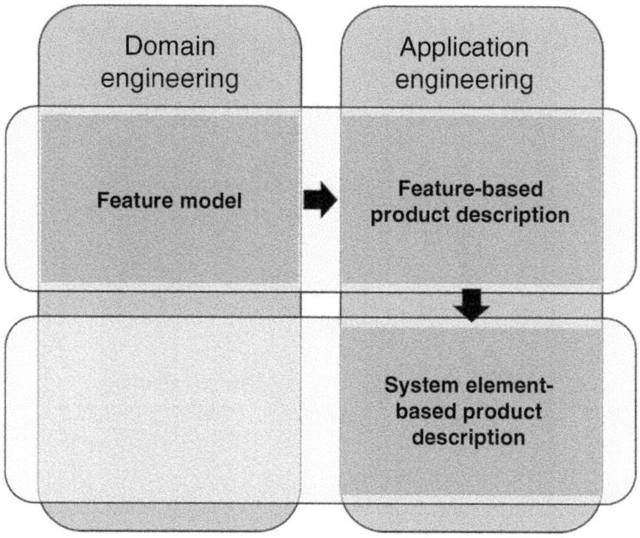

Figure 34.6 Variability management during the concept phase of a development project.

As Figure 34.7 summarizes, during the industrialization phase of a development project:

- The feature model is created to define the market variance offered to the customer. This is done in SAP VC (SAP 2024) using domain assets that describe the sales characteristics of the offered products.
- The configuration model is created as the basis for the variant creation during the sales process. Based on the sales characteristics required by the customer, the configuration model describes the system-element-based product description of a finished good. Since this logic needs to be executed during the sales process, the configuration model, as well as the feature and the variant model, are implemented in a product configurator (SAP VC).
- The system element-based product description is automatically derived by the product configurator, which has the configuration matrix implemented as well as the system elements and modules from the physical perspective. This is the basis for the bill of material of a production order for a dedicated finished product, including mechanical CAD models as well as other engineering documentation assets.
- The variant model can be implemented additionally to avoid the complex rule sets in the configuration model.
- The feature-based product description is provided in the product configurator as a so-called market description as an entry point of the configuration process of a finished product. This entry point predefines some sales characteristics to provide a certain preconfiguration of a finished product to the customer.

Since both variability management approaches fulfill different purposes (variability management definition for development vs. variant configuration during the sales process), the involved mechanisms and processes are different. Belimo is currently developing a comprehensive methodology to address these gaps within the domain engineering models. The to-be approach aims to enhance the end-to-end workflow and improve traceability throughout the development process.

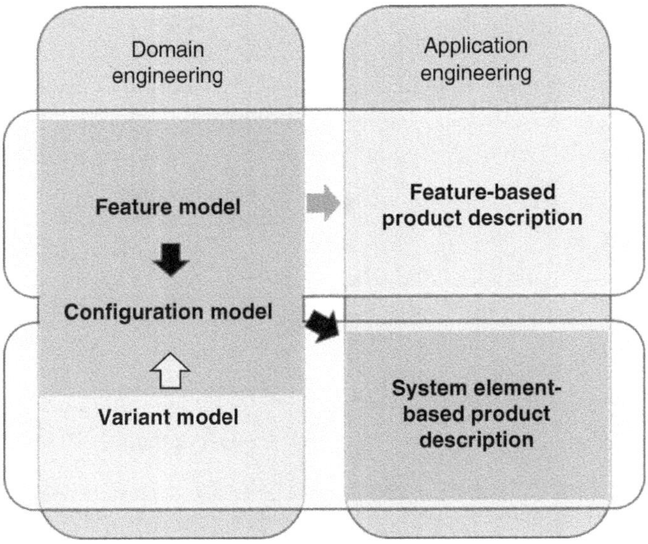

Figure 34.7 Variability management during the industrialization phase of a development project.

To sum up, variability management offers several benefits for Belimo. The main ones are listed below:

- Consistency: Adherence to predefined rules prevents invalid or incompatible feature and system element configuration combinations, ensuring reliable product configurations.
- Flexibility: The variability management tools allow for diverse product configurations, accommodating various customer preferences and technical constraints.
- Efficiency: With increased traceability through the variability management tools, during the different project phases the product development can be sped up and the likelihood of errors can be reduced.

By leveraging variability management, Belimo can efficiently manage product variability, delivering customized HVAC solutions that meet diverse market demands while maintaining consistency, flexibility, and efficiency.

34.5 Organizational Shift and Cultural Changes

Adopting MBPLE requires significant organizational and cultural changes. This section highlights the key shifts and processes that are implemented to ensure a smooth transition within our organization.

To tackle the general complexity's increase mentioned in Section 34.2, the organizational structure of the R&D function is adapted to facilitate simplified coordination and more efficient communication among different departments. This adaptation mainly focuses on a line organization structure aligned with technical processes of systems engineering, according to ISO/IEC 15288 (ISO/IEC 2023). In this structure, every department takes over clear responsibilities for executing the activities of their technical process scope. These responsibilities are carried out by defined roles, in cross-functional teams that realize the development of the product lines. A team that has methodological governance oversees the implementation and continuous improvement of the MBPLE approach in general. This setup of clear roles and responsibilities ensures that roles, process responsibilities, and line responsibilities are conflict-free among the employees.

Belimo focused on adapting the stage-gate development process for MBPLE. This ensures that the methodology can be properly executed within the adapted organization. The strong link between the stage-gate development process and the MBPLE methodology emphasizes collaboration, standardization, and continuous improvement, aligning with the company's commitment to innovation along an iterative and recursive mindset.

As usual, the organizational and process adaptations require a cultural change within the organization. To support this, training programs and workshops are conducted to equip the team with the necessary skills and knowledge. Additionally, on-the-job coaching takes place to support during the daily business. With those actions, Belimo fosters a culture of innovation and adaptability, encouraging employees to embrace new processes, methodologies, and technologies.

34.6 Case Study and Practical Insights

To illustrate the practical benefits of MBPLE, this section presents a case study from Belimo's MBPLE implementation for a "Damper Actuators product line," focusing on the concept phase of its development project. This example highlights how MBPLE can facilitate the development of configurable products, enhancing flexibility and responsiveness to market demands.

The referenced project aims to modularize and streamline a big part of the "Damper Actuators product portfolio" at Belimo. By applying MBPLE, Belimo effectively addressed various features for the development to incorporate communication protocols, movement types, torque/force requirements, cabling, and fail-safe mechanisms within proper product variants.

The "damper actuators product line" modularizes key aspects of market products from different product families using similar MBSE models for modules and system elements based on a set of reusable features and feature options. It includes the construction of a library for reusable requirements assets. In the past, these aspects were addressed through dedicated single product-oriented development projects with limited realization of synergies. The goal was to utilize a modularization approach to manage the commonalities more effectively, allowing for the creation of diverse products with shared assets.

The following steps were concluded during the concept phase of the development project in regard to the MBPLE approach:

- Features, feature options, as well as requirements, are elicited and included in the requirements domain assets pool in Codebeamer.
- The relevant features and feature options are addressed to the relevant product families of the "damper actuators product portfolio" in Codebeamer. Application-specific features and feature options as well as requirements are defined.
- Features and feature options relevant for the variant definition during the concept phase are defined and transferred to the product family projects of iQUAVIS. These relevant feature options do not consider things like housing color, cable length, or other aspects that have no influence on the architecture of the product line. During the industrialization phase of the development project, these aspects need to be considered for the feature model (see Figure 34.8).

Features		Feature options
Name	Name	Name
Product Family A features	Advanced functionality	Enhanced digital bus systems
		Digital bus systems
		Bus cascade
	Basic functionality	Analog control
		Belimo bus control
		Client control
	Feedback	Potentiometer
		Switches
	Power supply	Line voltage
		24 V
	Running time	x seconds
		y seconds

Figure 34.8 Overview of features and feature options belonging to a product family in iQUAVIS (simplified content).

Nota bene: The transfer of information from Codebeamer to iQUAVIS is currently manually realized. In 2025, an automated interface between both tools will be established.

- The **feature model** is created per product family in iQUAVIS. Therefore, the variability definition is done along the feature tree branches (Figure 34.9), and additional exclude or mandatory rules between the branches are included in a DSM. (Figure 34.10).
- With the built-in "variant manager" in iQUAVIS, a variant analysis per product family is done with the support of the tool. Based on this, the relevant market product configurations are automatically created and linked with the feature options to create the **feature-based product descriptions** (see Figure 34.11).

  The market products are created in the product families and linked with the feature options accordingly (Codebeamer). This allows the reuse of the requirements, which are referenced to the features and feature options.

  Nota bene: The transfer of information from iQUAVIS to Codebeamer is currently manually realized. In 2025, an automated interface between both tools will be established.
- The product line scope is defined by referencing the relevant market product configurations from the product family projects in iQUAVIS (Figure 34.12).
- The market product configurations are linked to reusable system elements and module models – **variant model** – to create the **system element-based product descriptions**. (Figure 34.12). Based on this information, interface specifications, and functional allocation are reused in iQUAVIS.

As described in Section 34.4, this simplified approach is chosen because there is no difference in market and technical variance considered to keep the development effort under control. This might limit the flexibility of later scope extensions of the product line. Additionally, this setup works quite well because it is suitable for both a brownfield approach, where we already know the market products of the product families, and a greenfield approach, where we analyze the feature model from scratch to define completely new market product configurations.

The application of MBPLE brought several key advantages:

Focused development: By reusing communication, gearbox, and actuator modules defined with MBSE models, as well as design assumptions from the prototype, the focus can be kept on optimizing the modular components and integrating them efficiently.

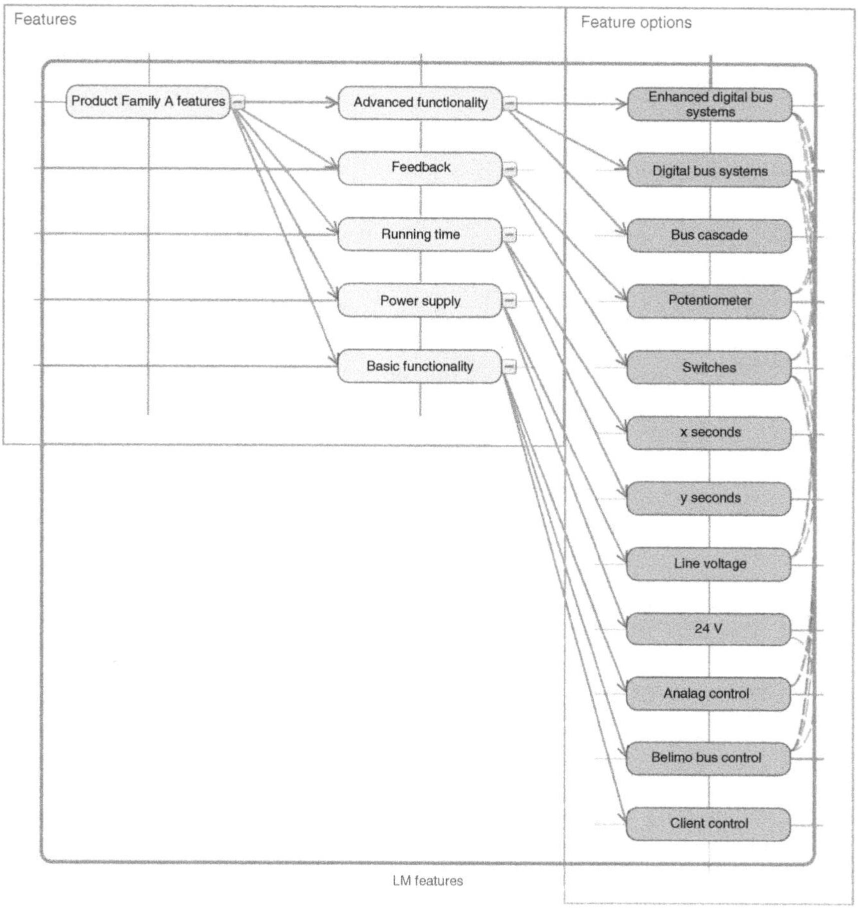

Features				Feature options	
Name	ID	Name	O/D/V	Name	O/D/V
Product Family A features	PRREQ–1045	Advanced functionality	Optional	Enhanced digital bus systems	Variant
				Digital bus systems	Variant
				Bus cascade	Variant
	PRREQ–897	Basic functionality	Default	Analog control	Variant
				Belimo bus control	Variant
				Client control	Variant
	PRREQ–886	Feedback	Optional	Potentiometer	Variant
				Switches	Variant
	PRREQ–898	Power supply	Default	Line voltage	Variant
				24 V	Variant
	PRREQ–899	Running time	Default	x seconds	Variant
				y seconds	Variant

Figure 34.9 Views on feature model in iQUAVIS (simplified content).

Simplified customization: The modular approach enables quick and easy build of applications by reusing requirements, MBSE models for customization to meet specific customer requirements, such as different communication protocols, torque ranges, and fail-safe mechanisms.

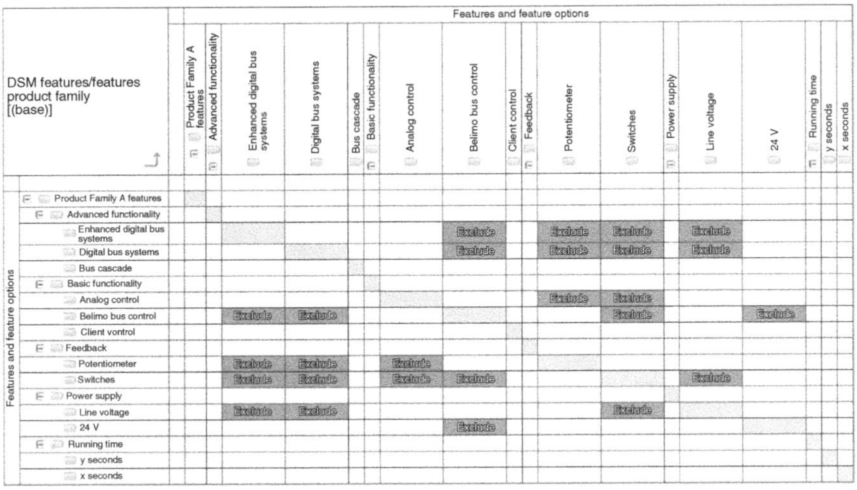

Figure 34.10 Feature model DSM in iQUAVIS (simplified content).

Product configurations	Features	Feature options
Name	Name	Name
Product Family A_Config_1	Basic functionality	Analog control
	Power supply	24 V
	Running time	x seconds
Product Family A_Config_2	Basic functionality	Analog control
	Power supply	24 V
	Running time	y seconds
Product Family A_Config_3	Basic functionality	Client control
	Power supply	24 V
	Running time	x seconds
Product Family A_Config_4	Basic functionality	Client control
	Power supply	24 V
	Running time	y seconds
Product Family A_Config_5	Advanced functionality	Enhanced digital bus systems
	Basic functionality	Analog control
	Power supply	24 V
	Running time	x seconds
Product Family A_Config_6	Advanced functionality	Enhanced digital bus systems
	Basic functionality	Analog control
	Power supply	24 V
	Running time	y seconds
Product Family A_Config_7	Advanced functionality	Enhanced digital bus systems
	Basic functionality	Client control
	Power supply	24 V
	Running time	x Seconds
Product Family A_Config_8	Advanced functionality	Enhanced digital Bus Systems
	Basic functionality	Client control
	Power supply	24 V
	Running time	y seconds
Product Family A_Config_9	Advanced functionality	Digital bus systems
	Basic functionality	Analog control
	Power supply	24 V

Figure 34.11 Feature-based product descriptions in iQUAVIS (simplified and limited content).

Products	Product configurations	Modules and system elements		Module and SE configurations
Name	Name	Class	Name	Name
Basic damper actuators with Arch A	Product Family A_Config_2	Module	Actuator base module	Base module 2
		Module	Actuator secondary module	Secondary module 1
	Product Family A_Config_1	Module	Actuator base module	Base module 1
		Module	Actuator secondary module	Secondary module 1
	Product Family B_Config_9	Module	Actuator base module	Base module 1
		Module	Actuator secondary module	Secondary module 1
		System element	Accessory	Specific Accessory B_Config_9
	Product Family A_Config_3	Module	Actuator base module	Base module 2
		Module	Actuator secondary module	Secondary module 2
	Product Family C_Config_1	Module	Actuator base module	Base module 2
		Module	Actuator secondary module	Secondary module 3
	Product Family B_Config_7	Module	Actuator base module	Base module 1
		Module	Actuator secondary module	Secondary module 2
	Product Family B_Config_8	Module	Actuator base module	Base module 1
		Module	Actuator secondary module	Secondary module 3
	Product Family C_Config_3	Module	Actuator base module	Base module 2
		Module	Actuator secondary module	Secondary module 3
		System element	Accessory	Specific Accessory C_Config_3
Enhanced damper actuators with Arch D	Product Family C_Config_2	Module	Actuator base module	Base module 4
		Module	Actuator secondary module	Secondary module 5
		Module	Logic module	Logic module 3
		System element	Accessory	Product line accessory
	Product Family A_Config_40	Module	Actuator base module	Base module 5
		Module	Actuator secondary module	Secondary module 5
		Module	Logic module	Logic module 2
	Product Family A_Config_41	Module	Actuator base module	Base module 3
		Module	Actuator secondary module	Secondary module 3
		Module	Logic module	Logic module 2
	Product Family A_Config_42	Module	Actuator base module	Base module 3
		Module	Actuator secondary module	Secondary module 2
		Module	Logic module	Logic module 2
	Product Family A_Config_48	Module	Actuator base module	Base module 4
		Module	Actuator secondary module	Secondary module 1
		Module	Logic module	Logic module 2

Figure 34.12 System element-based product descriptions in iQUAVIS (simplified and limited content).

Extended product portfolio: The modularization allows for future extensions of the product portfolio. A new communication module can be developed according to customer demand and integrated with limited effort together with the existing modules.

Broader use case realization: The platform approach enables the integration of actuators and other products emerging from the platform project into a broader context, facilitating more complex use cases at the product-of-products level.

Standardization of interfaces: To ensure a seamless integration of modules, standardized interfaces are defined, which cover a broader application context, such that similar modularization principles can be applied also in other product line development projects. These interfaces are managed within MBSE models in iQUAVIS to ensure the proper reuse of these assets during the development of the architectures.

Those advantages led to several projects notable successes, including:

- Enhanced product quality: Improved actuator performance due to focused development efforts and leveraging modular design principles.
- Software reuse: With streamlined hardware, the software development benefited from a platform approach, allowing for the direct reuse of software components, libraries, and functions across different products.

- Cross-application flexibility: Although this project focused on air applications, the same actuators can also be adapted with limited effort for water applications, demonstrating the versatility of the modular approach.
- Integration capabilities: The modular design with dedicated sensor interfaces allows for easy integration of sensors, enhancing the functionality and customizability of the actuators.

The modularization of the "damper actuators product line" through MBPLE has significantly transformed Belimo's approach to product development. By leveraging a modular architecture with standardized interfaces and reusable assets for MBSE models and requirements, Belimo achieved higher efficiency in development processes, further enhanced product quality, and greater flexibility to meet diverse customer requirements. The standardized interfaces facilitate the integration and reuse of modules across different product line projects, maximizing the utility of developed components and reducing redundant efforts.

The ability to reuse assets and integrate new technologies seamlessly has allowed Belimo to dynamically extend the product portfolio, ensuring a swift response to market demand and technological advancements. Moreover, the platform approach has opened new possibilities for integrating actuators with other products, enabling complex use cases and providing a robust foundation for future innovations. This case study demonstrates the strategic advantage of MBPLE in the context of large-scale product line projects with limited reuse of existing artifacts.

References

Belimo (2024). Corporate Webpage. https://www.belimo.com/ch/de_CH (accessed 10 July 2024).

iQUAVIS (2024). Software Webpage. https://www.two-pillars.de/en/iquavis/ (accessed 25 July 2024).

ISO/IEC (2021). Software and systems engineering – methods and tools for the feature-based approach to software and systems product line engineering (ISO/IEC/IEEE 26580: 2021).

ISO/IEC (2023). Systems and software engineering – system life cycle processes (ISO/IEC/IEEE 15288: 2023).

PTC (2024). Codebeamer Software. https://www.ptc.com/en/products/codebeamer (accessed 25 July 2024).

SAP (2024). SAP VC Software. https://www.sap.com/swiss/products/crm/variant-configuration-and-pricing.html (accessed 25 July 2024).

35

MBPLE in Action: What We Can Learn from the Five Industrial Cases?

35.1 Introduction

As industries evolve, so too must our approaches to managing complexity and variability within systems. This chapter analyzes how those five organizations adapt and implement model-based product line engineering (MBPLE) in response to their unique challenges.

The five cases presented in this chapter – Airbus, MBDA, Thales, Raytheon, and Belimo – highlight the diverse facets of MBPLE adoption and the necessity of adapting practices to fit specific industry needs. Each case sheds light on how these organizations address the complexity and variability inherent in their systems, illustrating that while MBPLE offers a robust framework, its application must be tailored to the unique demands of each sector.

Section 35.2 explains the selection and significance of these five cases as representative examples of MBPLE adoption in different industrial contexts.

Section 35.3 utilizes the MBPLE adoption quadrant introduced in Chapter 22. It applies it to the five cases to understand and analyze their relationships with complexity and variability and to derive the adoption patterns they followed. This section presents three alternative adoption paths.

Section 35.4 highlights the similarities and divergences among the five cases as well as how they adapted from the product line engineering (PLE) standards for the adoption of MBPLE.

We chose to include various perspectives in this section of the book, even those that do not entirely align with our understanding of MBPLE or fully conform to the standards. For example, we feature organizations that use model-based systems engineering (MBSE) tools not solely based on systems modeling language (SysML) or that explore alternative implementations of feature models and variation points. Our main motivation is to share diverse MBPLE practices unified by the core principles defined in the PLE standards. As MBPLE continues to evolve as an engineering approach, lessons learned from multiple industries are invaluable. Paraphrasing the joke from Chapter 7: "We may be methodologists, but you can still negotiate with us!"

35.2 Why Do These Five Cases Matter?

Throughout this book, we have emphasized that while we propose best practices for MBPLE learning, implementation, and adoption, starting from common motivation drivers, a one-size-fits-all approach is not feasible. Different industries require adaptations based on their unique needs, constraints, and contingencies. These adaptations may be influenced by technical factors as well as socio-economic and political considerations.

Model-Based Product Line Engineering (MBPLE): The Feature-Based Path to Product Lines Success, First Edition.
Marco Forlingieri et al.

All five cases meet the minimum criteria described in the Part V Introduction and come from three distinct industries: aviation, defense, and heating, ventilation, and air control.

Naturally, one might ask: Why focus on these specific industries and organizations? The reasons for our choices are outlined below.

Defense – MBDA, Thales, and Raytheon: The defense industry is a pioneering sector in the application of systems engineering, MBSE (Ducamp et al. 2022), and PLE (Lanman et al. 2011; Clements et al. 2014). Despite being considered a relatively new discipline, MBPLE has achieved a certain level of maturity within this field. The complexity and variability of systems such as MBDA, Raytheon missiles, and Thales radars are notably high, reflecting the complex nature of defense technologies.

Aviation – Airbus: The aviation industry shares several characteristics with the defense industry, such as large-scale program development, maturity in systems engineering and MBSE, high complexity, and the development of safety-critical systems. However, it also has its own unique aspects. For example, certain aircraft areas, such as cabin modules and systems, have a higher degree of customization. The industry also deals with multiple commercial clients, whose ultimate users are the passengers, and has a strong interdependence with the manufacturing and service dimensions (Forlingieri 2022).

Heating, ventilation, and air control – Belimo: This industry has great potential for the end-to-end application of system engineering practices due to the relatively short system life cycle phases. The same applies to MBPLE as a discipline of systems engineering. We chose to include this real-world example to illustrate the diverse applications and adoption strategies of MBPLE. Belimo, a market leader in this sector, produces a wide range of components such as sensing, control, and actuation solutions, catering to the high variability and diverse needs of numerous customers across several industries. While the products themselves are not as complex as those in the defense and aviation sectors, this relative "simplicity" allows for the observation of the MBPLE application along the entire product life cycle, from ideation to production, within the same team.

One limitation of this last part of the book is the absence of the automotive and railway, also among the first forerunners of (MB) PLE. Although the authors reached out to some of the key companies in these sectors that have adopted the MBPLE approach, time constraints and the priority of bringing this book to publication led to the decision to limit this edition to only five cases. We hope to welcome more industrial cases and update the existing ones in future editions.

The authors have also integrated their own experiences to address these limitations throughout the book. They have worked on MBPLE in Europe, Canada, and the Asia–Pacific region, supporting the automotive (e.g. Renault, Continental) and railway industries (e.g. Bombardier Transportation, Alstom).

35.3 The MBPLE Adoption Quadrant: Understanding Paths and Trajectories Toward MBPLE

This section describes the five systems of interest – aircraft and its systems, missiles, radars, and sensing, control, and actuation solutions – of the five organizations, using as metrics the level of complexity and variability, as introduced in Chapter 2. This premise is necessary to understand their paths and trajectories to adopt MBPLE.

Complexity: Aircraft and their systems, as well as missiles, exhibit a high level of complexity. This complexity arises not only from the advanced technologies and large scopes involved but also from the highly regulated environment in which they operate. These factors result in the development of large, complex systems within extensive, long-lasting programs, making the management of complexity crucial. This applies to both MBDA and Raytheon.

Radars, while still complex, have a lower order of magnitude compared to aircraft and missiles. Their complexity lies primarily in software parameterization and the capability to serve multiple contexts and scenarios despite being integrated into large mission programs.

Belimo's products, on the other hand, are the least complex among the cases discussed. While the scope-driven complexity is not as critical here, the integration of new technological advancements poses challenges in managing the complexity of these components.

Figure 35.1 illustrates how these products relate to varying degrees of complexity.

Variability: Aircraft are unique systems. They operate in standardized environments (airports, airspace, etc.) that limit and control the "external variability" – coming from the environment –, resulting in lower variation in components such as wings, landing gear, and cockpit. On the contrary, the cabin exhibits a high degree of variability due to its exposure to final customers – the passengers – and the diverse requirements of various airlines (see Chapter 2).

Missiles typically have less variability, but the portfolio and diverse mission capabilities of the systems can quickly increase their variation. Radars may exhibit higher levels of variability than missiles, particularly in software parameterization and due to the numerous scenarios they serve.

Finally, sensors, actuators, and control solutions demonstrate high levels of variability because they are integrated into numerous products across various industries.

Figure 35.1 also depicts the position of these products in relation to their degree of variability.

Figure 35.1 Complexity and variability degrees of aircraft, missile, radar, and HVAC solutions.

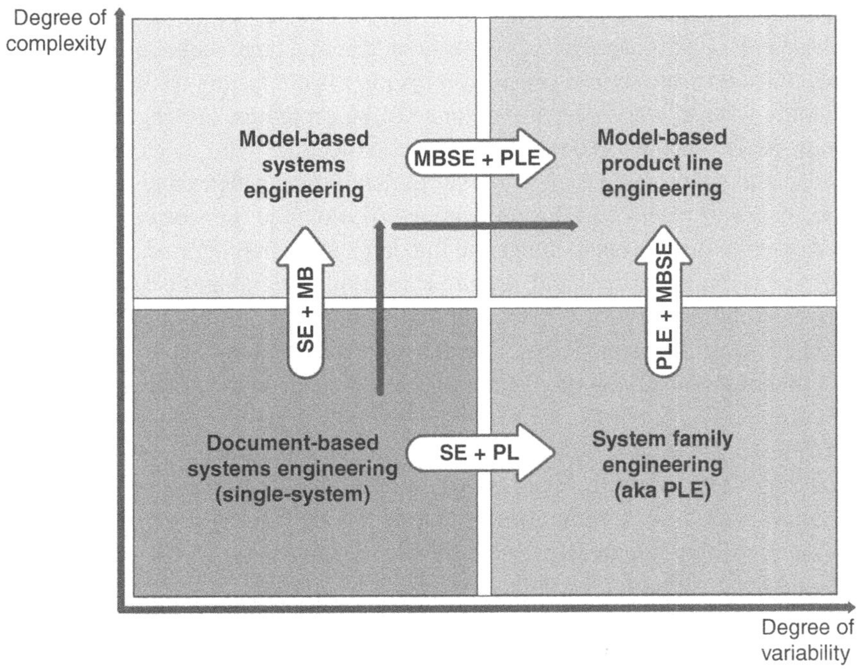

Figure 35.2 Path of "complexity-triggered adoption" of MBPLE at Airbus and MBDA.

MBPLE adoption paths: To understand this section, it is key to read Chapter 22, where the MBPLE adoption quadrant is explained. We use the "MBPLEAQ" to analyze and compare commonalities and variabilities in the MBPLE adoption paths of those five organizations. Three distinct patterns arise.

Figure 35.2 shows the first path that we call "complexity-triggered adoption." This applies similarly to the Airbus, MBDA, and Raytheon cases described in Chapters 30 and 31.

The three organizations started the adoption of MBSE first within a digital transformation that helped them move away from a document-based approach (introducing first SE + MB) while still focusing on single-system development.

The second phase of this transformation consisted of integrating some PLE concepts and mechanisms first into the SysML assets only (MBSE + PLE) to finally land into a broader adoption of MBPLE. The high level of complexity of their products and the large amount of documents posed the MBSE adoption as a priority. However, the increase in variability (e.g. cabin monuments and systems) and the need to reuse models – to justify the large investment in MBSE – pushed the organizations to slowly introduce the PLE component into the MBSE adoption and then to extend it to a more holistic model-based PLE approach (MBPLE). Although Raytheon is considered among the pioneers in adopting PLE in combination with MBSE (Young and Clements 2017), they do not adopt the naming "MBPLE" but refer just to feature-based PLE in combination with the "digital trinity" as shown in Chapter 33.

Figure 35.3 presents an opposite pattern that we call "variability-triggered adoption" and that applies to Thales, described in Chapter 32.

In this case, the increase of the radar portfolio, including the related variability within their systems and engineering artifacts (e.g. requirements, source codes, parameters, etc.), pushed Thales to move from single-system and document-based development to a system family

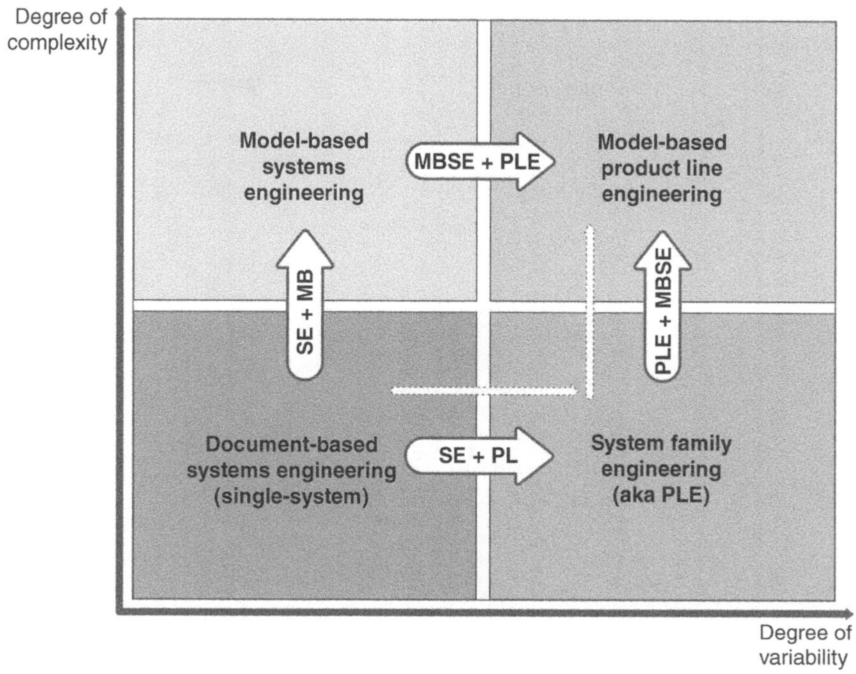

Figure 35.3 Path of "variability-triggered adoption" of MBPLE at Thales.

engineering approach, passing first through a clone-and-own approach (SE + PL), both still relying during the first stage on documents. Slowly, the introduction of MBSE at Thales Group to respond to the increasing complexity convinced the radar teams to experiment with MBSE but treat it at the same levels as other documents and assets (PLE + MBSE). Finally, with the full adoption of the Arcadia MBSE methodology and Thales in-house "orchestra suite" (Navas et al. 2021), the organization shifted to a model-centric PLE approach that we know as MBPLE.

Figure 35.4 illustrates the final pattern identified in our fifth industrial case, which we call the "Divide et Impera" (Latin for "divide and conquer") adoption, or more simply, "differentiated adoption." Considering Belimo's portfolio and its significant variability, the initial direction was to transition from a document-based, single-system approach to a system-family engineering approach (dotted lines).

This involved gradually introducing the concept of product lines and variability, relying on clone-and-own first, before implementing the PLE approach with a focus on the BOMs, requirements, and other models (PLE + MBSE), but without a unifying system architecture principle. This strategy aimed to better manage variability in the late stages of design, where quick wins could be achieved.

In a subsequent stage, the same team at Belimo recognized the necessity to invest more in system architecture and in a model-based approach to facilitate monitoring system evolutions and improve consistency, often hindered by the multitude of documents. This team focused on the concept and earlier design phases, moving from a document-based approach (through SE + MB first) – starting first with a few diagrams – to an MBSE approach (continuous lines). Gradually, the team introduced PLE elements – features and variation points – to control logical system architectures and other assets, primarily in the architecture models (MBSE + PLE).

The final "mile," which is still in progress, involves adopting an MBPLE approach from both the lower-right and upper-left quadrants. However, it is important to recognize that due to the relatively

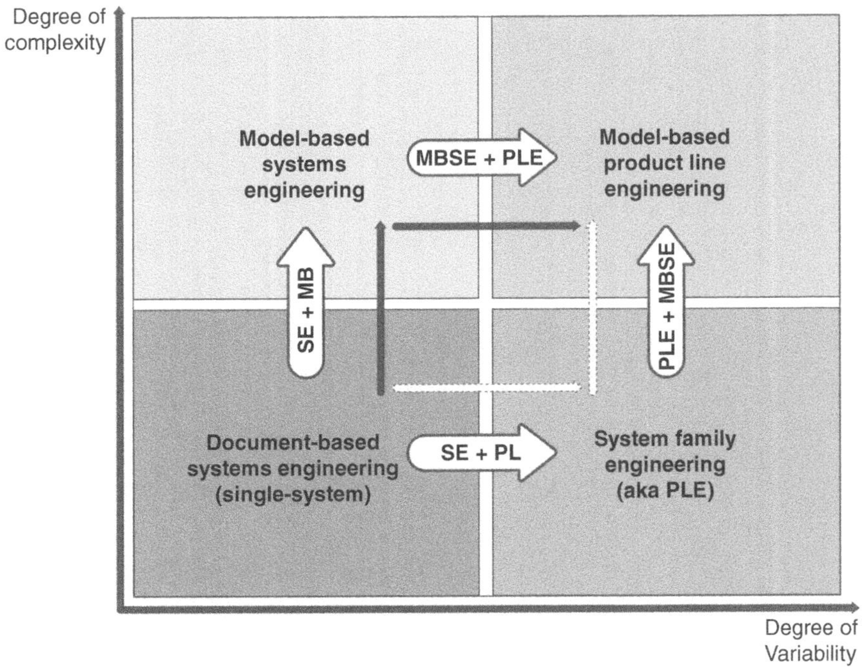

Figure 35.4 Path of "differentiated adoption" of MBPLE at Belimo.

low complexity of Belimo's components, the business case for a fully integrated Application Lifecycle Management (ALM) and Product Lifecycle Management (PLM) model-centric strategy is not as compelling compared to the other three major organizations and their more complex systems.

35.4 Commonalities and Divergences in the MBPLE Adoption

The five industrial cases, while covering the MBPLE adoption and providing a general overview of it, focus on diverse facets, going into the details of specific aspects of the adoption.

We opted for this approach to make them more attractive to the readers because a comprehensive treatment of each case within the limited space of this book, or a simple comparison between them (between apples and oranges), would not have done justice to the distinct ways those companies have implemented MBPLE. However, it is key to highlight some similarities and differences in the adoption. We use the MBPLE adoption framework described in Chapter 22 to ease this cross-case analysis. The information provided below is a synthesis of what can be found in the previous chapters about those five organizations and additional knowledge provided by the guest authors in the form of a questionnaire.

MBPLE process: At Airbus, while the approach itself is based on the ISO/IEC 26550 (ISO/IEC 2015) and 26580 (ISO/IEC 2021) standard family, some tailoring is performed to adapt to Airbus' needs and culture, as well as aviation-specific business processes. MBPLE is part of a larger transformation initiative called Digital Design Manufacturing and Services (DDMS) with a strong focus on company-wide systems engineering and product line-oriented practices.

Similarly, MBDA uses the well-known PLE standards as the basis for the MBPLE approach. The company implements MBPLE in an improvement program, named the "Greater Engineering Transformation Program," focusing on the technical management and engineering (MB)SE processes.

At Thales, MBPLE is integrated into define, develop, and qualify the solution (DDQS) processes that are accompanied by PLE instructions, primarily based on ISO/IEC 26550. In addition, the PLE approach is also applied to the bid management process and to customer service processes to deliver the customer's user documentation for the project, based on the features and instantiated assets.

RTX (parent company of Raytheon) provides a comprehensive "OneRTX Digital Engineering" solution using Digital Threads – including a mature MBSE solution – enabling engineering lifecycle activities for products in the RTX product portfolios from concept through retirement and disposal in line with the ISO/IEC 15288 (ISO/IEC 2023). OneRTX solution is based on a multi-year initiative and comprises a set of common, tailorable MBSE and feature-based PLE processes and guidelines with accompanying staff training boot camps. The OneRTX solution has been successfully used on numerous DoD contracts, compressing life cycles, enabling informed decisions using high-fidelity analysis models and simulations, and accelerating time-to-field for both new products and adding new product features to fielded systems.

Finally, Belimo, Innovation, and R&D processes are highly influenced by ISO/IEC 15288 (ISO/IEC 2023). In addition to that, to enable the reuse of artifacts and foster the definition of its modular architectures, the configuration management process is also central in the adoption of MBPLE – also based on ISO/IEC 26580.

The current focus at Belimo is only on the engineering processes, in particular, the "concept definition" and "system architecture definition processes" and the later "design processes," because of the differentiated application of MBPLE, described in Section 35.3 of this chapter and, more in detail, in Chapter 33.

MBPLE method: The MBPLE methodological approach used at Airbus focuses on a holistic 4-step approach – using a single variability model to drive different types of assets, in line with the MBPLE paradigm presented in Chapter 12. The shared assets currently in scope are: SysML models, governed within the Airbus' MBSE framework, requirements (textual and SysML-based), and 3D elements.

At MBDA, the SysML model is the master for any type of architecture, from operational to structural. For example, structural architecture provides the framework for mechanical and electrical/electronic architecture development. Since the structural architectures are variable, they are all controlled by a feature model and its feature configuration within the MBPLE approach.

Thales promotes a holistic PLE approach where the feature model is central and gives more emphasis to it than to the MBSE part. For instance, the company focused on formalizing the method for the extraction of features in an iterative way, where instead of creating digital feature models at first, spreadsheets and/or mind maps are often used to capture the initial variability, eliminating the concern for structure and hierarchy amongst variation points. As an example of another method formalization, Thales also separates the "need level" features and the "solution level" features (Navas et al. 2021) within the feature model.

Raytheon primarily creates and delivers artifacts pursuant to US DoD contract deliverables, which in turn are based on US DoD instructions, handbooks, etc.

For several years the US DoD has launched multiple digital transformation initiatives, deprecating document-based systems engineering, and with the publication of DoD instruction

5000.97 (DOD 2023), Raytheon transitioned to model-based engineering (MBE) comprising MBSE methods, plus model-based hardware and software design methods, model-based simulations, etc. for systems, systems of systems, and system families, by applying a feature-based PLE approach. The example provided in Chapter 33, "the hypothetical intelligence gathering system," shows a simplified application of Raytheon's approach in dealing with system family engineering and the so-called "digital trinity."

Belimo slightly differs from a traditional MBPLE method application. While still having the ISO/IEC 26580 as a reference, Belimo's features consist of "common" features (e.g. a cluster of common requirements) and feature options that express the variability and "rule" it in the architecture models. Feature models and architecture models are differentiated into two levels: a more abstract one, including features, requirements, and MBSE models, and a more detailed one, where features and BOMs are integrated within the product data management part.

MBPLE information model: Airbus integrates the current MBPLE framework elements into its internal data model for systems engineering (SECAM), which includes a meta-model for supported assets and employs SysML notation (Ducamp et al. 2022).

MBDA encompasses various features in its "E2EMBE information model," ranging from use cases to design choices, and includes different types of variation points such as atomic, starting, or propagated.

Thales has developed an "engineering data model" at the solution engineering level that includes specification references, product breakdown structure configuration items, functional chains structuration, integration, verification and validation references, and changes references. This model is structured into different levels: system needs, logical architecture, and physical architecture, incorporating variability and adhering to the "Arcadia methodology" (Voirin 2023). It is designed to promote co-engineering developments while remaining tool-independent and is not based on SysML but on a tool-specific notation.

The OneRTX digital engineering solution includes the definition of the components of the digital threads required to support engineering activities for a product, including capability allocation, requirements traceability, and blended virtual and physical integration, verification, and validation (IV&V). For each product in the RTX product portfolio, a digital thread definition activity is performed identifying the authoritative source of truth (ASoT) for each category of digital artifact used for the products. These tailored digital threads comprise the enduring, bidirectionally linked, authoritative sources of truth used by customers and RTX engineers to make informed decisions.

Belimo documents its methods in an ontology description. Unlike the other cases, Belimo's feature tree does not follow the recommended FODA-like (Kang et al. 1990) hierarchical notation for variability. Additionally, similarly to Thales, their MBSE models are not based on SysML.

MBPLE tool chain: The current tool chain at Airbus focuses on creating a holistic approach and an end-to-end agnostic flow of variability data across the organization and tools. PTC pure::variants (PTC 2024b) is used as the main hub, connecting to Cameo Systems Modeler (Cameo 2024) and IBM DOORS Classic (IBM 2024a). The 3DEXPERIENCE solution (Dassault Systèmes 2024) has its own variability management (not in a feature tree-like), with a mapping between PTC pure::variants and the 3DX references. As data is treated in the form of agnostic ontologies, the tool chain does not drive the implementation of the framework.

MBDA has a heterogeneous development environment with different tools. For this reason, an MBPLE tool that supports an open ecosystem was selected, and the choice fell on pure::variants from PTC. MBDA's tool chain includes IBM Rhapsody (IBM 2024b) and Capella (2024) as MBSE tools, Xpedition Designer (Siemens 2024) for ECAD, and the 3DEXPERIENCE platform for MCAD.

Thales uses the "orchestra suite," an internal set of integrated tools that support MBPLE methods, including PTC pure::variants, Capella, and Product and Asset Lifecycle Management (PALM) for the PLM and Enterprise Resource Planning (ERP) parts (Thales 2024). A holistic MBPLE approach is enabled by connecting both PLM and ERP-integrated tools with the inputs of the project variant coming from the feature model.

Raytheon's OneRTX enterprise integrated digital environment, consisting of integrated, best-of-breed engineering tools support engineering activities including: model-based acquisition, model-based mission engineering, model-based requirements engineering, model-based architecture, model-based product line engineering, model-based multidisciplinary analysis and optimization (MDAO), model-based hardware design (mechanical and electrical); and software design, model-based emulations, model-based low and high-fidelity simulations, as well as blended virtual and physical IV&V. Due to the impossibility of listing all the solutions used, we refer here mainly to IBM Rhapsody (IBM 2024b) used for the MBSE domain, and gears (BigLever 2024) as an integrated PLE tool.

Belimo has foreseen a roadmap for introducing MBPLE and related tools in the earlier stages of development. The main tools involved are Codebeamer (PTC 2024a) for requirements management, iQuavis (iQUAVIS 2024) for high-level feature modeling and architectural modeling, and SAP VC (SAP 2024) for later-stage development. SAP VC includes the product structure and related finished configurations, as well as separate features and assets from PLM.

MBPLE organization: At Airbus, the MBPLE framework does not lead organizational changes, but it serves as an important contact point for end-users, aiding acceptance and accelerating adoption. It is part of the DDMS program, a temporary organization, and works in synergy with the MBSE team and the team responsible for adapting Airbus to become a product line-based organization.

Similar to Airbus, MBPLE at MBDA is part of the "Greater Engineering Transformation Program" and within the MBSE team. At this stage, MBDA has deliberately decided to focus only on engineering management processes, and the E2EMBSE and E2EPLE teams primarily support the functions that perform such processes. Due to confidentiality, no other information could be shared.

At Thales SRA, we saw how the process puts the product at the center of the organization and how the product leads the business. The company formed two product teams for two different product lines, collaborating with project teams. For over 10 years in the Radar division, a dedicated resource was appointed to deploy MBPLE and support engineering teams.

Finally, in 2023, this resource will be integrated into the "SE method and tool" department. This service will bring support for all SRA SE and is composed of ten persons. Additionally, a new organization will be put in place at the end of 2024 with the creation of a Center of Competences, including around 50 persons.

Raytheon is on a digital transformation journey that will support business growth, drive operational excellence, and equip employees to perform their best. The digital transformation strategy is driven by leading-edge digital capabilities that will redefine how the company works, optimize its operations, and transform its products and services. A key digital transformation initiative enhances the product lifecycle by becoming a model-based enterprise (including MBPLE), connecting its product data from design through sustainment. Due to confidentiality, no additional or specific information concerning the MBPLE organization can be shared.

Table 35.1 Comparison of key MBPLE terms used in this book and in the five industrial cases.

ISO/IEC 26580	Feature catalog	Bill of features	Shared asset supersets	Product asset instances
This book	Feature model	Feature configuration	Shared asset supersets	Product models
Airbus	Feature model	Feature configuration	Product line assets	Member product assets
MBDA	Feature catalog	Bill of features	Shared asset supersets	Variants
Thales	Feature model	Project configuration	Product assets	Product variants
Raytheon	Feature catalog	Bill of features	Shared asset supersets	Product asset instances
Belimo	Feature model	Variant model	Feature-based product description	System element-based product description

At Belimo, as stated before, MBPLE is applied to two main life cycle stages. At the earlier stage (conceptual), the innovation system architecture (IAS) team is responsible for the methodology-wide implementation of MBSE/MBPLE from a method and tool perspective. This team provides training on the subject, including requirements, features, and architecture modeling. Comprising six people, the team handles methodological aspects with two dedicated members. At the later stage (more design-focused), product structure and related variability management are handled in SAP VC rather than from the IAP (product data management). Both teams belong to the same department, IA (innovation architecture).

Table 35.1 shows the key terms of the MBPLE 4-step approach used by the five organizations and compares them with our terms (the book's authors) and the ISO/IEC 26580's terminology.

This chapter summarizes the key commonalities and differences among the five cases. Among the divergences, is the centrality of the ISO/IEC 26580 standard in shaping the adoption of MBPLE in diverse organizations and industries.

References

BigLever. (2024). BigLever software gears. https://biglever.com/solution/gears/ (accessed 10 May 2024).

Cameo (2024). Cameo system modeler. https://www.3ds.com/products/catia/no-magic/cameo-systems-modeler (accessed 11 May 2024).

Capella (2024). MBSE capella. https://mbse-capella.org/ (accessed 11 May 2024).

Clements, P., Gregg, S., Krueger, C. et al. (2014). Second generation product line engineering takes hold in the DoD. Crosstalk. USA.

Dassault Systèmes (2024). 3DExperience Platform. https://www.3ds.com/3dexperience (accessed 11 May 2024).

DOD Office of the Under Secretary of Defense for Research and Engineering (2023). DOD Instruction 5000.97 Digital Engineering. Approved by H. Shyu. https://www.esd.whs.mil/DD/ (accessed 28 Aug. 2024).

Ducamp, C., Bouffaron, F., Ernadote, D. et al. (2022). MBSE approach for complex industrial organization program. *Systems Engineering*, first published 26 September 2022.

Forlingieri, M. (2022). The four dimensions of variability and their impact on MBPLE: How to approach variability in the development of aircraft product lines at Airbus. In: *Proceedings of the 16th International Working Conference on Variability Modelling of Software-Intensive Systems (VAMOS '22)*, (23–25 February). Florence, Italy: ACM, VaMoS.

IBM (2024a). IBM Engineering Requirements DOORS. https://www.ibm.com/products/requirements-management (accessed 28 July 2024).

IBM (2024b). IBM Engineering Systems Design Rhapsody. https://www.ibm.com/products/systems-design-rhapsody (accessed 11 May 2024).

iQUAVIS (2024). Software webpage. https://www.two-pillars.de/en/iquavis/ (accessed 25 July 2024).

ISO/IEC/IEEE (2015). Software and systems engineering – reference model for product line engineering and management (ISO/IEC/IEEE 26550:2015).

ISO/IEC (2021). Software and systems engineering – methods and tools for the feature-based approach to software and systems product line engineering (ISO/IEC/IEEE 26580:2021).

ISO/IEC (2023). Systems and software engineering – system life cycle processes (ISO/IEC/IEEE 15288: 2023).

Kang, K.C., Cohen, S., Hess, J. et al. (1990). Feature-Oriented Domain Analysis (FODA) feasibility study. *CMU/SEI-90-TR-021. Software Engineering Institute*. Carnegie Mellon University. http://resources.sei.cmu.edu/library/asset-view.cfm?AssetID=11231 (accessed 7 January 2023).

Lanman, J.T., Kemper, B., Rivera, J. et al. (2011). *Employing the Second Generation Software Product-line for Live Training Transformation, Interservice/Industry Training, Simulation, and Education Conference (I/ITSEC)*.

Navas, J., Bonnet, S., Voirin, J.L. et al. (2021). A value-driven, integrated approach to model-based product line engineering. In: *INCOSE International Symposium* 31: 95–110.

PTC (2024a). Codebeamer. https://www.ptc.com/en/products/codebeamer (accessed 11 May 2024).

PTC (2024b). pure::variants. https://www.ptc.com/en/products/pure-variants (accessed 10 May 2024).

SAP (2024). SAP VC Software. https://www.sap.com/swiss/products/crm/variant-configuration-and-pr icing.html (accessed 25 July 2024).

Siemens (2024). Xpedition designer.https://eda.sw.siemens.com/en-US/pcb/xpedition-enterprise/ (accessed 10 April 2024).

Thales (2024). Product & Asset Lifecycle Management.https://www.thalesgroup.com/en/worldwide/security/product-and-asset-lifecycle-management-palm (accessed 20 July 2024).

Voirin, J.L. (2023). Arcadia Reference: Workflow and Activities, Thales.https://mbse-capella.org/resources/arcadia-reference/Arcadia%20Reference%20-%20Activities.pdf.

Young, B. and Clements, P. (2017). Model based engineering and product line engineering: combining two powerful approaches at Raytheon. In: *27th Annual INCOSE International Symposium* (IS 2017), Adelaide, Australia.

36

Conclusion

This book has provided a comprehensive overview of the fundamental concepts, available technology, technical implementation, and strategic and organizational aspects of model-based product line engineering (MBPLE). These elements, along with the industrial case studies presented in Part V, provide useful guidance to understand and implement MBPLE in an organization.

Several key elements for the development and deployment of MBPLE were identified and addressed. These elements were first envisioned in the introductory chapters of the book, which presented the benefits of transitioning from a single-product to a product-line-based delivery approach and the necessary enablers (strategic, cultural, technological, and organizational) for the deployment of MBPLE. Subsequently, each element was further developed in later chapters of the book (in particular, Parts III and IV) to support this first view. The last part of the book also establishes how these different key elements can fit together and function as a whole within an MBPLE-oriented organization.

The first conclusion of this book is that the ISO/IEC 26580 (ISO/IEC 2021) standard should serve as a lighthouse for adopting MBPLE. At its core, MBPLE is "feature-based" product line engineering, where features act as a "single source of variability." Features are like the "conductor of an orchestra," guiding the implementation of variability within assets. Variability and commonality are the symphonies, aiming to reuse the same notes, while the score – the relationships and constraints of our feature model – ensures everything plays in harmony. The model-based aspect of MBPLE further optimizes this approach, akin to an orchestra performing in the world's finest theater, with superior acoustics and instruments, to deliver a flawless and cohesive performance.

This leads to the second conclusion of this book which is that the basic necessary standards, technologies, languages, and methods to implement an operationally viable "MBPLE factory" are already available and could be deployed in many organizations, albeit on a limited scope of shared assets. In any case, attention must be paid to implement the MBPLE factory at the speed of relevance, taking into account the maturity of teams and the priority given to particular engineering artifacts to be transformed into shared reusable assets.

A third conclusion is that, in order to operate MBPLE across all types of shared assets and obtain the maximum benefits, software tools still have to overcome some barriers to provide effective end-to-end digital continuity. This endeavor must be assumed by software editors and tool vendors of both authoring and Product Lifecycle Management/Application Lifecycle Management tools.

The essential conclusion of this book is that implementing MBPLE in an organization is far from being a purely technical issue. A successful deployment of MBPLE will undoubtedly rely on effective systems engineering practices. In particular, a very accurate formalization of the results of business and opportunity analyses is paramount. However, aligning all functions and sectors of the

Model-Based Product Line Engineering (MBPLE): The Feature-Based Path to Product Lines Success, First Edition.
Marco Forlingieri et al.

organization around clear business goals and a common delivery approach is of utmost importance. The business context, goals, and constraints provide the essential elements to perform product line architecture and align the product line architecture approach (and the organizational structure that should support it) to the business needs. It becomes evident, then, that the implementation of MBPLE should be considered a transformation initiative and executed gradually within transition plans, which require upfront investment and forethought.

We hope this book has equipped readers with the knowledge and tools necessary to build a compelling business case for MBPLE and to embark on a successful implementation journey. It is our strong belief that, by embracing MBPLE, organizations can achieve greater profitability, reduce lead time, improve product quality, and obtain a substantial return on investment, securing their position at the forefront of modern engineering practices.

As Sun Tzu wisely noted in the 5th century BC (Tzu 2010):

> *There are not more than five musical notes, yet the combinations of these five give rise to more melodies than can ever be heard.*
>
> *There are not more than five primary colours, yet in combination they produce more blues than can ever be seen.*
>
> *There are not more than five cardinal tastes, yet combinations of them yield more flavours than can ever be tasted.*

Variability is intrinsic to the world we live in. From quanta to DNA, from colors to music, everything is governed by combinations of common elements. The challenge lies in understanding and mastering the "rules" of control and reuse.

Similarly, organizations can unleash the power of variability, enabling innovation while maintaining control, managing complexity, and unlocking the full potential of their product lines. To achieve this, we believe organizations should embrace MBPLE, the feature-based path to product line success.

References

ISO/IEC (2021). Software and systems engineering – methods and tools for the feature-based approach to software and systems product line engineering (ISO/IEC/IEEE 26580: 2021).

Tzu, S. (2010). *The Art of War*. Chichester: Capstone Publishing.

Annex A: MBPLE Glossary

Bill of features See feature configuration.

Core element A core element is an element in a shared assets superset used for all member products of a product line.
Reference: VAMOS (Weilkiens 2016).

Domain asset ISO/IEC 26550 defines the domain asset, which is then redefined and named a shared asset in ISO/IEC 26580. See Shared Asset.
References: ISO/IEC (2015, 2021).

Feature A feature is a characteristic of a product that sets it apart from other products within the same product line.
Reference: ISO/IEC (2021).

Feature catalog See feature model.

Feature configuration A feature configuration is a valid set of selected features of a feature model for a member product. The ISO/IEC 26580 standard calls the feature configuration the bill of features.
Reference: ISO/IEC (2021).

Feature constraint A feature constraint specifies an expression about features that must always be true in the context of a feature configuration.
Reference: ISO/IEC (2021).

Feature group A feature group specifies the cardinality and optionally further constraints about a valid selection of alternative sub-features for feature configurations.

Feature model A feature model specifies a product line's variability by features organized in a hierarchical tree structure.
References: ISO/IEC 26580:2021 calls it a feature catalog (ISO/IEC 2021).

Feature tree A feature tree is a graphical notation of a feature model.

Member product A member product is a real-world product that belongs to a product line. It is specified by a product model.
Reference: ISO/IEC (2021).

Model-based product line engineering Model-based product line engineering (MBPLE) consists of applying feature-based PLE in combination with MBSE, where architecture models are central but not exclusive to the realization of the product line.

Model-Based Product Line Engineering (MBPLE): The Feature-Based Path to Product Lines Success, First Edition.
Marco Forlingieri et al.

Model-based systems engineering Model-based systems engineering (MBSE) is systems engineering with the formal application of models to make engineering information accessible to machines to support the stakeholders.
Reference: Weilkiens, Vinarcik, and Fischer (2023).

OR feature group A OR feature group has an upper cardinality larger than 1, which means that a feature configuration can select more than one sub-feature.

PLE factory configurator A PLE factory configurator is an automatic process deriving product models from shared assets supersets for a given feature configuration.
Reference: ISO/IEC (2021).

Product asset instance See product model.

Product line A product line represents a family of products, which includes a variability model, shared assets supersets, product models, and a product portfolio.
Reference: ISO/IEC (2021).

Product line development Product line development is the execution of tasks to develop a product line.

Product line engineering Product line engineering (PLE) is a discipline that involves developing similar products or systems with shared features.

Product model A product model is a model specifying a member product of the product line. There are more than one product model for a member product, for example, a SysML product model, a CAD product model, and so forth. It is derived from shared assets supersets based on a feature configuration. The ISO/IEC 26580 standard calls it a product asset instance.
Reference: ISO/IEC (2021).

Product portfolio A product portfolio defines the set of member products.

Root feature A root feature is the top-level feature of a feature model.

Shared asset A shared asset is a digital artifact that contributes to the architecting, design, fabrication, operation, maintenance, and retirement of a product (and of its components). It can be a member of one or more shared assets supersets.
Reference: ISO/IEC (2021).

Shared assets superset A shared assets superset contains all shared assets needed by all planned member products.
Reference: ISO/IEC (2021).

Sub-feature A sub-feature is a feature that acts as a specialized, usually more detailed, feature of a broader parent feature within the hierarchical tree structure of a feature model.

Variability model A variability model contains a feature model and feature configurations.

Variant A variant is a shared asset that implements a feature.

Variation A variation is a shared asset that has design choices. It is also called a variation point.

Variation point A variation point marks a shared asset that has design choices. It is also called a variation.

XOR feature group An XOR feature group is a feature group with lower and upper cardinality of 1, which means that only exactly one sub-feature of the feature group can be selected by a feature configuration.

Mapping of MBPLE Terms

MBPLE	VAMOS[1]	ISO/IEC 26550; ISO/IEC 26580
Feature	Variation, variant (implicitly)	Feature
Feature configuration	Variant configuration (implicitly)	Bill of features
Feature configurations (set)	Variant configurations (set; implicitly)	Bill of features portfolio
Feature constraint	Constraint	Feature constraint
Feature model	Variations, variants (set)	Feature catalog
Member product	–	Member product
PLE factory configurator	–	PLE factory configurator
Product line	–	Product line
Product model	Variant configuration	Product asset instance
Shared asset	Core or variant element	Shared asset
Shared assets superset	Core and variation model	Shared asset superset
Variant	Variant	Shared asset
Variation	Variation point	Variation point

References

ISO/IEC (2015). ISO/IEC 26550: 2015 Software and systems engineering – reference model for product line engineering and management. London: ISO/IEC.

ISO/IEC (2021). ISO/IEC 26580: 2021 Software and systems engineering – methods and tools for the feature-based approach to software and systems product line engineering. ISO/IEC: https://www.iso.org/standard/43139.html.

Weilkiens, T. (2016). *Variant Modeling with SysML*. MBSE4U.

Weilkiens, T., Vinarcik, M., and Fischer, C. (2023). *The Craft of MBSE*. Fredesdorf, Germany. MBSE4U.

1 Variant Modeling with SysML (Weilkiens 2016).

Index

Model-Based Product Line Engineering (MBPLE): The Feature-Based Path to Product Lines Success, First Edition.
Marco Forlingieri et al.